SETTING
NATIONAL
PRIORITIES
The 1974 Budget

SETTING NATIONAL PRIORITIES
The 1974 Budget

Edward R. Fried
Alice M. Rivlin
Charles L. Schultze
Nancy H. Teeters

with the assistance of
Henry J. Aaron, Edward B. Baker, Jr.,
Duran Bell, Martin Binkin,
Barry M. Blechman, Karen Davis,
Robert W. Hartman, John D. Johnston,
Arnold M. Kuzmack, Richard D. Lawrence,
Benjamin A. Okner, Alton H. Quanbeck,
Jeffrey Record, Robert D. Reischauer,
Michael Timpane, and William D. White

THE BROOKINGS INSTITUTION
Washington, D.C.

THE BROOKINGS INSTITUTION is an independent organization devoted to nonpartisan research, education, and publication in economics, government, foreign policy, and the social sciences generally. Its principal purposes are to aid in the development of sound public policies and to promote public understanding of issues of national importance.

The Institution was founded on December 8, 1927, to merge the activities of the Institute for Government Research, founded in 1916, the Institute of Economics, founded in 1922, and the Robert Brookings Graduate School of Economics and Government, founded in 1924.

The Board of Trustees is responsible for the general administration of the Institution, while the immediate direction of the policies, program, and staff is vested in the President, assisted by an advisory committee of the officers and staff. The by-laws of the Institution state, "It is the function of the Trustees to make possible the conduct of scientific research, and publication, under the most favorable conditions, and to safeguard the independence of the research staff in the pursuit of their studies and in the publication of the results of such studies. It is not a part of their function to determine, control, or influence the conduct of particular investigations or the conclusions reached."

The President bears final responsibility for the decision to publish a manuscript as a Brookings book or staff paper. In reaching his judgment on the competence, accuracy, and objectivity of each study, the President is advised by the director of the appropriate research program and weighs the views of a panel of expert outside readers who report to him in confidence on the quality of the work. Publication of a work signifies that it is deemed to be a competent treatment worthy of public consideration; such publication does not imply endorsement of conclusions or recommendations contained in the study.

The Institution maintains its position of neutrality on issues of public policy in order to safeguard the intellectual freedom of the staff. Hence interpretations or conclusions in Brookings publications should be understood to be solely those of the author or authors and should not be attributed to the Institution, to its trustees, officers, or other staff members, or to the organizations that support its research.

Foreword

IN ANY ONE YEAR, presidents seldom propose major changes in the scope and role of the federal government. Such changes do occur, but usually in small steps whose implications are realized only after several years have passed. The federal budget for the fiscal year 1974, however, is a striking exception. Faced with the prospect of a substantial excess of spending over revenues in a period when large budget deficits would clearly be inflationary, the President decided not only to reduce the level of federal spending but to change national priorities. While leaving the structure of federal taxes and the current defense posture unchanged, he recommended a sweeping series of reductions in the domestic expenditures of the federal government, including elimination or sharp curtailment of many programs. He also recommended a major set of revisions in the way the federal government deals with state and local governments, replacing numerous specific grants-in-aid with broad revenue sharing assistance under which federal controls over the use of grant funds would be substantially reduced.

The President's budget reflects a comprehensive view of the priorities to be given various national objectives and of the role of the federal government at home and abroad. But other views about what the federal government should do and how it should go about doing it are clearly possible and would have widely different effects on the future size and composition of the federal budget. Public debate about the budget, however, has not focused on fundamental choices or comprehensive alternatives. Rather it has concentrated on such matters as the pros and cons of specific budget cuts and the wisdom and legitimacy of presidential impoundment of appropriated funds. Moreover, most of the discussion in the Congress and the press revolves around what the budget implies for the year immediately ahead, whereas the major consequences of the choices made in the budget will show up in later years.

The very size and complexity of the federal budget tend to fragment discussion about it. The intricate structure of the tax laws, the thousands of individual federal activities, the mystique that surrounds the defense program, and the technicalities of the budget document itself discourage the development of comprehensive alternatives to the budget presented by the President. The authors of *Setting National Priorities: The 1974 Budget* have sought to make the problem of budgetary choice more intelligible by classifying, analyzing, and projecting into the future the components of the budget in a way which makes it possible to put together several comprehensive alternative budgets, each illustrating a different view of how the federal government could deal with national problems.

The first major section of the book discusses domestic programs grouped into five major "strategies" or roles of the federal government: (1) affecting the distribution of income through taxes and transfer payments; (2) helping people buy such essential goods and services as housing, medical care, and higher education; (3) providing grants to state and local governments for carrying out specific social programs; (4) investing in the physical environment (transportation, water resources, pollution control); and (5) general revenue sharing. Within each of these strategies current federal programs are analyzed, compared with several alternative approaches, and the costs of each projected forward to 1978 under several different sets of assumptions.

In the second section of the book the defense budget is analyzed, not only in the familiar terms of the cost and effectiveness of particular forces and weapon systems, but also in the context of alternative views about the world role of the United States and the mission of its armed forces abroad. Again, current programs are compared with alternatives and projections made of the costs of each alternative.

The final chapter builds on these materials to present a number of alternative budgetary futures, which differ from each other in several respects: the size of the total budget, the structure of taxes to support it, the split between defense and domestic programs, and the emphasis given to each of the various domestic strategies discussed earlier in the book. These comprehensive budgets illustrate widely divergent views about what the federal government ought to be doing.

While the number of alternatives developed in this final chapter is necessarily limited, readers—from the materials presented in the earlier chapters—can construct others to accord with their individual preferences.

In preparing many of the chapters, the authors relied on background material provided by other members of the Brookings staff and by outside experts. In many respects the defense section reflects the collective effort and ongoing studies of the Brookings Defense Analysis staff headed by Alton H. Quanbeck. The title page lists the names of those who contributed background material and analyses, and their assistance is acknowledged at the appropriate places in the text. In addition, the analysis of federal grant programs and general revenue sharing was greatly aided by contributions from Martha Derthick and Allen D. Manvel. The authors also benefited from the participation of Henry Owen in the planning of the foreign policy and national security section of the book and from his review of each of its chapters. Valuable comments on these chapters were also received from Robert R. Bowie, Morton H. Halperin, and William W. Kaufmann.

While this volume is in many ways a cooperative enterprise in which a large number of Brookings staff members and outside experts participated, the four authors bear full responsibility for the contents and conclusions of the chapters. The listing of a contributor's name does not necessarily imply his or her agreement with the authors' treatment of the subject.

Setting National Priorities: The 1974 Budget is the fourth in a series of Brookings publications dealing with the problems of choice posed by the President's annual budget. Research for the foreign policy and defense chapters was carried out under a continuing program of studies supported by a grant from the Ford Foundation. The project as a whole was supported by a grant from the Carnegie Corporation of New York.

The combined efforts of many people made it possible to publish this study on a very tight time schedule. Andrew D. Pike carried out the computer programs used in making economic and budgetary projections and in estimating the revenue consequences of various tax reforms and housing allowances. Harold Beebout and George Chow of the Urban Institute developed the costs for the alternative reforms of the cash transfer programs discussed in Chapter 3. Research assistance was provided by Robert M. Gordon and Daniel J. Sullivan. The risk of factual error in this volume, produced under a short deadline and with many tables and numerical references, has been minimized by the work of Evelyn P. Fisher and Louisa Thoron, who organized the checking of data in the domestic and defense chapters, respectively. Janet E. Smith, Shirley Hornbuckle, and Katy Matheson ably carried the major secretarial burden. Elizabeth H. Cross, assisted by other members of the Brookings publications staff, worked tirelessly under difficult conditions to edit the manuscript.

The views expressed in this book are those of the authors and should not be attributed to the trustees, officers, or other staff members of the Brookings Institution or to the Carnegie Corporation or the Ford Foundation.

KERMIT GORDON
President

July 1973
Washington, D.C.

Contents

5. Grants for Social Programs   170

6. Investing in the Physical Environment   233

7. General Revenue Sharing   266

FOREIGN POLICY AND NATIONAL SECURITY

*Prepared with the assistance of Barry M. Blechman and others
whose names are indicated in the sections to which they contributed*

8. The Rising Cost of Defense   290

9. Changes and Trends in the Defense Budget 305

10. Defense Budget Issues 336

11. Major National Security Options 388

BUDGET STRATEGIES AND NATIONAL PRIORITIES

12. Alternative Budgets for the Future 409

Appendixes

Tables

Chapter 4: Helping People Buy Essentials

Chapter 5: Grants for Social Programs

Chapter 6: Investing in the Physical Environment

Chapter 7: General Revenue Sharing

Chapter 8: The Rising Cost of Defense

Chapter 9: Changes and Trends in the Defense Budget

Chapter 10: Defense Budget Issues

Figure

1. The Federal Budget and National Choices

IN JANUARY 1973, President Nixon sent to Congress and made public his proposed budget for the fiscal year ending June 30, 1974, which embodied recommendations for federal expenditures totaling $269 billion. Setting a precedent, the President also made tentative proposals for the following year, indicating how he would spend $288 billion in fiscal year 1975.

Why the Budget Matters

This budget has received an unusual amount of attention and comment—both favorable and unfavorable—mainly because the President is proposing cuts in some existing programs and consolidation of others, on a scale far beyond anything presidents have recommended in the past. But any federal budget merits attention, examination, and debate, whether it cuts programs, adds new ones, or merely continues the federal activities of the previous year. Enormous resources are involved: $269 billion is 20 percent of the gross national product (GNP), one-fifth of the value of everything the nation produces. Where these resources come from and how they are spent matter a great deal. National life is profoundly affected by decisions to spend more federal resources for health care and less for highways, or more for strategic submarines and less for day care centers; to increase aid to old people and decrease that for children or farmers or Indians; to shift tax burdens from corporations to individuals or from the poor to the rich; to change the locus of decision making from Washington to state and local authorities or from government to individuals. All these types of decisions are reflected in the budget. It is the job of the President to propose a budget that embodies his priorities and judgments; it is the responsibility of the Congress and the public to consider its merits and demerits carefully and weigh it against alternative proposals for raising and spending federal funds.

Unfortunately, at least two factors inhibit informed debate on the budget and the policy problems inherent in it. First, the budget is incredibly complex and hard to understand—even for those who work on it full time. Federal funds are spent for thousands of different purposes, in thousands of programs, each with detailed rules and hidden ramifications. Revenues are collected under equally complicated tax laws. Perhaps because of the budget's complexity, neither Congress nor the public ever really focuses on it as a whole or on the basic questions it raises. The press emphasizes controversial issues, such as President Nixon's proposed cuts in ongoing programs, and citizens address themselves mainly to aspects of the budget that affect them most directly—as teachers or wheat farmers, veterans or city officials, defense workers or scientists. Congressional committees concentrate on the pieces of the budget for which they have responsibility. Indeed, under present procedures, Congress never votes on the budget as a whole. It appropriates funds for particular departments or activities and votes on separate revenue measures at various times during the legislative session.

Second, much of the budget reflects past decisions and commitments. Even if the Congress changes its procedures so that it can debate and vote on the budget as a whole, it will not be able to make dramatic changes in any one year, since most of the budget is made up of fairly firm commitments under long-standing policies—commitments to provide social security benefits, to maintain troops for the defense of Europe or Asia, or to add the next segment to an unfinished highway network. These policies should be continually reexamined, but decisions to alter them may not have much effect on the budget for several years.

In this book we have tried to contribute to informed debate on the federal budget in two ways. First, we have attempted to make it easier to view the budget as a whole and alternatives to it by sorting programs and purposes into a manageable number of categories so that the important issues can emerge. Second, we have focused on major long-run policy decisions affecting the budget and the decisions that must be made now if the budget is to be significantly altered four or five years from now.

Four Kinds of Choices

The federal budget reflects choices in at least four different dimensions. First, there are choices among *objectives*—what is the relative importance of the various things the federal government is trying to accomplish? The budget implies judgments about the seriousness of general problems facing the nation (problems abroad versus problems at home, poverty versus pollution) and about the relative weight to be given to more specific objectives (modernizing strategic forces versus maximizing conventional forces, improving health services versus improving housing).

Second, there are choices about major *roles or strategies*—how should the government act in pursuit of its objectives? The defense budget reflects judgments not only about the importance of potential threats to national security, but about the appropriate international roles and military strategies in response to them. Should war be deterred by nuclear or conventional forces, through forward defenses and alliances or through a U.S.-based strategy? How broadly should the United States define its security interests overseas? What kind of commitments should it make to other countries, and when should it be prepared to intervene abroad? Similarly, the domestic budget outlines the administration's idea of the appropriate role of the central government in a federal system and in the private economy. Should the federal government give general budgetary support to state and local units or should it specify how the funds are to be used? Should it give cash transfers to individuals or assistance in buying certain essentials, such as food or housing? To what extent should it intervene to alter the private market's delivery of health care or housing? These questions about role or strategy are emphasized in this book.

Third, there are choices about *distribution*—who should benefit from federal programs and who should pay for them? While some federal activities, such as national defense and space programs, presumably affect the whole population, others aid particular groups and represent public decisions about the relative importance or neediness of those groups (old and young, farmers and businessmen, poor and less poor). Particular taxes, moreover, fall more heavily on some groups than others.

Finally, there is the question of the overall *size* of the budget—how big a share of national output should be devoted to the activities of the federal government? In the short run, the level of federal expenditures or receipts may reflect judgments about the state of the economy and its need for stimulus or restraint. In the longer run, however, the size of the federal budget expresses a choice between public and private needs and between federal and state or local spending to meet public needs.

These choices interact and influence each other. How much is devoted to any governmental program is influenced by judgments about how large total government expenditures should be, which in turn are influenced by the urgency of the problems with which governmental programs deal. Questions of distribution affect the allocation of budgetary resources among roles or strategies, and vice versa. And none of these four kinds of choices is debated or made in the abstract. No one explicitly decides on the relative weights to be given to health and pollution control or on the proportion of the budget to be devoted to old people and children. Nevertheless, decisions do get made and they often involve choices in several dimensions at once. For example, a decision to reduce combat forces ready to fight land wars in Asia might be based on a judgment that threats to national security were declining, or that, declining or not, the importance of U.S. interests in Asia had diminished, either in absolute terms or relative to domestic problems.

Major Changes in Federal Activity

Recent changes in federal receipts and expenditures reflect at least implicit decisions in all these dimensions. Expenditures are shown in Table 1-1, classified by the major types of activity around which we have organized this book. As shown in the table, one-third of the budget is used for national security. The proportionate share of these expenditures has dropped sharply in recent years, but their absolute size continues to be very large despite the elimination of the Vietnam

Table 1-1. Federal Budget Expenditures, by Major Category, Selected Fiscal Years, 1950–74

Category	1950	1960	1970	Estimate 1973	Estimate 1974
	Billions of dollars				
Defense, space, foreign affairs	18.0	49.5	87.7	83.6	88.8
Cash income maintenance	6.7	20.6	45.8	74.3	81.3
Helping people buy essentials	2.7	1.1	14.6	23.3	27.2
Grants for social programs	0.3	1.3	8.8	14.9	14.0
Investment in physical environment	2.0	5.4	9.8	13.7	14.8
Revenue sharing[a]	...	0.1	0.5	7.3	6.6
Direct subsidies to producers	4.0	4.5	6.7	7.8	5.9
Net interest	4.8	6.9	14.4	17.4	18.7
Other programs	5.3	3.9	12.4	22.1	21.0
Financial devices and civil service retirement contributions	−0.7	−1.1	−4.1	−14.6	−9.6
Total	43.1	92.2	196.6	249.8	268.7
	Percentage of total				
Defense, space, foreign affairs	41.8	53.7	44.6	33.5	33.0
Cash income maintenance	15.2	22.3	23.3	29.7	30.3
Helping people buy essentials	6.3	1.2	7.4	9.3	10.1
Grants for social programs	0.7	1.4	4.5	6.0	5.3
Investment in physical environment	4.6	5.8	5.0	5.5	5.5
Revenue sharing[a]	...	b	b	2.9	2.4
Direct subsidies to producers	9.3	4.9	3.4	3.1	2.2
Net interest	11.1	7.5	7.3	7.0	7.0
Other programs	12.3	4.2	5.3	8.8	7.8
Financial devices and civil service retirement contributions	−1.6	−1.2	−2.1	−5.8	−3.6
Total	100.0	100.0	100.0	100.0	100.0

Sources: *The Budget of the United States Government*, relevant years; *The Budget of the United States Government—Appendix*, relevant years; *Special Analyses, Budget of the United States Government*, relevant years. Expenditures were reclassified by the authors. Figures may not add to totals because of rounding.
a. Includes small amounts of payments in lieu of taxes on federal lands.
b. Less than 0.05 percent.

war bulge. In fiscal 1974, expenditures for defense, space, and foreign affairs will amount to $89 billion.

Cash transfers to people, by contrast, have absorbed a growing proportion of the budget in the past four years. In fiscal year 1974 cash transfers—social security benefits, veterans' pensions, and the like—will amount to about $83 billion, or 31 percent of the budget, up from 24 percent in 1970. Most of this growth is attributable to increases in social security and other government programs for retired or disabled persons.

Thus national security and cash transfers consume two-thirds of the budget. When interest on the public debt, which amounts to 7 percent of the total, is added, almost three-quarters of the budget is accounted for. Where does the remaining one-quarter go?

Federal programs to help people purchase certain "essential" goods and services, such as food, housing, medical care, and higher education, which were negligible in 1960, will rise to $27 billion, or 10 percent of the budget, in 1974. Most of the growth has been in two health care programs: Medicare for the aged and Medicaid for the poor. Grants for social programs—education, manpower training, and other public services to people—also grew from very small amounts in 1960 to $15 billion in 1973. The President's proposed $14 billion for 1974 is 5.3 percent of the budget, about the same proportion as will be devoted to investments in the physical environment such as transportation, water resource programs, and environmental protection.

Producers' subsidies, chiefly farm programs, absorb a considerably smaller proportion of the budget than they did a decade or two ago. On the other hand, the enactment of general revenue sharing put a substantial new item in the 1973 budget.

Although it is not possible to say exactly how these shifts in federal activity have affected particular groups, clearly the aged and the disabled have received an increasing proportion of federal benefits. The relative shift from defense spending, which in theory benefits the nation as a whole, to cash transfers, which benefit mainly the aged and disabled, implies a decision to accord higher priority to the needs of these people. On balance, recent changes in federal expenditures have probably favored low-income groups. Most cash transfers go to the poor and near-poor as do federal subsidies to help people pay for essentials.

Changes in the revenue side of the federal budget, however, present a different picture: a heavy share of the federal tax burden falls on the poor and near-poor and that share is increasing. As may be seen in Table 1-2, the individual income tax is the largest source of federal revenues and has accounted for a fairly constant proportion of them in recent years. The individual income tax is moderately progressive; people with high incomes pay, on the average, larger fractions of their incomes than low-income people do, even though many of the well-to-do benefit from special privileges in the tax code (see Chapter 3).

The second largest—and most rapidly growing—source of federal revenues is payroll taxes, which are expected to account for nearly 31 percent of federal revenues in fiscal year 1974. These taxes, used to finance the social security system and related programs, are highly regressive; low-income people, on the average, pay larger fractions of their income than do high-income people. The rapidly increasing importance of payroll taxes as a source of federal revenue means that low-income earners bear a growing share of the federal tax burden. The growth in the share of payroll taxes has been offset by a decline in excise and corporation profits taxes, which together accounted for 36 percent of federal revenues in 1960 but only 21 percent in 1974.

With all these shifts in what the federal government does and where it gets the resources, what has happened to federal expenditures as a share of the nation's economy? The answer is, not much. Federal expenditures grew from 19 percent of GNP in 1955 to 21.4 percent in 1970 (see Table 1-3). The decline in national security expenditures as a percentage of GNP was offset by a rise in the proportion of the nation's total product devoted to federal civilian activities (including grants to state and local governments).

Table 1-2. Federal Budget Receipts, by Source, Selected Fiscal Years, 1950–74

Source	1950	1960	1970	Estimate 1973	1974
	Billions of dollars				
Individual income taxes	15.7	40.7	90.4	99.4	111.6
Corporation income taxes	10.4	21.5	32.8	33.5	37.0
Social insurance taxes[a]	4.0	14.7	45.3	64.5	78.2
Excise taxes	7.5	11.7	15.7	16.0	16.8
All other	3.3	3.9	9.5	11.6	12.4
Total	40.9	92.5	193.7	225.0	256.0
	Percentage of total				
Individual income taxes	38.4	44.0	46.7	44.2	43.6
Corporation income taxes	25.4	23.2	16.9	14.9	14.4
Social insurance taxes[a]	9.8	15.9	23.4	28.7	30.5
Excise taxes	18.3	12.6	8.1	7.1	6.6
All other	8.1	4.2	4.9	5.2	4.8
Total	100.0	100.0	100.0	100.0	100.0

Sources: Derived from *The Budget of the United States Government* and *Special Analyses, Budget of the United States Government*, relevant years. Some adjustments were necessary because of the change in budget concept from administrative to unified within the period covered by the table. Figures may not add to totals because of rounding.

a. Includes payroll taxes for social security and unemployment insurance, employee contributions for federal retirement, and contributions for supplementary medical insurance.

Table 1-3. Federal, State, and Local Budget Expenditures, Direct and Intergovernmental, as a Percentage of Gross National Product, Selected Fiscal Years, 1955–70ᵃ

Level of government and type of expenditure	1955	1960	1965	1970
All levelsᵇ	28.3	29.9	30.8	34.0
Federal, total	19.0	19.5	19.5	21.4
Grants-in-aid to state and local governments	0.8	1.4	1.7	2.4
Direct	18.1	18.1	17.9	19.0
Defense	10.6	9.3	7.6	8.4
Other direct civilian	7.5	8.8	10.3	10.6
State, total	4.9	5.9	6.6	8.5
Grants to local governments	1.6	1.9	2.2	3.0
Direct	3.3	4.0	4.5	5.4
Local, direct, totalᶜ	6.9	7.8	8.4	9.6

Sources: U.S. Bureau of the Census, *Census of Governments, 1967,* Vol. 6, No. 5, *Historical Statistics on Governmental Finances and Employment* (1969), Tables 2 to 6; Bureau of the Census, *Summary of Governmental Finances in 1955,* G-GF 55 (1956), and *Governmental Finances in 1970–71,* GF 71—No. 5 (1972); *The Budget of the United States Government, Fiscal Year 1974,* p. 370. Figures may not add to totals because of rounding.

a. There is some variation among state and local governments, especially in the earlier years, of the period covered within a governmental fiscal year.

b. Federal grants to state and local governments are spent by them and included in their expenditure totals. The same is true of state grants to local governments. As a consequence, total governmental expenditure, as a percentage of gross national product, is less than the sum of the percentages spent by each level of government.

c. Net of a small amount of local funds paid to state governments.

All Levels of Government

The federal government, of course, accounts for only part of the functions of government in the United States. Moreover, in recent years state and local governments have been growing faster—measured by the size of their expenditures and especially by the number of their employees—than has the federal government. Between 1955 and 1970 state and local spending rose from 10.2 to 15.0 percent of GNP. In the same period, state and local employment rose from 4.7 million to 9.8 million, and the ratio of state and local to federal civilian employees climbed from about 3 to 1 to nearly 5 to 1.

The figures on employment point up a major difference in the nature of state and local activities on the one hand and federal activities on the other. State and local governments—especially the latter—spend large portions of their budgets providing education, health care, fire and police protection, garbage collection, and other services directly to people. Demand for these services has increased rapidly in recent years as both population and aspirations have grown. In the decade between 1960 and 1970, rising expenditures for education accounted for almost half of the growth in state and local budgets, as the school-age population increased and teachers' salaries rose more rapidly than wages in general.

Except for defense, the federal government provides few services directly to anyone. The expansion in federal civilian expenditures, as has been noted, is chiefly the result of activities that involve transfers to individuals or grants to state and local governments, activities that require small numbers of federal employees.

When all three levels of government are taken together, the growth of the public sector in recent years emerges clearly. Total government expenditures rose from 28 percent to 34 percent of GNP between 1955 and 1970 (Table 1-3), and to an estimated 35 percent last year. One-third of national output is now devoted to public purposes, less than the proportion in Western Europe but higher than Japan's. Most of the growth has been at the state and local level. Direct federal expenditures—that is, total spending excluding grants-in-aid to state and local governments—only rose from 18 percent of GNP to 19 percent. About a third of the expansion in state and local expenditures has been financed by federal grants-in-aid. An even greater proportion of the expansion in local expenditures has been financed by increased grants from states to their local governments.

Major shifts occurred in the distribution by function of total public expenditures between 1955 and 1970, as the following data show. Income transfers have grown (mostly at the federal level) as has spending on education (mostly at the state and local level), while the proportion of GNP devoted to defense has declined.

Type of expenditure	*Percentage point increase in share of GNP*
All public expenditures	5.7
Defense	−2.4
Income transfers	3.8
Education	2.4
All other	1.9

On the revenue side, the share of total government receipts from individual income and property taxes has remained remarkably constant in the last fifteen to twenty years (see Table 1-4). Social security

Table 1-4. Distribution of Combined Federal, State, and Local Budget Receipts, by Source, Selected Fiscal Years, 1950–70

Percent

Source	1950	1955	1960	1965	1970
Individual income taxes	31	31	32	29	33
Corporation income taxes	18	20	17	15	12
Social insurance taxes	6	8	11	12	15
Excise and sales taxes	22	18	17	18	15
Property taxes	12	11	12	13	11
All other[a]	10	13	11	13	13
Total	100	100	100	100	100

Sources: *Economic Report of the President, January 1973*, pp. 268, 269, 277; *The Budget of the United States Government, Fiscal Year 1952*, p. 951, . . . *Fiscal Year 1957*, p. 1085; and . . . *Fiscal Year 1960*, p. 539. Figures may not add to totals because of rounding.
a. Includes customs, licenses, and miscellaneous receipts.

payroll taxes, however, have risen appreciably in the total tax picture, while corporation income taxes and excise and sales taxes have declined.

Why This Year's Choices Were So Hard

Making a budget always demands difficult decisions among competing objectives, but until recently budgetary choices at the federal level have been rendered at least superficially easier, in periods of peacetime prosperity, by the tendency of federal revenues to rise faster than the cost of ongoing federal activities. Federal tax revenues, especially income tax receipts, tend to rise faster than the GNP. In a normal peacetime year, the government could count on having both enough revenue to cover the increased costs of responsibilities already undertaken and some "fiscal dividend" left over to expand old programs or undertake new ones. Indeed, in the early 1960s (before the Vietnam buildup began) economists used to worry that the tendency of federal revenues to outrun expenditures was exerting deflationary pressure—a "fiscal drag"—on the economy. Some advocated federal tax cuts to reduce the fiscal drag; others thought it would be better to turn some federal revenues over to state and local governments in revenue sharing.

In the last several years, however, this problem has given way to a new one. In putting together his proposed budgets for 1971, 1972, and 1973, the President did not need to worry about the fiscal drag; he found himself in a different kind of bind: despite the gradual fall in the cost of the Vietnam war, hardly any money was available for new programs. Each year, as the President looked ahead to the next, he found that the expected costs of programs already on the books were rising nearly as fast as federal revenues. Some of these expected cost increases were "uncontrollable," at least from the point of view of the executive. Interest on the debt was rising. Some increases could not be avoided without changing the law—for example, rising obligations to social security and Medicare beneficiaries or federal responsibilities to match state or local spending for public assistance or Medicaid. Other increases, while not legally uncontrollable by the executive, reflected the "built-in" costs of carrying on existing programs in the face of rising prices, wages, and workloads.

At the same time substantial tax cuts in 1969 and 1971 reduced federal revenues. The revenue loss from these tax cuts in combination with a rapid growth of uncontrollable expenditures left the President with little room for new program initiatives when he prepared his 1971, 1972, and 1973 budgets.[1]

In preparing his budget for fiscal year 1974, however, the President faced an even more difficult problem. During fiscal year 1973 the budget picture had worsened. Expenditures rose well above the amount originally budgeted, as new legislation sharply increased social security benefits, veterans' pensions, and other transfer programs, while outlays for several other programs exceeded estimates. If nothing was done, the federal government would be running very large deficits in fiscal years 1974 and 1975, even on a full employment basis.[2]

The essence of the problem facing the President is shown in the top half of Table 1-5. Expenditures for existing programs plus estimated costs of new programs already proposed by the administration (such as welfare reform and health insurance) seemed likely to exceed revenues by $16 billion in fiscal 1974 and by $21 billion in fiscal 1975, even on a full employment basis.

1. A detailed analysis of these developments was provided in Charles L. Schultze and others, *Setting National Priorities: The 1973 Budget* (Brookings Institution, 1972).

2. On a full employment basis, federal revenues are measured as they would be at the level of income accompanying a 4 percent unemployment rate; federal expenditures for unemployment compensation are similarly calculated. The difference between revenues and expenditures so computed—the full employment surplus or deficit—is generally conceded to measure the federal budget's impact on the economy better than the actual surplus or deficit.

Table 1-5. The Problem Facing the Administration in Constructing the Budget, and Actions Taken to Remedy It, Fiscal Years 1974 and 1975[a]

Billions of dollars

Components of the problem and the remedy	1974	1975
The problem		
Anticipated revenues	268.0	290.0
Proposed expenditures	283.9	311.1
Existing programs	279.9	303.2
New programs proposed in 1972 by the administration	4.0	7.9
Deficit	−15.9	−21.1
Actions taken to eliminate the deficit		
Domestic expenditure cuts	10.2	13.2
Defense expenditure cuts	2.0	2.0
Elimination of proposed programs[b]	4.0	7.9
Resulting budget surplus	0.3	2.0

Sources: *The Budget of the United States Government, Fiscal Year 1974; The Budget of the United States Government, Fiscal Year 1973;* and authors' estimates.

a. All estimates are calculated on a full employment basis.

b. Fiscal year 1974 expenditures for the major new proposals submitted by the President last year, but not resubmitted this year, have been estimated at one-half the level shown for those programs in the 1973 budget; if they had been resubmitted, delays in enactment would have reduced the first year's spending. The 1975 estimate is taken, without adjustment, from the data in Table 16, pp. 540–42, of the 1973 *Budget*

This situation left the President with three major options: (1) he could propose a budget that implied a substantial deficit on a full employment basis; (2) he could propose a tax increase; (3) he could cut expenditures.

The revised budget the President presented for fiscal year 1973, the new one he proposed for 1974, and his tentative projections to 1975 manifest his decision to reject the first two options and to take measures that would reduce federal spending substantially below the projected levels. The results of these actions are summarized in the second bank of figures in Table 1-5. The 1974 budget was brought into balance on a full employment basis, and a slight surplus was projected for 1975. What reasoning led to this course of action?

Option 1: To Run a Substantial Deficit

The President's economic advisers contended that a sizable full employment deficit in fiscal 1974 would have a strong inflationary effect on an economy that was recovering rapidly from the slump of 1970 and 1971—and most economic analysts would agree. Although the economy is not yet back to full employment, a substantial recovery in economic activity is taking place. Output has grown rapidly and unemployment has declined. Real GNP rose by 6½ percent in 1972; the administration projects it will rise by 6¾ percent in 1973. An unusually strong consensus among private economic forecasters holds that the rates of economic growth in the official forecasts are reasonable and obtainable. The surveys covering business investment plans indicate a 13 percent growth in investment expenditures in 1973. The increased taxes yielded by economic recovery, coupled with revenue sharing, have increased the ability of state and local governments to undertake additional expenditures. Heavy consumer spending can be expected to continue, sustained by incomes augmented by higher transfer payments and an unusually large refund of individual income taxes. These forecasts assume the balanced full employment budget presented by the President. With full employment budget deficits on the order of $15 billion to $20 billion for fiscal 1974 and 1975, however, the economy would surge ahead at an even faster rate—at least for a while. And there is also fairly general agreement that this would be risky. In the short run, faster economic growth would intensify inflationary pressure and in the longer run too sharp a pace of advance would carry the serious danger of an unsustainable boom in business investment in plant, equipment, and inventories, with the possibility that a subsequent collapse would bring on a new recession.

In an economy with a GNP of $1,200 billion no one can say with confidence that a precisely balanced budget for fiscal 1974 is absolutely necessary, or that a federal deficit of a few billion dollars would bring on the consequences described above. But deficits of $15 billion to $20 billion are another matter. Incurring deficits of this size was not, in fact, a sensible option for the President.

On June 1, 1973, the administration released revised estimates of revenues and expenditures for fiscal 1973 and 1974. Principally because of a faster than anticipated inflation in the first half of calendar 1973, the projection of full employment budget receipts for fiscal 1974 was increased by $5 billion. The estimate of total expenditures was not changed. As a consequence, the balance in the full employment budget originally projected for fiscal 1974 became a $5 billion surplus. In the short run, at least, an acceleration of inflation tends to produce a more restrictive federal budget, as revenues respond faster to price increases than do expenditures. While the newly announced surplus did not signal a basic change in fiscal policy, it did reflect the administration's decision to let this restrictive effect occur, rather than to increase expenditures to match the higher revenues.

Option 2: Raising Taxes

Economic reasoning ruled out the first option, and the President's political and value judgments ruled out the second—raising taxes. Increasing federal taxes by the amount needed to secure a balanced budget would have meant taking an additional 1 percent of GNP out of the private sector to pay for federal programs. The President apparently judged that the federal programs that could have been bought by these additional taxes were not worth the sacrifice of private income. The lack of support for a tax increase among politicians of both major parties was undoubtedly another major influence.

But there is no *economic* reason for foreclosing this option. If the nation so chooses it can devote an additional 1 percent of its income to federal taxes, as an alternative to cutting federal expenditures, without placing any strain on the economy or significantly lessening its growth.

Collections of federal income and corporation profits taxes have been reduced sharply by recent changes in the law. If the tax cuts of 1969 and 1971 had not taken place, federal revenues anticipated for 1974 would have been higher by $16 billion, about the amount needed to balance the 1974 budget on a full employment basis. On the other hand, social security payroll taxes have been raised by about $19 billion since 1969, leaving the net tax burden essentially unchanged. Indeed, during the 1972 election campaign, when both major parties were promising to avoid any general tax increase, the Congress passed and the President signed an $11 billion increase in social security taxes, with no apparent political repercussions or even awareness that taxes had been increased. But all the increases in payroll taxes are now channeled into growing social security benefits and are not available for easing the fiscal problem caused by the expansion of other federal programs.

An alternative means of increasing revenues without a general tax increase is tax reform. Under current tax laws various forms of income —from capital gains, oil, and other mineral investments, interest on state and local bonds, and earnings reduced by accelerated depreciation—are taxed at a lower effective rate than other kinds of income. Abolishing this preferential treatment would significantly raise federal revenues.

This route toward solving the fiscal problem was not proposed by the President. Moreover, the Democratic chairman of the tax-writing Ways and Means Committee stated in early 1973 that he did not expect his committee to recommend any tax changes that, on balance, will raise federal revenues. Tax reform nevertheless can be a method both of increasing federal revenue and of shifting the burden of taxation. Chapter 3 of this book discusses a number of tax reform measures from both of these viewpoints.

Option 3: Expenditure Reductions—the President's Choice

To reduce the full employment budget deficit in 1973 and eliminate it in 1974 and 1975—without raising or reforming taxes—the President had to cut expenditures.[3] Major built-in increases were scheduled to occur in a number of programs, such as social security, Medicare and Medicaid, veterans' pensions, public assistance, and interest on the debt. Pay increases had to be provided for military and civilian employees of the federal government. And increased outlays were scheduled for a number of ongoing weapon systems. Part 1 of Table 1-6 shows the major areas in which budget expenditures were scheduled to rise, before the cuts. Part 2 of the table indicates that, even after substantial cuts in a number of programs, expenditures are expected to rise sharply in fiscal 1974 over 1973. Budget outlays, after the cuts, will rise from $249.8 billion to $268.7 billion, a growth of $19 billion. About $5 billion of the rise, however, results from the relative unavailability in 1974 of the various financial devices that are treated as negative expenditures and were used extensively to hold down expenditures in 1973 (sales of mortgages from government portfolios, royalties from offshore oil leases, and so on). Apart from these changes in financial transactions, expenditures on federal programs, defense and civilian, will rise by $14 billion.

Where the Cuts Were Made

The President's budget cuts will reduce expenditures on existing federal programs by $3.6 billion in 1973, $12 billion in 1974, and $15 billion in 1975.[4] Many of the actions necessary to realize these reductions have already been taken, since the President has ordered a

3. The discussion in this section concentrates on the effect of the budget cuts in fiscal 1974 and 1975. Changes made in the 1973 budget are discussed in Appendix A.

4. These estimates of the reductions in expenditures are somewhat smaller than those published in the budget. The reasons for the differences are given in Appendix B.

Table 1-6. Federal Budget Expenditures, before and after Administration Cuts, by Program, Fiscal Years 1973 and 1974[a]

Billions of dollars

Program	1973	1974	Change
1. Expenditures before budget cuts	253.4	284.9	31.5
Military	74.8	81.0	6.2
Vietnam costs	5.9	4.1	−1.8
Baseline military expenditures	68.9	76.9	8.0
Civilian	190.0	210.4	20.4
Major "built-in" increases	123.4	137.2	13.8
Administration proposals for new programs	0	4.0	4.0
All other civilian	66.6	69.2	2.6
Financial devices	−11.4	−6.5	4.9
Less:			
Reductions in existing programs	−3.6	−12.2	−8.6
Elimination of new programs[b]	0	−4.0	−4.0
2. Expenditures after cuts	249.8	268.7	18.9
Military	74.8	79.0	4.2
Civilian	186.4	196.2	9.8
Financial devices	−11.4	−6.5	4.9

Sources: *The Budget of the United States Government, Fiscal Year 1974* and *Special Analysis, 1974; The Budget of the United States Government, Fiscal Year 1973;* and authors' estimates. Figures may not add to totals because of rounding.

a. Actual expenditure estimates rather than full employment estimates are used in this table.

b. Fiscal year 1974 expenditures for the major new proposals submitted by the President in fiscal year 1973, but not resubmitted for fiscal year 1974, have been estimated at one-half the level shown for those programs in the 1973 *Budget.* If they had been resubmitted, delays in enactment would have reduced the first year's spending.

freeze on new commitments under a number of programs. The savings will be modest in fiscal 1973, but will grow to sizable amounts in 1974 and 1975.

Table 1-7 shows the breakdown of the reductions by the categories used throughout this book to classify government programs. Budget reductions are calculated as cuts in expenditures below the levels that otherwise would have obtained. Of the $12 billion in 1974 budget cuts, $2 billion represented reductions in the military budget. The other $10 billion fell in domestic programs, widely distributed among all the major categories of spending except general revenue sharing. In addition, as noted earlier, the President withdrew or substantially modified his proposals for several major new programs: the family assistance plan for welfare reform, on which the Congress failed to act last year, was not resubmitted; the special revenue-sharing proposals, which last year included an allowance for substantial additional funds, this year dropped the request for additional funding; and

Table 1-7. Federal Budget Expenditure Reductions to Eliminate Deficit, by Category, Fiscal Years 1974 and 1975

Billions of dollars

Category and component	1974	1975
Budget cuts		
Defense, space, foreign affairs	2.3	2.5
Defense	2.0	2.0
Space, atomic energy, foreign aid	0.3	0.5
Cash income maintenance	1.5	1.5
Public assistance	0.8	0.8
Veterans' pensions and compensation	0.4	0.4
Other	0.3	0.3
Helping people buy essentials	1.8	3.0
Medicare and Medicaid	1.1	2.0
Housing subsidies	0.3	0.6
Education	0.3	0.3
Food	0.1	0.1
Grants for social programs	2.8	3.0
Education	0.3	0.4
Health	0.4	0.4
Manpower training	1.0	1.0
Social service	0.6	0.6
Community action programs	0.3	0.4
Other	0.1	0.2
Investment in physical environment	1.9	2.8
Transportation	0.3	...
Water resources	0.6	0.8
Waste treatment	1.0	2.0
Direct subsidies to producers	1.0	1.6
Farm price supports	0.6	0.9
Rural electrification loans	0.4	0.7
Other	0.9	0.9
Total cuts	12.2	15.2
Withdrawal of previously proposed programs[a]		
Health insurance[b]	0.6	1.1
Family assistance plan	2.0	4.0
Supplements to special revenue sharing	1.4	2.8
Total withdrawals	4.0	7.9

Sources: Same as Table 1-5. Figures may not add to totals because of rounding.

a. See Table 1-5, note b.

b. The President's 1974 budget indicated that some form of health insurance program would be forthcoming, at a much lower net budgetary cost than the program he proposed in the fiscal 1973 budget. The figure in the table represents the difference between the costs of the two programs.

the budget allowance for a new health insurance plan included in the 1974 budget is much lower than that provided in last year's budget.

Almost all the budget cuts were made in civilian programs, especially those whose expenditure levels are easiest for the executive branch to control. (Programs such as social security cannot be controlled through the budget process but require changes in the law.) Indeed, after account is taken of the inevitable rise in prices in the next year, the real value of expenditures for those civilian programs in which outlays are relatively controllable will fall by some $3.6 billion from 1973 to 1974 (see Table 1-8).

In contrast, cuts in defense programs were small. In fact, after allowance is made for pay and price increases and for the declining cost of Vietnam, military expenditures on peacetime forces will rise by about $2 billion between 1973 and 1974.

Of the $10 billion cut in domestic programs in the 1974 budget, about $3 billion represents a general scaling back of a wide range of activities in such areas as space, atomic energy, transportation, and the national parks, and a modest reduction in the rates of growth for vocational rehabilitation, agricultural extension services, and other programs. In general, these reductions raise no major questions of national policy and constitute only marginal changes in the scale of the affected programs (although views may, of course, differ on the wisdom of such changes).

Another $2 billion of the cuts involve long-standing programs that

Table 1-8. Significant Changes in Federal Budget Outlays from Fiscal Year 1973 to Fiscal Year 1974

Billions of dollars

Description	Amount of change, 1973 to 1974
Civilian expenditures	14.7
Reduced use of financial devices	4.9
Major built-in increases	11.4
Allowance for inflation in relatively controllable programs	2.0
Change in real purchasing power of relatively controllable programs	−3.6
Military expenditures	4.2
Allowance for inflation and military retirement	3.7
Vietnam expenditures	−1.8
Change in real purchasing power of non-Vietnam programs	2.3

Source: *The Budget of the United States Government, Fiscal Year 1974*, and authors' estimates.

have been politically popular but criticized by outside evaluators as inefficient and poorly targeted. Price support subsidies to farmers will be cut back; the $700 million rural electrification program, under which the government made 2 percent loans to electric cooperatives, has been converted to a loan-guarantee program with higher interest rates; and outlays for traditional water resource investments—irrigation, navigation, and flood control—will be curtailed.

The remainder of the cuts are heavily concentrated among the newer programs of the federal government that deal with social and environmental problems—manpower training, education, health care, housing, urban development, social services, and environmental pollution. These cuts cannot be evaluated one by one, solely from the standpoint of program efficiency. They raise much broader questions about what the government's objectives ought to be and what role it ought to play in dealing with national problems. The proposed cuts in the Medicare program, for example, would be achieved by requiring that beneficiaries pay a larger fraction of their "normal" medical expenses but a smaller fraction of very large medical bills. This proposal would help provide incentives for better use of scarce medical resources. But unless accompanied by a health insurance program that assured reasonable access to medical care for the poor, the change would place part of the burden of balancing the federal budget on those least able to afford it. What ought, therefore, to be the federal role in furnishing medical care to the poor and the near-poor? The 1974 budget cuts in Medicare cannot be judged except in this broader context. The same kind of considerations arise in the other areas. It is a major purpose of this book to place the 1974 budget proposals in that larger framework.

The Longer-Term Impact of the 1974 Budget

A projection of federal revenues and expenditures to fiscal 1978, which assumed that the President had *not* made his budget cuts, that the new programs he proposed last year had been resubmitted and adopted, and that current tax rates were continued, shows large full employment budget deficits in 1974 and 1975, which then grow smaller but do not disappear in the subsequent three years.[5]

5. The projections of full employment revenues and expenditures in this book were based on roughly the same assumption of moderate price increases (2.5 to 3 percent per year) as were made by the administration in presenting its original budget estimates in

Table 1-9. Projected Full Employment Revenues and Expenditures, before and after Budget Cuts by the Administration, Fiscal Years 1974–78

Billions of dollars

Revenue or expenditure item	1974	1975	1976	1977	1978
Projections before budget cuts					
Revenues	268	290	315	342	370
Expenditures[a]	284	311	334	357	378
Existing programs	280	303	325	347	368
New programs	4	8	9	10	10
Deficit	−16	−21	−19	−15	−8
Projections after budget cuts					
Revenues	268	290	315	342	370
Expenditures[a]	267	288	308	329	348
Surplus	1	2	7	13	22

Source: Brookings Budget Projection Model.

a. Full employment expenditures assume a level of outlays for unemployment insurance consistent with a 4 percent unemployment rate, and hence differ from actual expenditures in any year when unemployment is higher or lower than that.

If the President's budget cuts remain in effect, the level and growth of expenditures will be substantially smaller, producing approximately balanced budgets in fiscal 1974 and 1975, and then potential budget surpluses, growing to $22 billion by 1978 (see Table 1-9).

The central lesson of these projections is that the budget cannot simply be restored to where it was before the President's budget cuts were proposed. Such a restoration would mean large and highly inflationary budget deficits for the next three to four years. There are indeed alternatives to the course of action proposed by the President. But any realistic alternative will require major changes in current policies on taxes, defense spending, and domestic programs. This book seeks to identify the options that do exist and to examine their implications for national policy.

The Major Budgetary Issues

Although the President's proposed budget cuts are controversial, it would be a sad mistake to limit debate on the 1974 budget to the pros and cons of these particular cuts. As noted, far more important

January. Even if the larger than anticipated inflation in the first half of calendar 1973 soon slows down to the more moderate pace assumed earlier, full employment revenues will be higher than shown in our estimates throughout the projection period, 1974 to 1978. But the higher than expected rate of inflation in 1973 will also eventually show up in larger expenditures than we have projected. As a consequence, the basic budgetary situation portrayed by the projections should not be fundamentally altered.

issues are involved: What should the government be doing? How much should it do? How should the benefits and costs be distributed?

Moreover, discussion of these questions should not be limited to one year, because it is almost impossible to make major changes in the budget in a single year. If debate on budget issues is to have any impact on what actually happens, it must focus on major options for the next three to five years. Once a longer-run budget strategy is mapped out, it can be translated into specific first steps that might be taken in the 1974 budget.

The central purpose of the balance of this book is not only to analyze the 1974 federal budget but also to present a set of building blocks that the reader can use to construct alternative budgets for the next five years. These budgets can differ in overall size, in the relative priorities for defense and domestic programs, and in their underlying concepts of the appropriate role of the government.

It is not our intention to judge whether one set of national priorities is better or worse than another. The allocations of resources between public and private uses, between competing public uses, and between various groups in society must come from decisions that can be made only through political processes. Quite probably, no two people have exactly the same set of priorities. It is the resolution of conflicting goals through elected representatives at all levels of government that results in public policy decisions. But we hope that the presentation of alternative courses of action will help to inform the debate from which those decisions arise.

The first major section of the book, Chapters 2–7, discusses domestic policy, analyzing it in terms of four broad strategies, or ways of doing things:

• Affecting the distribution of income by cash transfers, such as social security, unemployment benefits, veterans' compensation, and pensions; by changes in taxes; and by subsidized employment.

• Helping people buy essentials, such as food, medical care, housing, and higher education.

• Providing categorical grants to carry out social programs, such as education, manpower training, and delivery of health care, and making available either through grants or direct expenditures money for improving the physical environment, including transportation networks, environmental protection, and water resources.

• Sharing revenue with other levels of government to provide financial assistance for their programs.

Each of these strategies has advantages and disadvantages. The rationale, advantages, and problems of each are discussed. Alternatives within each strategy have been developed, illustrating what programs could be undertaken at various levels of expenditures.

The second major section, Chapters 8–11, reviews the national security programs requested in the 1974 budget and their cost implications for future budgets. These programs are then analyzed in terms of the purposes for which the United States maintains forces and the cost consequences of changes either in the purposes themselves or in the ways of achieving them. On the basis of these analyses, alternative defense budgets are developed along with an estimate of the consequences for foreign policy and national security associated with each.

The final chapter puts together the building blocks, developed earlier, in a variety of combinations designed to illustrate major budget options for the next five years. Budgets are worked out that have different levels of federal spending, differing emphases on defense versus domestic programs, and different combinations of domestic strategies. Other combinations can be developed by the reader from the materials in the earlier chapters.

2. Domestic Strategies

THE FEDERAL BUDGET for domestic programs is large and exceedingly complicated. Through thousands of domestic programs with a wide variety of objectives, the government aids many different groups of people and interacts constantly and in various ways with state and local governments and private institutions. Altogether the domestic activities of the federal government will cost about $180 billion in fiscal year 1974, or about 15 percent of the gross national product.

What, Who, and How

There are several ways to cut through the complexity and organize a discussion of domestic programs from which the options can become clear. One way is to focus on various functions of government, such as providing education, improving health, reducing pollution, and alleviating poverty; to describe possible national objectives in each of these areas; and to lay out alternative federal programs for moving toward these objectives together with estimates of their potential accomplishments and costs. Such a discussion would help the reader decide what he thinks future federal budgets should be, based on the weight he gives the various objectives. The domestic sections of previous volumes of *Setting National Priorities* were organized in this way.

A second way would be to focus on particular groups in the population, such as the elderly, children, people of working age, the poor, farmers, or Indians; to define their special needs and alternative ways of meeting them, and to examine the advantages, disadvantages, and

23

costs of each. This approach would also aid the reader in choosing his preferred future federal budget, based on the importance he assigns to particular groups. Such a discussion would be provocative but hard to prepare, because the groups overlap and information on how federal programs affect them is often unobtainable.

We have chosen to organize this discussion of budget options in a third way: to focus on alternative "strategies" the federal government might adopt to achieve a variety of domestic objectives. By "strategies" we mean the kind of action the federal government takes—the role it plays in the federal system and the private economy. Does it deal with individuals or with other levels of government? Does it simply redistribute resources among people and governments or does it specify how these resources are to be used? In other words, we are organizing the choices not around *what* the government does or *who* benefits from its actions, but around *how* it acts.

We have identified four major strategies that are being followed now and might receive varying degrees of emphasis in the future.

1. *Redistributing cash income among individuals.* This strategy involves taxes, cash transfers, and employment programs through which the federal government affects the distribution of income among persons and families without attempting to influence what they do with the money. Social security is an example of this.

2. *Helping people buy "essentials."* This strategy involves transfers or tax advantages that help people buy specific goods and services, such as housing or medical care, that are normally sold in the private market. Food stamps, Medicare, college scholarships, and tax advantages for homeowners are examples.

3. *Increasing specific public services.* This strategy usually involves "categorical" grants to state and local governments—for instance, grants for libraries or highways or vocational education—that specify fairly narrowly what is to be produced or who is to receive the services. In exceptional cases it may include direct federal services, such as national parks and water resource projects.

4. *Revenue sharing.* This is a new strategy involving federal efforts to increase the resources available to state and local governments without concern for how the money is spent—except perhaps in the broadest terms—or for whom.

The purpose of this section of the book is to explore the rationale and limitations of each of these strategies and illustrate what could be done and who would benefit under each of them, at various levels of spending, so that the reader will have some building blocks for constructing future budgets that correspond to his preferences and priorities and the total level of federal activity that he regards as desirable.

Goals and Strategies

We have organized the discussion in this way because current political controversy about federal domestic activities reveals deeper disagreements over strategies, or how the federal government should act, than over the general objectives of federal activity. Indeed, on a level of broad generalities, political leaders and citizen spokesmen agree about the goals the federal government should be seeking or at least about the direction of desirable change. Serious dissent on these three general goals of federal domestic activity would be unlikely:

• reducing poverty and inequality, both in income and in access to essential public and private services;

• improving the effectiveness of public services;

• creating a cleaner, more attractive physical environment.

A generation or two ago these goals would not have been thought appropriate to the federal government. Before the 1930s the existence of poverty, the quality of education or police protection, or the deterioration of the environment were generally considered no business of the central government. But in the last forty years that attitude has changed dramatically. Presidential candidates of both major parties now make speeches about the need to reduce poverty, improve education and health care, clean up pollution, rebuild cities, and reduce crime. Recent political debate has not been over whether the federal government should be concerned with these objectives, but over what it should do and how much. In other words, the controversy now is over alternative strategies and the levels at which these strategies should be carried out.

Some strategies with wide support in other countries have little appeal in the United States. Socialists argue that public ownership of major industries and of transportation and communications networks is a good way to reduce inequality, improve the quality of services, perhaps even reduce pollution. But this kind of socialism has negligible support in the United States. The consensus that private capitalism should be regulated, but not replaced to any extent by public ownership, appears to be so widespread that socialist strategies are not worth discussing in a book about feasible alternatives for the federal budget.

Similarly, with a few special exceptions, there appears to be little support for direct provision by the federal government of public services, especially such human services as education, health care, and law enforcement. Advocates of a national education system or a federal police force do not command much attention. For all its faults, a system that leaves these services largely to state and local government enjoys wide support. The relevant arguments center on how much money the federal government should furnish state and local governments to increase or equalize the provision of these services and how extensively it should regulate the use of its grant funds—not on whether the central government should assume these functions.

The four general strategies we have identified as worth discussing are all being followed to some degree and hardly anyone would suggest that one strategy be adopted to the exclusion of others. The issues, rather, are emphasis and relative importance. Should incremental federal resources for the next several years be channeled mainly into programs designed to carry out a cash income strategy—and if so, what kind?—or should they go chiefly toward helping people pay for essentials? Should categorical grants be cut back in favor of revenue sharing, or vice versa?

Current Domestic Strategies

The federal domestic budget is now dominated by programs that provide cash transfers to people and programs to help individuals buy essentials. Together these account for $108 billion in the 1974 budget, or more than three-fifths of all domestic spending (Table 2-1). Moreover, expenditures taken by themselves are misleading. Taxes also affect the distribution of income and many provisions of the tax code assist people to buy "essentials" such as housing and medical care.

Measured by budget outlays, the most important thing the federal government does is to redistribute income by writing checks to individuals, especially those retired or disabled and survivors of deceased workers. Cash transfers to individuals amount to $81 billion in the 1974 budget, or some 45 percent of domestic spending. Social security benefits account for $54 billion of these transfers, and other

Table 2-1. Domestic Federal Budget Expenditures by Major Category, Selected Fiscal Years, 1950–74

				Estimate	
Category	1950	1960	1970	1973	1974
	Billions of dollars				
Cash income maintenance	6.7	20.6	45.8	74.3	81.3
Helping people buy essentials	2.7	1.1	14.6	23.3	27.2
Grants for social programs	0.3	1.3	8.8	14.9	14.0
Investment in physical environment	2.0	5.4	9.8	13.7	14.8
Revenue sharing[a]	...	0.1	0.5	7.3	6.6
Direct subsidies to producers	4.0	4.5	6.7	7.8	5.9
Net interest	4.8	6.9	14.4	17.4	18.7
Other programs	5.3	3.9	12.4	22.1	21.0
Financial devices and civil service retirement contributions	−0.7	−1.1	−4.1	−14.6	−9.6
Total	25.1	42.7	108.9	166.2	179.9
	Percentage of total				
Cash income maintenance	26.7	48.2	42.1	44.7	45.2
Helping people buy essentials	10.8	2.6	13.4	14.0	15.1
Grants for social programs	1.2	3.0	8.1	9.0	7.8
Investment in physical environment	8.0	12.6	9.0	8.2	8.2
Revenue sharing[a]	...	0.2	0.5	4.4	3.7
Direct subsidies to producers	15.9	10.5	6.2	4.7	3.3
Net interest	19.1	16.2	13.2	10.5	10.4
Other programs	21.1	9.1	11.4	13.3	11.7
Financial devices and civil service retirement contributions	−2.8	−2.6	−3.8	−8.8	−5.3
Total	100.0	100.0	100.0	100.0	100.0

Sources: *The Budget of the United States Government*, relevant years; *The Budget of the United States Government—Appendix*, relevant years; *Special Analyses, Budget of the United States Government*, relevant years. Expenditures were reclassified by the authors. Figures may not add to totals because of rounding.
a. Includes small amounts of payments in lieu of taxes on federal lands.

programs for retired and disabled workers are also large. Civil service retirement, veterans' pensions and compensation, railroad retirement, and federal contributions to public assistance for the aged, blind, and disabled total $17 billion, and this figure does not include military retirement, which accounts for $5 billion in the defense budget for fiscal year 1974. Relative to other programs, cash transfers grew most rapidly in the 1950s, when the social security system began to pay out substantial benefits and coverage was being extended to new groups. Spending for cash transfers, which grew more slowly than the rest of the domestic budget in the 1960s, spurted up again in the 1970s, mainly because of large increases in social security benefits. Programs to help people buy essentials grew more rapidly than total domestic spending in the 1960s, mostly because of the enactment and rising costs of the Medicare and Medicaid programs. Federal programs to help people buy food, housing, and postsecondary education also grew and have continued to expand in the 1970s.

Two major sets of programs to increase the output of specific public services account for another sizable portion of the federal budget: grants for social programs, such as education and manpower training, and efforts to improve the physical environment, including transportation, water resource programs, and reduction of pollution. Together these two sets of programs have consumed somewhat less than 20 percent of federal domestic spending since 1960, but their patterns of growth were radically different.

Grants for social programs, which were negligible in 1960, grew sharply in the next ten years as the federal government took on new responsibilities for education, health care, manpower training, community action, and social services for the poor. The War on Poverty of the 1960s emphasized grants for services rather than income transfers to the poor. Other Great Society programs, such as educational innovation and regional medical programs, not designed especially for the poor were also enacted; and some older programs, such as vocational education, were broadened. Grants for social programs continued to expand between 1970 and 1973, somewhat faster than the budget as a whole. However, these programs, while highly controversial, have never accounted for more than 9 percent of domestic spending. The less controversial physical investment programs are about the same size, but they were already substantial in 1960 and in the past decade have grown less rapidly than the social grant programs. Since 1960, however, the emphasis has shifted away from highways and toward development of other modes of transportation and control of pollution.

The recently enacted general revenue sharing program accounts for about 5 percent of federal domestic spending in 1973 and will drop slightly in 1974 since some retroactive payments made in 1973 will not recur.

Some federal programs do not fall into any of these categories—for example, subsidies to producer groups such as farmers. As may be seen in Table 2-1, such subsidies were far more important in the budget in 1950 (before other programs expanded) than they are now. The 1974 budget shows an absolute drop in farm programs, but even in the 1973 budget subsidies to producer groups amounted to only 5 percent of the domestic budget as against about 16 percent in 1950. Confining attention to the expenditure side of the budget may be particularly misleading in this area, however, since tax benefits to specific producer groups are substantial.

Rethinking Current Programs

While sorting current federal programs by the type of federal action involved and grouping them into "strategies" is a useful approach, it is important to remember that these "strategies" do not reflect carefully considered, coherent plans. Rather they are collections of programs enacted at different times for different purposes—programs that are often inconsistent with each other, that sometimes overlap, and that frequently leave gaps in coverage. Indeed, it will be a recurrent theme of the next five chapters that no matter what the relative emphasis among strategies for the future, there is an urgent need for rethinking the programs *within* each strategy to make them both more equitable and more effective.

For example, programs affecting the distribution of income are extremely uneven in their impact. Cash transfer programs, as we have seen, primarily benefit retired and disabled persons and survivors of workers. Programs to assist younger families and their children are extremely limited; virtually no cash assistance is available to low-wage workers. Federal taxes also need examination in light of their impact on the distribution of income. Special treatment under the income tax of various kinds of income and expenditures leads to unequal tax burdens on people in similar economic circumstances and generally lowers effective tax rates paid by high-income people. Payroll taxes, used to finance transfer programs, are a heavy and growing burden on low-wage earners.

Programs to help people buy essentials are especially uneven in their coverage and impact. Medicare is a purely federal program providing broad coverage for the ordinary medical expenses of old people (but not for prolonged hospitalization or nursing home care for the chronically ill). Medicaid, however, is a joint federal-state program to help low-income people pay for medical care, under which the states make rules about eligibility and the federal government shares the cost. Some states define beneficiaries fairly generously, while equally needy people in other states are not helped.

Current housing programs are similarly erratic. Several programs provide federal subsidies for housing, mostly new housing, to be rented or sold to low-income people. But new construction is expensive, especially in cities, and the number of units built under these programs is small relative to the number of low-income people. The result is that a small minority of the poor and near-poor now receive fairly substantial housing subsidies while the majority receive nothing. Federal programs for child care and student aid also provide examples of inequities: substantial benefits for some and no help for others in similar circumstances.

Federal efforts to increase specific public services over the years have also left a legacy of ad hoc solutions, reflecting no coherent strategy. A large number of categorical grant programs for social purposes have been created (though mostly without large funding) until almost everyone agrees that, whatever their individual merits, there are too many separate programs for effective administration, from either the federal or the state and local point of view. Investment in the physical environment furnishes especially clear examples of the influence of historical accident on the development of federal policy. In transportation, for example, the federal government bears a large share of the cost of constructing state and locally owned highways, but provides no subsidies for their maintenance. Private railroads own and operate their systems without subsidies for the carriage of freight, although much intercity passenger traffic is now carried by a private, but governmentally sponsored, corporation which receives federal operating subsidies. Airports, though owned and operated by state and local governments, receive construction assistance from the federal government.

In combating environmental pollution, the federal government gives large grants to assist municipalities in constructing sewage treatment plants to reduce water pollution, but none for controlling the air pollution caused by municipal incinerators. Through the tax system, it subsidizes the investment by industry in some kinds of pollution control equipment but not others, even though in many cases the subsidized investment is less efficient than the unsubsidized.

In the case of water resource investments the federal government constructs local flood control projects, chiefly at federal taxpayers' expense. It offers moderate subsidies to hydroelectric power projects by lending capital at low interest rates, provides much larger subsidies for irrigation projects, and constructs navigation projects at no cost to the user. Serious reexamination of the effects of these disparate policies is clearly in order.

Strategies for the Future

Making intelligent budget choices involves not only rethinking existing programs but considering the potential benefits, costs, and limitations of emphasizing particular strategies in the future. Each of the four major strategies we have identified has a plausible rationale, whose persuasiveness depends on one's values and assumptions. Each also has limitations and inherent problems that must be resolved if the strategy is to be translated into specific programs. These points are discussed briefly here and at greater length in subsequent chapters.

Aid to People

REDISTRIBUTING CASH INCOME. A strong case can be made for using increments in federal resources during the next few years to reduce disparities in individual money incomes, especially by raising incomes at the low end of the scale. One could argue that the huge difference between the affluent and the poor—especially when it means that many live on incomes well below what most people regard as a decent minimum—is both inherently inequitable and a cause of other serious social problems, such as high crime rates and decaying neighborhoods.

Enthusiasm for the cash income strategy implies priority for reducing inequality and poverty over other possible objectives of the federal government. It implies respect for the individual's ability to make choices about how to spend his income and rejection of the idea that the government ought to make choices for people, especially poor people, by providing them with food stamps, housing, or medical care rather than money. It implies skepticism about the feasibility of reducing poverty by offering services, such as education or manpower training—or at least a recognition that services take time to have an effect—and a preference for the quicker, more direct methods of narrowing income disparities through tax and cash transfer programs or subsidizing employment.

Designing specific programs to reduce disparities in income is difficult, however, in part because this objective may conflict with two other objectives: maintaining incentives to work and treating people in equal circumstances equally. These problems arise in connection with tax reform: shifting the entire federal tax burden to a steeply progressive income tax, for example, would narrow disparities in after-tax incomes, but might also reduce efforts to earn and invest. Reforming cash transfer systems poses even more difficult problems. A system that provides an adequate basic income for everyone may discourage some from working, while a system that assists only certain groups of people judged "unable to work" is likely to be arbitrary and to leave out many in real need. Further discussion of these problems and some specific illustrations of future federal programs to affect the distribution of income are presented in Chapter 3.

HELPING PEOPLE BUY ESSENTIALS. One could also make a strong case for emphasizing federal efforts to help people buy such essentials as food, housing, medical care, and higher education, instead of (or in addition to) efforts to alter the distribution of income per se. Adequate food and shelter and essential medical care can be regarded as necessities of life, while access to higher education may be viewed as an opportunity for upward mobility that ought to be available to anyone who can profit from it. One might also argue for national concern about the distribution of housing, for example, not just on equity grounds, but because the community as a whole suffers when some part of it is housed in slums or other substandard dwellings.

The choice of transfers in kind over cash transfers implies a belief that, even if they had adequate incomes, some people would not buy "enough" of certain goods and services either because their values are different from those society thinks desirable—they would buy beer for themselves rather than milk for the children—or because expenditures such as medical care and higher education often come in large lumps and are difficult to budget for. One might also argue for transfers in kind on purely political grounds, since they may attract the support of producer lobbies, such as the housing industry, that general income transfers could not command. One could also, of course, argue for making health care or housing a public service, but the strategy of helping people buy essentials assumes that the private market (perhaps with some stimulation or regulation) operates reasonably efficiently and that the major need is to give people access to it.

The rationale for this strategy is sometimes extended to other services, such as elementary and secondary education, for which no important private market now exists. The argument is that schools that had to compete for students would be more effective than monolithic public school systems serving a captive audience, and hence that parents should be given vouchers entitling them to purchase education at the school of their choice. The same argument has been made about manpower training services.

In implementing this strategy, as with others, some problems keep cropping up no matter which service is under consideration. First, there is the problem of income testing and its effects on incentives to work. If benefits under a service program are greatest for the poor and decline as incomes rise, the effect is the same as that of an income tax. While the same problem exists with cash transfers based on need, the separate establishment of a number of service programs may lead to an unintended multiplication of this effect. Indeed, a family participating in several programs at once may find that an increase in income reduces medical care, housing, and child care benefits so much that they would be better off without it.

The second problem is that government financing of individual services may put strong upward pressure on their costs. Third-party payment reduces the price awareness of consumers and the incentives of producers to be efficient. The experience with Medicare and Medicaid has convinced even the most ardent advocate of national health insurance that wider coverage should not be undertaken without strong measures to keep costs down, either through direct control or through changing the incentives faced by medical care producers. Housing allowances, increased federal aid to students, or child care allowances might also drive up the prices of these services and necessitate controls.

Moreover, the cost problem is complicated by public pressure on the government to specify high standards for the services it finances— no second-rate service at public expense. Standards for public housing have been relatively high, but the problem is even more evident in child care where professional groups have insisted that publicly supported programs meet far higher standards, in number and qualifications of personnel, than generally prevail for privately financed child care. These higher standards, of course, mean higher cost; and since budgetary constraints usually prevent rendering high-cost service to everyone who needs it, the result has to be some form of rationing, through waiting lists or restrictive definitions of eligibility. Hence, the poorest, or some of them, may end up with better service than the near-poor can buy with their own resources. This situation characterizes current federal programs in housing, child care, and higher education. More generous public funding could avoid this "leapfrogging," but only at a high cost to the taxpayer.

Government Services

So far we have been dealing with the rationale for a heavy federal emphasis on assisting individuals to buy goods and services that are usually produced in the private market—by altering either the distribution of income in general or the individual's ability to purchase specific goods and services. These are the strategies, as has been shown, that currently account for two-thirds of the domestic budget. But a strong case can also be made—bolstered by another set of arguments and relying on another set of values and premises—for emphasizing provision of public services, generally through grants to state and local governments but in a few cases through direct federal provision of services. The general argument emphasizes the national importance of the service in question, the reasons that state and local governments without federal assistance will not produce enough of it or distribute it equitably, and, in the case of some services, the reasons for producing it publicly rather than privately. The specifics of the argument differ somewhat, depending on whether one is arguing for expansion of social services, for improvement of the physical environment, or for the general expansion of public services at the state and local level through revenue sharing.

GRANTS FOR SOCIAL PROGRAMS. A decision to emphasize federal grants for social services might reflect a concern with alleviating poverty along with a belief that cash transfers are not a feasible or perhaps even a desirable answer to the problems of the poor. Instead, perhaps because of the high value placed on self-reliance, one might advocate expansion of services designed to help the poor function better and earn more income in the future: compensatory education, day care and child development, physical and mental health services, manpower training, vocational rehabilitation, and various types of community action programs. The argument for *federal* grants to encourage such services is that concern with alleviating poverty is felt more strongly at the national level than at the state and local levels, where the poor have historically had little voice.

The case for emphasizing grants for social programs, however, need not be focused exclusively on the poor, but may reflect the belief that the stimulus of federal grants is necessary to improve the quality and quantity of services offered at the local level and to equalize their distribution—for everyone. State and local resources vary widely and even areas with adequate resources may undervalue certain social services because some of the benefits go to other districts. This is particularly so for new or risky ventures—small areas may be reluctant to undertake research and development of social services that would largely benefit other areas if successful—and for services to groups likely to migrate out of the area.

Such federal grants, however, also create perplexities. One is how tightly the federal government should police what is done. Loose guidelines or controls may allow state and local governments to waste the money or spend it according to their own, rather than national, priorities. Tight guidelines, on the other hand, might stifle local initiative, impose high administrative costs, and lower the effectiveness of the services. Moreover, once in place, specific social service grants tend to develop constituencies of their own and may be perpetuated after the national need that gave rise to them has diminished.

INVESTMENT IN PHYSICAL RESOURCES. Federal investment in physical resources is justified by concern for the quality of the physical environment, rather than for poverty or unequal distribution of income. The rationale for federal involvement does not rest primarily on the powerlessness of specific groups at the local level; it stems mainly from the tendency of the benefits of physical investment to spill out of small areas. Hence, individual communities—even states— have little incentive to undertake such programs. Why, for example, should a community situated on a river tax itself heavily to treat its sewage for the benefit of communities located downstream? In the case of some types of communications and transportation—the interstate highway network, for example—federal involvement is almost a physical necessity. Fifty state systems that did not mesh would be a disaster.

Although the case for federal intervention in physical investment is strong, the difficulties of designing appropriate policies are severe.

There is serious risk of creating perverse incentives: grants for treatment of waste may discourage the search for industrial processes that generate less waste; flood control projects may encourage uneconomic location of homes and industries; or grants for construction of transportation systems may foster excessive capital investment and inadequate maintenance.

REVENUE SHARING. Revenue sharing provides a means for expressing the national interest in increasing or equalizing public services while leaving the choice of services to the state and local governments that are closest to the people to be served. Since state and local governments depend on taxes that are less progressive and less responsive to economic growth than the federal income tax, the argument runs, the federal government should put its superior resources into general revenue sharing and perhaps also into block grants to support broad functions of government, but should not distort local spending decisions by specifying how the funds are to be used.

This strategy too has its problems, some of them arising from the conflict between the goal of maximizing local autonomy and the goal of preserving accountability to the federal taxpayer. Local governments may indeed not act in the national interest and may even waste the money. On the other hand, efforts to control local uses of such funds violate the spirit of the revenue sharing strategy—that local citizens are the best judges of what they need from the government. While federal controls may foster rigidity and stifle initiative, their absence can imply irresponsibility toward those paying the federal tax bill.

Competition and Complementarity

While different values and priorities would lead to different combinations of strategies, almost no one advocates concentration on any one of these strategies to the exclusion of the others. Even if substantial narrowing of income disparities were accomplished, financing medical expenses that are large as a percentage of family income would remain a problem. Even if families had funds for essential goods and services, supplies would be inadequate in some areas. Even with comprehensive national health insurance, medical facilities might be lacking in low-income or rural areas. Moreover, narrowing differences in individual incomes would not necessarily do much to alter disparities in publicly provided services such as elementary and secondary education. And even if local revenues were substantially equalized through revenue sharing, there would still be a national interest in encouraging particular kinds of services whose benefits spill over to other communities, such as pollution control, or in channeling services to recipient groups that are relatively powerless, such as the poor.

On the other hand, these strategies are to some extent alternative ways of solving the same problems or of moving toward the same federal objective. A decision to emphasize one strategy may mean less need for spending on another. For example, a high level of cash transfers would reduce the need for transfers in kind; and a high level of revenue sharing would reduce the need for federal subsidies for public services, except where national priorities were radically different from those of states and localities. In some cases competing strategies call for the delivery of the same service in different ways. Federal support of child care, for example, could be provided either through a voucher scheme that directly helped mothers purchase day care services or through grants to selected child care centers enabling them to offer their services free or at reduced prices. Better health care for the poor could be made available through a federally supported insurance system, under which the poor bought medical care wherever they wished, or through federal grants to health centers in low-income neighborhoods.

The next five chapters explore these strategies in more detail. They discuss what the federal government is now doing and some options for the future.

3. Redistributing Income

THERE ARE THREE DIRECT WAYS in which the government can affect the distribution of cash income among people: collecting taxes, providing cash transfers to individuals, and subsidizing employment and earnings in either public or private jobs. This chapter begins by examining the argument for an income strategy—for using these three tools in a major effort to reduce poverty and narrow disparities in individual incomes. It first discusses recent trends in poverty and income inequality and then the three sets of tools. The tax section gauges the impact of the current tax system on the distribution of income and describes the potential effect of three types of tax reform: reform of the federal individual income tax; reform of the social security payroll tax; and federal efforts to reform local property taxes. The next section focuses on the cash transfer system, discussing its present impact and explaining two ways in which it might be reformed: scrapping much of the current system in favor of a negative income tax and—less drastic—"filling the cracks" in current programs. The discussion then turns to proposals for reducing poverty by creating public jobs or subsidizing employment in the private sector.

Rationale for a Cash Income Strategy

Advocates of a direct cash income strategy argue, first, that poverty and inequality in the distribution of income are matters of national concern whose reduction deserves high priority among possible federal objectives. Second, they argue that taxes, transfers, and subsidized employment policies are more appropriate or more feasible than other possible tools for achieving these objectives.

Eliminating poverty and reducing inequality are related but not identical. The statement that people are "poor" means that they have too little income to purchase the minimum goods and services that most people in our society regard as essential to a decent life. Thus, to eliminate poverty it is necessary to raise the incomes of those at the bottom of the income distribution, bringing them up to some minimum level. The prevailing notion of what constitutes an acceptable standard of living changes over time—some people regarded as poor today would have been considered quite well off a hundred or even thirty years ago—but this does not make it impossible to eliminate poverty. It is of course impossible to alter the income distribution so that no one is at the bottom. Nevertheless, the federal government can take steps to ensure that no one falls far below the general standard of living by arranging its tax, transfer, and subsidized employment programs to guarantee everyone a substantial fraction—say, 40 or 50 percent—of the median income.

The argument for a major national effort to eliminate poverty rests partly on compassion, on the desirability of reducing the human misery that goes with deprivation. It also rests partly on the belief that there is a connection between poverty and other ills of society—that poverty breeds crime, disease, blighted neighborhoods, and other problems whose costs fall on the nonpoor as well as on the poor.

Even if poverty were eliminated, many would consider the persistence of large disparities in incomes undesirable. For a small group to enjoy incomes many times larger than that of the average family strikes many as unfair. Moreover, extreme differences in the incomes of parents give children unequal chances. Richer parents can provide better educational opportunities for their children, give them access to better jobs, and possibly pass on inherited wealth. Great disparity in incomes tends to rigidify the social structure.

There are many possible approaches to reducing poverty and inequality. One approach advocates in-kind transfers to low-income people, transfers designed to make sure that everyone has food, medical care, and housing. This approach is discussed in Chapter 4. Another strategy proposes increased investment in worker productivity

—giving the poor public services such as health care, education, and training designed to increase their future earning power. The War on Poverty of the 1960s attacked the problem this way; it encompassed federal programs for compensatory education, manpower training, preschool education, and the like. These programs are discussed in Chapter 5.

Those who advocate a direct income strategy as a solution to the poverty problem stress their belief that the principal need of the poor is an increase in their general purchasing power. They reject the idea that the government make choices for poor people by giving them food, housing, and medical care rather than money. The question, of course, is one of emphasis. A generous cash transfer program that eliminated poverty would reduce the need for transfers in kind but would not eliminate the argument that the government should help people buy certain kinds of essential services, such as medical care and higher education, which occur in large, infrequent lumps and may cause financial distress even for those who are not poor.

Those who advocate an income strategy rather than social services for the poor argue that taxes, transfers, and subsidized employment can change the income distribution directly and quickly, while investment in worker productivity may not pay off for a long time. They stress the relative ease with which income programs can be administered by the federal government and the potential difficulties of effectively administering social service programs. Here again the question is one of emphasis. Major reliance on an income strategy would only reduce, not eliminate, the need for social services.

Recent Trends in the Distribution of Income and in Poverty

However one measures income and its distribution among individuals and families, two facts stand out. First, the distribution of income is highly unequal. Second, even in a society of generally high incomes, a large number of people are still poor.

Distribution of Income

As can be seen in Table 3-1, the distribution of income among families is very far from equal. The 20 percent of families at the top of the income scale receive about 42 percent of all family income while

Table 3-1. Percentage Share of Aggregate Money Income Received by Each Fifth of Families and Unrelated Individuals, Ranked by Income, Selected Years, 1950–71[a]

Income rank	1950	1960	1970	1971
Families				
Lowest fifth	4.5	4.9	5.5	5.5
Second fifth	12.0	12.0	12.0	11.9
Third fifth	17.4	17.6	17.4	17.4
Fourth fifth	23.5	23.6	23.5	23.7
Highest fifth	42.6	42.0	41.6	41.6
Top 5 percent	17.0	16.8	14.4	n.a.
Unrelated individuals				
Lowest fifth	2.3	2.6	3.3	3.4
Second fifth	7.0	7.1	7.9	8.1
Third fifth	13.8	13.6	13.8	13.9
Fourth fifth	26.5	25.7	24.5	24.2
Highest fifth	50.4	50.9	50.5	50.4
Top 5 percent	19.3	20.0	20.5	20.6

Source: U.S. Bureau of the Census, *Current Population Reports*, Series P-60, No. 85, "Money Income in 1971 of Families and Persons in the United States" (1972), Table 14.

n.a. Not available.

a. Money income includes earnings, transfer payments, and income from property, but excludes income from the sale of capital assets.

the 20 percent at the bottom receive less than 6 percent. The distribution of income among "unrelated individuals" is even more uneven: the richest 20 percent receive about half the income and the other 80 percent share the remaining half.[1]

Moreover, these percentages have remained virtually unchanged since World War II. The share of before-tax money income received by the top 5 percent of families declined slightly, from 17 to 14 percent, between 1950 and 1970, but the share of the bottom 20 percent increased only from 4.5 to 5.5 percent in the same period.

Many people are surprised when they learn where they stand in the income distribution. In 1971, the lowest 20 percent of all families had money incomes of $5,263 or less, while the highest 20 percent had incomes of $17,513 or more. The top 5 percent—the affluent—had incomes of $27,128 or more. Only 20 percent of single persons had incomes over $7,600. Since these data are for 1971, it is appropriate to

1. Income is equal to money receipts as defined by the Census Bureau. It includes transfer payments, earnings, and income from property but excludes income from sales of capital assets. The term "unrelated individuals" is also a Census Bureau definition covering persons of fourteen years or more who are not living with relatives. An unrelated individual may be a person living by himself, living in a household of one or more families or other unrelated individuals, or living in group quarters such as a rooming house.

Table 3-2. Number of Poor and Near-Poor, Percentage of Total Population, Poverty Line Statistics, and Median Income, 1960–71

	Poor				Poor and near-poor				All families
Year	Number of people (millions)	As percentage of total population	Poverty line for four-person non-farm family	Poverty line as percentage of median income	Number of people (millions)	As percentage of total population	Near-poor poverty line[a]	Near-poor income line as percentage of median family income	Median family income
1960	39.9	22.2	$3,022	53.8	54.6	30.4	$3,778	67.2	$ 5,620
1961	39.6	21.9	3,054	53.2	54.3	30.0	3,818	66.6	5,737
1962	38.6	21.0	3,089	51.9	53.1	28.8	3,861	64.8	5,956
1963	36.4	19.5	3,128	50.0	50.8	27.1	3,910	62.6	6,249
1964	36.1	19.0	3,169	48.2	49.8	26.3	3,961	60.3	6,569
1965	33.2	17.3	3,223	46.3	46.2	24.1	4,029	57.9	6,957
1966	28.5	14.7	3,317	44.2	41.3	21.3	4,146	55.3	7,500
1967	27.8	14.2	3,410	42.8	39.2	20.0	4,262	53.4	7,974
1968	25.4	12.8	3,553	41.2	35.9	18.2	4,441	51.4	8,632
1969	24.1	12.1	3,743	39.7	34.7	17.4	4,679	49.6	9,433
1970	25.4	12.6	3,968	40.2	35.6	17.6	4,960	50.3	9,867
1971	25.6	12.5	4,137	40.2	36.5	17.8	5,171	50.3	10,285

Sources: U.S. Bureau of the Census, *Current Population Reports*, Series P-60, No. 80, "Income in 1970 of Families and Persons in the United States" (1971), Table 11; Series P-60, No. 86, "Characteristics of the Low-Income Population, 1971" (1972), Tables L, 1, 2; Series P-60, No. 83, "Money Income in 1971 of Families and Persons in the United States" (1972), p. 3.

a. Defined as 125 percent of the poverty line.

raise them by about 10 percent to reflect price and income changes since then. Still, many readers who consider themselves members of average, middle-income families may be surprised to find that in fact they are in the high-income group.

The surprising constancy in the degree of income inequality over the last two decades may hide some extremely important, offsetting changes that have occurred. A recent study by Peter Henle indicates that disparities in the distribution of wage and salary earnings became appreciably greater between 1958 and 1970.[2] This development may have been obscured in the aggregate data by increases in transfer payments which equalized incomes during the period and by the growing tendency of wives to work.

Poverty

The line between being poor and not being poor is an arbitrary one. A family with an income so low as to be considered poor in Boston would probably be quite well off in Bangladesh. And even within communities, views differ about what constitutes an acceptable standard of living.

In the early 1960s when poverty reemerged as a major national concern in the United States, there were many differing estimates of how many people were poor—and who and where they were—and it became evident that an official definition of poverty was needed for measuring progress toward the goal of eliminating it. Accordingly, the Social Security Administration developed a set of poverty-income levels for farm and nonfarm families of various sizes and composition; and families with incomes below these levels were officially considered "poor." Families with incomes below 125 percent of the poverty level were designated as "near-poor." The poverty-income levels have been adjusted annually to reflect changes in the general cost of living. In 1971, a nonfarm family of four was considered poor if it had an annual cash income of less than $4,137.

Under the official definition, 25.6 million people, or about 12 percent of the population, were considered poor in 1971 (see Table 3-2). Poverty, however, is by no means randomly distributed throughout the population. Blacks are more likely to be poor than whites. House-

2. "Exploring the Distribution of Earned Income," *Monthly Labor Review*, Vol. 95 (December 1972), pp. 16–27.

holds headed by women are more likely to be poor than those headed by men. Nevertheless, about 70 percent of the poor population in 1971 were white and over half lived in households headed by men (see Table 3-3).

Between 1960 and 1969, the number of poor people dropped substantially, from 40 million to 24 million. Most of the decline occurred in households headed by men (see Tables 3-2 and 3-3). These were the households that benefited most from the economic growth of the 1960s. The number of poor people living in households headed by white women declined by 700,000 between 1960 and 1969, but the number in households headed by nonwhite women increased by 400,000 during the period. Between 1969 and 1971 the decline in the

Table 3-3. Persons below the Poverty Income Level, by Family Status, Sex, and Race of Head of Household, Selected Years, 1960–71

Millions

Family status, sex, and race	1960	1965	1968	1969	1970	1971
Families with male head; male unrelated individuals						
White, total	21.1	15.4	11.0	10.1	10.7	10.6
Heads of families	4.9	3.6	2.6	2.5	2.6	2.6
Children and others related to heads of families	15.1	10.8	7.4	6.6	7.0	6.9
Unrelated individuals	1.1	1.0	1.0	1.1	1.1	1.2
Negro and other nonwhite races, total	8.1	6.7	4.0	3.6	3.6	3.5
Heads of families	1.4	1.2	0.7	0.7	0.7	0.6
Children and others related to heads of families	6.3	5.2	3.0	2.6	2.6	2.5
Unrelated individuals	0.4	0.3	0.3	0.4	0.3	0.4
Families with female head; female unrelated individuals						
White, total	7.2	7.1	6.4	6.5	6.8	7.1
Heads of families	1.3	1.2	1.0	1.1	1.1	1.2
Children and others related to heads of families	3.0	2.9	2.5	2.5	2.7	2.9
Unrelated individuals	2.9	3.0	2.8	3.0	3.1	3.0
Negro and other nonwhite races, total	3.5	4.0	4.0	3.9	4.3	4.3
Heads of families	0.7	0.7	0.7	0.8	0.9	0.9
Children and others related to heads of families	2.2	2.7	2.7	2.5	2.9	2.8
Unrelated individuals	0.5	0.5	0.5	0.6	0.6	0.6

Source: Bureau of the Census, "Characteristics of the Low-Income Population, 1971," Table 1. Figures may not add to totals because of rounding.

number of poor people was reversed—their number actually increased, reflecting the relatively high unemployment levels and sluggish economy of this period. The trend in the number of near-poor people was similar; a substantial decline in their number occurred between 1960 and 1969, followed by a slight increase between 1969 and 1971. Decreases in the numbers of poor and near-poor, reflecting improvements in the employment picture, are expected when figures for 1972 and 1973 become available.

If poverty is thought of in absolute terms—lack of a market basket of necessary goods and services—the gains of the 1960s are impressive. Far fewer people now have incomes too small to buy that basket. But it should be remembered that average income has increased greatly during the period. Hence if poverty is defined as relative to some measure of average income, the picture is far less encouraging. For example, if the poverty-income line for a family of four is defined as 50 percent of the median income for families of that size (see Table 3-2), there were 36 million poor people in 1963. In 1971, there were by that definition still 36 million poor. These figures suggest that although poverty in the market-basket sense has been declining the number of people receiving relatively low incomes may not have been reduced at all.

Taxes and the Distribution of Income*

Taxes have several functions. They allocate the cost of public goods and services among persons; they play a role in stabilizing the economy; and they affect the distribution of income.

Although views differ about what constitutes a fair system of taxation, one principle that commands wide support is that the general expenses of government should be distributed among persons on the basis of their ability to pay. This principle suggests that taxes should be progressive—that is, high-income people should pay a larger fraction of their incomes in taxes than low-income people, because people with high incomes give up luxuries to pay their taxes while those with low incomes give up necessities. The ability-to-pay principle also suggests that the poor should pay no taxes, since by definition they have less than enough money to buy the bare essentials and no way of contributing to the general costs of government. Accordingly, the ideal

* Prepared with the assistance of Benjamin A. Okner.

tax would be a progressive income tax from which the poor were exempt.

There are, however, both practical and philosophical arguments against sole reliance on such a tax. One is that if tax rates rise too rapidly as income rises, economic incentives may be impaired. People may make less effort to earn or invest if they have to give up a very large portion of their increased income to the government. Moreover, since middle- and high-income people are more vocal and politically powerful than the poor, it may be more difficult to raise income tax rates to obtain additional revenue than to derive it from other sources. It can also be argued that some taxes should be related to specific benefits received; for example, a tax on gasoline used to pay for roads helps allocate the cost of better roads to those who use them. More-over, people may be more willing to pay a tax when it is more appar-ently linked with specific benefits. The surprising willingness of wage earners to pay rising social security taxes may be related to the fact that many people link payment of these taxes with specific benefits they expect to enjoy themselves.

The present federal tax system is far from the ideal system that would be supported by those who believe in taxation according to the ability to pay. Taxes on the poor are heavy, and the tax system as a whole does little to alter the very unequal distribution of before-tax income. Although close to half of all federal receipts are derived from the individual income tax, which is moderately progressive and largely exempts the poor, this progressivity is offset by the effect of the pay-roll tax, which accounts for 30 percent of federal revenue and falls heavily on the poor. The payroll and individual income taxes taken together will account for almost three-quarters of total federal receipts in fiscal year 1974 and will do virtually nothing to alter the income dis-tribution.

The regressive effect of the payroll tax may be seen clearly in Table 3-4. The combined income and payroll tax of a four-person family with one earner is actually a smaller percentage of income if the family earns $25,000 than if it earns $10,000. While the affluent family pays a higher percentage in income tax, this is more than offset by the lower percentage of its income it pays in payroll tax.

The net effect of other federal taxes on the distribution of income is harder to identify. Estate and gift taxes are progressive, but account for only 2 percent of federal receipts. Corporation income taxes,

Table 3-4. Federal Individual Income and Payroll Taxes for a Four-Person Family with One Earner, Selected Earnings, 1963, 1968, and 1973

Earnings and tax items	1963	1968[a]	1973
$5,000 earnings			
Income tax	$420	$308	$98
Payroll tax[b]	348	440	585
Total tax	768	748	683
Effective income tax rate	8.4	6.2	2.0
Effective payroll tax rate[b]	7.0	8.8	11.7
Total effective tax rate	15.4	15.0	13.7
$10,000 earnings			
Income tax	$1,372	$1,198	$905
Payroll tax[b]	348	686	1,170
Total tax	1,720	1,884	2,075
Effective income tax rate	13.7	12.0	9.0
Effective payroll tax rate[b]	3.5	6.9	11.7
Total effective tax rate	17.2	18.8	20.8
$25,000 earnings			
Income tax	$4,889	$4,362	$3,890
Payroll tax[b]	348	686	1,264
Total tax	5,237	5,048	5,154
Effective income tax rate	19.6	17.4	15.6
Effective payroll tax rate[b]	1.4	2.7	5.0
Total effective tax rate	20.9	20.2	20.6

Sources: Calculated by authors from statutory individual income and payroll tax rates. Figures may not add to totals because of rounding.
a. Includes income tax surcharge.
b. Includes both employer and employee taxes.

which account for about 14 percent, are probably progressive, although some economists would question this. Customs duties, excises, and miscellaneous receipts probably have little net effect on the distribution of income.

Over the last few years the federal tax structure has become more regressive. Reliance on the payroll tax has increased from 16 percent of total revenue in fiscal 1960 to 30 percent in 1974, while the importance of the corporation income tax has declined from 23 percent of federal revenues in 1960 to 14 percent in 1974.

In the last four years changes in the individual income and social security payroll taxes have dramatically increased the burden on those with very low wages and reduced the burden carried by lower-middle-income groups. In 1969 a four-person family with one earner making $3,000 paid no income tax and was subject to a social security payroll

Figure 3-1. Changes between 1969 and 1973 in Federal Income Taxes and Social Security Payroll Taxes Levied on the Wages of a One-Earner Four-Person Family

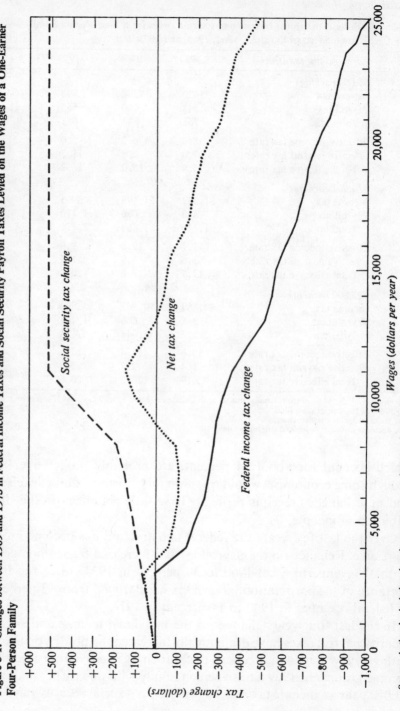

Source: Authors' calculations based on statutory requirements in each year.

tax of $288.[3] In 1973, the same family still pays no income tax but its payroll tax has grown to $351—a 22 percent increase. Figure 3-1 illustrates how the changes in income and social security taxes since 1969 have affected single-earner, four-person families with incomes below $25,000. The combined effects of the two tax changes have increased tax liabilities for families with incomes below $3,530; decreased the combined liabilities of families with incomes of $3,530 to $8,900; and increased taxes for those with incomes of $8,900 to $13,000. For incomes above $13,000 the combined taxes have declined, since income tax reductions for the higher-income groups have more than offset increased social security taxes.

Taken together, the individual income and payroll taxes do not change the distribution of income significantly, as may be seen in Table 3-5.

Individual Income Tax

More than any other federal tax, the individual income tax conforms to the ability-to-pay principle. The rate schedule is progressive. The marginal tax rate (the rate paid on increments of taxable income) for earned income rises from 14 percent in the lowest tax bracket to 50 percent in the highest. Rates for unearned income go from 14 to 70 percent. The combined effects of the personal exemption, the standard deduction, and the low-income allowance ensure that most poor families pay no income tax and that effective tax rates (taxes as a percentage of total income) paid by the near-poor are low.

Over the years, however, many special provisions have been written into the tax code to provide favorable tax treatment for particular types of economic activities. Some kinds of income are excluded from taxation or taxed at preferential rates. State and local bond interest is exempt from taxation—an exclusion that is usually defended on the grounds that the federal government has an interest in enabling state and local governments to borrow money at relatively low interest rates. Generous depletion allowances permit income from oil, gas, and other mineral production to be taxed at low effective rates—a preference that is usually defended on the grounds that it is in the national interest to encourage domestic production of oil and other minerals. Capital gains are taxed at much lower rates than ordinary

---

3. For reasons explained below (pp. 57–58), this includes both the employer and the employee payroll tax contributions.

Table 3-5. Combined Effect of Federal Individual Income and Payroll Taxes and Transfer Payments on the Distribution of Income, 1972

Population category and income quintile	Total income before taxes and transfers (1)	Total individual income and payroll taxes paid (2)	Total income after income and payroll taxes (3)	Cash transfers received[a] (4)	Total income after taxes and transfers (5)
			Percentage distribution		
Total population					
Lowest 20	1.7	1.1	1.8	40.2	6.3
20 to 40	6.6	5.0	7.0	26.8	9.1
40 to 60	14.5	13.3	14.8	13.1	14.6
60 to 80	24.1	22.8	24.4	10.3	22.8
80 to 100	53.1	57.9	51.9	9.6	47.1
Total	100.0	100.0	100.0	100.0	100.0
Sixty-five and over					
Lowest 20	0.7	0.4	0.8	27.6	4.0
20 to 40	1.3	0.7	1.4	15.4	2.9
40 to 60	1.5	1.2	1.5	4.6	1.9
60 to 80	1.8	1.7	1.8	3.1	1.9
80 to 100	3.0	2.6	3.0	2.7	3.0
Total	8.2	6.6	8.6	53.4	13.7
Under sixty-five					
Lowest 20	1.0	0.7	1.0	12.6	2.4
20 to 40	5.4	4.2	5.6	11.3	6.2
40 to 60	13.0	12.1	13.3	8.5	12.7
60 to 80	22.4	21.1	22.7	7.2	20.9
80 to 100	50.1	55.3	48.9	6.9	44.0
Total	91.8	93.4	91.4	46.6	86.3
Total dollar amount, in billions	772.1	151.7	620.4	80.1	700.5

Source: Based on the Brookings MERGE file of family units with incomes projected to calendar year 1972 levels. Figures may not add to totals because of rounding.
a. Includes old-age, survivors, and disability insurance, unemployment and workmen's compensation, public and general assistance (welfare), veterans' benefits, and military retired pay.

income, and capital gains on assets held until death escape the individual income tax altogether. Moreover, certain personal expenditures—charitable contributions and large medical bills, for example—are deductible in computing taxable income. The deduction for charitable contributions is defended as a means of encouraging private philanthropy and the deduction of large medical expenses as a means of easing the financial burden of serious illness. But whatever the justifications offered for these preferences and deductions, taken together they have three important effects: they reduce the revenue raised from the income tax; they make the tax less progressive; and they result in unequal treatment of persons in similar economic circumstances.

If present federal income tax rates were applied to all income received by individuals and families—with substantially reduced personal deductions and exemptions—income tax yields would be considerably higher. Joseph A. Pechman and Benjamin A. Okner have estimated that present rates applied to such a comprehensive tax base would have yielded an additional $77 billion in 1972. Alternatively, tax rates could have been cut by 43 percent and the same amount of revenue raised—for example, with rates ranging from 8 percent to 44 percent—if the lower rates had been applied to the more comprehensive base.[4]

A decision to exclude certain types of income or expenditures from the tax base or to allow certain personal deductions when computing taxes reduces the amount of funds that would otherwise be available to the government. Such a reduction is in fact a "tax expenditure" and its objectives and effects are similar to the actual expenditures that appear in the budget. The decision to make heavy medical expenses deductible in the computation of taxable income is no different from a decision to create a special government program to provide financial assistance to taxpayers with large medical bills. Both reduce revenues available for other purposes; but such a program would explicitly appear on the expenditure side of the budget whereas the "tax expenditure" does not appear anywhere. For this reason tax expenditures are subjected to far less critical scrutiny by the executive branch, the

4. Joseph A. Pechman and Benjamin A. Okner, "Individual Income Tax Erosion by Income Classes," in *The Economics of Federal Subsidy Programs,* A Compendium of Papers submitted to the Joint Economic Committee, 92 Cong. 2 sess. (1972), Pt. 1, pp. 13–40 (Brookings Reprint 230).

Congress, and the public than are budgetary expenditures. Another difference between explicit expenditures and tax expenditures is that the latter are more beneficial to high- than to low-income taxpayers because of the ascending marginal tax rate schedule. And tax expenditures provide no benefits at all to people too poor to pay income tax.

Tax preferences generally make the tax system less progressive. Many high-income people derive a large portion of their income from sources that receive preferential tax treatment or have large deductible expenses. Indeed, a great deal of their time and effort goes into ensuring that they receive their income in preferential form. As a consequence they pay astonishingly little tax. In 1969 a "minimum tax" provision was enacted with the intent of making sure that people with large amounts of preference income paid at least a minimum tax. Despite this provision, 276 returns filed in 1971 with adjusted gross incomes of $100,000 or more showed no federal tax liability whatever. Far more important, as may be seen in the first column of Table 3-6, these preferences make the individual income tax much less progressive than an examination of the statutory rate schedule might indi-

Table 3-6. Current Effective Federal Individual Income Tax Rates and Rate Increases under Two Reform Packages, by Income Class, 1974 Income Levels

Income class[a] (thousands of dollars)	Current law	Effective rate (percent)		Increase in effective rate (percentage points)	
		Package 1[b]	Package 2[b]	Package 1[b]	Package 2[b]
0–3	0.8	0.9	0.9	*	*
3–5	4.6	4.7	4.8	0.1	0.2
5–10	8.6	8.8	9.2	0.2	0.6
10–15	10.9	11.1	11.6	0.2	0.7
15–20	12.8	13.1	13.9	0.3	1.2
20–25	14.5	15.0	16.2	0.5	1.8
25–50	17.3	18.2	20.3	1.0	3.0
50–100	23.8	26.2	29.2	2.4	5.4
100–500	24.6	30.7	34.8	6.1	10.2
500–1,000	27.2	41.3	48.3	14.1	21.1
1,000 and over	29.8	46.7	54.9	16.9	25.1
All classes[c]	13.1	14.0	15.2	0.9	2.1

Source: Estimated from the Brookings file of 1970 individual income tax returns with data projected to calendar year 1974 levels.
* Less than half of 0.1 percent.
a. Income is equal to adjusted gross income as defined in the Internal Revenue Code, modified to include the full amount of capital gains plus items receiving preferential treatment.
b. The changes included in tax reform packages 1 and 2 are shown in Table 3-7.
c. Includes negative income class not shown separately.

cate. On the average, even extremely rich people—those with incomes over $1 million—pay less than a third of their income to the government in personal income tax despite top-bracket rates of 50 percent on earned and 70 percent on unearned income.

Various reforms of the income tax designed to reduce preferences and broaden the tax base have been proposed. Such reforms would have three characteristics. First, they would generate increased revenue without requiring a general increase in tax rates (or alternatively, they would permit a reduction in tax rates without loss of revenue). Second, they would make the tax more progressive, increasing the effective tax rates paid by high-income people and shifting a larger share of the tax burden onto those most able to pay. Third, they would reduce inequities in the tax, so that two persons with similar incomes would no longer pay very different taxes simply because their incomes came from different sources or because their expenditure patterns differed.

One simple reform would convert the personal exemption into a uniform tax credit. Under current law an exemption is worth more to high-income taxpayers ($525 for a taxpayer in the 70 percent bracket) than to those with lower incomes ($105 to a taxpayer in the 14 percent bracket and zero to a person with income too low to be taxable). But a uniform credit would be worth the same amount to each taxpayer. For example, a $150 nonrebatable credit in lieu of the present $750 personal exemption would have no effect on revenue but would reduce liabilities for all four-person families with adjusted gross incomes of less than $10,580, while increasing them for higher-income units.

A drastic reform would be to eliminate all exclusions and deductions and apply a single (and considerably lower) rate schedule to all forms of income, whatever the source. The resulting tax would be more progressive, more equitable, and infinitely simpler to comprehend and administer than the present one.

Two less drastic reforms are illustrated here. Each is a package of changes designed to reduce the preferential treatment of income and personal expenditures allowed by the present law. Package 1 consists of (1) increasing from 50 to 60 percent the portion of capital gains subject to tax and removing the alternative tax provisions; (2) reducing the amount of charitable contributions allowed as an itemized deduction by disallowing deductions for contributions amounting to less than 2 percent of income; (3) eliminating the current exclusion from income of the first $100 of dividends; (4) reducing by half the preferential treatment of income from mineral production and accelerated depreciation on real estate; and (5) increasing the preference-income base and taxing preferences at half the ordinary income tax rates. Package 2 incorporates all the changes in package 1 but stiffens most of them so as to produce more revenue. In addition, it includes (1) eliminating personal deductions for gasoline taxes, real estate taxes, and mortgage interest; (2) reducing the deduction for medical expenses; and (3) removing the investment tax credit. As shown in Table 3-7, the package 1 reforms would raise about $8 billion in additional income tax revenue in 1974, $11 billion in 1976, and almost $16 billion in 1978. Approximately 84 percent of the 1974 revenue increase would come from taxpayers with incomes of $20,000 and over.

Reforms that substantially increase effective tax rates for upper-income individuals and corporations have to be evaluated in the light of their possible impact on incentives, investment, and economic growth. And reasonable men can reach different judgments in balancing these economic considerations against the equity arguments for reform. But the case against tax reform cannot rest on the grounds, sometimes alleged, that it is impossible to raise much money unless one eliminates personal exemptions, charitable deductions, deductions for real estate taxes and mortgage interest, and other provisions that benefit large numbers of taxpayers in the middle range of the income distribution. Of the $15.7 billion that would be raised by package 1 reforms in 1978, only $2.8 billion (from reducing charitable deductions) would come from altering provisions that affect large numbers of middle-income taxpayers.

The package 2 reforms would raise considerably more revenue than those in package 1—$18 billion in 1974, $25 billion in 1976, and $33 billion in 1978. In this package, more of the changes would affect the average low- or moderate-income taxpayer: eliminating the deduction of gasoline taxes and homeowners' deductions for mortgage interest and property taxes, and reducing deductions for medical expenses. Such changes would affect a large number of families at all income levels, but the higher the level, the greater the effect.

Some of the reforms would also raise additional revenues from corporations—particularly the changes in capital gains taxation, the reduction of depreciation and depletion allowances, and the repeal of the investment tax credit. Adoption of the smaller tax reform package

Table 3-7. Revenue Effect of Various Structural Reforms of the Individual Income Tax under Two Reform Packages, 1974, 1976, and 1978

Billions of dollars

	1974		1976		1978	
Reform provision	Pack-age 1	Pack-age 2	Pack-age 1	Pack-age 2	Pack-age 1	Pack-age 2
Remove maximum tax on earned income	0.1	0.1	0.2	0.2	0.3	0.3
Remove alternative tax on realized capital gains and increase percentage included in adjusted gross income to:						
60 percent	1.6	...	1.9	...	2.1	...
75 percent	...	4.2	...	4.9	...	5.5
Eliminate deduction of gasoline taxes	...	0.7	...	0.9	...	1.2
Eliminate deduction of real estate taxes and mortgage interest	...	6.4	...	8.4	...	10.4
Remove dividend exclusion	0.3	0.3	0.4	0.4	0.4	0.4
Depreciation and depletion advantages						
Remove 50 percent of excess	0.1	...	0.2	...	0.2	...
Remove 75 percent of excess	...	0.2	...	0.3	...	0.3
Remove investment tax credit	...	0.8	...	1.0	...	1.1
Place floor on charitable contributions deduction						
2 percent	1.9	...	2.4	...	2.8	...
3 percent	...	2.3	...	2.8	...	3.3
Raise floor on itemized medical expense deduction to 5 percent	...	1.5	...	2.0	...	2.4
Tax unrealized gains transferred by gift or bequest in excess of $5,000	0.5	0.5	1.9	1.9	3.9	3.9
Revise preference income base[a] and tax at:						
One-half the regular income tax rates[b]	3.4	...	4.0	...	4.6	...
Three-fourths the regular income tax rates[b]	...	5.3	...	6.2	...	7.1
Total revenue effect[c]	7.6	17.7	11.2	24.7	15.7	32.9

Source: Estimated from the Brookings file of 1970 individual income tax returns with data projected to calendar years 1974, 1976, and 1978 income levels.

a. Revision of preference income base involves inclusion of state-local bond interest as a preference item and removal of the $30,000 exemption and the deduction for current-year taxes paid.

b. The regular income tax rates range from 14 percent to 70 percent. One-half these rates would therefore be a schedule ranging from 7 percent to 35 percent; three-fourths would be a schedule ranging from 10.5 percent to 52.5 percent.

c. The total revenue effect of each package is not equal to the sum of the components because various provisions interact with one another.

would add about $5 billion to corporation profits tax liabilities in 1974 and $7 billion in 1978. The larger reform package would increase corporation profits taxes by $10 billion in 1974 and $13 billion in 1978.

The progressivity of the individual income tax is moderately increased by the package 1 reforms and substantially increased by the package 2 changes (see Table 3-6). Under both packages, effective tax rates for those with incomes below $50,000 are affected only slightly. However, the increases in effective tax rates for those at the top of the income scale would be very large, especially with reform package 2, under which effective tax rates would increase from about 27 percent under current law to 48 percent for taxpayers with incomes of $500,-000 to $1 million; and for those with incomes of $1 million or more, effective rates would increase by 25 percentage points.

Administration Proposals

On April 30, 1973, the Nixon administration presented its proposals for tax change to the Congress. These include a number of changes—some involving tax reform, some tax relief, and others dealing with tax simplification. Several of the reforms and simplifications are clearly desirable; for example, elimination of the dividend and sick pay exclusions and the retirement income credit, reducing itemized deductions for medical expenses and casualty losses, instituting a limitation on accounting losses (tax shelters), providing a new and more effective form of the minimum tax, and giving states and localities a subsidy incentive to issue taxable rather than tax-exempt bonds. Other provisions, however, would apparently increase rather than reduce the inequities of the income tax. The tax credit for property tax relief of the elderly is of questionable merit (see discussion below, pages 64–68) as is the credit for parochial school tuition.[5] Additional tax relief for oil producers is an inefficient (and probably ineffective) way to help solve the nation's energy problems. And the proposed "miscellaneous deduction allowance," part of the simplification package, would lose revenue and amount to a standard deduction for taxpayers who itemize. A more straightforward approach would have been simply to disallow the deduction of certain personal expenditures.

5. In fact, the U.S. Supreme Court on June 25, 1973, ruled that such credits are unconstitutional. See also Robert D. Reischauer and Robert W. Hartman, *Reforming School Finance* (Brookings Institution, 1973), Chaps. 5, 6.

Major reforms that would significantly raise effective tax rates on high incomes (for example, raising taxes on capital gains) were not included in the administration's package. On balance, the administration's reform package will result in a loss of revenue. It is estimated that two reform provisions—a new form of minimum tax and restrictions on tax shelters—will raise about $800 million in the first full year. All the other administration proposals reduce receipts: according to Treasury Department estimates, tax relief for oil and gas producers will cost $50 million; property tax relief for the elderly, $500 million; a tuition credit for children in nonpublic schools, $450 million; and tax simplification, $400 million. In total, the Nixon proposals are estimated to cost $600 million.

In contrast to these proposals, the two tax reform packages discussed above would raise substantial additional revenue. They would also make the individual income tax a more effective instrument for income redistribution. On equity grounds, serious consideration might be given to income tax reform even if there were no need for additional revenue, in which case the tax reforms could be accompanied by an across-the-board cut in rates.

The Payroll Tax

After the individual income tax, payroll or employment taxes are the second largest source of federal revenue, and they are growing fast. In fiscal year 1974 payroll taxes are expected to bring in $78 billion, or 30 percent of all federal revenue, up from $22 billion, or 20 percent, ten years ago. This spectacular growth results primarily from rising wages, higher tax rates, and increases in the ceiling on the wages to which the tax applies.[6]

Unlike the individual income tax, the social security payroll tax is regressive—low-income families pay a much higher proportion of their income in payroll tax than do high-income families. The social security tax rate is now 11.7 percent and applies to the first $10,800 of wages earned in covered employment (scheduled to rise to $12,000 on January 1, 1974).[7] The tax is paid by employers, with half of it de-

---

6. The discussion in this chapter is limited to social security payroll taxes. Other payroll taxes for unemployment insurance and other purposes are a very small percentage of total revenues and are not discussed here.

7. The rate for self-employed persons in 1973 is 8 percent and applies to the first $10,800 of net business earnings.

ducted from the employee's paycheck. Thus the employee is aware of only half the tax. But economists generally agree that the whole tax actually comes out of wages: if there were no such tax, wages would be higher by approximately the amount paid by employers.[8]

Also unlike the income tax, the payroll tax is levied on the first dollar of earnings; no personal exemption or standard deduction is allowed. The result is a tax that bears heavily on persons and families in the lower half of the income distribution—because wages make up a large portion of their income and because the total amount of their wages is below the payroll tax ceiling. For high-income groups, the payroll tax drops to insignificance because wages and salaries constitute a smaller proportion of total income and because wages above the ceiling are exempt from the payroll tax. Moreover, since there is no pooling of family earnings—each earner pays the tax on his own wages up to the ceiling—the tax discriminates against families with more than one earner. At present, a family with two earners, each of whom is making $10,800, would pay twice as much tax as a single-earner family with the same $21,600 income.

As may be seen by comparing the first column of Table 3-8 with the first column of Table 3-6, effective rates for the payroll tax show a pattern that contrasts sharply with that of the income tax rates. Payroll taxes are a much greater burden to low-income families than income taxes. Indeed, up to about $12,000 a year, a four-person single-earner family pays more payroll tax than federal income tax.

Since the payroll tax constitutes such a heavy burden on wage-earners—and especially those earning low wages—it is surprising that it has aroused so little opposition, even from spokesmen for the poor. One reason may be that taxpayers are aware only of the half of the tax that is deducted from their paychecks and do not realize that the other half probably reduces their earnings by a like amount. A second and perhaps more important reason is that many people do not think of the payroll tax as a tax; rather, they regard it as an insurance premium or a personal contribution to a trust fund that will give them or their survivors a vested right to benefits in the event of death, disability, or retirement. This analogy to private insurance has done much to make the social security system popular but has obscured important issues about the way it is financed.

8. John A. Brittain, *The Payroll Tax for Social Security* (Brookings Institution, 1972), Chaps. 2, 3.

Actually, the analogy between the social security system and a private insurance or annuity scheme is strained. Social security "contributions" are compulsory, not voluntary, and the benefits received by a person are only loosely related to payments made in the past. Over the years, Congress has raised social security benefits so that workers who retired some years ago are receiving considerably higher benefits than would be justified on the basis of their contributions. Moreover, benefits have been raised more at the low end of the scale than at the high end, so that the average ratio of benefits to contributions is much higher for workers with low wages than for workers with high wages. The notion that the social security trust fund is a kind of bank into which a generation of workers puts money that can be drawn out later is far from the truth. Reserves in the trust fund are not much larger than needed to pay the current year's benefits (when a surplus builds up, Congress usually raises benefits). In any case, there is no mechanism by which a generation can put away real purchasing power in a public retirement system such as ours and retrieve it in the future. Real purchasing power transferred to social security benefi-

Table 3-8. Current Effective Social Security Payroll Tax Rates and Rate Changes with a Full Reform Package,[a] by Income Class, 1974 Income Levels

Income class[b] (thousands of dollars)	Effective rate (percent)		Changes in effective rate as result of reform package
	Current law[a,c]	Reform package[a]	
0–3	4.6	0.9	−3.7
3–5	4.8	1.3	−3.5
5–10	7.4	3.7	−3.7
10–15	8.7	6.0	−2.7
15–20	7.8	7.3	−0.5
20–25	6.7	7.8	1.1
25–50	5.3	7.7	2.4
50–100	2.4	6.2	3.8
100–500	0.6	3.6	3.0
500–1,000	0.1	1.4	1.3
1,000 and over	*	0.5	0.5
All classes[d]	6.3	6.2	−0.1

Source: Based on the Brookings MERGE file of family units with incomes projected to calendar year 1974 levels.

* Less than half of 0.1 percent.

a. The full reform package includes a $1,300 deduction plus $750 per capita exemption and removal of the taxable earnings ceiling. The effect on revenues is shown in Table 3-9.

b. Income is equal to money income plus realized capital gains.

c. Effective tax rates include the total of employee and employer contributions.

d. Includes negative income class not shown separately.

ciaries in any given year gives them command over economic resources that are no longer available for other uses. To the extent that the tax used to finance social security benefits falls on low-wage earners, resources in any year are transferred from these earners to social security beneficiaries.

It is misleading to think of payroll taxes as individual contributions destined to be returned to the contributor at a later date; it is far more accurate to think of the social security system as a national pension scheme, whose benefit levels are determined by the national priority accorded to the needs of the retired, the disabled, and survivors and whose costs are paid for by a tax on current earners. Once this point of view is accepted, there is no logical reason why the tax used to support the pension system should impose hardship on the poor. The arguments for financing pensions out of a progressive tax that exempts the poor are just as strong as those for financing other government expenditures in this way.

One possibility would be to abolish the payroll tax and finance social security out of general revenues. This would necessitate a drastic increase in other tax rates; for example, an increase of about 65 percent in income tax rates would be needed to compensate for the revenue lost by abolishing the social security payroll tax. A far less disruptive option would be to keep the payroll tax but make it progressive. Two straightforward reforms would do this. The first would involve introducing exemptions and deductions so that the poor are not taxed. There are two ways of incorporating exemptions and deductions into the payroll tax: allowing all taxpayers to claim them, as on the income tax, or providing them for lower-income taxpayers only. The second would remove the ceiling on taxable earnings. The first reform would reduce the revenue yield of the payroll tax and the second would increase it.

Estimates of the revenue effects of these reforms are shown in Table 3-9 for calendar years 1974, 1976, and 1978. The effect of the first type of reform (introducing into the employee portion of the payroll tax a $750 personal exemption and a $1,300 minimum standard deduction, the same as under the individual income tax) is shown in line 1a. Families with more than one earner would be allowed to pool their exemptions. Thus a single worker would be exempt from the payroll tax until his earnings exceeded $2,050. A married couple with two children would be exempt from tax until their earnings exceeded $4,300 (they would be able to deduct $1,300 plus four times $750). Under this reform all earners would pay less payroll tax than they do now, because all would benefit from the exemptions and deductions. The revenue loss in 1974 would be about $13 billion.

The second type of reform would restrict to low-income people the benefit of the exemptions and deductions by phasing them out as income rose. For example, a four-person family with earnings of less than $4,300 would benefit from the full amount of the exemptions and deduction and would pay no tax. As their earnings rose, however, the combined allowance (exemptions and deductions) would be reduced

Table 3-9. Revenue Effect[a] of Various Structural Reforms of the Social Security Payroll Tax, 1974, 1976, and 1978
Billions of dollars

Reform provision	1974	1976	1978
Personal contributions[b]			
1. Retain taxable earnings ceiling and:			
a. Introduce a $1,300 deduction and $750 per capita exemption	−12.9	−13.5	−14.1
b. Introduce a full deduction and exemption, but phase it out by $1 per $1 of earnings above basic allowance	−3.0	−2.8	−2.6
2. Remove taxable earnings ceiling and:	11.1	17.0	21.2
a. Introduce a full deduction and exemption as in 1a	*	3.2	6.8
b. Introduce a phased-out deduction and exemption as in 1b	10.1	14.2	18.6
Employer contributions			
3. Retain taxable earnings ceiling and:			
a. Introduce a full deduction and exemption as in 1a	−12.0	−12.6	−13.2
b. Introduce a phased-out deduction and exemption as in 1b	−2.6	−2.4	−2.3
4. Remove taxable earnings ceiling and:	10.3	13.4	16.8
a. Introduce a full deduction and exemption as in 1a	−1.7	0.8	3.7
b. Introduce a phased-out deduction and exemption as in 1b	7.6	11.0	14.6
Comprehensive reform			
5. Full deduction and exemption and removal of taxable earnings ceiling, applied to both personal and employer contributions (sum of 2a and 4a, above)	−1.7	4.0	10.5

Source: Based on the Brookings MERGE file of family units with incomes projected to calendar years 1974, 1976, and 1978 levels.
  * Less than $500 million.
  a. The revenue effect shown is the difference between collections estimated for each year under current law and amount under the reform provision. All amounts are calculated under the same growth and price assumptions used in Chapter 1.
  b. Includes contributions of the self-employed.

dollar for dollar. If the earnings of a family were $5,300, the allowance would be reduced by $1,000 to $3,300 and tax would be levied on $2,000. At the $8,600 earnings level, the allowance would fall to zero and tax would be levied on the full amount earned. With this modification, revenue losses would be reduced to about $3 billion in 1974 (see Table 3-9, line 1b). The burden of the tax would be removed for the poor and reduced for the near-poor. The disadvantage of this approach is that families in the phase-out range ($4,300 to $8,600, in the example) would face a double tax on increased earnings. For each additional dollar earned they would not only have to pay the tax but would lose part of their exemption. To avoid this problem it might be preferable to give the exemption and the deduction to all taxpayers and to offset part or all of the revenue loss by raising the tax rate.

Another way to raise more revenue and at the same time make the tax more progressive would be to remove the ceiling on taxable earnings. Indeed, revenue losses from the introduction of exemptions and deductions could be more than offset by removing the ceiling (Table 3-9, lines 2a and 2b). Simply removing the ceiling would increase personal tax collections in 1974 by over $11 billion. If the ceiling were removed and the full exemption enacted, total payroll tax collections in 1974 would be about the *same* as under current law, while removal of the ceiling and introduction of the phased-out exemption for personal tax contributions would increase 1974 collections by $10.1 billion.

The revenue effects of similar changes for the employer tax contributions are roughly of the same size and direction. However, removing the taxable earnings ceiling for employers results in less additional revenue than removing it does for personal contributions because the latter taxes include those paid by the self-employed. Many people in this category have very large earnings (for example, doctors and lawyers), and removing the taxable earnings ceiling on personal contributions therefore brings in a large amount of additional revenue.

For 1974, it is estimated that comprehensive reform of the payroll tax, including the introduction of the full exemption and deduction plus elimination of the taxable earnings ceiling, would cost about $1.7 billion (this includes the changes in both the personal and employer tax). Over the next few years as income and earnings rose, however, the reforms would result in increased collections: for 1976, an estimated $4.0 billion increase and for 1978, an estimated rise of $10.5

billion. These increases would reflect, first, the decline of the revenue
loss from the deduction and exemption as earnings rose and then very
large increases in revenue from the removal of the taxable earnings
ceiling in an economy with rising wages.

Not only can a reformed social security payroll tax raise more than
sufficient revenue to meet requirements for future benefit payments,
but at the same time the existing regressivity of the tax can be eliminated. Effective payroll tax rates under existing law are compared with
the rates under a fully reformed system in Table 3-8. Under current
law, the rates are low at the bottom of the income scale because a large
proportion of income received by people in these groups is not subject
to tax; much of it is income from transfer payments or from work not
covered by social security. At high income levels, current effective tax
rates are low both because of the taxable earnings ceiling and because
a large proportion of income is derived from property earnings—divi-
dends, interest, royalties, capital gains—not subject to tax.

Under the comprehensive payroll tax reform, effective rates are reduced for families with incomes under $20,000 and increased for fam-
ilies with incomes above that level. As can be seen, tax rates remain
relatively progressive up to the $100,000 income level and then fall for
the richest families—again, because earnings constitute a small proportion of total income at the top of the income scale.

Federal Action to Reform the Local Property Tax

Since the federal government collects no property tax, reform of the
property tax at first glance hardly seems to be a federal budget issue.
Nevertheless, during the 1972 presidential campaign both candidates
promised some form of federal assistance to relieve the burden of the
local residential property tax and several bills with this objective have
been introduced in the Congress.

The property tax has long been the mainstay of local government
financing. In 1972 local property tax collections amounted to $44 bil-
lion, or 38 percent of the revenues raised by local governments from
their own sources. About 45 percent of the support for public schools
in the United States is derived from the local property tax.

The property tax is an unpopular tax and its unpopularity appears
to have risen in recent years. Taxpayers' resentment—sometimes described as a "taxpayers' revolt"—has frequently taken the form of

negative votes on increases in property taxes for school support or on school bond issues thought to require higher property taxes in the future.

Actually, property tax collections have not been rising as fast as state and local taxes as a whole, but taxpayers appear to be more aware of property tax increases than of the rise of other taxes. This may be because property taxes are usually collected in large chunks once or twice a year, because reassessments of property may occur in infrequent large jumps, and because property tax rate increases are frequently subject to referendum. Hostility to the property tax may result as much from the inequities of its administration as from the level of the tax itself. Assigning a fair value to a piece of property is a difficult task. Even honest well-trained assessors may estimate the value of the same property very differently, and corruption and sloppy administration of the tax are by no means unknown. Resentment of the property tax also stems from the widely held beliefs that it is a regressive tax and that it weighs particularly heavily on older people with low incomes. Although economists do not agree that the property tax is regressive, there is no doubt that it constitutes a heavy burden for some old people who continue to live in houses they bought when their families and their incomes were larger and who now find that property taxes take a sizable fraction of their reduced income.

Whether accurate or not, the public's perception of the property tax as inequitable and regressive has led to widespread demands for state and federal action to improve property tax administration, to reduce the burden of the tax, especially on old people, and to provide other ways of financing local services, especially schools.

One approach to reform, often called a "circuit breaker," is designed to relieve the burden of the property tax by providing a payment or income tax credit to those whose property tax payments are a high proportion of their income. Eighteen states now have circuit breaker provisions, fifteen enacted since 1970, but most apply only to the aged. Only Michigan, Vermont, Oregon, and New Mexico have comprehensive programs for all low-income taxpayers.

In 1972 the Nixon administration explored the idea of combining property tax relief with aid to elementary and secondary education. In his State of the Union Message in January 1972, President Nixon promised a "revolutionary" new program "for relieving the burden of property taxes and providing both fair and adequate financing for our children's education."[9] The idea was to replace the portion of both local and state residential property tax revenues used for schools with a new program of federal grants for education, possibly financed by a new federal tax. The proposal did not move beyond the idea stage, however, largely because its dual objectives—relieving the property tax and reforming school finance—proved to be somewhat incompatible. Replacing the portion of the property tax used for schools with federal grants would require channeling large amounts of federal funds into districts with high property tax collections, and these are the districts least in need of assistance in financing schools. A program to equalize resources available to education would require quite a different formula—one that channeled larger amounts of money into districts with low property tax collections relative to school funding needs. It would be possible to design a program that accomplished both objectives, but only at a higher cost to the federal government than the administration was willing to contemplate.

During the 1972 election campaign the President switched to a more modest proposal, a federal circuit breaker to assist the elderly. This proposal was part of the package of proposals for tax changes submitted to the House Ways and Means Committee in April 1973. Under the administration's proposal, elderly homeowners would get a federal tax credit for property tax payments in excess of 5 percent of their income, up to a maximum amount of $500. Elderly renters would get a similar credit, computed on the assumption that 15 percent of the rent they pay is for property taxes. Both homeowners and renters with incomes up to $15,000 a year would receive a full credit. Those with incomes of $15,000 to $25,000 would get a partial credit, and those with incomes over $25,000 would get no credit. The credit would be rebatable—taxpayers whose property tax credit exceeded their income tax liability before credits would receive a cash refund from the government.

As an alternative to building a circuit breaker directly into the federal tax structure, the federal government might provide states with incentive grants to establish state circuit breaker programs. For example, the federal government could agree to reimburse states for some fraction of the cost of a state program that conformed to federal

9. *Weekly Compilation of Presidential Documents*, Vol. 8 (Jan. 24, 1972), p. 71.

guidelines. This is the approach taken in the Muskie-Percy Property Tax Relief and Reform Act (S. 1255) introduced in March 1973. Under S. 1255 the federal government would reimburse states for half the property tax relief provided to low-income homeowners and renters in those places that take appropriate action to reform the administration of their property tax. Thus the states would be offered a "carrot" to induce them to modernize and upgrade their property tax assessment procedures as well as to introduce circuit breaker provisions.

Under the most generous state circuit breaker for which federal aid would be given by S. 1255, states would rebate property taxes paid in excess of 3 percent of household income for those with incomes under $3,000; the percentage would rise as income rose to 6 percent for those with incomes of $10,000 to $15,000. No rebate would be given to those with incomes over $15,000. Under this formula a homeowner with an income of $2,000 would receive a rebate for any property tax in excess of $60 (3 percent of $2,000) and a family with an income of $12,000 would get a refund for any property tax in excess of $720. Similar relief would be provided for renters.

The administration's circuit breaker proposal would probably cost the federal government about $900 million a year. Estimates of the distribution of benefits by income class are shown in Table 3-10. The federal share of the cost of S. 1255 could be as much as $1.3 billion a year, although the actual cost would depend on how the states responded.

Table 3-10. Estimated Cost of the Administration's Proposed Circuit Breaker for the Aged, and Distribution of Benefits by Income Class, 1972

Income class (thousands of dollars)	Benefits		
	Total (millions of dollars)	Average (dollars per taxpayer)	Percentage of taxpayers benefiting
0–3	231	128	27
3–5	239	182	35
5–10	343	234	34
10–15	62	204	24
15–20	17	171	19
20–25	2	112	13
25 and over	...	...	...
All classes[a]	893	179	29

Source: Based on the Brookings MERGE file of family units with incomes projected to calendar year 1972 levels. Figures may not add to totals because of rounding.
a. Includes negative income class not shown separately.

The circuit breaker proposed by the administration does not channel the most aid to those at the bottom of the income distribution. As may be seen in the second column of Table 3-10, average benefits rise with income up to a point. Moreover, under all circuit breakers, higher average payments go to households with higher net worth within any income class. This is not surprising; people with more valuable houses generally pay more property tax.

A national circuit breaker would also distribute benefits unevenly among taxpayers in various regions. Among homeowners the major beneficiaries would be those in the northeastern states, which tend to rely more heavily on property taxes than do other parts of the United States. Benefits to homeowners in the South, which customarily has had low rates, would be negligible unless states in that region raised property taxes by a large amount.[10] For renters, however, the regional distribution of benefits would be the opposite. If a uniform percentage of rent was attributed to property tax in all localities, renters in the South would generally get credit for more tax than was actually reflected in their rent and renters in the Northeast would get credit for less than their true share.

The merits of a circuit breaker depend on which of several objectives one has in mind. If the principal objective is to lessen opposition to the property tax by making sure no one pays property taxes that are an excessively high portion of current income, some form of circuit breaker is a plausible mechanism, but in that case there is no apparent reason for limiting the aid to the aged. If, on the other hand, the objective is to assist those whose incomes are low relative to the cost of adequate housing, the circuit breaker is a poor mechanism indeed. It singles out property taxes from other costs of housing for no apparent reason and fails to channel aid to those who need it most. This objective would be much more efficiently served by a housing allowance that would give aid to those whose income was low relative to the cost of adequate housing in their community. The "low benefit" housing allowance discussed in Chapter 4 would cost about $2.5 billion if made available to all needy households. It would be far more effective than S. 1255 in distributing aid to low-income people whose need for housing was great. A similar housing allowance limited to the aged

10. A federally sponsored circuit breaker might indeed have this effect. Since it would shift some of the cost of the property tax to the federal government, it would encourage heavier reliance on the property tax in general.

would cost about $600 million—in other words, it would cost less than the administration's proposal and be far more effective in helping the needy aged.

If the objective is to reduce state and local tax burdens on low-income people, the circuit breaker is again a poor tool. Property taxes are not as clearly regressive as state and local sales taxes. If the federal government wants to make a serious effort to reduce the regressivity of state and local taxes, the most efficient means available is to disallow the deductibility of state and local general sales taxes in computing federal income taxes. Such a change would yield additional federal tax revenue of over $2 billion annually. Eliminating the deductibility of these taxes would give the states and local governments a powerful incentive to switch from sales taxes to income taxes to meet their revenue needs. If accompanied by federal action to allow a credit against federal liability (up to a maximum amount per family) for state income taxes, these changes could have a strong effect on the structure of state and local taxes and the distribution of individual incomes.

Cash Transfers

A second major way in which the federal government affects the distribution of income is by cash transfers under such programs as social security, veterans' pensions, and public assistance. Cash transfers are a large and growing fraction of federal expenditures. They tripled between fiscal 1950 and 1960, going from $7 billion to $21 billion (see Table 3-11). By fiscal 1970, expenditures had reached nearly $50 billion, and they are expected to rise to $86 billion in 1974. Total cash transfers in fiscal 1974 will be equal to 32 percent of the budget and 6.6 percent of the gross national product; in 1960 they were 23 percent of the budget and 4.3 percent of GNP.

A large proportion of federal cash transfers goes to people at the lower end of the income distribution, especially old people with low and moderate incomes (see Table 3-5). Indeed, cash transfers go farther toward equalizing the distribution of income than do federal taxes (compare columns 1, 3, and 5 of Table 3-5).

The current cash transfer "system," however, is not designed to ensure everyone a minimum income. Indeed, it is not really a system at all, but a hodgepodge of different programs enacted at various times for various purposes and mainly benefiting the aged and disabled. If

Table 3-11. Federal Expenditures for Cash Transfers, by Program, Decennial Fiscal Years, 1940–70, and 1974

Billions of dollars

Program	1940	1950	1960	1970	1974
Retirement and disability	**0.7**	**4.7**	**18.0**	**43.3**	**76.9**
Old-age, survivors, and disability benefits	a	0.7	10.8	29.0	53.5
Public assistance to aged, blind, and disabled	0.2	0.9	1.3	1.9	3.3
Miners' benefits in connection with black lung disease	...	...	...	...	1.0
Veterans' compensation and pensions	0.4	2.2	3.4	5.3	6.5
Federal civilian government retirement	a	0.3	0.9	2.6	4.9
Railroad retirement	0.1	0.3	0.9	1.6	2.5
Military retirement[b]	a	0.2	0.7	2.8	5.1
Other	**0.1**	**2.2**	**3.3**	**5.4**	**9.6**
Unemployment compensation	0.1	2.0	2.4	3.2	5.2
Public assistance under Aid to Families with Dependent Children	a	0.2	0.6	2.2	4.3
Total cash benefits	**1.0**	**6.9**	**21.3**	**48.7**	**86.4**

Sources: *The Budget of the United States Government*, and accompanying *Appendix* and *Special Analyses*, various years. Figures may not add to totals because of rounding.

a. Less than $500 million.

b. Military retirement is included in this table to give a complete accounting of the cash income maintenance programs. Military requirement is included in defense expenditures in Table 1-1 and in the tables showing total outlays in Chapter 8.

it was decided to pursue a cash income strategy in the future—to put major federal emphasis on reducing poverty and narrowing disparities in cash income—a thorough redesign of cash transfer programs would be in order. Two principal approaches to reform are explored here: replacing all or part of the current system with a new national income support program, similar to a negative income tax; and filling the cracks in present programs to make them more equitable and more effective in reaching those in need.

The Development of the Current System

The major federal cash transfer programs had their origin in the Great Depression of the 1930s. The tremendous economic dislocations of that period brought massive unemployment, sharp drops in earnings, and widespread destitution. The shock convinced the nation that major new programs were needed to protect people from income losses beyond their control.

The transfer programs that developed were strongly influenced by the philosophy of social insurance. Social insurance advocates believed that work should be the primary protection of individuals against poverty, but that people should contribute part of their wages to a trust fund and receive in exchange protection for themselves and their families against loss of income caused by old age, death of the breadwinner, unemployment, or disability. Benefits paid in the event of such losses would not be charity based on need but earned rights based on past contributions. The social security, railroad retirement, and unemployment insurance systems enacted in the mid-1930s all reflect this social insurance philosophy. They are financed from payroll taxes and provide benefits related to past wages to those whose eligibility has been established by prior contribution. The civil service and military retirement programs, established earlier, are also "earned right" programs.

The depression also focused attention on the immediate plight of destitute people who could not wait for future benefits under the new social insurance programs. Efforts were made to stimulate the private economy and to provide temporary public employment for those who could not find jobs in the private sector, but cash transfer programs were also established for needy people who could not work. The same act that set up the social security system in 1935 began federal contributions to "welfare" or public assistance programs run by the states for the benefit of aged, blind, or disabled persons with low incomes and for children in families with no breadwinner. These programs were expected to wither away as the economy prospered and social insurance programs matured.

Over the last four decades these depression-born programs have grown and changed, but three facts stand out in their history. First, the "earned right" programs have been far more popular and less controversial than the "welfare" programs, even though the difference between them is largely a fiction. Social security benefits, for example, have been raised far beyond the levels that would be justified by the actual contributions of retirees, so that a large fraction of social security payments are in effect welfare benefits. Second, the aged and disabled poor have been treated far more generously (even under welfare programs) than people who have low incomes for other reasons. Third, even with prosperity and social insurance, the problem of poverty has not withered away.

Retirement and Disability Programs

Benefits for retired and disabled people dominate current expenditures for cash transfers. Social security is by far the largest program, accounting for $54 billion in expenditures in fiscal year 1974, or 60 percent of federal cash transfers. Other programs primarily for retired and disabled people bring the total to $77 billion, or 89 percent of total cash transfers in 1974. These programs have gone a long way toward eliminating income insecurity resulting from old age and disability. The earned rights programs augmented by the newly enacted supplemental security income program, which begins January 1, 1974, have effectively put a national floor under the incomes of aged and disabled people.

SOCIAL SECURITY. Social security provides income to workers who have retired or been disabled and to survivors of deceased workers. Benefits go almost entirely to those who have established eligibility by paying social security taxes on their wages for a specified length of time (and to their survivors), although Congress has legislated a few exceptions; for example, minimum benefits are available to everyone over seventy-two, whether otherwise eligible or not. The size of a beneficiary's social security check is only roughly related to past earnings. The benefit schedule has been "tilted" over the years to favor workers with low average wages—they get benefits that are higher in relation to their past contributions than do those with high average wages.

When it was first enacted, social security provided modest benefits for a minority of the population. Only workers in industry and commerce were covered, retirement benefits went to the retiree only (with a small lump-sum payment to his estate on his death), disability was not covered, and there were no continuing payments for survivors or dependents. Until about 1950 expenditures under the program were small because benefits were low and few were eligible. In the last two decades, however, both expenditures and beneficiary rolls have grown rapidly. About 30 million people, or 15 percent of the population, will receive social security checks in fiscal year 1974.

This growth is attributable to several factors. First, the list of occupations covered by social security has been successively expanded, so that almost all workers are now covered, the exceptions being federal employees and a few employees of state and local governments and religious organizations. Second, various categories of dependents and survivors were added to the list of beneficiaries, and benefits for the disabled were initiated in 1956. Third, benefit levels have been steadily increased.

Periodic across-the-board increases in benefits have adjusted payments to compensate for increases in the cost of living and, especially in recent years, have augmented real benefits as well. Congress enacted across-the-board increases in benefits of 15 percent in 1970, 10 percent in 1971, and 20 percent in 1972. As a result, the typical benefit for a retired worker and spouse has risen from $2,300 a year in 1968 to $3,500 in 1973. This is an increase of more than 50 percent over a period in which consumer prices rose by only 26 percent.

The 1972 social security legislation not only provided a 20 percent benefit increase, but also liberalized eligibility rules, raised widows' benefits, and provided a new mechanism for automatic benefit increases in the future. Beginning in 1975, social security benefits may be increased annually to reflect rises in the consumer price index if the index has risen at least 3 percent since the last increase.

Social security benefits have been effective in reducing poverty among the aged and disabled. In 1966, according to Benjamin Okner, 60 percent of all social security payments went to people who would have fallen below the poverty line if they had not received such income. Over 90 percent of the elderly who would otherwise have been poor were saved from this by social security.[11] It does not follow, however, that *further* increases in social security would be an efficient way to reduce poverty. On the contrary, across-the-board increases are extremely expensive and only a small fraction of the extra money goes to the poor; most of it goes to people who, partly thanks to social security, are no longer poor. Raising the minimum benefit is not an efficient way of reaching the aged poor either, since many of those eligible for minimum benefits are not poor; they are people with another source of income, such as federal retirement, who worked for only a relatively short time in jobs covered by social security. Programs specifically targeted to assist the aged poor, whether they re-

11. Benjamin A. Okner, "Transfer Payments: Their Distribution and Role in Reducing Poverty," in Kenneth E. Boulding and Martin Pfaff (eds.), *Redistribution to the Rich and the Poor: The Grants Economics of Income Distribution* (Belmont, Calif.: Wadsworth Publishing, 1972), pp. 67, 73.

ceive social security or not, reach far more needy people per dollar expended than do further increases in social security.

SUPPLEMENTAL SECURITY INCOME PROGRAM. In the social security amendments of 1972, without much public notice, the Congress enacted a guaranteed annual income for the elderly and the disabled. Under these amendments, public assistance for the aged, blind, and disabled—the so-called "adult categories"—will be assumed by the federal government on January 1, 1974, renamed the supplemental security income (SSI) program, and administered by the Social Security Administration. Under SSI an aged, blind, or disabled person with no other income is entitled to $130 a month, or $1,560 a year, and a married couple to $195 a month, or $2,340 a year. The first $20 of any other income received (including social security benefits) will be disregarded in determining eligibility and an additional $65 a month of earned income will also be disregarded. Beyond this point, benefits will be reduced $1 for every $2 of additional earnings. Uniform federal eligibility standards and definitions are to be used in all states under SSI.

In the past the states have generally paid more generous benefits under the adult categories than under Aid to Families with Dependent Children, but benefits under the adult programs still vary enormously, not only from state to state but from category to category. For example, in late 1972, average benefits for aged welfare recipients ranged from $55 a month in Tennessee to $172 a month in New Hampshire; for the blind, from $67 in Mississippi to $165 in New Hampshire; for the disabled, from $64 in Louisiana to $170 in Alaska.

The new federal program will mean substantial increases in income for most beneficiaries. Some of the apparent increase is illusory, however, because SSI beneficiaries will no longer be eligible for food stamps.[12] This restriction could result in a loss of benefits worth $144 a year to an aged person with no income other than SSI and $240 for a similarly situated couple.

Even with the large increase in average payments provided by the program, SSI benefits will be insufficient to lift beneficiaries over the poverty line unless they receive additional income from some other source. An aged person with no income except SSI payments would need an additional $600 a year to reach the poverty line in 1974 and an

12. See pp. 107–08, below.

aged couple would need about $400 a year more. Retaining eligibility for food stamps for SSI beneficiaries would narrow, but not eliminate, the gap between their incomes and the poverty line.

OTHER RETIREMENT AND DISABILITY PROGRAMS. An additional $20.1 billion will be spent in fiscal year 1974 to finance other benefits that go primarily to aged or disabled people. These include veterans' compensation and pensions, and the military, federal civilian, and railroad retirement programs.

Military retired pay, which is financed out of general revenues, will cost about $5.1 billion in fiscal 1974 and is expected to grow rapidly over the next few years.[13] Federal civilian retirement, financed partly by a payroll tax on civilian employees and partly from federal revenues, will cost about $4.9 billion in 1974. Both military and civilian government retirement benefits are adjusted automatically for increases in the cost of living. Railroad retirement is a separate system, primarily because it was established before social security. The tax rate used to support this program is higher than the payroll tax rate and the benefits are larger than under social security. Railroad retirement benefits also were increased by 20 percent in fiscal 1972.[14]

Veterans' programs, financed from general funds, will cost about $6.5 billion in fiscal 1974 and are expected to rise substantially in the next decade as World War II veterans reach retirement age. Compensation is paid to veterans for disabilities incurred in the service and to their survivors in case of death while in the service. Pensions are paid to veterans on the basis of nonservice-connected disabilities and need. A veteran is automatically considered disabled if he is sixty-five or older. Legislation passed in 1972 provided 10 percent increases in disability and dependency compensation and a 6.5 percent increase for nonservice-connected pensions.

Veterans' pensions stand midway between the earned right programs and welfare. The pension can be considered a deferred payment for military service, hence an earned right. Although the veteran must show that he is needy to get the pension, the means test is administered in a simple, dignified way and receiving the pension does not appear to carry the stigma of being on welfare.

13. See Chapter 10, below.
14. For a more detailed discussion of the various programs, see Charles L. Schultze and others, *Setting National Priorities: The 1973 Budget* (Brookings Institution, 1972), Chap. 6.

Assistance to People Who Can Work

Cash transfers to people who are neither aged nor disabled will account for only $9.6 billion in fiscal year 1974, or 11 percent of all cash transfers. They are far more controversial, however, than the more costly retirement and disability programs, primarily because a conflict arises between two widely held values: (1) that people in need should be helped and (2) that everyone who can should work. The two major programs for such people—unemployment insurance and Aid to Families with Dependent Children (AFDC)—are run by the states, have widely differing benefit levels, and are generally conceded to be in need of reform. Controversy rages, however, over what constitutes "reform," especially for the AFDC program.

UNEMPLOYMENT INSURANCE. This complicated program, enacted along with social security, was part of the social insurance initiative of the 1930s. The idea was that employers would contribute to a special fund that would be used to finance benefits to those who became unemployed. Unlike social security, however, unemployment insurance is run by the states and benefits are set by each state (usually a percentage of previous wages with a ceiling set on the amount payable). The tax rate is also set at the state level, although the receipts are deposited with the U.S. Treasury and appear in the federal budget. The tax rate varies not only from state to state but from employer to employer within states, as each employer is given an "experience rating" based on past unemployment among his employees.

Weekly benefits are paid to experienced workers during limited periods of unemployment. The recipient must register for work and be willing to accept suitable employment. Federal law requires the states to have a basic program under which benefits are paid for up to twenty-six weeks. Legislation passed in 1970 stipulated that an additional thirteen weeks of benefits are to be made available if the unemployment rate among insured workers for the nation as a whole is 4.5 percent or higher for three consecutive months. Extended benefits can also be triggered in an individual state if the state unemployment rate of insured workers is as high as 4 percent for thirteen consecutive weeks and the unemployment rate is at least 20 percent above the rate in the preceding two years.

High unemployment rates pushed expenditures under the program up to $6.8 billion in fiscal 1972. They dropped to $6.0 billion in fiscal

1973 as economic conditions improved and are expected to be $5.2 billion in fiscal 1974.

In May 1973, the administration sent to the Congress proposals for improving unemployment insurance benefits. At present, states individually establish the level of benefits, which in general are equal to 50 percent of a person's previous wages, subject to a maximum amount. However, the maximum amounts set by the states are so low that two-fifths of all workers covered by the program receive benefits lower than 50 percent of previous wages. The new proposal would require the states to pay 50 percent of previous wages with a ceiling equal to at least two-thirds of the average weekly wages of covered workers in the state. The estimated cost of this provision would be approximately $800 million in fiscal 1974, rising to $960 million by 1978 (on the assumption of a 4 percent unemployment rate). The administration also proposes extending coverage to farm workers other than those who work on small farms.

Even if the administration's reforms were adopted, large disparities in the level of unemployment benefits among states would remain. Moreover, a few occupations are still not included. Coverage for domestic workers, for example, is still not mandatory and only three states provide it. Two other gaps are inherent in the nature of the program: (1) it provides no benefits for the inexperienced unemployed, new entrants into the labor force who are unable to find jobs; and (2) it provides no assistance for the long-term unemployed, those who have exhausted their benefits.

Controversy about unemployment insurance turns mainly on the conflicting objectives of ensuring an adequate income for those who cannot find work and of encouraging unemployed people to find another job. There have been various proposals to make the program more generous—to raise benefit levels, add supplementary payments for dependents, or make thirteen or more weeks of extended benefits available to all the unemployed regardless of the state or national unemployment rate. Opponents argue that the current system already reduces incentives for people who lose their jobs to find new jobs quickly and that making the program more generous would intensify the problem.

Martin Feldstein points out in a recent paper that the unemployment insurance system may operate to lengthen the average duration of unemployment and increase the unemployment rate.[15] Since unemployment benefits are not taxable, the unemployed worker drawing an unemployment check worth half his previous wages may be nearly as well off as when he was working and had to pay federal income and payroll taxes, and perhaps state income tax, union dues, and other work expenses. Especially in a two-earner family, the earner who loses a job may have little incentive to take another one as long as the unemployment insurance checks continue. Moreover, the existence of unemployment insurance may make workers less reluctant to take seasonal jobs and give employers less incentive to organize their operation on a full-year basis than they would otherwise have. Feldstein suggests making the employee's benefits taxable and shifting the basis of the experience rating from the firm to the individual, so that a worker who draws unemployment insurance benefits knows that his wages will be subjected to a higher tax rate in the future. This last suggestion would be difficult to administer, since the employer would have to keep separate records on each employee, depending on his prior unemployment experience. And while that experience may to some extent have been within the control of the employee, it will largely have been determined by events over which he had no influence. Moreover, during periods of high prosperity the number of workers drawing unemployment insurance falls to a very low percentage of the covered labor force, and the average duration of unemployment becomes very short. This suggests that in a strong labor market workers do not take advantage of unemployment insurance to remain away from work—or at least, that this effect is not very pronounced.

AID TO FAMILIES WITH DEPENDENT CHILDREN. By far the most controversial federal cash transfer program is Aid to Families with Dependent Children. It was set up in the 1930s to deal with what was thought to be a relatively small problem—the plight of needy children in families with no male breadwinner, families in which the father had died or was absent for a long time. Originally the aid went only to children, but in 1950 assistance was extended to the adult, usually the mother, responsible for the children.

The AFDC program is administered by the states, which establish

15. Martin Feldstein, "Lowering the Permanent Rate of Unemployment," Discussion Paper 259 (Harvard Institute of Economic Research, Harvard University, 1972; processed), pp. 79–80, 84, 95–96.

the level of benefits and, within broad federal guidelines, who is eligible. The federal government then reimburses the states for a certain percentage of the costs. As with the adult categories of welfare, there is wide variation in the average size of the benefits from state to state. In December of 1972, the average monthly benefit for the country as a whole was $53.95 per recipient. Since families receiving AFDC averaged 3.5 persons per family, the average family benefit was approximately $191 a month. Benefits per recipient ranged from $14.41 in Mississippi to $95.01 in Massachusetts.

When the program was set up, the prevailing view was that men should be strongly encouraged to work—unless physically unable to do so—but that mothers should be encouraged to stay home. This view was reflected in the AFDC program. Aid was not available to families, no matter how poor, with an able-bodied male adult at home, and if the mother went to work, her welfare payments were reduced by the full amount of her earnings. By the 1960s, however, attitudes had changed and critics were pointing out that both these features might have perverse effects. Fathers might be induced to desert their families (or not marry the mother) in order to make them eligible for welfare, and mothers able to work might be discouraged from doing so. Hence, the 1962 amendments gave states the option of providing aid to needy families dependent on an unemployed father. The 1967 amendments changed the rules about earnings. Since then, families have been allowed to keep the first $30 of earnings each month without any reduction in their benefits. Above this amount, benefits are reduced by $2 for each $3 earned. From the family's point of view, this amounts to a tax of 67 percent on earnings over $30 a month—more than the top-bracket rate on earnings under the individual income tax.

For the first three decades of its existence AFDC involved a relatively small number of recipients—the number fluctuated between 1 and 1.5 percent of the population until the late 1950s. As the recessions of 1958 and 1960 developed, the proportion of the population receiving AFDC benefits rose from 1.4 percent in 1958 to 2.2 percent in 1964. In the late 1960s, however, despite the fact that the economy was prospering and unemployment rates were low, the proportion receiving AFDC began to rise rapidly. The recession of 1971–72 led to further increases. By 1972, 11 million persons, or 5.3 percent of the population, were receiving AFDC benefits. The AFDC rolls are constantly changing, however. The average length of time on welfare is not very long; one-fourth of the cases "close" every six months and one-third every year. For many mothers receiving AFDC the problem is not permanent lack of work but sporadic unemployment and low wages.

The rising welfare rolls focused attention on the cost of AFDC to federal and state taxpayers as well as on its inequities and perverse incentives and led to widespread demands for welfare reform. Some "reformers" simply wanted to cut costs by tightening eligibility rules and reducing benefits. Others wanted to reduce disparities among the states by putting a federal floor under welfare payments, to extend aid to families with low incomes headed by men ("the working poor"), and to increase work incentives by allowing families to retain a larger portion of their earnings.

In 1969 the Nixon administration proposed a major welfare reform that would have put a federal floor under the income of all families with children and extended aid to the working poor for the first time. The original family assistance plan would have provided federal assistance of $1,600 a year to a family of four. A family could earn up to $60 a month before its benefits were reduced, and the reduction would have been at a rate of 50 percent on earnings above that amount. The proposal, in a modified form, was passed by the House of Representatives but ran into difficulty in the Senate Finance Committee. A revised welfare reform proposal, reflecting the House version, was reintroduced during the Ninety-second Congress. The bill (H.R. 1) would have provided an annual income of $2,400 for a family of four but would have eliminated food stamps and kept the marginal tax rate at 67 percent. This bill also passed the House. It again ran into difficulties in the Senate Finance Committee, where one group of legislators wanted to provide a more generous program and another group was interested in tightening up and reducing the existing program. Late in the legislative session, the bill was brought to the floor of the Senate. No agreement could be reached on the AFDC portion of welfare reform, so it was dropped; only the liberalization of social security benefits and the reform of the adult categories of welfare (the new SSI program discussed above) were enacted into law. The administration did not renew its request for reform of the AFDC program in the 1974 budget.

Reforming Cash Transfers

Despite the recent growth in cash transfer programs, substantial numbers of people are still poor and many others live close to the poverty line. What should be done? Should the cash transfer system be reformed so that everyone's income is brought at least up to the poverty line? Or should efforts be made to solve part of the problem by subsidizing employment or by some other means?

The approximately 26 million people with incomes below the poverty line in 1971 were an extremely diverse group. About 20 million were members of families, and of these, nearly half were children. About 12 million poor people lived in families in which the head worked, 5 million of them in families in which the head worked full time all year, and 7 million in families where the head worked part of the year. Of the family heads not working year round, some were elderly, some disabled, some unable to find work, some had still other reasons. In other words, some families were poor because the head did not or could not work, others because family earnings were not sufficient to raise them above the poverty line.

As noted, the approach to the poverty problem reflected in current cash transfer programs is to devise separate cash transfer programs for various categories of people in need of income. The result is a hodgepodge of programs within which most aid goes to categories of the poor judged "unable to work," especially the aged and disabled, and little aid is available for those who do work but remain poor. Even within aided categories, benefit levels often vary greatly from state to state.

The categorical approach has come under increasing attack in recent years on the grounds that it is inherently inequitable to treat equally needy people in such different ways and that the present categories make little sense. With so many nonpoor mothers joining the work force, even when their children are small, it seems anachronistic to have a welfare system that treats men so differently from women and discourages welfare recipients from working by taxing their earnings at a high rate.

A NEGATIVE INCOME TAX. Dissatisfaction with the categorical approach has generated proposals for a drastic reform: scrapping existing transfer programs (and perhaps some service programs as well) and replacing them with a single comprehensive program, such as a negative income tax. A new program of this sort would guarantee everyone a basic minimum income, the amount depending on family size, but would encourage people to work by allowing them to retain a substantial fraction of their earnings.

This drastic solution is tremendously appealing at first glance. Instead of the present incredibly complex patchwork of programs that affect different people so erratically and are so demonstrably inequitable, there would be a single comprehensive system based only on need and administered in a dignified, impersonal way, perhaps by the Internal Revenue Service. For example, the national program might guarantee a family of four $4,000 a year and reduce the guarantee by one dollar for each two dollars earned. No one would be destitute, and everyone would have an incentive to work, because families with earnings would always be better off than those without.

Attempts to translate the idea into specific legislation, however, have revealed some difficulties that are inherent in any income transfer program of this type. First, there is the problem of balancing work incentives for those who are able to work against the needs of those who cannot. A guarantee level that is adequate to the needs of those who cannot work may tempt some workers to drop out of the labor force or at least to reduce their effort. Allowing people to keep a sizable fraction of their earnings should encourage work, but it also means that benefits go to people with substantial earnings, which sharply increases the cost of the program. For example, if the guarantee was $4,000 and benefits were reduced only by one dollar for each three dollars earned, families with incomes up to $12,000 would get some benefits.

A second problem that must be faced in designing this type of income transfer system is how to balance the competing claims of large and small families. The basic guarantee reflects a judgment about what people need to maintain an adequate standard of living. Big families clearly need more income than small families. The difficulty is that, if the guarantee rises with family size, there will be some income levels at which individuals and small families will pay taxes while larger families with the same earnings receive cash transfers from the government. A couple with one child and $8,000 in earnings might wind up paying substantial taxes to provide benefits to another couple with the same (or even larger) income and five children. If having an additional child is regarded as primarily a voluntary act—like buying an additional car—one might question whether such transfers are equitable. Moreover, if a low rate of population growth is thought desirable, one might ask whether substantial transfers from small to large families do not set up perverse incentives.

A third problem arises because of the disparities in price levels and standards of living between the North and the South and between rural and urban areas in the same region. A family of four would clearly have difficulty living on $4,000 a year in New York City; the same sum would not only buy more in rural Alabama, but would compare far more favorably with the prevailing standards of living. This is not an argument against a generous negative income tax but a reason for developing meaningful indexes of wage levels and living costs in different parts of the country. Such indexes would make it possible to have a high average benefit, with variations from place to place in accordance with prevailing costs and standards of living.[16]

Finally, there is the problem of meshing the new income transfer system with existing contributory programs, such as social security, and with in-kind transfers, such as Medicaid and public housing. The most drastic solution would be not to try—to scrap these programs or change their nature so that they were supplementary to the basic cash transfer program. For example, if the cash transfer program could be relied on to provide a minimum income for all aged persons, social security could be revamped into a strictly wage-related insurance program whose purpose was simply to ensure higher retirement income (or survivors and disability benefits) to those with higher wages, not to keep people out of poverty. Since the social security benefits would then be supplementary to the minimum income provided by the negative income tax, they would not need to be as large as they are now, and the payroll tax could be reduced and a comparable amount added to the individual income tax to help pay the costs of guaranteeing the minimum income. However, such a wholesale dismemberment of popular existing programs in favor of unknown new ones seems unlikely to appeal to politicians or voters.

The cost of a negative income tax depends both on the level of the guarantee and on the rate at which benefits are reduced as income rises (the marginal tax rate). Table 3-12 shows estimates of the cost (above that of existing welfare programs) of a universal negative in-

16. For a discussion of this point, see Schultze and others, *Setting National Priorities: The 1973 Budget*, pp. 208–10.

come tax in 1976. Three guarantee levels are shown—$2,400, $3,600, and $4,800 a year for a family of four. The estimates assume that if the family receives benefits from any other income maintenance program, such as social security, such benefits would reduce negative income tax payments dollar for dollar. In other words, such benefits would be subject to a marginal tax rate of 100 percent. All other income, such as wages, would be subject to a lower tax rate. For each guarantee level three alternative marginal tax rates are shown: 33, 50, and 67 percent.

As may be seen in the table, a negative income tax with a $2,400 guarantee and a tax rate of 67 percent would cost the federal government less in 1976 than continuing current public assistance programs. This is not surprising; $2,400 is an extremely low benefit for a family of four with no other income. Benefit levels under public assistance programs are now substantially higher than this in most states, and

Table 3-12. Net Federal Cost of a Universal Negative Income Tax and Cost of Assistance to the Poor under Existing System, Fiscal Year 1976

Income for family of four under negative income tax, and existing benefit	Marginal tax rate (percent)	Total cost in 1976 (billions of dollars)
Negative income tax: guaranteed income[a] (dollars)		
2,400	67	6.2
2,400	50	6.9
2,400	33	9.1
3,600	67	12.1
3,600	50	14.8
3,600	33	22.0
4,800	67	21.1
4,800	50	27.1
4,800	33	43.3
Existing system of benefits to poor		
Cash assistance[b]	...	10.3
Federal	...	6.9
State and local	...	3.4
Food stamps	...	2.4

Source: Unpublished material developed by Harold Beebout and George Chow with the TRIM model at the Urban Institute.

a. The $2,400 level of guarantee assumes $800 per year per person for the first two persons, $400 per person for the third through the fifth, and $300 per person up to the eighth.

The $3,600 guarantee assumes $1,200 for the first two family members, $600 for the third through the fifth, $500 for the sixth and seventh, and $400 for the eighth.

The $4,800 proposal assumes $1,600 for the first two family members, $800 for the third through the fifth, $600 for the sixth and seventh, and $500 for the eighth.

b. Uses an annual accounting period (see Jodie T. Allen, "Designing Income Maintenance Systems: The Income Accounting Problem," Working Paper 958-9 [Washington: Urban Institute, 1972; processed]) and does not exclude the first $360 of earned income as in the existing system.

the projections of public assistance costs assume that benefit levels will increase in the future at least as fast as the cost of living. Substituting such a program for current public assistance programs would extend small amounts of aid to some needy individuals and childless couples not covered by present welfare programs, but would by no means eliminate poverty and would make most families now on welfare worse off, unless the states supplemented the benefits of the national program from their own sources. Lowering the tax rate to 50 or 33 percent would enhance work incentives, increase benefits for the working poor and near-poor, and make the program more expensive. A negative income tax with a $2,400 guarantee and a 33 percent tax rate would be of substantial help to families with moderate earnings. A family of four with earnings of $3,600 a year would have its total income boosted to $4,800 by a negative tax payment of $1,200 ($2,400 minus one-third of $3,600). Smaller benefits would be available to families of four with earnings up to $7,200. Families without earnings, however, would not benefit from the lower tax rate.

Even a program with a $3,600 guarantee would not eliminate poverty for those who have no other income, since the poverty line for a family of four is likely to be about $4,750 by 1976. If a 50 percent tax rate was applied, a family of four with $2,400 in earned income would be lifted to just above the poverty line, and if a 33 percent rate was applied, they would be lifted over the poverty line ($5,200). Single adults who are aged or disabled would be worse off than under existing legislation and couples slightly better off. This second program would, however, substantially increase the incomes of families on welfare in states with low benefit levels and greatly ease the plight of the working poor. With a $3,600 guarantee and a 50 percent tax rate, some aid would go to families of four with incomes up to $7,200. The total costs would be considerably higher: $15 billion with a 50 percent tax rate, $8 billion more than the estimated federal cost of the cash maintenance programs for 1976. However, if food stamps were eliminated, the net cost would go down by $2.4 billion.

A program with a $4,800 guarantee for a family of four, by contrast, would entirely eliminate poverty, improve the position of almost everyone now on welfare, and give major aid to the working poor and near-poor. Even with a high tax rate (67 percent), some aid would be provided to families with incomes up to nearly $7,200. But the total cost would be $21 billion, or $14 billion above the estimated federal costs of the current programs and $11 billion above the total costs (including state and local expenditures). Single adults with no other income would be marginally better off ($1,600 a year rather than $1,560) and adult couples notably better off ($3,200 a year rather than $2,340). The cost of the $4,800 guarantee rises rapidly as the marginal tax rate is reduced.

In view of the difficulties of picking a single guarantee level high enough to be adequate for those with no other income and low enough not to impair incentives, one might propose a two-level system. The aged and disabled would be given a fairly generous guarantee—$3,200 for a couple and $4,800 for a family of four—but their earnings would be taxed at 67 percent, since preserving their work incentive would not be crucial. Other families would be given a lower guarantee— $2,800 for a family of four, for example—but their earnings would be taxed at only 33 percent to provide a strong incentive to work. A mother with three children, for example, who worked part time and earned $2,100 would have a total income of $4,200—$2,100 from her earnings and $2,100 from the negative income tax. A man who had a wife and two children and earned $3,000 a year would end up with a total annual income of $4,800, an amount just above the poverty line estimated for 1976.

Such a two-tiered system would cost $6.5 billion to $7 billion more in 1976 than the cost of the existing public assistance program. This rough estimate does not count the cost of the child care that would have to be provided for many mothers of young children if they were to work, even part time. The system would have several big advantages. It would entirely eliminate poverty among the aged and disabled. It would steady the income of the sporadically employed and provide substantial help to those who can command only low wages or can work only part time. However, it makes two questionable assumptions: (1) that society expects everyone who is not aged or disabled, even mothers of small children, to work at least part of the time, and (2) that everyone who is not aged or disabled can find some kind of job at least part time or for part of the year. If jobs are not in fact available (or made available through public job-creation programs, discussed in the next section), families without earnings would remain in poverty and many families now on welfare in the more generous states would suffer a sharp drop in their incomes.

FILLING THE CRACKS. Although drastic reform of the cash transfer system has much to recommend it, it would be extremely difficult to accomplish in practice. The idea of a guaranteed income, even if supplemented by strong incentives to work, strikes many as undermining basic values such as self-reliance and the work ethic. The existing cash transfer programs, particularly the earned right programs, have a constituency and many would argue against replacing or undercutting them. Hence, from a practical point of view it seems useful to consider whether a more satisfactory income transfer system could not be obtained by improving existing programs—filling the cracks, so to speak, in the existing cash transfer system. Such improvement might involve: (1) retention of social security and other retirement and disability programs with only minor reforms, and (2) introducing into both AFDC and unemployment insurance a national standard of benefits and eligibility and improved work incentives.

If no legislative action is taken to change existing cash transfer programs, total expenditures will still continue to rise. More people become eligible for social security each year, and new beneficiaries generally have higher benefits than persons already on the rolls.[17] This is also true for railroad, federal civilian, and military retirement. In addition, under recent legislation these programs, except railroad retirement, are to be adjusted automatically for increases in the cost of living. As the labor force grows, an increasing number of people will also become eligible, even at full employment, for unemployment benefits. Table 3-13 shows the projected growth in cash transfer programs from 1974 to 1978. The projections assume some further increase in the number of welfare recipients, but at a much slower pace than in the recent past. All the benefits have been adjusted for future increases in the cost of living.

If the reductions proposed in the 1974 budget do not take place, these programs could be expected to grow from the $83 billion estimated in 1974 to more than $112 billion by fiscal 1978. The cuts proposed for these programs would only reduce them by $1.5 billion in fiscal 1974 and $1.6 billion in 1978.

RETIREMENT AND DISABILITY PROGRAMS. In the past, social security, veterans', and railroad retirement benefits have been adjusted

17. For example, a person who retired in 1965 never paid social security tax on more than $4,800 of his or her annual wages, and benefits are calculated accordingly. A person retiring in 1972 could have had wages of up to $9,000 in his record because of increases in the ceiling on taxable earnings.

Table 3-13. Projected Cost of Existing Federal Cash Transfer Programs, Fiscal Years 1974–78[a]

Billions of dollars

Description	1974	1975	1976	1977	1978
Cost before reductions proposed by the administration	82.8	91.3	97.9	104.9	112.4
Proposed reductions	1.5	1.5	1.6	1.6	1.6
Cost after proposed reductions	81.3	89.8	96.3	103.3	110.8

Sources: *The Budget of the United States Government, Fiscal Year 1974; The Budget of the United States Government—Appendix, Fiscal Year 1974; Special Analyses, Budget of the United States Government, Fiscal Year 1974;* and authors' estimates.

a. Excludes military retired pay.

on an ad hoc basis not only for increases in the cost of living but to increase real benefits also. If across-the-board increases in real benefits of 5 percent were legislated for these three programs to go into effect in January 1975 and again in January 1977, they would add $3.6 billion to fiscal 1976 and $8.0 billion to fiscal 1978 expenditures. Increases of 10 percent on the same dates would double the budgetary costs, adding $16 billion to expenditures in 1978. The latter, more generous increases would roughly duplicate the actual gains that occurred between fiscal 1969 and 1973. Across-the-board increases in benefits under retirement programs are clearly expensive. Moreover, as pointed out earlier, they are not an efficient way of eliminating poverty among the aged, because so much of the increase in benefits goes to people who are not poor.

Another type of proposal, enacted several times in the past, is an increase in the minimum benefit under social security. The minimum benefit is the smallest benefit payable, and quite often it goes to persons who have major pension rights in other systems, such as federal or state retirement programs. People frequently retire under these programs and then work in employment covered by social security just long enough to meet minimum requirements for eligibility. Raising the minimum benefit is quite expensive and is not very effective in reducing poverty. An increase in the minimum from the current $84.50 a month to $109.50 a month would cost $900 million if fully effective in calendar 1974.

However, some of the people receiving the minimum benefit have worked at very low wages and paid social security taxes for a long period of time. The 1972 legislation devised a special minimum benefit to long-term low-paid workers.[18] Increasing this special minimum by 20 percent would cost only about $130 million and would be far more effective in reaching the needy than an increase in the general minimum.

The 1972 legislation provided that the earnings record for men retiring in the future would include the record up to the age of sixty-two, instead of sixty-five as in the past. Women's benefits have been calculated this way since 1956. The effect of the provision is to raise benefits, since earnings between sixty-two and sixty-five tend to be lower than at younger ages. Extending this feature to those already retired and not now entitled to it would cost $1.2 billion in calendar year 1974 and would grow to $1.3 billion by 1978 because of the cost-of-living adjustments.

Another proposal for expanding social security benefits is to remove the age limitation (now fifty) on eligibility for disabled widows and widowers and to provide full benefits for them. If benefits are taken at fifty, a widow now receives half the amount she would be entitled to at sixty-five. A related modification would be to permit the disabled spouse of a retired worker to receive benefits even if the disabled person had not yet reached sixty-two. These proposals would cost $375 million in the first full year and would rise to $417 million by 1978.

The most direct way of eliminating poverty among the aged and disabled, however, would be to increase benefits under the new supplemental security income program, scheduled to start in calendar 1974. Raising benefits under this program to $180 a month for individuals and $225 for couples would be a major step in this direction and would cost only about $1 billion in addition to amounts already projected for the program. Adding benefits for dependents of the disabled would also be desirable.

These SSI increases, plus the three minor improvements in social security discussed above (increasing the long-term minimum, computation for all men at the age of sixty-two, and full benefits for disabled widows and spouses) would give the United States an almost complete system of providing for at least the minimum needs of the aged and

18. This benefit is calculated by multiplying the number of years over ten in covered employment by $8.50. A worker with twenty years of low-paid employment would be just slightly better off if he chose the special minimum ($85 a month) rather than the regular minimum benefit. Low-paid workers with more than twenty years of covered employment would be better off—$127.50 a month with twenty-five years, $170 a month with thirty years.

disabled. Big gaps, however, would remain in coverage of people who are needy for other reasons.

Working-Age People and Their Families

Filling the cracks in programs for needy people who are *not* aged or disabled is much more difficult because there are far larger cracks to fill. The two existing programs (unemployment insurance and AFDC) have benefit levels that vary greatly from state to state and some state-to-state differences in coverage. Moreover, large groups of needy people are not covered by either program. Unemployed persons are not covered if they have not worked long enough to establish eligibility for unemployment insurance (UI) benefits, if they work in the few still-uncovered occupations, or if they have exhausted their benefits. Only a few of the families with unemployed fathers are covered by AFDC. The other large groups not helped by either program are the working poor: people, mostly men, who have jobs but do not earn enough to keep themselves and their families out of poverty.

Some of these people would be assisted if UI benefits were raised in the states where they are now lowest. The administration's proposal for raising UI benefits, discussed above, would move in this direction. So would proposals to put a national floor under AFDC benefits and extend the program to all families with children. Estimates of the cost of moving to a schedule of federally set minimum benefits for an expanded AFDC program are shown in Table 3-14 for various levels of minimum income and marginal tax rates. Excluded from this program are unattached individuals and childless couples of working age. Again, the estimated cost of guaranteeing $2,400 for a family of four in 1976 is below the cost of the current program because the average benefits would be lower and the $360 annual income currently disregarded is not included. Adoption of the $4,800 minimum would eliminate poverty for families with children, and the cost would range from $16 billion with a marginal tax rate of 67 percent to $35 billion with a marginal tax rate of 33 percent. It would thus cost considerably more than the total cost (federal, state, and local) of the current AFDC program, which is estimated to reach $7.3 billion in 1976.

An even more restricted program would be to provide a guaranteed minimum income only to households headed by women that include children. In effect, this version of reform converts AFDC into a separate negative income tax applicable only to mothers with dependents.

Table 3-14. Federal Cost of Alternative Annual Income Guarantees to Families with Children, by Various Marginal Tax Rates, Fiscal Year 1976

Income for family of four under guarantee plan, and existing benefit	Marginal tax rate (percent)	Total cost in 1976 (billions of dollars)	
		All families with children	Female-headed families with children
Aid to families with children: guaranteed income (dollars)			
2,400	67	4.7	3.3
2,400	50	5.3	3.5
2,400	33	7.2	4.0
3,600	67	9.2	5.8
3,600	50	11.4	6.3
3,600	33	17.6	7.2
4,800	67	15.6	8.7
4,800	50	20.8	9.5
4,800	33	34.6	10.9
Existing Aid to Families with Dependent Children			
Cash assistance	...	7.3	...
Federal	...	4.0	...
State and local	...	3.3	...

Source: Same as Table 3-12.

The costs of this approach, at various benefit levels and marginal tax rates, are also shown in Table 3-14. The estimated costs for low levels of benefits are below those of the current program, in part because some families—those with an unemployed father, which are now eligible in some states—would be excluded.

The advantages and disadvantages of various ways of providing cash transfers for the poor, except to the aged and severely disabled, depend on the extent to which employment and reasonable wages are available to the disadvantaged groups that make up most of the poor population. The programs to provide employment and subsidize wages discussed in the next section can be considered both a supplement to and a partial substitute for the kinds of cash transfers discussed so far.

Public Employment and Wage Subsidies*

For those of the poor who are neither aged nor disabled—and they are the majority—the lack of decent, steady jobs is the chief cause of poverty. The various cash transfer programs discussed earlier attempt

* Prepared with the assistance of Duran Bell.

to meet this problem by supplying income to those out of work and by supplementing the low earnings of those with jobs. Public employment and wage subsidies have been seen as another means of dealing with these problems. But there are a number of widely different variants of this approach, each with different objectives.

• A public service employment program can be used as a means of furnishing work for those who cannot find other jobs. In such cases, the federal government would act as the "employer of last resort." The public service jobs would be specially created and would not be part of the regular civil service.

• A more limited and carefully structured public employment program can be a means of providing entrance into career public service jobs for many disadvantaged workers, who have high unemployment rates and low earnings even in periods of prosperity. Targeted on groups with high unemployment, a program of this sort might also be a means of reducing the unemployment rate without increasing inflationary pressures.

• A countercyclical public employment program can provide temporary employment for those out of work in economic recessions. The great majority of this group are not the long-term poor, but workers who in normal times have incomes above the poverty line. While it had other objectives, the current emergency employment assistance program, enacted in 1971[19] and proposed for termination in the 1974 budget, is of this nature.

• Wage subsidies combined with a public employment program can be viewed as a means of replacing part of the current public assistance program and offering income support to the working poor. In 1972 the Senate Finance Committee reported out a proposal (the Long bill) that incorporated wage subsidies and a public employment program as an alternative to the administration's family assistance plan.

The Federal Government as Employer of Last Resort

A broad public service employment program could be designed so as to make the federal government the employer of last resort. Everyone able to work would be guaranteed a job. If a person could not find a private job, a public service job would be available. At first glance such a guarantee has much appeal. Raising the income of the

---

19. Emergency Employment Act of 1971 (Public Law 92-54).

poor by giving them jobs is much more acceptable politically than providing a straight cash transfer that carries no work obligation. And an affluent society ought to ensure that anyone who wants to work can find a job. But on further examination this approach raises a number of major problems. At one end of the scale, if the public service jobs were separate from regular public service employment, offered low wages, and lacked career advancement, the program would not come to grips with the residual unemployment and the job-related problems of the poor that exist even in periods of prosperity. As pointed out in an earlier section of this chapter, the major problem for most of the poor is not long-term joblessness but sporadic short-term unemployment and low wages. This is particularly the case for young people and mothers with dependent children, who cannot secure steady work with job security and career advancement. Dead-end public service jobs would serve them little better than the jobs already available. (Public service jobs, which welfare recipients would be required to take as a condition of receiving benefits, are discussed later in this chapter.)

On the other hand, if the government acted as employer of last resort with a special public employment program that offered wages significantly higher than those available in the regular jobs now filled by disadvantaged workers, it would attract not only the unemployed but also large numbers of workers from existing jobs. Budgetary costs would be huge, and the transfer of workers from regular jobs to the public service employment rolls would exert severe upward pressures on wages and be highly inflationary.

Entry into the Career Public Service

There is another kind of public service employment program, however, which might prove useful in reducing the periodic unemployment, improving the skills, and raising the earnings of many disadvantaged workers, without adding to inflationary pressure (indeed, it might alleviate such pressure). Rather than creating a special set of public jobs, it would aim at moving disadvantaged workers into regular public service careers. In the 1960s one out of every four new jobs was in the public sector, principally among state and local governments. In the 1970s that trend is likely to continue. If retirements and normal turnover are taken into account, some 10 million to 12 million new workers will have to be hired by the public sector in the next five years, about half of them in education. While many of these jobs now require professional training, many could be filled by appropriately trained disadvantaged workers. The jobs are steady, pay good wages, and in general offer advancement and rising earnings over much of a jobholder's working life.

A training program, with a regular public sector job at the end of training and further on-the-job training in the first years of work, would tie the disadvantaged worker directly to a career job. This would not be a make-work program or a disguised income transfer with minimal training content. Although entrance standards would take into account the background of the disadvantaged and some probationary period would be necessary, standards of performance and effort would have to be high. Some trainees would not make it. But it would be critical for the success of such a program that both the trainees and the public officials for whom it was a source of labor accept the program as one that made high demands on people and in return offered substantial rewards.

Most of the expansion in public service jobs will come not in the federal but in the state and local sector. A public service entry program, therefore, would have to tie into state and local hiring needs. It might have several characteristics. First, state employment services or other sponsors would make agreements with state and local governments to identify specific hiring needs. Second, training courses would be set up to match specific jobs, and a job would be available at the end of training; federal grants would cover the cost of training, counseling, and administration. While a small proportion of the jobs might require fairly extensive training, the majority would not. Third, federal grants would also give to the hiring public agency a declining on-the-job training subsidy for the first and second years of regular employment. Fourth, a bonus would be paid if the employee remained on the job for the full two years. Finally, for all trainees except those with family responsibilities, training would be at night or part time and only a small living allowance would be paid.

Under several assumptions—training courses of varying length with an average cost of $2,000 per trainee, an on-the-job subsidy of $2,500 in the first working year and $1,500 the second, an attrition rate of 30 percent during training and another 30 percent in the first two years of work—some 350,000 disadvantaged workers could enter the program each year for an annual federal cost of $1.4 billion. At the end of five years, perhaps 800,000 to 900,000 formerly disadvantaged workers could be holding secure, productive, and well-paying jobs. (For each 100,000 workers entering the program, about $400 million must be added to the average annual costs.) To be successful such a program would have to be worked out in careful detail and expanded gradually. The number of successful placements assumed in the estimate given above might prove to be too optimistic, but the limits of such a program need not be written small in advance—actual experience can be a guide.

While an impressive number of disadvantaged workers might be placed in career jobs over a five-year period, the fraction of total public service employees from disadvantaged backgrounds would still be quite modest. The program would not convert public service employment into a special "haven" for the disadvantaged.

Several additional aspects of the program should be noted. Some persons from disadvantaged backgrounds would have entered public service employment in any event, without the assistance of the program. Any estimate of the number of disadvantaged workers that would be placed in career public service jobs by the program therefore overstates its potential net contribution to the hiring of disadvantaged workers. But this is true of virtually any kind of program aimed at improving the lot of the disadvantaged. It would be crucial to make sure that participants in the program were in no way treated differently from other public service employees in terms of wages, working conditions, or membership in unions. But public service unions might object to the program since it would increase the supply of labor for the jobs their members hold; if the program was large, they might view it as a threat to their ability to secure wage increases.

As disadvantaged workers filled more of the jobs in the rapidly expanding public service sector, some less disadvantaged workers, who might otherwise have entered those jobs, would seek work in the other sectors of the economy. Upward wage pressures should diminish, and economic policy could aim at a lower overall level of unemployment. At the same time the supply of workers for the low-paid, casual, and dirty jobs of society would shrink. Many of those jobs would have to be upgraded. Automation of such jobs would increase; pay would have to be raised and working conditions improved. Some indirect benefits should therefore accrue to disadvantaged workers who are not a part of the public service employment program.

A Public Service Program for Recessions

In 1971 the Congress enacted a federal grant program designed principally to provide regular public service jobs during periods of high unemployment. The public employment program (PEP) supplied federal grants covering the wages or salaries (up to $12,000) of unemployed persons hired by state and local governments. All such governments are eligible for this public employment grant when the national unemployment rate is at or above 4.5 percent. Even when the national rate is below that level, a smaller grant is available to communities whose unemployment rate equals or exceeds 6 percent. Funds are allotted to the various states and communities by a formula that takes into account the number of unemployed in each state and in the communities within a state. The jobs made available under PEP are supposed to be transitional, providing work for the unemployed until permanent positions can be found on public or private payrolls. Preference is given to Vietnam and Korean veterans, disadvantaged workers, and certain other groups.

The PEP program was put into effect with remarkable speed. Within six months of passage, some 140,000 unemployed workers had been hired.[20] Because the program was enacted after most state and local governments had settled on their annual budgets and hiring decisions, it is quite likely that most of the jobs represented additions to state and local payrolls, rather than federal support for jobs that would have been filled anyway. Once such a program has lasted for several years, however, enabling state and local officials to count on the grants in making up their budgets, it is problematical how many new jobs it will create.

About 37 percent of those hired under PEP were disadvantaged workers—less than the fraction of the total unemployed that these workers represent. PEP, in other words, has been a program generally aimed at hiring those put out of work by a recession, rather than one targeted specifically at hiring disadvantaged workers.

As a countercyclical device, PEP has two advantages over other forms of federal spending. Recent experience shows that it pumps funds into the economy quickly and that it is likely to perform much better on this score than most other federal programs, in which, for a

20. Sar A. Levitan, "The Emergency Employment Act: A Progress Report," *Conference Board Record*, Vol. 9 (September 1972), p. 46.

variety of reasons, there are usually long lags before federal spending actually takes place. Moreover, PEP funds are fully spent on hiring people—in the short run, at least, there tends to be more employment per dollar of spending than for other programs.

So long as recessions are short, PEP retains these advantages. In longer recessions PEP money is likely to substitute, in part at least, for other state and local spending rather than represent a net addition to hiring. But postwar recessions in the United States have usually been short, and any other countercyclical aid to state and local governments during longer recessions would run into the same substitution problem. So PEP is better in the short run and has no more disadvantages in the longer period than other programs. The current PEP program does not taper off gradually as unemployment recedes. Once the national unemployment rate falls below 4.5 percent, no further grants may be made (except for the small program providing assistance to areas with unemployment of 6 percent or more). As a consequence, a small change in the unemployment rate from slightly above to slightly below 4.5 percent can cause the grants to be terminated; a slight shift in the other direction can bring the program back into operation. A more appropriate countercyclical program would match the size of the grants to the excess of unemployment over some target rate. In this way the program could gradually expand or contract as economic conditions worsened or improved.

It is important not to confuse PEP's function as a countercyclical device with a permanent public employment program designed to relieve poverty or to provide opportunities for disadvantaged workers. PEP does not fulfill those roles, although the language of the act indicates that the program should be especially aimed at the disadvantaged. A combination of PEP, available as a purely countercyclical device, and a long-term program for entry of the disadvantaged into public service careers is more likely to deal successfully with the two different objectives than would an attempt to use either of the programs by itself to meet both.

In its 1974 budget the administration proposes that PEP be allowed to expire without renewal. (The current authorization for funds ran out on July 1, 1973.) If the national unemployment rate should fall below 4.5 percent, most of the grants would have ceased in any event. But allowing the program to expire assumes that it would not be a useful standby device in case of future recessions.

An alternative to the administration's proposal would be a reauthorization of PEP, leaving it principally as a standby countercyclical measure that would automatically come into operation should unemployment begin to rise. And the "triggering" formula in the current law might well be modified along the lines suggested earlier to allow a gradual expansion or contraction of the program as the unemployment rate moves up or down. If the program were extended, small budgetary costs would continue even in periods of high employment as communities with particularly high unemployment rates continued to draw the special grants.

Wage Subsidies and Public Employment as an Alternative to Welfare

Some have viewed public employment and wage subsidies as a replacement for part of the current AFDC system and as an alternative to negative income taxes. Under this approach, those of the poor who are classified as "employable" would no longer receive direct cash transfers. Wage subsidies would be paid to those working at low wages in regular public or private jobs. If regular jobs could not be found, employable persons would be given work in specially created public service jobs. Wages in the public service jobs would be set below those in regular employment to provide incentives for recipients to seek the latter kind of work.

The Long bill was a proposal of this kind. Under it, current AFDC recipients would be divided into two categories. Mothers with dependent children under six years old would be considered unemployable, as would single parents who were incapacitated, attending school full time, or living in areas remote from job opportunities. They would receive cash transfers ($2,400 for a family of four), but after a modest "disregard," the payments would be reduced dollar for dollar with outside earnings—a 100 percent marginal tax rate. States that, with federal assistance, now pay welfare benefits higher than this would not be required to make up the difference between $2,400 and their current benefit level nor would they receive federal assistance to do so.

All others currently eligible for AFDC, principally mothers with dependent children over six, would be classified as employable. For them, no direct cash transfer would be available. But they, together with other employable adults in families with children, would be eligible for a number of employment-related benefits. A new federal employment corporation (FEC) would be established to administer this aspect of the program. All eligible and employable family heads would be guaranteed a job by the FEC. Three options would be available. First, the participant could be placed in a regular job paying the minimum wage (currently, $1.60 an hour). Second, if such a job was not available, the FEC could place the participant in a regular job paying at least three-quarters of the minimum and pay him or her a subsidy equal to three-fourths the difference between the wage and the minimum. Thus, a man placed in a job paying $1.20 an hour would receive an extra 30 cents an hour from the FEC, bringing his effective wage up to $1.50.[21] In either of these two situations the FEC would pay an additional earnings bonus, equal to 10 percent of the earnings of a family head and his wife, up to an earnings level of $4,000 (with a schedule for phasing the bonus out completely at $5,600). In effect, this would mean returning to the worker most of his social security payroll tax (the portions paid by both employer and employee).

Finally, if the participant could not find a regular job at a wage equal to at least three-quarters of the minimum wage, he or she would be placed in a specially created public employment program either arranged or operated by the FEC. The participant would be paid three-quarters of the minimum wage and guaranteed thirty-two hours of work a week (not even sufficient at present to yield $2,000 a year). Neither the wage subsidy nor the earnings bonus would be paid. Clearly, the intent is to make public employment less desirable than the other options.

It is estimated that costs under the Long bill would be $12 billion to $15 billion more than the cost of the AFDC and food stamp programs it would replace. The specific provisions of the Long bill could, of course, be varied with higher or lower benefits, different eligibility requirements, and modified incentive structures. But the bill illustrates the basic aspects of this kind of approach.

The approach embodied in the Long bill differs from the cash transfer systems discussed earlier in three major ways: (1) for those classified as employable no income is provided except in conjunction with wages earned on the job; (2) since experience with the labor market

21. The minimum wage will probably be raised to at least $2 in the relatively near future. Three-quarters of the minimum would be $1.50, and the FEC would pay wage subsidies equal to three-quarters of the difference between that amount and $2.

even in periods of relatively high prosperity indicates that steady jobs in the private or public sector are not available for all disadvantaged workers, the program establishes a special public service employment program under which the federal government acts as employer of last resort; (3) however, to induce eligible recipients to seek employment at regular jobs rather than remain in the special public service program indefinitely, it sets the wages in that program significantly lower.

The public service job program would offer little to the young disvantaged worker who now has at least sporadic access to private jobs with equal or better pay. The main clientele of the program would be the current AFDC recipients who would be classified as employable —principally mothers with dependent children over six. The annual income paid on these jobs would be low, and since the states are neither required to supplement this income nor given federal assistance to do so, the many AFDC recipients living in states with AFDC benefits higher than this would take a substantial cut in income. Moreover, if no income supplements were available, except on the job, it would be impossible to fire anyone. Under these conditions, the job content of the public service employment program would become less and less, and the program would soon become a means of paying relatively low income guarantees under the guise of wages (while still incurring the cost of child care subsidies necessary for many of the recipients to participate in the program).

At the same time, the income supplements provided to those who work in regular jobs at low wages are relatively generous under the Long approach—or at least would be if minimum wages are increased, as seems likely in the 1973 session of Congress. Little income assistance is now available for this group, which constitutes a large fraction of the poor.

While a number of changes could be made in the specific provisions of the Long bill to deal with some of the problems outlined above, substantial changes would soon begin to destroy the structure of the approach. States might be required to supplement the income of families currently eligible for AFDC so that those now on the welfare rolls would not suffer sharp reductions in income under the new program. But in states where such supplements were large, the income of those in the public service employment program would equal, even exceed, that of people in regular jobs, removing the incentives built into the program for recipients to take regular jobs. The wages in public service employment programs could be increased, but as pointed out in an earlier section, if carried very far this could make jobs under the public program more attractive than regular jobs and siphon off a significant number of workers from their regular employment, with serious inflationary consequences and very large budgetary costs.

In an economy in which most disadvantaged workers, including mothers with dependent children, could find steady work in regular jobs and appropriate day care facilities for their children if needed, the Long approach would be more attractive. The public service job component of the program would be only something to fall back on temporarily for people who would shortly secure regular employment. Wage subsidies could supplement income in low-paying regular jobs. The consequent tying of income assistance to jobs would be more acceptable politically than straight cash transfers unrelated to work, and it might therefore be much easier to raise the incomes of the poor. But experience to date with programs seeking to place AFDC recipients in regular jobs has been disappointing. There is little basis for assuming the existence of conditions that would make the public employment–wage subsidy approach a workable substitute for the alternative cash transfer systems discussed earlier.

4. Helping People Buy Essentials

THE LAST CHAPTER EXPLORED various ways in which the federal government could directly alter the distribution of cash income or general purchasing power among people through tax policy, cash transfers, and subsidized employment—letting individuals decide how their income should be spent. This chapter explores a different type of assistance: federal transfers or tax advantages to help people pay for specific kinds of "essential" goods and services.

The chapter begins by outlining the general strategy of helping people buy essentials and then turns to more detailed discussions of five types of goods and services that either are or could be dealt with in this way: food, housing, medical care, higher education, and child care. Each of the five discussions gives the case for singling out this particular good or service and spells out the nature of current federal programs. It then outlines one or more alternative proposals, estimates their costs, and suggests what each might accomplish or fail to accomplish.

Rationale and Problems

The basic argument for helping people buy essentials is that certain goods and services are so important the federal government ought to ensure that everyone has at least a minimal amount. Food, shelter, and medical care are necessities of life; no one should be denied an adequate diet, decent housing, or medical help when sick or injured.

101

Higher education and child care arrangements may be essential to increasing a person's earnings and allowing him or her to move up the socioeconomic ladder.

But saying that a good or service is important does not prove the case for the government's helping people buy it. People with incomes buy what they think is important without government prodding. Why not simply redistribute income and let people buy what they think they need?

To argue for helping individuals buy specific goods and services, one has to believe that many will not spend as much of their income on the particular good or service as society thinks they should. They may skimp on food or housing so they can buy a car or a television set. They may find it difficult to budget for expenditures, such as medical care, that come in unpredictable large lumps. They may attach a higher value to present consumption and a lower value to future income than society thinks they should, spending too little for higher education for themselves or their children. If, for any of these reasons, people seem likely to spend a lower proportion of their income on a particular good or service than the group as a whole thinks they should, then earmarked assistance can be justified.

But the earmarked assistance need not be given to the consumer. One way to increase consumption is to produce the good or service publicly and give it away free or even force people to use it. This is the approach taken to elementary and secondary education. Another possibility is to give a public subsidy to private producers to enable them to sell below cost. Federal aid for college buildings or assistance to hospitals is of this sort.

The decision to subsidize demand rather than supply—to give people earmarked purchasing power and let them seek their own supplier—is appropriate when (1) consumer choice and competition among suppliers seems desirable; (2) when the public interest is in increasing the consumption of some general class of items, such as "food," not in specifying an exact diet; or (3) when the assistance is directed at a particular group, such as the poor, but it seems demeaning or inefficient to segregate them in charity hospitals or public housing and hence preferable to give them financial assistance and let them find their own physician or apartment.

There are several mechanisms the government can use to help individuals buy essentials. Perhaps the most obvious is a voucher, essentially a special kind of money good only for a particular class of purchases. Food stamps are vouchers. A government promise to reimburse suppliers for certain types of services rendered to eligible beneficiaries is much like a voucher. Medicare and Medicaid work this way. A tax deduction or credit is similar in effect—the taxpayer is partially or fully reimbursed for a class of expenditures he has made.

These mechanisms have two important common elements. First, eligible individuals are *entitled* to receive the voucher or other assistance by virtue of age, income, military service, or some other criterion determined by law; it is not up to the supplier or a government bureaucrat to decide who gets federal assistance. Second, the individual can shop around. He chooses the supplier; the supplier does not choose him.

The voucher or entitlement mechanism is quite different from many of the mechanisms now used by the federal government to affect the distribution of essential goods and services. While food stamps are vouchers, commodity distribution is another matter. The recipient of surplus commodities gets no choice of suppliers, items, or brands. Veterans' education benefits are essentially vouchers. Eligibility is determined by military service and the eligible veteran can shop around among schools. However, civilian student aid (except for the Basic Opportunity Grant program not yet started) is given to the college or university. Tax deductions for housing costs, medical expenses, and child care—which primarily aid middle- and upper-income people—are similar to vouchers, but many programs to subsidize the same services to the poor channel the subsidy to the supplier. The middle-income mother is entitled to her child care deduction if she meets the law's requirements, and she is allowed to choose her own day care arrangement. Under Head Start, however, the subsidy goes to the supplier of care, who determines, within limits, who will be served.

A number of common themes run through the specific sections that follow. One is the inequity and inefficiency of income tax concessions as a means of helping people buy essentials. At the present time special tax treatment for medical expenses, homeownership, and child care cost at least $16 billion a year. But tax advantages have no value to the poor, who most need assistance, because their incomes are so low they pay no income tax. Moreover, for those who do pay, the value of the concessions grows as income rises—a $1,500 deduction for mortgage interest, for example, is worth $750 to a high-income tax-payer in the 50 percent tax bracket and $210 to a working man in the 14 percent bracket. As a means of helping people buy essentials, therefore, the tax system is inefficient because it does not concentrate the assistance where it is needed most; much of the Treasury's funds are "wasted" on upper-income taxpayers.

Another theme of this chapter is the need to weigh the advantages of voucher or entitlement approaches against the advantages of sub-sidizing suppliers. It is easier to make a voucher system equitable. Eligibility rules can be written to ensure that everyone who meets the same objective criteria gets assistance. In principle, similar rules could be written for supplier subsidies by requiring the supplier to serve everyone who meets the objective criteria. In practice, however, there is usually not enough of the subsidized service to satisfy demand. Suppliers—public housing managers, student aid officers, or Head Start project leaders—have to ration federal assistance. The result is uneven treatment of people. In general, the supply subsidy approach has meant fairly generous assistance for a small fraction of those eligible, no service for the rest, and big differences in selection criteria from one place to the next. Shifting to a voucher approach would be fairer, but it would also be more expensive, because covering everyone who is eligible would cost more than covering just a fraction of them unless the amount of assistance per person was drastically cut.

In principle, the voucher approach should lead to greater efficiency and greater consumer satisfaction if in fact adequate supplies of the service are available and suppliers compete for the business. But there may be barriers that keep the market from responding and make it desirable to subsidize supply. The market may not supply doctors and medical facilities in urban ghettos or poor rural areas. Even if all low-income people have adequate housing vouchers, blacks may be restricted by discrimination to certain areas and have to pay higher rents.

Two other themes or common problems of this strategy recur in what follows. One is the conflict between the objective of assisting those most in need and the objective of preserving incentives to work. If food or medical care or housing subsidies fall rapidly as family income rises, the effect is the same as a steep tax on increased income. Moreover, the problem is compounded if a household is getting bene-fits from several programs at once. A family whose income rose by a thousand dollars might lose more than a thousand dollars' worth of benefits—the "tax" would be more than 100 percent of additional income. If benefits are reduced gradually as income rises, there will be more incentive for families to increase their income. This lowering of the "tax" rate, however, extends aid to people higher in the income distribution, who presumably need it less, and raises the cost of the program.

The second set of problems has to do with the nature of control over suppliers. Should there be price controls? Should there be quality standards? Voucher-type programs that add to demand without increasing supply may bid up prices. This is clearly a problem in medical care and might be in housing and child care if a major program were undertaken. Moreover, public subsidy leads to demands for controls on the quality of the suppliers' product, the argument being that public funds should not be used to purchase substandard housing or second-rate medicine or education or child care. Setting quality standards high, however, will raise costs and may lead to a situation in which people with federal assistance can buy better services than are available to people with higher incomes and no federal assistance.

Food

Although the United States has not enacted a guaranteed annual income, the food stamp program has recently been transformed, without much public notice, into a guaranteed annual income for food. It is essentially a negative income tax earmarked for food, with national standards of eligibility depending only on income and family size. A major budgetary question for the next several years is what to do about the food stamp program. If an income strategy is chosen, food programs could be eliminated and the funds applied to cash transfer programs. If an income strategy is rejected, however, the food stamp program could be continued and perhaps increased as a basic element in a strategy to help people buy essentials.

Why Help People Buy Food?

Food is a necessity of life and there is clearly a national interest in making sure that no one goes hungry. Nevertheless, people do not normally starve themselves or their children unless they are too poor to pay the grocer, so it is hard to make a strong case for giving needy people food or even food vouchers rather than money. Food is a predictable daily expense and the arguments about expenditures that come in unpredictable large lumps which are used to justify special treatment of medical bills, for example, do not apply to food

But while economists may find the case for choosing food programs rather than cash transfers weak, politicians appear to find it strong. Recent Congresses, which have rejected major welfare reform, have been more than willing to reform and expand food programs. This political preference for food subsidies may reflect distrust of the ability of the poor to spend money wisely. It may also reflect the fact that food subsidies are handled by agricultural committees and have the support of farm lobbies.

Current Programs

Three major federal programs now provide food to needy people (see Table 4-1). The smallest long-standing program is the distribution of surplus commodities to institutions and low-income people. These commodities are given away free to people who meet the eligibility criteria, but the recipient has to take whatever commodities

Table 4-1. Federal Outlays for Food Assistance Programs, Fiscal Years 1970, 1973, and 1974, and Alternative Programs, Fiscal Years 1976 and 1978

Millions of dollars

Program	1970	1973	1974	1976	1978
Surplus commodity distribution	571	798	736	400	420
Schools and institutions[a]	280	415	383	400	420
Other needy people	291	383	353	0	0
Child nutrition programs[a]	383	699	787	830	870
Food stamps	577	2,192	2,196	3,960	4,350
Current program	577	2,192	2,196	2,370	2,570
Conversion of distribution program to food stamps	...	...	...	370	390
Continuing adult welfare recipients' eligibility	...	...	...	200	220
Expansion of beneficiaries[b]	...	...	...	920	970
Additional adjustment for food prices[c]	...	...	...	100	200
Total food assistance outlays	1,531	3,689	3,719	5,190	5,640

Sources: From or derived from data in *The Budget of the United States Government, Fiscal Year 1972—Appendix*, pp. 141, 145–47; *Budget . . . 1974—Appendix*, pp. 199, 204, 206–07.

a. Assumes continuation of present program, adjusted only for changes in overall price level.

b. Assumes an increase of 8 million in the number of beneficiaries at 75 percent of the average subsidy to current beneficiaries.

c. Assumes that food prices rise 1 percent faster than general price level.

happen to have been declared surplus. The second is the child nutrition program (formerly called the school lunch program), which subsidizes meals served in schools. The food stamp program, begun in 1961, is now the largest of the three.

Until 1971, states were allowed to set their own eligibility rules for food stamps. In that year eligibility requirements and benefits were made uniform for all participating governments, all benefits to be paid from federal funds. Participation by state and local governments is voluntary. Food stamp and surplus food distribution programs can not be operated simultaneously without special permission, which is usually reserved for disaster areas.

Any household receiving public assistance is eligible for food stamps. In addition, other families, not on welfare, can purchase food stamps if their monthly income does not exceed the maximum allowable amount. This is the first federal program to base eligibility strictly on income.

Under the program low-income families and individuals may purchase food stamps in various denominations and use them like cash when they shop in the supermarket. The store is then reimbursed by the government. The amount of food stamps that may be purchased varies with the size of the family. A four-person family can buy stamps worth $112 a month, or $1,344 a year. The cost of the stamps depends on the family's size and income. Four-person families with income (minus allowable deductions) of less than $30 a month receive the stamps free; that is, they get a subsidy of $1,344 a year. If their income rises, the cost of the stamps rises. If they have an income of $1,200 a year, they pay $300 for the $1,344 worth of stamps, receiving a subsidy of $1,044; if their income is $2,400, they pay $636, receiving a subsidy of $708. For every dollar of increased income (after deductions) a family loses about 30 cents in food stamp benefits; thus, the marginal tax rate is about 30 percent. In computing income for food stamp eligibility a family may deduct income and social security taxes, child care costs (if required to enable an adult to work), and certain other expenses. Because of the items excluded from the definition of monthly income, families may be eligible for food stamps at income levels above the poverty-income line and after they have become ineligible for public assistance.

The food stamps may not be used to purchase alcoholic beverages, tobacco, and imported foods. Elderly people, unable to prepare their own meals, can use the stamps to purchase food from meal delivery services. All adult recipients between the ages of eighteen and sixty-five must register for work unless they are disabled, mothers with children under eighteen, students, or working at least thirty hours a week. The beneficiaries must live in an area that has a food stamp project, and not all areas do. Some have surplus food distribution programs instead. Localities can switch from the surplus food distribution program to food stamps, and many have done so recently. Only 125 counties out of more than 3,000 did not have either program in March 1972.

In January 1973, 12.5 million people were receiving food stamps. The average family of four received $1,273 worth of food stamps a year for which it paid $580. Thus a participating family of four would on the average be receiving $693 in additional purchasing power a year.

Under legislation passed in 1972, state welfare programs for the aged, blind, and disabled—the adult categories—will be assumed by the federal government in January 1974 and uniform national benefits will be paid (see Chapter 3). Unless the law is changed before the program goes into effect, beneficiaries of this new federal supplemental security income program will not be eligible for food stamps. Many recipients will be better off than under current programs, even allowing for the loss of food stamp benefits. Some who live in states with currently high benefit levels will, however, be worse off unless those states take steps to supplement their benefits.

Whether the food stamp program should be abolished, continued without change, or increased depends partly on decisions made about welfare reform. Food stamps are currently being purchased by 4.9 million people who are not on the public assistance rolls. If a comprehensive welfare reform covering the working poor were enacted, a strong case could be made for abolishing food stamps and using the money for welfare benefits on the grounds that it is desirable to allow people freedom of choice in the allocation of their resources. If cash benefits were not extended to the working poor, however, the argument for retaining the food stamp program would be far more persuasive.

Alternative Proposals for Food Stamps

A number of actions could be taken to expand the food stamp program. The eligibility of adult welfare recipients could be restored. The value of the stamps could be raised periodically with increases in food prices (rather than with increases in the general cost of living, as is now the case). The shift from the distribution of surplus commodities to the food stamp program could be accelerated.

Finally, a major effort could be undertaken to expand the use of food stamps. Presumably, all of the 25.6 million persons officially below the poverty line in 1971 are eligible to purchase stamps, but fewer than half are participating. Many people may not know that they are entitled to food stamps. An active effort to inform them of their eligibility might expand the program markedly. However, among the lowest-income families, which need the stamps most, participation is probably high already, and the new recipients would have a higher average income level and receive a lower average subsidy than the present beneficiaries. If all these steps were undertaken, the program could reach a $4.4 billion level by 1978, or $1.8 billion more than is now projected for that year (see Table 4-1).

Health*

The case for federal programs to help people pay for medical care is far stronger than the case for special programs to help them buy food, and larger federal resources currently go into programs to finance health care. Expenditures for Medicare and Medicaid are expected to be $17 billion in fiscal year 1974, and income tax deductions for medical expenses are expected to provide subsidies of about $5.6 billion to taxpayers. Current programs, however, are extremely uneven in their coverage—some people receive substantial assistance while equally needy people are unaided—and are not designed to foster efficient use of medical resources. On both equity and efficiency grounds, a persuasive case can be made for replacing current programs with some form of national health insurance.

Why Help People Buy Medical Care?

While medical care is only one factor contributing to health, it is often a critical factor—sometimes a matter of life and death. Denying care to someone because his income is low is not the same as rationing cars or clothes or television sets on that basis. Society has increasingly

* Prepared with the assistance of Karen Davis.

come to the view that adequate medical care is a basic right, to be neither denied nor treated as charity to those who are poor. Moreover, people have more than an altruistic interest in seeing that others get medical care. Communicable diseases are reduced by immunization and treatment, healthier children do better in school, and a healthier work force means a more productive economy.

Without public help many people will be unable to finance needed medical care or will be able to do so only with hardship. Unlike food bills, medical bills often come in large unpredictable amounts. Private insurance mitigates but does not solve the problem of paying for health care. The poor are unlikely to have insurance provided as a fringe benefit at work and are unable to afford it themselves. Hence they are apt to postpone care except in emergencies. For the middle class, average medical bills and standard health insurance coverage do not take an impossibly high share of income, but major health catastrophes can suddenly bring financial distress, even ruin. Most private insurance policies do not offer adequate protection against such expenses. Even "major medical" policies usually contain limits on the expenditures that will be covered and require individuals to pay a sizable fraction of the expenditures that are covered.

In addition, private insurance is typically so designed that it encourages inefficient use of medical resources. Many insurance policies provide "low dollar" coverage against normal medical expenses; they have neither a substantial "deductible" amount (to be paid by the patient before the insurance benefits begin) nor a "coinsurance" rate (percentage of the medical bill paid by the patient himself). Low dollar coverage may encourage excessive use of medical services. The patient who has paid his insurance premium regards care as essentially free and uses more of it than he would if he were sharing the cost. Moreover, many policies cover only expensive forms of care— inpatient but not outpatient hospital services, hospitals but not nursing homes—and this encourages use of the more expensive forms of care. A doctor may put a patient in the hospital for tests or other procedures simply because the patient's insurance policy will cover these expenses only if incurred in a hospital.

Attempts to foster innovative methods of organizing and delivering health care services, particularly for low-income people, are hampered by inadequate financing. Efforts to encourage physicians, clinics, or health maintenance organizations to locate in medically underserved areas are unlikely to succeed if people in those areas cannot pay, either directly or indirectly through third parties, for health services.

Current Federal Programs

Since the mid-1960s the federal government has played a major role in financing individual medical care services through the Medicare and Medicaid programs. The Medicare program provides a basic hospital insurance plan for all people sixty-five and over covered by the social security program and pays half the cost of a supplementary medical insurance plan covering physicians' services and certain other benefits. Under the Medicaid program, the federal government shares with the states the costs of providing medical care for welfare recipients and the medically indigent. In addition, the federal government subsidizes the purchase of health insurance and the payment of medical expenses through special tax provisions. Under the personal income tax, one-half the cost of health insurance premiums up to $150 plus all medical expenses (including the remaining premiums) that exceed 3 percent of income may be deducted on each tax return. These provisions benefit high-income people more than low-income people, because those with high incomes face higher tax rates and are more likely to itemize deductions.[1] Moreover, the fact that employers' contributions to health insurance for employees are not included as income on the employees' income tax returns results in loss of revenue to the government. The federal government thus subsidizes the purchase of health insurance both by individuals and by employers on employees' behalf.

These three programs for financing individual medical care services have filled many gaps in private health insurance coverage. Medicare has brought insurance to many elderly people who would otherwise have lost their insurance coverage on retirement. Medicaid has helped the poor, a group with little private health insurance coverage. Only a third of the poor have any private insurance protection whereas 90 percent of the families with incomes of $10,000 or more do have it.

---

1. Coverage of out-of-pocket expenses under the personal income tax is equivalent to providing for each taxpayer who itemizes deductions an insurance policy that has a deductible equal to 3 percent of the taxpayer's income and a coinsurance rate that is 100 percent minus his marginal effective tax rate.

The tax provisions provide relief for families with high medical expenses who itemize deductions on their personal income tax.

As shown in Table 4-2, federal expenditures under both Medicare and Medicaid go primarily to low-income groups. This is hardly surprising since Medicaid is explicitly designed to aid the poor and Medicare to aid the elderly population, which is disproportionately represented at the low end of the income scale. By contrast, tax subsidies give only a little relief to the poor—primarily to the working poor with health insurance. Most of the tax benefits go to those in the middle and upper brackets. If one puts all three programs together, about 46 percent of the total benefits go to people in families with incomes below $5,000. This concentration of benefits on low-income groups, however, is largely attributable to sizable expenditures for low-income old people. Of the $5 billion in benefits for people under sixty-five in 1970, only 29 percent went to people with incomes under $5,000, while 45 percent went to people with incomes of more than

Table 4-2. Distribution of Federal Medical Care Benefits under Medicare, Medicaid, and Income Tax Subsidies, by Family Income and Age, 1970

Family income class		Program			Age	
	Total federal benefits	Medi-care payments	Medic-aid payments	Federal individual income tax sub-sidies	Under 65	65 and over
			Millions of dollars			
All classes	14,224	7,494	2,930	3,800	4,994	9,230
			Percentage distribution			
Under $5,000	46	54	67	13	29	55
$5,000–$9,999	27	26	24	31	26	27
$10,000–$14,999	16	14	5	26	23	12
$15,000 and over	12	7	4	30	22	7
Total	100	100	100	100	100	100

Sources: Total Medicare and Medicaid payments are from U.S. Social Security Administration, Office of Research and Statistics, *Compendium of National Health Expenditures Data*, DHEW (SSA) 73-11903 (1973), p. 73; the distribution is derived from unpublished estimates of payments by family income.

The amount of tax subsidy is from Bridger M. Mitchell and Ronald J. Vogel, "Health and Taxes: An Assessment of the Medical Deduction" (1973; processed), pp. 21, 31; the distribution is based on data in ibid., p. 34, and Martin S. Feldstein and Elizabeth Allison, "Tax Subsidies of Private Health Insurance: Distribution, Revenue Loss and Effects," Discussion Paper 237 (Harvard Institute of Economic Research, Harvard University, April 1972; processed), p. 5.

Medicaid payments for persons over sixty-five are distributed as 67 percent to the "under $5,000 class" and 33 percent to the "$5,000–$9,999" class. All Medicare payments are distributed to the group sixty-five and over. Tax subsidies for ages over and under sixty-five are estimated from the Brookings file of 1970 individual income tax returns.

Figures are rounded and may not add to totals.

$10,000. Indirect payment of medical services for middle- and upper-income families, therefore, substantially exceeds that made by the government on behalf of the poor under the age of sixty-five.

Problems with Current Programs

Current federal programs help millions of people pay for medical care, but they have three major flaws: they are extremely uneven in coverage and benefits; they provide little protection against catastrophic medical expenses; the tax subsidy program offers large benefits to the rich and little to the poor.

In comparison with other groups, the elderly have been treated generously under federal health financing programs. Medicare provides substantial benefits for hospital and physicians' care for retired persons covered by social security no matter where they live or what their income. In addition, a substantial portion of Medicaid money in some states is spent for medical services to impoverished old people not covered by Medicare.

These programs do not, however, relieve old people of all medical expenses. In fiscal 1972 private medical payments by persons over sixty-five averaged $404 per capita (including $67 in Medicare premiums). Those high out-of-pocket expenses are partly attributable to the fact that Medicare does not protect old people from the expenses of prolonged hospitalization or extremely serious illness. Under the hospital portion of Medicare, after the first sixty days the individual pays $18 a day. After the ninetieth day, he may use a lifetime reserve of sixty hospital days, making a contribution of $36 a day. However, once he has been in the hospital for one hundred and fifty days, the program makes no further payments (or after ninety days if he has already used up the lifetime reserve), and the individual is forced to pick up all expenses. Under the physician portion of Medicare, people must pay 20 percent of the physician's charge even if it runs into many thousands of dollars. Other benefits such as private nursing care and out-of-hospital drugs are not covered at all. If an old person is sick enough long enough, he may incur bankrupting out-of-pocket costs.

Medicaid has been plagued from its inception by the federal-state nature of the program. Since states set the benefits, low-income people in some geographical areas have complete protection against virtually

Table 4-3. Regional Distribution of Medicare and Medicaid Benefits under Current Programs and Recipient Groups, 1970

Region	Medicare		Medicaid	
	Number of elderly	Medicare payments	Number of poor	Federal Medicaid payments
	Millions			
All regions	20	$7,494	27	$2,930
	Percentage distribution			
Northeast	25.9	28.6	17.8	39.6
North Central	28.5	27.7	21.9	19.2
South	30.1	25.7	45.7	16.7
West	15.4	18.0	14.6	24.5
Total	100.0	100.0	100.0	100.0

Sources: For amount of payments, see Table 4-2. Population data are from U.S. Bureau of the Census, *Statistical Abstract of the United States, 1972* (1972), Tables 36 and 542. Payments distributions are from U.S. Social Security Administration, Office of Research and Statistics, *Health Insurance Statistics*, HI-41, "Health Insurance for the Aged: Monthly Reimbursements per Person by State, 1970" (1973), Table 1; and U.S. Department of Health, Education, and Welfare, National Center for Social Statistics, "Numbers of Recipients and Amounts of Payments under Medicaid and Other Medical Programs Financed from Public Assistance Funds, 1970," NCSS B-4 (CY 70) (1972; processed), Table 01. Figures are rounded and may not add to totals.

all medical expenses and low-income individuals in other areas have only limited Medicaid benefits or none at all.[2] As shown in Table 4-3, 46 percent of the poor live in the South, yet only 17 percent of Medicaid payments go to people in that area. Three states—New York, Massachusetts, and California—spend 50 percent of all Medicaid funds. In addition to geographical inequities created by the Medicaid programs, the tying of benefits to eligibility for welfare means that many poor people without adequate private health insurance coverage—the working poor, childless couples, low-income families with an unemployed father in states that do not provide cash assistance for such families—receive no coverage from Medicaid.

Existing tax subsidies for health insurance and medical expenses also have erratic effects. First, they devote substantial federal revenues to helping taxpayers buy health insurance, an expense that could be met by most nonpoor persons without undue financial burden. Of the $4.4 billion in tax subsidies for medical expenses in 1972, $2.5 billion stemmed from tax treatment of health insurance premiums. Second, tax provisions covering direct medical expenses do not adequately protect people from catastrophic expenses. If a family with an income

2. See Charles L. Schultze and others, *Setting National Priorities: The 1973 Budget* (Brookings Institution, 1972), pp. 218–20, for a more complete discussion.

of $10,000 incurred $4,000 of medical expenses, its taxes would be reduced by $703. While this is some compensation, it is far from adequate protection against excessive medical bills. Third, the deduction mechanism is an inequitable method of compensating people for financial losses from ruinous medical expenses. If a family with an income of $40,000 incurred the same $4,000 of medical expenses, its taxes would be reduced by $1,176.[3] The federal government "pays" a higher share of the medical expenses of the family whose income is four times as high and who presumably could better afford the $4,000 expenditure. In short, tax deductions provide little assistance for the poor, nor do they provide either adequate or equitable protection against the catastrophic expenses that are the real financial problem for middle-income families hit by serious illness.

Recent and Proposed Changes in Current Programs

The 1972 amendments to the Social Security Act extended eligibility under the Medicare program to 1.7 million social security recipients under sixty-five, who have been eligible for social security disability benefits for two years, and to persons covered by social security and their families requiring treatment for chronic kidney disease. Approximately $1.8 billion will be spent in 1974 under Medicare for care of the disabled, while another $127 million will be spent on treatment of chronic kidney disease of people under sixty-five. Expenditures on the treatment of chronic kidney disease are expected to rise substantially once the program is fully implemented.

The administration's budget for fiscal 1974 proposes cutbacks in Medicare that will result in the elderly paying a larger share of bills for hospital care and physicians' services. Specific legislative proposals are not yet available, but some details have been revealed. Coinsurance under the physician portion is to be increased from 20 percent to 25 percent and the deductible increased from $60 to $85. This change will result in substantially higher costs for all Medicare beneficiaries using physicians' services. Those incurring physicians' bills of $2,000 under current law pay $450 toward those bills. Under the proposed law, they would pay $560.

3. Since only expenses in excess of 3 percent of income can be deducted, the high-income family has lower total medical deductions. However, the higher marginal tax rate faced by the family with a $40,000 income results in a greater tax saving. Comparison here applies to a family of four.

Under the hospital part of Medicare, the present system of copayments will be replaced by a requirement that patients pay 10 percent of the total charges for hospital care for all covered days. Most Medicare beneficiaries with hospital stays of a hundred or more days would face somewhat lower charges than under current law, and for very long stays the reduction in charges would be quite significant. However, since 99 percent of all Medicare hospital stays are less than a hundred days in length, most Medicare patients would be required to pay higher charges:

	Length of hospital stay (days)					
	10	20	30	60	90	150
Percentage of stays of greater duration (HEW estimates)	50	21	10	2	1	0.06
Total payment by a patient in 1974 under current legislation (dollars)	84	84	84	84	714	3,234
Average total payment by a patient in 1974 under proposed legislation (dollars)	167	281	392	678	864	1,163

Under current law, a patient hospitalized for thirty days, for example, would pay only the initial deductible, estimated to be $84 in 1974. Under proposed legislation, if he incurred average hospital bills he would be required to pay almost $400.

The administration estimates that these changes in the Medicare law will reduce federal expenditures by $500 million in fiscal year 1974 and by $1.3 billion in 1975, the first full year covered by the change.

Greater use of coinsurance features in health insurance coverage can have desirable consequences. Coinsurance on hospital charges, for example, encourages patients and physicians to select less expensive hospitals and reduce excessively long hospital stays, and by so doing discourages hospitals from charging exorbitant fees. The proposed changes in cost sharing under Medicare are particularly inappropriate, however, because (1) they are not related to income; (2) they contain no ceiling on coinsurance payments; and (3) savings generated by the coinsurance provisions are not used to provide better protection against catastrophic expenses—such as an increase in covered hospital days or coverage of out-of-hospital prescription drugs.

Any discussion of cost-sharing provisions must be in the context of reasonable ability to pay such charges. Few elderly people have sufficient income to pay any sizable coinsurance amount: only 18 percent of the elderly had family incomes above $10,000 in 1970. In addition, the elderly already pay twice as much out-of-pocket for medical services as do other population groups. Under proposed legislation, an elderly couple with one member hospitalized for thirty days and physicians' bills of $2,000 could expect to pay medical expenses of at least $1,500 (including Medicare premiums, benefits not covered, such as drugs, and normal medical expenses for the other family member). Most would agree that such an out-of-pocket payment is excessive for any family whose income is below $10,000, and thus for more than four out of five elderly people.

It might be argued that greater use of coinsurance under Medicare would not cause financial burdens because the Medicaid program could pick up coinsurance amounts for the elderly poor. Experience with the Medicaid program gives little hope that it can be relied upon to protect the elderly poor from excessive bills (and the wide variation in benefits across geographical areas jaundices one's view even more). Furthermore, many elderly persons who would face serious financial burdens under the proposed changes are not sufficiently poor to qualify for Medicaid. Only 19 percent of the elderly are currently covered by the program.

Moreover, recent and proposed changes cut back Medicaid benefits substantially. Under the 1972 amendments, premium, copayment, and deductible requirements imposed on Medicaid recipients are expected to reduce federal expenditures by $90 million. Another provision permits states to reduce the benefits they offer under Medicaid. If states actually cut back their own outlays, matching payments by the federal government will be reduced. Altogether, it is estimated that the poor will receive about $1.3 billion less in Medicaid benefits in 1974 because of these changes. The cut in federal expenditures alone will be about $715 million.

In addition to the sizable cutbacks in the Medicaid program made possible by the 1972 amendments to the Social Security Act, new legislation proposed by the administration will result in some further small cutbacks. Dental benefits for adults are to be eliminated, at a saving of $75 million in 1974. Extension of coverage to clinics not associated with hospitals will offset $20 million of this saving and increases in Medicaid expenditures for the elderly necessitated by changes in the Medicare program will offset another $44 million—resulting in total savings of $11 million.

The total effect of recent and proposed changes in Medicare and Medicaid, therefore, is to provide additional medical benefits for the disabled and persons with chronic kidney disease, while increasing considerably the medical costs payable by the elderly and the poor.

Recently, the administration has proposed changes in the tax provisions affecting health insurance and medical expenses. In testimony before the House Ways and Means Committee on April 30, 1973, Secretary of the Treasury George P. Shultz indicated that as part of a plan to simplify the personal income tax the administration proposes elimination of the special treatment of individual health insurance expenses. In its place the administration wants to put a single deduction for all medical expenses, health insurance premiums, and casualty losses; an itemized deduction would be permitted only if, and by the amount that, the combined total exceeded 5 percent of the taxpayer's adjusted gross income. No change in tax treatment of employer contributions to health insurance premiums is proposed.[4] While this change would in effect reduce tax subsidies for medical expenses (which go in large part to higher-income groups), inequities arising from the greater value of a deduction to higher-income persons would remain.[5]

A superior alternative would be to replace all existing tax benefits for health insurance and medical expenses with a tax credit for all medical expenses in excess of some percentage of income. For example, taxes could be reduced by one dollar for each dollar of medical expenses in excess of 10 percent of income. In this case, a family with an income of $20,000 and medical expenses of $4,000 would have its taxes reduced by $2,000. A family with an income of $40,000 and the same medical expenses would receive no reduction in taxes. Such an approach would have several advantages over a tax deduction. First,

4. U.S. Department of the Treasury, *Proposals for Tax Change* (1973). Originally, the detailed explanation of tax changes included a requirement that employer contributions to health insurance plans be counted as taxable personal income; this requirement is marked "deleted" in the report and presumably is no longer an administration proposal (p. 114).

5. Under proposed legislation, a family of four with an income of $10,000 and medical expenses of $4,000 would receive a tax reduction of $665, while a family with a $40,000 income and the same medical expenses would receive a tax reduction of $840.

tax benefits would be concentrated on those for whom medical expenses pose the most serious financial burden. Second, people's payments for medical expenses would be guaranteed not to exceed some reasonable fraction of income; any additional expenses would be "paid" by the federal government. Third, the government would no longer be paying a higher share of medical bills for higher-income persons.[6]

Table 4-4 illustrates the costs and distribution of benefits by income class in 1974 under existing legislation, legislation proposed by the administration, and several alternative tax credit schemes. The proposed legislation would reduce tax subsidies arising from personal income tax deductions from $2.6 billion in 1974 to $860 million.[7] A refundable full tax credit on all medical expenses in excess of 10 percent of income would result in a tax subsidy of $3.4 billion—if only those who currently itemize medical expenses took advantage of the tax credit. However, since many with low incomes who do not currently itemize deductions would be eligible for benefits under a tax credit plan, the costs are underestimated. The estimates also do not consider any changes in prices, use of medical services, or health insurance coverage that would be induced by the credit. Final cost of the scheme, therefore, could substantially exceed $3.4 billion. Benefits under the tax credit plan would be funneled much more heavily toward low-income people. Under current law, 21 percent of the personal income tax benefits for medical expenses go to people with incomes of less than $10,000.[8] Under proposed legislation, one-third of the benefits would go to such people. Under a refundable full tax

6. The major disadvantage of such a tax credit plan is the absence of any controls on expenditures above 10 percent of income. The range over which individuals have some incentive to contain costs could be extended by a tax credit which reduced taxes by 50 cents for each dollar of expenditures between 7 and 15 percent of income, and dollar for dollar for all expenditures over 15 percent of income. Another possibility is a tax credit reducing taxes 80 cents for each dollar of expenditure over 8 percent of income. This would maintain some incentive for a person to contain costs over the entire expenditure range but would leave him vulnerable to excessively high costs.

7. Total tax subsidy, including $3.0 billion in 1974 attributable to exclusion of employers' contributions to health insurance plans from taxable personal income, would be $5.6 billion under current legislation and $3.9 billion under proposed legislation.

8. This differs from the 44 percent given in Table 4-2 because it applies only to individual health insurance premiums and medical expenses deducted from the personal income tax. Tax subsidies of employer contributions to health insurance premiums, which are excluded here, are concentrated more heavily on low- and middle-income workers.

Table 4-4. Estimated Tax Subsidies for Medical Expenses under Current Law and
Alternative Proposals, by Income Class, 1974[a]

Adjusted gross income class	Current law	Proposal 1	Proposal 2	Proposal 3	Proposal 4	Proposal 5
	Millions of dollars					
All classes	2,625	860	2,227	3,399	789	1,476
	Percentage distribution					
Under $5,000	2.1	4.2	27.4	23.4	9.6	7.3
$5,000–$9,999	18.7	29.7	43.3	43.2	40.4	39.3
$10,000–$14,999	21.6	19.4	9.7	13.1	14.2	20.5
$15,000 and over	57.7	46.7	19.4	20.3	35.9	32.9
Total	100.0	100.0	100.0	100.0	100.0	100.0

Source: Derived from the Brookings file of 1970 individual income tax returns with data projected to calendar year 1974 levels. Percentages may not add to 100 because of rounding.

a. *Proposal 1:* Itemized deduction of all health insurance and medical expenses in excess of 5 percent of income (administration proposal, omitting casualty losses).

Proposal 2: Full tax credit for all health insurance and medical expenses in excess of 15 percent of income, with credit in excess of tax refundable.

Proposal 3: Full tax credit for all health insurance and medical expenses in excess of 10 percent of income, refundable.

Proposal 4: Full tax credit for all health insurance and medical expenses in excess of 15 percent of income, nonrefundable.

Proposal 5: Full tax credit for all health insurance and medical expenses in excess of 10 percent of income, nonrefundable.

None of the plans include the $3 billion tax subsidy in 1974 attributable to the exclusion of employer contributions to health insurance plans from taxable personal income.

Estimates are based on individuals who currently itemize medical deductions. Many low-income individuals who do not now itemize deductions would be eligible for benefits under a tax credit plan. Tax subsidies shown, therefore, are underestimated—particularly for laws 2 and 3, which would refund any excess of the credit over total tax liability. The estimates do not consider any changes in prices, use of medical services, or health insurance coverage induced by the credit.

credit for all medical expenses in excess of 10 percent of income, two-thirds of the tax benefits would go to those with incomes below $10,000.

National Health Insurance

Because of their major flaws, a strong case can be made for shifting from present programs to a new system of national health insurance designed to move toward three objectives: (1) ensuring that everyone has access to essential medical care regardless of income, location, or type of family; (2) protecting everyone from medical expenses that are high relative to income; and (3) reducing costs and encouraging efficiency in the delivery of medical care.

A variety of national health insurance plans that would move toward one or more of these objectives have been proposed.[9] They

9. For discussion of several such plans see Schultze and others, *Setting National Priorities: The 1973 Budget*, pp. 236–50.

range from relatively inexpensive plans, which provide protection only against extremely high medical expenses, to full coverage of all medical expenses for everyone. For example, Senator Russell B. Long has proposed an insurance plan that deals with the problem of catastrophic expenses. It would provide coverage for approximately 75 percent of hospital costs after the patient had been in the hospital for sixty days. Coverage of physicians' bills and other medical services would begin only after a deductible of $2,000, and individuals would pay coinsurance of 20 percent on expenses above $2,000. However, once patients had paid the deductible amounts (sixty days of hospital care and $2,000 in physicians' bills), further payments would be limited to $1,000. Such a plan would be of little help to the poor or the near-poor, but it would provide needed protection against medical catastrophe for high-income people. Compared to the more comprehensive plans that have been offered, it would not be costly. Senator Long estimates it would cost $3.6 billion a year at current medical prices.

At the other extreme are proposals, such as the Kennedy-Griffiths bill, for complete coverage of most medical expense without any deductibles or coinsurance. Such a plan meets the objectives both of assuring adequate financial access to medical care for all and of protection against catastrophic medical expenses. At the same time it gives the federal government an opportunity to control all aspects of the medical care market through its role as sole purchaser of medical care services. The administrative problems of managing such a complex system would be immense, however, and so would the federal cost. The Department of Health, Education, and Welfare has estimated that enactment of the Kennedy-Griffiths bill would result in federal expenditures of about $60 billion in 1974 in addition to those that would be made under existing federal programs. Benefits are not related to a family's income under either the Long or the Kennedy-Griffiths bill.

In between these extremes lie many other proposals that differ in conception as well as in cost. The type of proposal that seems best adapted to meeting all three criteria of equity, protection, and efficiency is a national health insurance plan with income-related benefits. Under such a plan, both deductibles and coinsurance would be related to income so that people would be protected against expenses that were high relative to their income. To prevent undue financial burdens a ceiling related to income could be placed on the out-of-pocket expenses a family would have to pay. One advantage of such an approach is that a single plan would serve the dual purpose of protecting the poor against normal expenses and protecting higher-income people against heavy expenses; hence, no stigma would be attached to receiving benefits under the plan. Benefits would depend solely on the relationship between the expense incurred and a family's income, not on arbitrary factors such as the geographical location or the makeup of the family. The fact that people would normally be paying part of the expenses themselves could be expected to lessen wasteful use of medical resources by encouraging both doctors and their patients to use less costly types of care. This effect would be weakened, however, if most people bought supplementary insurance to cover expenses not covered by the federal plan.

In designing a plan of this type (or any national health insurance plan) several questions would have to be answered.

1. Who should be covered?

Since one of the major objectives is to reduce the inequities of the present system, the argument is strong for including the whole population. The cost of the plan could be reduced by restricting it to certain groups (for instance, families with children or people covered by social security), but any such restriction would be arbitrary and likely to omit groups for whom assistance is particularly crucial (for example, unrelated individuals or migrant farm workers not covered by social security).

2. What services should be covered?

This is a difficult question, about which many would disagree. Preventive health services, for example, might have high payoff in improving health and reducing the need for treatment; moreover, people are likely to skimp on prevention if it is not covered by insurance. Comprehensive physical examinations, however, can be expensive, and conclusive evidence on the value of regular checkups is not yet available. Similarly, the exclusion of mental health benefits could create severe financial strain for some families. Yet coverage of such expenses could inflate the cost of the plan unless strong incentives to discourage excessive use were retained. Custodial nursing home care for the elderly is another example of the type of expenditure that can strain personal financial resources and for which no private health insurance coverage exists. Yet including such a benefit in a national health insurance plan might lead to a big increase in the use of such services and take needed budgetary resources away from younger groups in the population. It is important to cover a range of services wide enough to avoid creating incentives for the use of more expensive medical resources. For example, covering inpatient but not outpatient hospital care might lead to greater use of high-cost medical resources when less expensive methods would be equally effective.

3. What measures should be taken to reduce costs and encourage efficiency?

Coinsurance and deductibles should encourage patients and physicians to weigh the costs of alternative medical resources (such as inpatient hospital care versus outpatient care; care by a primary physician versus care by a specialist). The plan might also provide financial incentives to encourage the growth of certain organizational forms; for instance, higher benefits could be offered people enrolled in health maintenance organizations. There is some reason to be skeptical, however, about whether market incentives of these kinds can be relied on to hold down costs. Direct governmental controls over reimbursement rates and other medical prices might prove necessary. To avoid overuse of costly facilities, some procedure for review of their use during long hospital stays would clearly be necessary.

4. How should the plan be financed?

Three methods of financing national health insurance are generally discussed: general revenue financing, payroll taxes, and premiums. Of the three, premium payments are the most regressive—and fall most heavily on the working poor. To the extent that it is a substitute for wages, the premium is actually borne by the worker, even when the employer nominally pays it. Since the premium is per worker rather than per dollar of earnings, it is equivalent to a head tax and constitutes a larger fraction of income for the low-income worker than for the high-income worker. The payroll tax, while not as regressive as the premium method of financing, is more regressive than financing from general revenues, which come in large part from progressive income taxes.

5. What role should be played by private insurance companies?

A public plan with little or no role for private health insurance companies can greatly affect the way in which the medical care market operates. Instead of dealing with the providers of medical care indirectly through a multitude of private health insurance companies, the federal government could itself set standards of reasonable payment for services rendered, enforce quality controls (with eligibility for payment contingent on maintaining minimum standards of quality), and use financial incentives to encourage desired patterns of distribution, uses of medical resources, and organizational forms. Counterarguments favoring a larger role for private health insurance companies include their experience in dealing with medical care providers and the greater efficiency of operation that might result from competition among health insurance companies.

6. How steeply should benefits drop as income rises?

If the principal objective of the plan was to help low-income people pay for care and give upper-income groups protection only against genuinely catastrophic expenses, then coinsurance and deductibles should be low or zero for the poor and near-poor but rise sharply in the middle-income ranges. Such a schedule, however, would involve high marginal tax rates and might impair incentives to work. More gradual increases in coinsurance and deductibles would lower marginal tax rates but raise the total cost of the plan and give a higher proportion of the benefits to those who need it less.

One plan meeting the general criteria set forth here was recently set forth in a staff paper by the U.S. Department of Health, Education, and Welfare (HEW).[10] This plan, called Maximum Liability Health Insurance (MLHI), illustrates one possible set of deductibles and coinsurance that vary with income. It has a deductible equal to 10 percent of income for all middle- and upper-income families. In addition, these families face a coinsurance of 50 percent on all medical expenditures in the range of from 10 to 20 percent of income. The maximum out-of-pocket payment a family would be required to make, therefore, is limited to 15 percent of family income. More generous coinsurance and deductible provisions are provided for lower-income families. For example, families with incomes below $2,400 would be required to pay 5 percent of all medical bills up to $720, so that the maximum out-of-pocket payment would be $36. Table 4-5 shows the deductible and coinsurance provisions for each income class (plan 1).

The cost of such a plan would depend on the specific benefit pack-

10. *Caspar W. Weinberger to be Secretary of Health, Education, and Welfare,* Hearings before the Senate Committee on Labor and Public Welfare, 93 Cong. 1 sess. (1973), Pt. 2, Appendix, pp. 23a–38.

age and the structure of coinsurance and deductibles. HEW has estimated that its illustrative staff plan would cost $35.2 billion in 1976. With normal increases in medical expenditures, the cost in 1978 should be about $43 billion. But since the plan would replace the existing Medicare and Medicaid programs and would presumably be accompanied by repeal of the current tax laws that provide indirect subsidies for the purchase of medical care, it could be implemented at a net cost to the government of $11 billion. The costs of this comprehensive health insurance plan are relatively low, largely because few people with incomes above $12,000 would incur medical expenses in excess of 10 percent of income. The following table provides an estimate of the net budgetary cost (in billions of dollars) of plan 1 in 1978:

Cost in 1978	43
Offsetting federal expenditures	
Medicare	16
Medicaid	8
Tax subsidies	8
Subtotal	32
Net cost	11

This plan would increase access to medical care for many of the poor, especially those who live in states with low Medicaid benefits, and provide protection against extraordinary expenses for everyone. Some of the poor would receive fewer benefits than under Medicaid, and most high-income elderly people would also be worse off under the plan.

Much more generous plans of the same general kind could be devised. One possibility would be a plan with no coinsurance or deductible for people with family incomes below $5,000 and better protection against catastrophic expenses for middle- and upper-income families. Such a plan is illustrated in the bottom half of Table 4-5. Under this plan the poor would receive substantially greater benefits than under plan 1, and almost all of them would be considerably better off than they are now.

Plan 2 would cost approximately $10 billion more than plan 1, or about $53 billion in 1978. With offsets from the Medicare and Medicaid programs and the elimination of tax subsidies, the net additional federal cost would be $21 billion.

Table 4-5. Costs to Families under the Maximum Liability Health Insurance Plan of the Department of Health, Education, and Welfare (Plan 1) and Alternative Health Insurance Proposal (Plan 2), by Income Class

Family income class (dollars)	Family pays	Of medical bills up to	Plus	Of additional bills up to	Maximum liability	
					Amount	Percentage of income[a]
Plan 1[a]						
Under 2,400	5 percent	$ 720	...	...	$ 36	3.0
2,400–3,599	20 percent	720	...	...	144	4.8
3,600–4,799	50 percent	720	...	...	360	8.5
4,800–5,999	75 percent	720	...	...	540	10.0
6,000–7,199	100 percent	720	...	...	720	10.9
7,200–8,399	100 percent	780	25 percent	$ 780	975	12.5
8,400–9,599	100 percent	900	25 percent	900	1,125	12.5
9,600–10,799	100 percent	1,020	25 percent	1,020	1,275	12.5
10,800–11,999	100 percent	1,140	25 percent	1,140	1,425	12.5
12,000 and over	100 percent	10 percent of income	50 percent	10 percent of income	...	15.0
Plan 2[a]						
Under 5,000	Nothing	...	...	...	0	0
5,000–6,999	25 percent	$1,000	...	...	$ 250	3.6
7,000–8,999	50 percent	1,000	...	...	500	6.3
9,000–11,999	100 percent	1,000	10 percent	$1,000	1,100	10.5
12,000–14,999	100 percent	1,000	50 percent	1,000	1,500	11.1
15,000–17,999	100 percent	1,000	75 percent	1,000	1,750	10.6
18,000 and over	100 percent	1,000	100 percent	1,000	2,000	10.0

Sources: Caspar W. Weinberger to be Secretary of Health, Education, and Welfare, Hearings before the Senate Committee on Labor and Public Welfare, 93 Cong. 1 sess. (1973), Pt. 2, Appendix, p. 39a, and authors' estimates.

a. Calculations are based on the midpoint of each income class. At the upper end of the distributions, the maximum liability is 15 percent of income for plan 1 and 10 percent for plan 2.

Problems Not Solved by Financing

While adequate financing is essential in assuring access to medical services and preventing financial burdens arising from large medical bills, an insurance program cannot be relied on to solve all the problems of the health care system. Experience with existing financing programs clearly suggests that even with comprehensive national health insurance some groups—especially residents of central cities and farms—would get substantially less care than others unless special efforts were made to increase the access to care of these groups.

Under Medicare, for example, uniform benefits are available to all participants, but average expenditures are substantially lower for blacks than for whites. Although 9 percent of the elderly belong to a black or other nonwhite race, they receive only 6 percent of the payments made by the program. Most of this discrepancy is explained by the fact that elderly whites receive more services—more hospital stays and doctors' visits—than do elderly persons of other races, even though elderly whites enjoy better health than elderly nonwhites (see Table 4-6).[11] Since comprehensive financing apparently does not eliminate racial disparities, it is urgent that supplementary measures be undertaken on the supply side to improve the physical access of blacks to medical resources—such as increasing the supply of physicians who will practice in minority neighborhoods, placing more black physicians on hospital staffs, training minority group paraprofessional personnel to work in community health organizations, subsidizing health care organizations to locate in minority neighborhoods, and improving and expanding hospital outpatient facilities.

Evidence suggests that special efforts are needed to improve access to medical care in central cities and farm areas. In rural areas, the most efficient solution may well involve better medical transportation systems to link rural residents with the health facilities and manpower available in urban areas. For central cities, programs to encourage the growth of medical care organizations such as neighborhood health

11. Indeed, the poor health of blacks, reflected in their high mortality rate, reduces the chance that they will live long enough to benefit from Medicare at all. Present life expectancies imply that only 56 percent of black babies will live to sixty-five as against 74 percent of white babies. U.S. Department of Health, Education, and Welfare, National Center for Health Statistics, *Vital Statistics of the United States, 1969*, Vol. 2, Sec. 5, *Life Tables* (1973), p. 58.

Table 4-6. Use of Medical Services by the Elderly, and Their Health Status,
by Race, 1969

Service, use, and health status	White	All other races
Hospital care		
Discharges per 1,000 Medicare enrollees	312	237
Hospital days per 1,000 Medicare enrollees	4,150	3,491
Hospital charges per day per Medicare patient	$65	$60
Medicare payments per elderly person	$215	$150
Physicians' services		
Annual visits per person	6.2	5.1
Percent of visits in hospital clinics	5.4	15.3
Medicare payments per elderly person[a]	$105	$79
Health status[b]		
Days of restricted activity per person per year	33.1	47.6
Days of bed disability per person per year	13.1	20.5
Percent with limitations due to chronic conditions	41.6	51.4
Percent unable to carry on major activity[c]	15.1	25.0

Sources: Medicare payments are calculated from population data in *Statistical Abstract of the United States, 1972*, Table 37; payments data in U.S. Social Security Administration, Office of Research and Statistics, *Health Insurance Statistics*, CMS-25, "Current Medicare Survey Report, Hospital Insurance Sample: Inpatient Hospital Utilization, 1969" (April 2, 1973), p. 12; and physicians' data from Social Security Administration, unpublished tabulation.

Other Medicare data are from *Health Insurance Statistics*, CMS-25, p. 9. Other data in the table are from U.S. Department of Health, Education, and Welfare, Health Services and Mental Health Administration, *Age Patterns in Medical Care, Illness, and Disability, United States, 1968–1969*, Vital and Health Statistics—Series 10—No. 70 (April 1972), pp. 10, 15, 32, 39, 45.

a. Payments to physicians are for 1970 and are based on unpublished tabulations from the Current Medicare Survey sample of the Social Security Administration. Data on physician payments by race for all Medicare beneficiaries in 1968 are $79 per elderly white person and $45 per elderly person of other races (U.S. Social Security Administration, *Medicare: Health Insurance for the Aged, 1968*, Section 1, Summary, *Utilization and Reimbursement by Person* [1973]).

b. Based on 1968–69 data.

c. Major activity refers to ability to work, keep house, or engage in other normal activities.

centers, to train residents as paramedical personnel, and so forth, may be more effective in reducing physical barriers to care.

An insurance program that leads to higher medical expenditures may drive medical prices up if nothing else is done. Voucher-type subsidies work best in competitive markets, where increases in demand for services will not result in substantial price increases, at least in the long run. The medical care market, clearly, is not competitive, and without supplementary measures, the benefits of improved financing are likely to be dissipated by price increases. Some of the inflationary impact may be lessened by appropriate design of insurance coverage, but a financing strategy must be combined with other strategies to assure success.

The insurance system itself can be designed to reduce the inflationary impact, by encouraging the development of more effective ways of delivering health care. Medicare and Medicaid have actually discouraged many innovational changes. For example, the Medicare program will not pay for services rendered by paraprofessionals. Medicaid frequently will not pay for services rendered in neighborhood health centers. Neither program was originally set up to reimburse organizations providing comprehensive medical services to enrollees in exchange for an annual payment. But reimbursement techniques can be designed to prevent these negative effects and to promote the growth of new forms of organizing the delivery of medical care. Even a carefully structured insurance program, however, cannot do the job alone. Resistance within the medical profession and the financial obstacles facing new organizations in their formative years are likely to obstruct any major changes without direct federal efforts to foster their development.

Closely related to the problems of inflation and efficiency is the problem of assuring an adequate supply of medical manpower. Because of the long lag in training medical personnel and professional resistance to the expansion of certain types of medical manpower, federal intervention may be required to increase the supply of certain types of personnel. Without intervention, for example, medical schools are likely to continue to place greater emphasis on training specialists than on turning out primary-care physicians who are instrumental in preventive care programs, to restrict openings to medical school, and to limit admissions of women and students from minority groups. Without adequate financial support, many groups, such as minority students, will probably be unable to attend medical schools in any case. Federal initiative in providing incentives to medical schools and other health profession training schools to yield socially desirable outcomes must be a complementary part of any attempt to improve financial access to medical services. These approaches are discussed further in Chapter 5.

Housing*

Some kind of shelter from the elements is, like a minimum amount of food, a necessity. But current American ideas of what constitutes adequate housing, like ideas about an adequate diet, go far beyond

* Prepared with the assistance of Henry J. Aaron.

what is necessary to sustain life and health. The quality of a person's house and the neighborhood that surrounds it have a major impact on the quality of his life. People forced to live in crowded, rundown, dreary buildings, surrounded by other crowded, rundown, dreary buildings, consider themselves deprived and are so considered by others. "Adequate housing" has come to mean at the very least a sound structure with central heating, plumbing that works, cooking facilities not shared with another household, approximately one room per person, and that important but hard to define attribute, a decent neighborhood.

Besides its importance in everyone's life, two aspects of housing make it a special object of public concern: building or buying a house is a big investment for the average family, and a family's housing is extremely visible to others.

Since the construction or purchase of a house is a large investment for the average family, people need to be able to borrow money easily to finance the purchase of a house and pay it back over a long period of time. Otherwise, homeownership will be largely restricted to people with substantial income or wealth. The widespread idea that people ought to have an opportunity to own their own homes has provided much of the impetus behind government efforts to make housing credit widely and easily available.

The visibility of housing means that people care more about other people's housing than they do about other people's furniture or more private types of consumption. Especially in a city, housing that is dilapidated, unsightly, or rat-infested is detrimental, not just to those who live there, but to their neighbors as well. This fact provides a rationale for public efforts to help all people upgrade their housing, especially for efforts to upgrade the housing of the poor.

People with very low incomes simply cannot afford either to rent or to buy housing that comes up to the standard most of the population regards as minimally acceptable. A successful income strategy would alleviate this problem—just as it would the nutritional problem—but one can also make a case for a separate effort to assure everyone of a decent dwelling. The argument is simply that, since society cares more about the housing of the poor than about other things they consume, it is more efficient to intervene directly in the distribution of housing than to redistribute income. There may also be political advantages to housing aid: the housing industry is likely to support a housing subsidy with more enthusiasm than a general subsidy to low-income families. Moreover, subsidizing housing may give the public some leverage on the industry itself and an opportunity to set standards of quality or to carry out other policies, such as fostering racially integrated housing, along with the basic policy of ensuring that everyone has a decent house.

There are two basic approaches to helping people buy housing. One is to subsidize demand, perhaps by giving people housing vouchers similar to food stamps. The other approach is to subsidize suppliers of housing so that they are able to sell at lower prices or offer lower rents than would otherwise prevail.

Either demand or supply subsidies can be targeted on low-income groups—or on other special groups such as the elderly. Housing vouchers can go just to the poor or suppliers can be offered special subsidies for renting or selling housing to low-income people.

A program that subsidizes demand is easier to make equitable. Assistance can be given to everyone who meets certain income, age, or other criteria. Moreover, demand subsidies give the consumer of housing the choice of where he wants to live and the type of housing he prefers. The argument for demand subsidies is that the consumer is the best judge of what he needs and that if he has the funds to make his demand effective the market will supply these needs.

The market, however, may fail to respond. There may be no housing available to blacks or low-income people in some neighborhoods even if they have housing vouchers. Supply subsidies may make it possible for the government to ensure that housing actually becomes available, to control its quality, or to carry out related policies such as rebuilding a whole section of a city at once. On the other hand, if the subsidy goes to the supplier, the consumer has less choice; he may have to stay in the same building to retain his subsidy. Moreover, if there is not enough subsidized housing, suppliers will choose who gets it, perhaps from a long list of eligible claimants. Since different suppliers will evolve different rules, it will be difficult to keep the program fair.

At present the largest federal housing program subsidizes demand: tax breaks given to homeowners under the income tax are similar in effect to giving housing vouchers primarily to middle- and upper-income people. Most federal housing subsidies for low-income people work through the supply side.

The Development of Federal Housing Programs

Until 1968, federal housing policy consisted of: (1) the creation of major federal institutions to improve the operation of the housing market, especially to increase the volume of credit for home purchases; (2) substantial assistance to homeowners under the income tax system; (3) rather small efforts to subsidize the construction of low-rent housing for the poor. Since 1968, efforts to help the poor have been substantial, although federal help to low-income groups is still far smaller than the assistance provided to middle- and upper-income groups through the tax system.

IMPROVING THE HOUSING MARKET. Prompted by the mortgage foreclosures of the Great Depression, the housing shortages during and after World War II, and public desire to assist returning veterans, the federal government established a network of institutions designed to make it both easier for home-buyers to borrow money at reasonable rates with low down payments and safer for lenders to lend. The Federal Housing Administration and the Veterans Administration insure and guarantee home mortgages. The Federal National Mortgage Association (now a privately owned company), the Government National Mortgage Association, and the Federal Home Loan Mortgage Corporation buy, sell, and hold home mortgages, thus providing a secondary market for mortgages that both stabilizes and augments the flow of funds into mortgage lending.

These institutions have revolutionized housing credit practices and greatly increased both the rate of home construction and the proportion of Americans who own their own homes. These activities are not further discussed here, because they are not particularly controversial and do not involve major budgetary resources.

TAX EXPENDITURES. The income tax laws strongly favor homeowners over renters. If two taxpayers have the same income and total assets and live in dwellings of comparable value, but one owns and the other rents, the owner will have a substantially lower tax bill. The renter may have his assets invested in stocks or bonds from which he gets an income, but he has to pay tax on that income. The owner has part or all of his assets invested in his house. He gets income from this investment too, in the form of rent-free housing, but does not pay tax on this income. Furthermore, before figuring his tax he can deduct from his income both the interest on his mortgage and the real estate taxes he pays.

These tax advantages to homeowners were small before World War II when income tax rates were low, but they are now substantial. Tax subsidies to homeowners in 1972 are estimated to cost the government about $10 billion, making this "program" by far the largest federal housing subsidy program. Most of the benefit goes to middle- and upper-income taxpayers. Nearly three-fifths of these tax concessions accrue to families with incomes over $20,000 and only 7 percent to families with incomes under $10,000. Concentration of the benefits at the upper end of the income scale results from two factors: (1) people with higher incomes are more likely not only to own houses but to own more valuable houses, and to itemize their deductions; (2) a dollar of tax deduction is worth more to a taxpayer in a high tax bracket than to a taxpayer in a lower one.

In effect, the tax treatment of homeownership is equivalent to a program in which the government issues vouchers to homeowners to pay part of their housing cost, these vouchers being more valuable, on the average, to high-income than to low-income taxpayers. If Congress were confronted with a proposal for an expenditure program with identical effects, it is doubtful whether a single representative or senator could be found to vote for so bizarre a scheme.

HELPING THE POOR. Under the low-rent public housing program, established in 1937, the federal government provides funds to local housing authorities for the construction of low-rent housing. Only low-income families are eligible to live in these projects—when a family's economic fortune takes a turn for the better it has to move out. Rent is adjusted to family income. Under current federal regulations the rent cannot exceed 25 percent of a family's income, but it may be less, depending on the rules of the local housing authority.

Public housing has had an erratic history full of conflicts about the purpose of the program. It did not begin to make a significant dent in the housing needs of the poor until it became part of the big new housing thrust of the late 1960s.

The rediscovery of poverty in the mid-1960s prompted some federal efforts to involve the private sector in producing more housing for low-income families. One result was the rent-supplement program, enacted in 1965, under which the government can contract with nonprofit corporations or cooperatives to provide housing for low-income families. The contractor charges rents at prevailing rates, the tenant pays 25 percent of his income (after an adjustment for minor children), and the government pays the difference as a "rent supplement" on behalf of the tenant.

Even with public housing, rent supplements, and a couple of other small subsidy programs, total subsidized housing starts never reached 100,000 units a year from 1950 to 1967. They totaled only 856,000 units for the eighteen-year period, or only 3 percent of all starts.

A new stage of federal housing policies began in 1968 with enactment of the Housing and Urban Development Act of 1968, which declared that the construction or rehabilitation of 26 million housing units from 1969 to 1978 was a national goal—6 million with federal assistance and 20 million without. The goal implied federal assistance in the construction or rehabilitation of 600,000 units a year, more than twelve times the average rate in the period 1950–67.

This act also created two new programs to assist lower-middle-income and low-income families to buy or to rent adequate housing. Under the homeownership assistance program residents in an approved project pay at least one-fifth of their adjusted income toward mortgage amortization; they may deduct 5 percent of gross income as an offset to social security taxes and exclude from income $300 for each minor child. If the homeowner's payment is less than enough for amortization, the government pays the difference up to a specified maximum.

The rental assistance program requires renters in approved projects to pay one-fourth of their adjusted income as rent. The government pays the difference between this amount and fair market rents up to a specified maximum. The maximum government payment is frequently too low to make it economically feasible for the project to rent to tenants with very little income. However, up to 20 percent of the units in a project may be occupied by tenants who also receive assistance under the older rent-supplement program, under which the government can accommodate very low-income families.

The enactment of the housing goal and the programs to implement it resulted from the historical coincidence of two largely unrelated housing problems. First, a much increased rate of new family formation was expected. This projection came at a time when there had been two years during which tight money had inhibited residential construction. As a result many people feared that a general housing

Table 4-7. Federally Subsidized and Unsubsidized Housing Starts, 1950–72

Starts in thousands

| Period | Total, all housing starts | *Conventionally constructed starts* | | | Mobile homes |
		Total	Subsidized	Subsidized, as percentage of total	
1950–59, annual average	1,597	1,505	41	2.7	91
1960–68, annual average	1,617	1,434	68	4.7	183
1969	1,913	1,500	197	13.1	413
1970	1,868	1,467	431	29.4	401
1971	2,581	2,084	426	20.4	497
1972[a]	2,954	2,378	336	14.1	576

Sources: 1950–70, Anthony Downs, "Federal Housing Subsidies: Their Nature and Effectiveness, and What We Should Do About Them: Summary Report" (Chicago: Real Estate Research Corporation, October 1972; processed), p. 8; 1971–72, data obtained from U.S. Department of Housing and Urban Development, Office of Economic Analysis.

a. Preliminary.

shortage might occur. Second, the growing awareness of poverty and urban decay made the middle- and upper-income orientation of federal housing policies seem particularly inappropriate.

Actual performance since 1968 has fallen somewhat short of the housing goal, but it has been spectacular by historical standards. Total starts have averaged over 2 million units a year since 1969, a sharp increase over the performance of preceding years. As may be seen in Table 4-7, the number of subsidized starts has climbed sharply since 1968.

As the flow of housing assistance to low- and moderate-income families swelled, serious administrative and political difficulties appeared. First, investigative reporting turned up instances of corruption, bad administration, or poor judgment in several cities. Only some of these allegations involved programs of housing assistance; many involved unsubsidized programs that operated in low-income areas. Although the dubious or dishonest procedures occurred in only a few communities, the reports triggered concern about the entire system of federal housing assistance. The financial soundness of housing built with homeownership and rental assistance came into question although over 90 percent of rental assistance housing is not in financial difficulty and only a small minority of units under the homeownership assistance program is in default.[12]

12. Anthony Downs, "Federal Housing Subsidies: Their Nature and Effectiveness, and What We Should Do About Them: Summary Report" (Chicago: Real Estate Research Corporation, October 1972; processed).

In retrospect, the assumption that programs to subsidize housing for the poor or to assist construction in low-income areas could operate as do other programs of the Federal Housing Administration (FHA) seems unrealistic. The FHA should have anticipated that default rates would be higher and that low-income families would make more mistakes than middle-income families. Workloads for FHA offices should have been reduced; in fact, they have increased. Counseling services should have been mandatory for home-buyers; in fact, they are meager and spotty. Rigorous cost control on new construction should have been instituted; in fact, controls were loose and easily circumvented. Following the revelations of scandals, administrators in the Department of Housing and Urban Development began requiring extensive reporting, checking, and verification by would-be builders and HUD field offices. As a result, the flow of subsidized starts in 1972 was much below the 1970–71 average.

On January 8, 1973, Secretary George W. Romney announced that the government would stop making new commitments under all housing assistance programs; only the projects that had already been evaluated as financially feasible would be allowed to proceed. This announcement was to have no immediate effect on the number of assisted housing starts, which come months or years after evaluation for financial feasibility, the lag varying from program to program. During the ensuing months the number of starts would taper off first in the homeownership program, later under rental assistance, and still later under low-rent public housing. Completions would follow the same pattern with even longer lags.

Since expenditures under these programs only occur after occupancy of completed housing units, the secretary's announcement had essentially no budgetary impact during fiscal 1973 and will reduce expenditures in fiscal 1974 only slightly. Hence, it is clear that the administration's decision to halt new commitments under assisted housing programs is not primarily a response to current budgetary stringency. Rather it reflects real concern about the equity and efficiency of these programs.

Problems with Current Programs

The administration has frozen new commitments under four existing programs that provide subsidized housing for people with low and moderate incomes: low-rent public housing, rent supplements, homeownership assistance, and rental assistance. Details of these programs differ but the basic concept is the same. Groups of housing units are newly constructed or renovated for the express purpose of being sold or rented to low- and moderate-income people. Families apply for such housing; if they are accepted, they pay a percentage of their income in rent or mortgage repayments. The difference between what they actually pay and the market rate for such housing is a subsidy paid on their behalf by the government.

There is no doubt that these programs have assisted the groups for which they were intended. The typical tenant in low-rent public housing has very modest means. In 1969 about 69 percent of the benefits from the program went to families with incomes under $4,000. Families in the rent-supplement program tend to be smaller, but they have even lower incomes than those in public housing. The home-ownership and rental assistance programs reach a group with slightly higher incomes; the benefits are concentrated on those with incomes of $4,000–$7,000.

There is also little question that the housing built under these programs has been a substantial improvement over the housing that would have been available to participants without the programs. Despite the bad image that "public housing" has among the nonpoor, long waiting lists for most assisted housing projects attest to the consumers' judgment that such housing is more desirable than what they could afford on their own.

Three main criticisms can be leveled at the design of current housing assistance programs. First, they are inequitable. They provide substantial subsidies to a small number of the poor and near-poor but no assistance at all to other equally needy people. The average annual benefit under the homeownership and rental assistance programs is about $830. The median rent-supplement payment is $1,260, and the average benefit in low-rent public housing about $2,100. These substantial benefits now go to about 2.5 million families, most of them with incomes under $8,000. Only one out of seven of the families in this income class is a beneficiary.

Second, since the subsidy is tied to the housing unit, the consumer has only a take-it-or-leave-it choice. If he moves in search of a better job or a better school or because of changed family circumstances, he loses the subsidy and is unlikely to be able to get another one. Hence, the programs tend to restrict mobility and keep people in housing units they might not choose if they could take the subsidy with them and shop around.

Third, the housing subsidies are tied to new construction, which makes them unnecessarily expensive per unit. Especially in cities, the cost of constructing new dwelling units is extremely high, and hence placing families in new housing is considerably more expensive than finding them acceptable housing in existing structures.

On grounds of both equity and efficiency a case can be made for reducing the scope of existing housing assistance programs and introducing some form of housing allowance designed to ensure that all low-income families have access to decent housing. The next section discusses how such an allowance might work and what it might cost.

Housing Allowances

Housing allowances can be designed in different ways for different purposes, but a typical formula rests on two assumptions: (1) that it is reasonable to expect all families to spend a specified proportion of their income—say, a quarter—for housing; and (2) that estimates are available of the cost of "basic" or minimally acceptable housing for families of various sizes in each community. Under this type of allowance, the government would pay families the difference between their expected contribution and the cost of basic housing in the community. For example, if basic housing for a family of four was estimated to cost $1,800 a year, a family with $3,000 a year would get a housing allowance of $1,050 ($1,800 minus $750). If the family's income rose to $5,000, its housing allowance would drop to $550 ($1,800 minus $1,250).

The cost of such an allowance to the taxpayer, as well as the benefit to recipients, obviously depends on three factors. The first is the definition of basic housing—in other words, the level of benefit available to families with zero income. The percentage of income that a family is assumed able to pay in rent is the second. This percentage can also be regarded as a marginal tax rate. If a family is judged able to spend 25 percent of its income on housing, its housing allowance will be reduced $25 for each additional $100 of earnings, which is equivalent to a 25 percent tax on income. The proportion of eligible households that apply is the third factor. This proportion in turn depends in part on the nature of restrictions put on households to ensure that the housing allowance is not spent on other goods.

In the design of any housing allowance a number of important issues would have to be resolved. First, how closely should the government supervise expenditures by recipients to ensure that housing allowances resulted in higher expenditures on housing? At one extreme, the government might avoid all supervision. In that case, the housing allowance would in fact be an unrestricted cash grant whose value would vary from community to community according to housing costs. At the other extreme, the government might closely supervise expenditures to make sure that housing allowances were not spent for other purposes. One way to do this would be to pay the allowances in the form of vouchers good only for payment by the recipient to his landlord (in the case of renters) or lender (in the case of homeowners). A further effort to make certain that the allowances were used for housing expenditures might be the requirement that all but the most impoverished families put up some money of their own to purchase rent vouchers—as they do for food stamps.

Second, designers of a housing allowance would have to decide what measures should be taken to deal with the most common and most serious objection to housing allowances—that landlords would respond to them by jacking up rents, a response that would lead to higher incomes for property owners but not to better housing. This objection rests on presumed answers to the two crucial questions about the operation of housing markets.

1. How will recipients respond to allowances? Will they stay put in existing residences? Will they seek better housing but within present, narrowly defined neighborhoods? Will they seek better housing outside present neighborhoods? There is little firm evidence on exactly what recipients would do. Some badly deteriorated neighborhoods, already experiencing high vacancy and abandonment rates, might be swept by mass exodus. Residents of poor but stable neighborhoods might seek better housing nearby. Decisions will be influenced by vacancy rates; by the composition of the local housing stock; and for blacks, Chicanos, Puerto Ricans, and other minorities, by the relative strength of discrimination in local housing markets and the vigor with which open housing legislation is enforced.

2. How will landlords respond to increased housing demand? Are they monopolists who will extract much or most of the allowances in higher rents? Or will they, like other competitive producers, respond to higher demand by increasing supply? It is vital to remem-

ber that changes in the total supply of housing do not depend entirely on new construction; they depend also on the tens of millions of maintenance, repair, and improvement decisions made by landlords and homeowners each year. Although evidence about the probable response of property owners to a housing allowance is unavailable, a considerable amount of information suggests that, with certain possibly serious exceptions, they will behave more like competitors than monopolists. The market for rental housing in most large urban areas is highly competitive; ownership of the low-cost housing stock is widely diffused among thousands of owners, most of whose holdings are quite small. Contrary to common impressions, available evidence suggests that most owners try hard to manage their units well and fairly, that judicious maintenance is good business, and that average profit rates are low. This evidence suggests that property owners would respond to increased demand, particularly if goaded by the threat of vacancies, by raising rents primarily to cover the costs of the improvements and better maintenance that tenants would be in a position to demand.

A third issue concerns the manner in which housing allowances should be introduced. A generous universal system of allowances could be introduced simultaneously throughout the nation, largely replacing increments to existing programs. On the other hand, a system of allowances could be introduced gradually as a supplement to, or a partial replacement for, increments in existing subsidy programs. Gradual introduction could be managed in various ways. Housing allowances might be paid only to certain groups, such as the aged. They could be introduced only in metropolitan areas, other urban areas, or rural districts in which there were sufficient vacant standard units to ease transition. They could be introduced subject to budget limitations so that within each housing market only some of the eligible families received them at the outset. In all cases, the limitations of the allowance would minimize the chance that a large increase in demand would disrupt housing markets or drive prices up even temporarily. Continued construction under existing subsidy programs could be used to solve any remaining transitional problems.

A fourth issue is deciding what measures should accompany allowance payments to promote improved housing standards. Such measures might range from serious efforts at code enforcement to specific evaluation and approval of each unit occupied by the recipient of an allowance. The question is how much red tape and administrative expense is justified by the desire to protect the unwary.

To examine the effects of housing allowances, the Department of Housing and Urban Development is undertaking three ambitious experiments. These experiments contain safeguards to ensure that housing occupied by allowance recipients meets minimum standards. In one experiment, selected families in two metropolitan areas, Pittsburgh and Phoenix, will receive allowances under several different allowance formulas. The purpose of the experiment is to discover precisely how the demand for housing changes in response to various allowances. Do families move? If so, how far, and to what kinds of neighborhoods? How much do they change housing expenditures? How sensitive are each of these kinds of behavior to the different allowance formulas?

The second experiment, to measure the response of housing suppliers to a housing allowance, is far more difficult and important. In this experiment, all families in a small number of carefully chosen metropolitan areas who are eligible on the basis of income will receive housing allowances. The experiment will test the allegation that a large-scale system of allowances will drive costs up instead of improving housing quality. By introducing a large-scale system of allowances abruptly, this experiment will examine these allegations on grounds most favorable to critics of housing allowances. The supply experiment is far more costly and harder to design than the demand experiment and is at an earlier stage of development.

The third experiment will deal with administration. Which kinds of allowance are easiest to administer? Which agencies seem best able to handle them? What are the administrative costs and how are they affected by efforts to secure certain kinds of data such as those on net worth?

The appropriate size of a housing allowance depends on what is done about welfare reform. If a cash income strategy is rejected—if current programs limp along as they are but no major new effort is made to put a floor under incomes on a national level—a housing allowance could play a major role in reducing poverty. A substantial housing allowance plus food stamps and an adequate health insurance program could serve as a guaranteed annual income—a negative income tax in kind instead of in cash.

On the other hand, if a substantial cash transfer program is en-

Table 4-8. Benefits and Number of Households Assisted under Three Housing Allowances, by Eligible Groups, 1974 Levels[a]

| | Benefits (billions of dollars) | | | | | | Number of households receiving benefits (millions) | | | | | |
| | High benefit | | Low benefit | | Medium benefit with welfare reform | | High benefit | | Low benefit | | Medium benefit with welfare reform | |
Eligible group	No price change	Prices rise 10%	No price change	Prices rise 10%	No price change	Prices rise 10%	No price change	Prices rise 10%	No price change	Prices rise 10%	No price change	Prices rise 10%
All households	12.3	15.5	1.9	2.5	3.7	5.3	20.3	22.7	7.8	9.0	13.3	15.5
All families	9.0	11.6	1.2	1.7	2.4	3.6	13.2	15.0	4.1	5.0	7.9	9.5
Families with children	6.6	8.5	0.9	1.2	1.8	2.7	8.5	9.7	2.7	3.2	5.2	6.3
All renters	6.6	8.3	1.1	1.4	2.1	3.0	11.0	12.2	4.3	5.0	7.6	8.8
Nonfarmers	11.4	14.4	1.7	2.3	3.4	4.9	19.2	21.5	7.2	8.4	12.7	14.8
Aged only	2.8	3.6	0.4	0.6	0.9	1.3	6.0	6.5	2.5	2.9	4.2	4.8

Source: Authors' estimates.

a. *High benefit allowance:* basic housing benefit (family of four with zero available resources) = $1,650–$2,100 a year, depending on location of residence. Available resources = money income, plus one-fourth of assets in excess of $10,000 a year ($5,000 for households with aged head), less $300 for each household member working at least twenty hours a week, less social security taxes. The basic allowance is reduced by one-fourth of available resources.

Low benefit allowance: basic housing benefit = one-half the level of the high allowance, reduced by one-fourth of available resources.

Medium benefit allowance combined with welfare reform: negative income tax rate = 50 percent on earnings above $720 annually (excluding social security taxes); basic benefit (family of four) = $2,400 (benefit varies with household's size—all households are eligible); allowance = three-fourths of high allowance for a family with no available resources.

No price change assumes that housing costs are unaffected by the housing allowance.

Prices rise 10 percent assumes that housing costs increase 10 percent because of the housing allowance.

acted, a housing allowance, though a smaller one, might still be useful. The major source of cost-of-living differences throughout the United States is variation in housing costs. Housing allowances would be a logical way to build some regional differentiation into a broad income-maintenance system without varying the basic support level.

Estimated costs of three hypothetical housing allowances based on different assumptions about who would be eligible and what would happen to housing prices are shown in Table 4-8. The first, the "high benefit" allowance, would set a basic housing benefit for a family of four with zero available resources within a range of $1,650 to $2,100 a year, depending on where they lived. The allowance would be reduced by one-fourth of available resources. "Available resources" is defined as total money income plus one-fourth of assets in excess of $10,000 a year ($5,000 for households of which the head is elderly), less $300 for each household member working at least twenty hours a week, less social security taxes. The second, the "low benefit" allowance, would set the basic benefit at one-half the level of the high allowance. The benefit would also be reduced by 25 percent of available resources. The third, the "medium benefit" allowance, assumes that welfare reform is enacted and that the reform consists of a negative income tax with a basic benefit of $2,400 for a family of four and a 50 percent tax rate on earnings above $720 a year (excluding social security taxes). All households are included. Welfare reform costs are not included in the table. The medium allowance is set at three-fourths of the high allowance for a family with no available resources. For a family of four on welfare with no other source of income, the combined housing allowance and welfare benefit would equal $3,150 a year. If that same family had one member at work earning $3,000 a year, the combined housing and welfare payments would equal $1,600, and the family's income would be raised to $4,600 a year.

The costs of each allowance are estimated under two assumptions about cost. The first assumes that housing costs are unaffected by the housing allowance. The second assumes that costs rise by 10 percent.

As may be seen in the table, the high allowance is extremely expensive. If it was applied to all households and if prices were assumed to rise, the high allowance would cost about $15.5 billion in 1974. The reason for the large expense is that the high allowance would, in effect, constitute a moderate negative income tax with a very low—

25 percent—tax rate. The low allowance is very cheap. It is a very small negative income tax—about $900 for a family of four with no other income—again with a very low tax rate. The medium allowance with welfare reform is the most interesting of the three, from a policy viewpoint. The costs are in the range of the estimated cost of achieving the 1968 housing goal under existing programs. The allowance could be used to introduce regional variation into welfare reform. Note that, if welfare reform was limited to families with children, the true costs would be higher than shown in the table (for all groups except families with children).

Allowance costs are quite sensitive to price rises, in part because price rises increase benefits and in part because new households become eligible for benefits as prices rise.

Problems Not Solved by Housing Allowances

Although housing allowances would permit low-income people to pay for better houses and apartments than they can now afford, such allowances could not be expected to solve all the problems associated with poor-quality housing. Many "housing" problems have less to do with the quality of individual dwellings than with the quality of neighborhoods—the condition of streets, the availability of health services, the educational standards of schools, the accessibility of parks and open spaces, the level of crime, the attitude and effectiveness of the police, and the proximity to stores and public transportation. Even a substantial infusion of new income into a low-income neighborhood, as a result of generous housing allowances or some other policy, could not be expected to affect these neighborhood characteristics directly.

If the federal government is to have an impact on the quality of neighborhoods, it will have to act not only to improve housing but to improve public services at the local level. Revenue sharing is one vehicle for increasing the resources available for state and local services. Making resources available, however, will not necessarily improve services in the neighborhoods that need them most unless some mechanism is developed for targeting the funds on poor neighborhoods or for fostering institutions, such as community action agencies, to give low-income people a voice in public decision making and to put pressure on state and local governments to respond to their needs.

Moreover, efforts to improve public services one at a time may be doomed to failure in neighborhoods with multiple problems. Good schools will not be enough to make a neighborhood attractive if the crime rate remains high—in fact, it may be nearly impossible to operate high-quality schools in crime-ridden neighborhoods. This interdependence of neighborhood characteristics strengthens the argument for coordinated and concentrated effort to improve public services and enhance the attractiveness of an area all at once. Grants for urban community development (discussed in Chapter 5) might be a vehicle for such an approach.

Higher Education*

A major federal program to help students pay for education beyond high school would seem a logical inclusion in a federal strategy of helping people buy essentials. Indeed, legislation passed in 1972 authorized the Basic Opportunity Grant program, which, with some changes and additional funding, could become the basis for a federal program to help all needy students pay for higher education.

Why Help People Buy Higher Education?

Education beyond high school, though clearly not a necessity in the same sense as food and medical care, can make a profound difference in a person's life. A college or professional degree increases earning capacity, on the average, and is a prerequisite for many rewarding high-status careers. But the fact that higher education is beneficial to the recipient does not necessarily mean that the government ought to intervene to help people buy it. The case for public subsidies rests on two further contentions. First, the contributions of educated people are not reflected entirely in their incomes; others gain as well. Highly educated people advance science and the arts and raise the general cultural and intellectual level of a community. Hence, there is a public interest in expanding higher education beyond the level it would reach if students had to bear the full cost.

The second contention is that restricting the opportunity for higher education to those who can afford to pay for it is inequitable, wasteful of talent, and harmful to society generally. Denying higher education to the poor restricts their chances of moving up the social and economic ladder and tends to rigidify the social structure. Hence, there is

* Prepared with the assistance of Robert W. Hartman.

a public interest in equalizing opportunities for higher education among income groups.

A college or professional education is extremely expensive and is typically concentrated in a few years at the beginning of a person's working life. Paying the full cost of a college or professional education is out of the question for a poor family, and it may be an impossible burden even for a middle-income family, especially one with several children seeking a higher education at about the same time.

If students can borrow, they can spread the cost of their education over several years and pay for it out of the increased future earnings they hope will result. But even if the government intervenes to make credit for higher education widely available, many families, especially poor families, may buy less higher education than society as a whole thinks they ought to. Both the financial and the cultural benefits of higher education lie in the future, and some people may not place a high value on these future benefits or they may fear heavy indebtedness and inability to repay educational loans.

These considerations suggest that *some* level of government should subsidize higher education and make it available at a price lower than its cost, especially to students from low-income families. But why should this task fall to the federal government? State and local governments have a long tradition of support for higher education. Indeed, public institutions, ranging from state universities to community colleges, now enroll a majority of students. These institutions receive support from state and local taxpayers and charge tuitions far below cost.

The argument for *federal* subsidies to higher education is simply that state and local governments, left to their own devices, may fail to act in the national interest in at least four respects. First, a state or locality may spend less on higher education or do less to expand enrollment than would be in the national interest because it may take into account only the benefits to future residents of the area. But educated people are mobile and often move out of the area that subsidized their education. Hence, there may be a federal interest in increasing the resources flowing to higher education and encouraging additional enrollment by lowering the price to everyone. This objective might be accomplished by subsidizing either supply or demand. The federal government could give grants to colleges and universities to help them cover their costs and enable them to keep their tuitions lower than would otherwise be possible, or it could give a subsidy directly to students to help them meet the expenses of higher education.

Second, states and localities may not respond adequately to nationally perceived needs for people with particular skills, such as language specialists or research scientists. Consequently, there may be a federal interest in subsidizing particular types of education, either by giving grants to institutions to pay for such programs or by giving aid to students who want to go into certain specialties.

Third, states and localities may fail to provide enough opportunities for low-income students to pursue a higher education. Traditionally, state-supported institutions of higher education have charged low tuition to in-state students but have made little effort to help students pay for their living expenses. Public institutions are often located far from centers of population, and those with the largest subsidy derived from taxes often have entrance requirements that effectively exclude the poor. A large part of the state subsidy goes to students from middle- and upper-income families that could afford to pay a larger share of the cost. Community colleges are more accessible to low-income students but spend less per student and rarely help students pay for living expenses. Thus there may be a need for federal programs to equalize opportunities by reducing the cost of higher education to low-income students. Once again, this objective could be met by giving grants to colleges and universities enabling them to assist low-income students or by giving grants based on ability to pay directly to the students.

Finally, state and local support for public institutions of higher education may weaken the private sector of higher education. As recently as 1951 students were about evenly divided between public and private institutions. In the last two decades, however, enrollment has expanded rapidly in the public sector, especially in public junior colleges, and the proportion of students enrolled in private institutions has dropped to about 25 percent. While some private colleges and universities are strongly supported centers of intellectual excellence, many others are finding it increasingly difficult to compete for faculty and students with the heavily subsidized public institutions and are appealing for public assistance on the grounds that their continued financial health is in the national interest.

Although preserving private institutions is unlikely to be the sole focus of any federal effort, it may be desirable to pursue the other objectives mentioned above in ways that will enhance rather than further damage the relative position of private institutions. Federal grants to colleges and universities can be structured so that private institutions get a disproportionate share of the money, or programs of aid to students can be designed so that students who choose high-tuition institutions get additional funds to help pay the extra cost. From the students' point of view such a grant program would narrow differences in price between public and private institutions. Alternatively, the federal government could attempt to get at the root of the private sector's problem by inducing states to shift their methods of support to ones that treat nonpublic schools more evenhandedly. For example, the federal government could design grant programs to induce states and localities to aid students in both public and private institutions.

In sum, there are at least four possible objectives of federal subsidies to higher education: increasing enrollment and resources in higher education generally; enhancing education in particular fields of national interest; equalizing opportunities for students from low-income families; and preserving diversity in higher education by strengthening private institutions. Each of these objectives could be furthered by subsidizing institutions or state and local governments, or by giving aid directly to students to help them pay for higher education.

Current Federal Programs

A long list of federal programs affecting higher education has accumulated over the years, enacted at various times for a wide variety of purposes and administered by different agencies. As shown in Table 4-9, outlays for higher education programs in fiscal year 1974 are expected to be about $5.8 billion, not counting most of the federal funds that support scientific and other research projects in colleges and universities.

"Institutional support" includes programs for construction of classroom buildings, libraries, and laboratories; funds for special kinds of education of interest to the federal government, such as foreign language and area studies; funding of special institutions, such as support for military academies and a small contribution to the budgets of land grant colleges. Commitments to spend under many of these institutional aid programs are sharply reduced in the President's 1974 budget proposals. The cuts, if sustained, would reduce future outlays.

Three-quarters of current federal aid to higher education now goes to student support, and this proportion is expected to rise in the future. The President's 1974 budget emphasizes aid to students, though only at the undergraduate level. Fellowship programs for graduate students as well as training grants in several fields have been cut back on two grounds: first, that there is an oversupply of scholars trained at the doctoral level and, second, that federally guaranteed loans, rather than grants, should be used to help graduate and professional students pay for their education.

The largest and fastest-growing component of federal support for higher education is aid to undergraduate students, budgeted at $3.7 billion in the 1974 budget. A large share of this money—about $2.3 billion—will go for two programs that receive little attention in regular budgetary deliberations: the student aid programs administered by the Social Security Administration and the Veterans Administration. Education benefits under social security are available to full-time students eighteen to twenty-two years old who are survivors of workers covered by social security or dependents of retired or disabled beneficiaries. Veterans' education benefits are available to men and women who have fulfilled specified requirements of military service. Under both programs, applicants who have the necessary characteristics for eligibility are "entitled" to support, provided they attend approved

Table 4-9. Federal Outlays for Higher Education, by Type of Support, Fiscal Years 1972–74ᵃ

Millions of dollars

Type of support	1972	1973	1974
Institutional	**1,389**	**1,403**	**1,452**
Student	**3,375**	**4,227**	**4,231**
Graduate	561	658	508
Undergraduate	2,814	3,569	3,722
Office of Education	881	1,010	1,227
Social Security Administration	521	659	758
Veterans Administration	1,247	1,683	1,592
Other	165	216	145
Other	**119**	**98**	**101**
Total	**4,883**	**5,728**	**5,784**

Source: *Special Analyses, Budget of the United States Government, Fiscal Year 1974*, pp. 113–14. Figures may not add to totals because of rounding.

a. Higher education as used here excludes almost all research, the exception being a small amount of educational research.

institutions. There is no test of the applicant's need or scholastic ability.

These two programs are "automatically" financed. Outlays for education benefits under social security are paid out of the social security trust fund. Veterans' benefits are appropriated by Congress, but if more veterans apply than expected, Congress simply makes up the difference through a supplemental appropriation. Hence, those who are entitled to benefits under either of these programs are assured of getting them.

The structure of the three college-based student aid programs administered by the Office of Education—the Educational Opportunity Grant (EOG) program, the College Work-Study (CWS) program, and the National Defense Student Loan (NDSL) program—is quite different.[13] Under these programs no student is "entitled" to anything. The funds appropriated, which regularly fall far short of amounts needed to accommodate all eligible students, are allocated to colleges and universities by a complex procedure described below and then rationed to student applicants by college student aid officers. The EOG program provides grants to low-income students. The CWS program pays 80 percent of the wages of needy students in on-campus or off-campus jobs; the employer, often the college itself, puts up the other 20 percent. The NDSL program provides loans to needy students at subsidized low interest rates. In all three cases, "need" is defined in relation to the cost of attending the particular college at which the student is enrolled—students at expensive colleges "need" more.

All three programs operate as follows. First, appropriated funds are allocated among states by a formula set by the law. Second, funds are allocated to colleges and universities within states by regional panels made up of student aid officials convened by the Office of Education. Third, once the funds arrive at the educational institutions, student aid officers allocate them to students who have applied for assistance, guided by Office of Education rules designed to establish national priorities as to who should receive federal aid.

Inequities can arise at all three stages. First, funds come much closer to meeting need (as perceived by the regional panels) in some states than others. In 1972, panel-approved requests for EOGs were

13. Changes in these programs enacted in 1972 are discussed in the next section.

$340 million, but appropriations were $210 million. The average fraction of a panel-approved request funded was therefore about 62 percent. But Utah got 87 percent of its approved requests while Maine received only 38 percent. Second, within states biases may arise in the allocation of funds among institutions. A recent study shows that schools with representatives on the panels fare remarkably well compared with others.[14] Finally, when the funds arrive at the college, student aid officers have considerable discretion in assessing the ability of a student and his family to contribute to his education and in determining which of the student's expenses are "necessary." This discretion is often defended on the grounds that student aid officers are close to students and good judges of what individual students really need. On the other hand, giving this much discretion to student aid officers may result in very unequal treatment of students in similar economic circumstances as well as great uncertainty for individual students, who have no way of estimating in advance how much aid they will be able to obtain.

Federal student aid is not effectively concentrated on the lowest-income students, partly because of the judgmental nature of the process and partly because need is related to expenses at the college attended. Students at public community colleges receive little help even if they come from very low-income families. A recent study estimated that 17 percent of students from families with incomes under $5,000 are enrolled in public two-year colleges but that these students receive only 7 percent of EOG funds. By contrast, the 11 percent of students from families with incomes under $5,000 that are enrolled in private universities and four-year colleges receive 42 percent of the funds. Among students who receive help under the three programs, the average amount received does not appear to vary greatly by income level. A recent study of recipients of CWS made these estimates:[15]

14. Nathalie Friedman, Lois W. Sanders, and James Thompson, "The Federal College Work-Study Program: A Status Report, Fiscal Year 1971" (U.S. Office of Education, November 1972; processed), Chap. 10, p. 24.

15. Derived from ibid., Table A.2.3(b).

Students were placed into income categories by the amount of money their families could afford to contribute toward college expenses. "Poverty level" families could make no contribution; "near-poor" families could contribute up to $500 a year; "higher income" families could contribute over $500. The average aid received includes amounts received by CWS recipients from CWS, EOG, and NDSL.

Income level	Average annual aid received
Poverty level	$1,426
Near-poor	1,245
Higher income	1,252
All income groups	1,341

Besides the three college-based aid programs, the Office of Education also administers the Guaranteed Student Loan program designed to increase the volume of funds available for student borrowing from banks or other eligible lenders. The federal government either directly or indirectly through a state agency insures the lender against default on the loan. In addition, until the spring of 1973 the program provided for interest subsidies to enrolled students if their family's taxable income was less than $15,000. The program has made it easier for students to borrow but has by no means ensured that funds will be available to all who want them. Many students have difficulty obtaining loans, especially those who live in one state and attend college in another.

The 1972 Amendments

In 1972 the Congress passed new legislation that changed the menu of federal student aid programs substantially. The legislation was a compromise between two sets of forces. On one side were those who wanted a basic grant program under which students would be entitled to aid in specified amounts, to be determined by their family's ability to pay but independent of tuition at their chosen college. Under such a program students could be sure of the aid to which they were entitled and could use it at any college that would admit them. The other side wanted to retain the existing college-based student aid programs and to give student aid officers additional flexibility in awarding funds.

In an evident compromise four steps were taken.

1. The legislation created a new student aid program—the Basic Opportunity Grant program. Under it, an undergraduate student is entitled to receive $1,400 minus an expected family contribution based on the income and assets of the student and his parents and on family size. The size of the grant does not depend on the cost of attending a particular college except that no student may receive more than half the cost of attendance. (The effect of this provision is to lower the

grant entitlement for low-income students who attend low-cost institutions.)

2. The EOG program was renamed the Supplemental Opportunity Grant program and wording restricting the grants to "low-income" students was removed.

3. Language limiting subsidies under the Guaranteed Loan program to students from families with incomes under $15,000 was also eliminated. In its place was put a vague requirement that a student demonstrate "need" for educational assistance no matter what his family income.

4. In a last-minute compromise reached in conference, Congress inserted a provision in the law that $653 million had to be spent on the old college-based programs in any year before funds could be spent on the Basic Grant program.

These changes, reflecting deep conflicts within the Congress, left the student aid picture muddy and confused. On the one hand, the Basic Grant program promised greater uniformity in student aid and more emphasis on low-income students. On the other hand, retention of the college-based programs and elimination of low-income requirements not only perpetuated the old inequities but reduced the extent to which subsidies would be targeted on low-income students.

If funding was ample for all programs, the compromise would not appear unreasonable. The Basic Grant program would ensure that low-income students could at least go to low-cost colleges, and the other programs could be used to assist both low- and middle-income students who wanted to attend more expensive colleges.[16] Since funds are likely to be limited, however, the provision that old programs be funded first creates a serious problem. Full funding of the Basic Grant program is estimated to cost about $1.7 billion.[17] If $653 million were spent on the old programs, total spending would be $2.353 billion, or roughly three times the 1972–73 spending for these programs. If less was appropriated (as seems likely), the Basic Grant program would have to be scaled down. Unfortunately the law also provides that if

16. However, the half-cost limitation would necessitate some self-help or borrowing by poor students even in the lowest-cost schools.

17. The administration has estimated that full funding of basic grants would be $959 million in fiscal 1974 (*The Budget of the United States Government—Appendix, Fiscal Year 1974*, p. 430). Our estimates are much higher, apparently because of the administration's expectation that many students will lose eligibility or have their grants greatly reduced because their families have substantial assets which are taken into account in determining the size of the grant.

the Basic Grant program receives much less than full funding student entitlements are reduced proportionately. Funds for the lowest-income students with the highest entitlements get cut by the largest absolute amount. With a total appropriation of $1.253 billion, for example, only $600 million would be left for basic grants after the required $653 million was spent on old programs and the poorest students would receive basic grants of less than $500, not enough to make college possible for a student otherwise unable to go. By passing this combination of provisions the Congress put both the administration and itself in a curious box: if funds for student aid were not substantially increased, the Basic Grant program would fail to accomplish its purpose.

Student Aid in the 1973 and 1974 Budgets

The first showdown came over an emergency fiscal year 1973 supplemental budget for higher education passed in April 1973 to fund programs for the academic year 1973–74. The administration, as may be seen in Table 4-10, had ignored the requirement that old programs be

Table 4-10. Office of Education Outlays for Student Aid Programs, Academic Years 1972–73, 1973–74, and 1974–75[a]

Millions of dollars

| | | 1973–74 | | |
Program	1972–73	Proposed by administration	Enacted	1974–75, proposed
Supplemental Opportunity Grant[b]	218	0	210	0
College Work-Study[c]	258	262	270	250
Direct Student Loan	306	22	293	5
Basic Opportunity Grant	...	622	122	959
Subtotal	782	906	895	1,214
Guaranteed Student Loans Subsidies	247	320	n.a.	n.a.
Total	1,030	1,227	...	...

Sources: Col. 1, U.S. Office of Management and Budget, estimate as of June 1973; col. 2, *Special Analyses, 1974*, pp. 114, 116; col. 3, *The Chronicle of Higher Education*, Vol. 7 (April 23, 1973), p. 2; col. 4, *The Budget of the United States Government—Appendix, Fiscal Year 1974*, p. 430. Figures may not add to totals because of rounding.

n.a. Not available.

a. Academic year 1972–73 corresponds to Office of Education fiscal year 1973; 1973–74 to fiscal 1974; and 1974–75 to fiscal 1975.

b. In 1972–73 this program was called the Educational Opportunity Grant program.

c. Includes Cooperative Education, which subsidizes cooperative study and work programs.

funded first and proposed a modest start on basic grants and almost no money for the old programs, except CWS. Congress, however, responded to the anguished cries of colleges and universities that were likely to lose under this arrangement, particularly the private universities and four-year colleges whose students receive a relatively high share of funds under the old programs. Under an avalanche of letters from colleges that claimed probable loss and under pressure to act quickly as the start of the school year approached, Congress voted to continue existing programs at their 1972–73 levels for the 1973–74 academic year. Fearful of a veto if their appropriations exceeded the President's request, the Congress had only a $122 million margin left for the Basic Grant program.

Since $122 million divided among so many students will buy only a minuscule average basic grant, Congress passed legislation providing that, in its first year of operations, the Basic Grant program be limited to full-time students attending college for the first time. This provision allows the program to offer assistance of up to $300–$350 to the neediest *freshmen*, on the assumption that all eligible students apply. This is a far cry from the $1,400 for all needy undergraduates specified in the authorizing legislation, but perhaps enough to get the program started.

The whole scene seems likely to be replayed when Congress considers the administration's proposals for fiscal year 1974 (academic year 1974–75). As shown in Table 4-10, the administration has substantially increased its request for Basic Grant funds but has continued to regard the program as a substitute for the old programs, except CWS.

Options for the Future

Among the many roles the federal government could play in the financing of higher education during the next few years, a strong case can be made for giving priority to programs designed to equalize opportunity for higher education among students from various income groups. Pursuit of this objective suggests a major program of grants to students based on income, under which students who could gain admission to accredited institutions of higher education would be entitled to support if they met the law's test of need. The student would be free to shop around among schools and to use his grant wherever he was admitted.

The program would be similar in conception to the Basic Grant program.[18] First, a maximum grant would be established that represented the cost to a student of attending college full time for a year; second, a schedule of family contributions would be drawn up, indicating how much families of various sizes, asset holdings, and income levels could be expected to contribute to the cost of the student's education; and third, the student would receive a grant equal to the difference between the maximum grant and the contribution expected of his family. To avoid involving the government in writing a lot of small checks to people with very low entitlements, it would be sensible to establish a minimum grant of, say, $200 a year.

The cost of such a program to the government clearly depends on several factors: (1) the level of the maximum grant and whether the maximum is the same for everyone or higher for those who attend high-tuition institutions; (2) the size of the family contribution expected at various income levels; (3) the extent to which enrollment increases as a result of the program; (4) the extent to which institutions of higher education increase their tuition.

The top half of Table 4-11 shows estimates of the cost and the number of students who would be aided under "low" and "high" grant programs with a fixed maximum grant (not adjusted to tuition actually paid). The "low" annual maximum is $1,400, which is a conservative estimate of the amount a student would need to maintain himself while attending a tuition-free college such as a local community college. The "high" maximum is $1,800, which is estimated to be enough to enable a student to attend a state college in his own state but not enough for him to attend most private institutions or state universities without additional help. The estimates of the total funds needed for both programs assume that families with incomes below the poverty line ($4,300 for a family of four) are unable to contribute and would be eligible for the maximum grant. Families with higher incomes would be expected to contribute more and would receive smaller grants. Under both programs, students from families with incomes of $11,100—approximately the national median income—would be

18. The major differences between the programs described in this section and the Basic Grant program are: (1) the provision in the Basic Grant program limiting student grants to half the cost of attendance has been eliminated here; (2) the program described here preserves relatively light taxation of family and student assets, on the grounds that in the relevant income classes a tough tax on assets would be impossible to administer.

Table 4-11. Number of Students Aided and Cost of Alternative Federal Student Grant Programs, Academic Years 1973–74 and 1977–78

Type of program and student and cost items	1973–74		1977–78	
	Low grant	High grant	Low grant	High grant
Fixed maximum grant[a]				
Number of students aided (millions)	2.55	2.55	2.95	3.25
Average grant (dollars)	786	1,016	885	1,189
Total cost (billions of dollars)	2.00	2.59	2.61	3.86
Maximum grant plus one-half of excess tuition[b]				
Number of students aided (millions)	2.55	...	2.95	...
Average grant (dollars)	835	...	1,165	...
Total cost (billions of dollars)	2.13	...	3.44	...

Sources: Authors' estimates. See discussion in text.

a. The low maximum grant is $1,400 for an academic year, the high, $1,800. Families below the poverty line are eligible for the maximum, those with higher incomes receive proportionately less, until at about the median income eligibility ceases.

b. The grant maximum is the greater of $1,400 or one-half the cost of attendance, with family income restrictions as in note a.

eligible for the minimum grant of $200, and those with higher incomes would get nothing.[19]

As may be seen in the table, it is estimated that the cost of these programs would range between $2.0 billion and $2.6 billion in fiscal 1974. These estimates assume that eligibility extends to all postsecondary students, including those in proprietary vocational schools, but that enrollment is not increased as a result of the programs

Table 4-11 also shows the costs of the low and high grant programs projected to 1977–78. Under the low grant program it is assumed that enrollment will grow as currently projected by the Office of Education; that within the total enrollment the proportion of students eligible for grants will be the same in 1977 as in 1973; and that the average grant will increase by 3 percent a year. Under the high grant program, we have assumed that total enrollment will increase by 1977–78 to 10 percent above the Office of Education projections; that the percentage of students eligible will be the same in 1977–78 as under the high grant program in 1973–74; and that the average grant will grow by 4 percent a year to account for rising tuition charges as well as other student costs. The two programs range in cost, under these assumptions, from $2.6 billion to $3.9 billion in 1977–78.

19. The $11,100 figure is for a family of four; also eligible are a few students from larger families with incomes up to $15,000. In addition, estimates of the total cost of such a program include 582,000 students classified as "independent" who are eligible.

If the grant maximum is the same for all students regardless of tuition paid, the extra cost of attending a more expensive college will be the same for grant recipients as for nonrecipients. That is, if public universities' charges (including room and board) are about $500 more than charges at a community college, that same differential will apply to all students, no matter how rich or poor. The grant program will make it easier for low-income students to go to college but will not lower the additional cost of attending more expensive colleges. Under such a program, it is unlikely that many low-income students would attend high-tuition private institutions unless the institutions themselves provided additional scholarship aid.

If one objective of the program is to achieve a mixture of students from different income groups in private as well as public colleges, then the provision of additional funds to those attending high-cost colleges may be in order. One way to do this is to have the government pay part of the tuition at very expensive institutions. A simple way to design such a program is to supplement the low grant program as follows. The student's grant maximum would be set at $1,400 or one-half of the cost of attendance, whichever was *greater*. From this maximum, as before, the family contribution would be subtracted to determine the student's entitlement. For students attending schools costing less than $2,800, the program is no different from a program with a fixed maximum grant of $1,400. For students at schools whose attendance costs exceeded $2,800, the federal government would pay half the charges, less the family contribution. The extra benefits would therefore accrue entirely to students attending private institutions. Estimates of the cost of such a program in 1973–74, average grant sizes, and the number of students aided are shown in the lower half of Table 4-11, under the assumption that enrollments and tuitions are unchanged by the program. This special supplementary program for the private sector would initially cost very little. However, if such a program were to bring about enrollment or tuition increases in the private sector, the incremental costs could mount considerably. The 1977–78 estimate for this program shown in the table assumes a shift of 10 percent of the grant recipients to the private sector and a rise in private sector tuitions of 10 percent a year, in addition to the adjustments made before. Under these assumptions a federal grant program would cost about $3.5 billion in 1977–78.

A grant program that increased the number of poor students in private institutions would hardly be a financial boon to the private sector. A college does not gain by having a poor student with a government grant replace a rich student paying his own way. A federal grant program would ease the financial plight of private institutions only to the extent that (1) some otherwise vacant places were filled with government-aided students; (2) institutions were relieved of some student aid cost that they would otherwise regard as necessary; (3) public institutions were induced to raise their tuitions, thus narrowing the gap between the price to the student of public and private education and making it easier for the private institutions to compete for students. The latter development would be more likely at higher grant levels.

If the preservation of a financially healthy private sector in higher education is considered an important objective of federal policy, other approaches might be considered. One possibility would be the use of federal leverage to induce states and localities to shift the form of their support of higher education away from subsidies to public institutions toward student aid that would support students in both public and private institutions. A program under which the federal government would match state funds spent for scholarships usable in either state or private institutions might be expected to increase state spending for scholarships and induce state-supported institutions to raise their tuitions to a level closer to that of private institutions.[20]

Problems Not Solved by Student Aid

The student aid programs outlined above would move a long way toward equalizing opportunities for postsecondary education, but even this objective cannot be achieved by student aid alone. For example, students from low-income families may need special help in college to make up for past educational deficiencies, and colleges may be unwilling to provide this assistance without incentives from the federal government.

Moreover, the process of equalizing opportunity for postsecondary education has to begin much farther down the educational ladder. If low-income students are to take advantage of postsecondary opportunities, they must have high-quality elementary and secondary education, as well as sensitive counseling and realistic information about the opportunities available.

20. The education amendments of 1972 authorized a program with these general characteristics, but the administration did not seek funding for it in the 1974 budget.

A second objective, that of increasing resources and enrollment, would be furthered by a major student aid program. Indeed, aid for low-income students is an effective way of increasing enrollment, since their enrollment rate is lowest at present and they are presumably those most likely to be deterred by financial considerations. There are, however, many other ways of increasing the resources devoted to higher education, such as institutional grants of various sorts, mechanisms generally preferred by academic administrators.

Although a student aid program with additional funds for high-tuition institutions would have some tendency to strengthen private institutions, the fundamental problems of the private sector cannot be solved in this way. As noted earlier, if private higher education is to be significantly strengthened, state and local governments will have to shift the form of their support from heavy reliance on subsidizing public institutions to more evenhanded programs.

The objective of fostering particular kinds of education, such as scientific specialties, is clearly not furthered by a system of general undergraduate student aid. To further this objective, quite specialized programs—either institutional support or earmarked fellowships, or both—would be required.

Finally, the federal government has another possible objective for higher education that is much discussed but rarely defined: namely, fostering innovation and improved teaching and learning. There is currently evidence of widespread dissatisfaction with the sameness of American higher education—the so-called "lock step" of the four-year college curriculum, its lack of relevance to real world jobs and problems and the impersonality and pedantry frequently found in academic institutions. Although complaints are rampant, no one is quite clear about how to change this situation. Federal grants for experimental and innovative programs, if imaginatively handled, perhaps by the new Fund for the Improvement of Postsecondary Education created by the education amendments of 1972, constitute a possible approach.

Child Care

Day care for children of working mothers is a new addition to the list of goods and services considered sufficiently "essential" to warrant public concern and financing, and pressures for increased federal funding for day care have been mounting rapidly. Federal concern could take the form of increased grants to state and local governments to help them provide more day care services. Alternatively, however, the general strategy of helping people buy essentials could be applied to day care. The federal government could issue vouchers to working mothers to help them buy child care for their children.

Why Help People Buy Child Care?

Until quite recently care of children below school age or during hours not in school was not thought to be a public responsibility except in emergencies. A generation ago few mothers worked, and those who did, from either choice or necessity, were assumed able to make arrangements for some kind of child care. In the last generation, however, and especially in the last ten years, several concurrent developments have changed public attitudes dramatically and aroused substantial support for public programs to help mothers, especially working mothers, pay for day care for their children.

First, the proportion of mothers in the labor force has risen rapidly. In 1950 only 22 percent of mothers with children under eighteen were in the labor force; by 1970 the proportion had risen to 42 percent. Over half the mothers of school-age children now work either part time or full time, as do about a third of the mothers of preschoolers. In 1971 about 26 million children, nearly 6 million of them under six years old, had mothers in the labor force. Pressure for assistance with child care has come not only from mothers having difficulty finding and paying for satisfactory child care, but from others concerned about the dubious, even dangerous, arrangements some mothers make.

Second, some women now see publicly supported day care as necessary to equality of the sexes. They argue that mothers as well as fathers ought to have career opportunities and that only if child care of good quality is available will women have a genuine choice between staying at home and going to work.

Third, the rapid rise in the welfare rolls since the mid-1960s has led to efforts to encourage welfare mothers to take jobs and become self-supporting. These efforts in turn have led to concern about child care, since lack of adequate arrangements is an important impediment to employment for many mothers.

At the same time educators were becoming increasingly concerned about the importance of early education and the possible influence of early learning experiences on the child's later development. Families who could afford it were sending their children to nursery schools and educators were hypothesizing that some of the learning difficulties that poor children often experience in school could be avoided if they had extra attention in the preschool years.

There are different views of what constitutes "good" day care, but it is generally agreed that small children need plenty of attention from responsive adults and that they benefit from a safe, healthy environment and access to toys and educational stimulation. Unquestionably, high-quality care is expensive. Full day care for a preschooler in a day care center with an educational program, a low ratio (say, 6 to 1) of children to adults, and a full range of health and counseling services costs about $50 a week, or $2,500 a year. Estimates of "adequate" care in a center run between $1,500 and $2,000 a year. Caring for preschool children in private homes would cost this much too if "caregivers" were trained and paid wages comparable to what they could earn in other work. After-school and summer programs for school-age children are less expensive, but well-staffed programs still cost perhaps $800 to $1,000 a year.

Most working mothers cannot and do not pay anything approaching $2,500, or even $1,500, a year for day care for a preschool child, especially if they have more than one child. Indeed, a majority of working mothers currently pay little or nothing for child care. They leave the child with relatives, either in their own home or the relatives' home, or simply let him look after himself. Others pay varying amounts—usually less than $1,000 a year—for care in private or nonprofit day care centers or by nonrelatives in private homes.

The quality of existing day care is difficult to judge. Information on day care centers indicates that proprietary centers tend to have high ratios of children to staff and that their staffs are paid low salaries and have low education levels. Nonprofit centers (often run by agencies of local government) have high ratios of staff to children, better-trained and -paid staff, and offer richer educational programs. The nonprofit centers generally serve lower-income families and receive subsidies from state, local, or federal resources. Day care centers, however, care for only a small percentage of the children of working mothers—just over 10 percent of such children were in day care centers in 1970.

Most care is provided in homes—the child's own or someone else's—and little information exists about its quality.

In sum, the basic argument for public subsidy of day care goes as follows. It is important both to mothers and children and to society as a whole that children be well cared for while mothers work; many mothers, especially those with low incomes, cannot afford to pay for the quality of care that society thinks children ought to have; therefore the government should take steps to see that adequate care is available, especially to low-income families who need it most and can least afford it.

Like higher education, day care is a problem only for families with children of a particular age. It is not a need—like the need for food or housing—that might easily be met by a generous cash transfer program.

As in the case of higher education, government subsidies for day care could take several forms. One possibility would be to subsidize supply, either by supporting a system of public day care centers (extending the public school system to provide day care) or by underwriting part of the cost of private day care suppliers, enabling them to keep their charges low for everyone or to serve the poor at less than cost. Alternatively, the subsidy could go to purchasers of day care, perhaps in the form of vouchers. Either approach could be used to provide special help to the poor. Publicly subsidized day care centers could charge fees related to income, in the manner of public housing subsidies. The value of vouchers could be higher for those with lower incomes, in the manner of income-related student aid or food stamps.

Current Federal Programs

Although no comprehensive federal day care program exists, the federal government currently subsidizes day care, directly and indirectly, in a variety of ways. At least three programs subsidize day care services for low-income families, especially welfare mothers.

The Work Incentive Program (WIN) provides funds for day care for welfare mothers who are in job-training programs and for former WIN participants when they get a job. In fiscal 1974, 155,000 children will be receiving care under this program, at a cost of $117 million.

Grants to states for social services under the welfare program provide more substantial day care funding, although surprisingly little is known about how these grants have been used or might be used in the future. In fiscal year 1972 social service grants to the states totaled about $1.7 billion, of which about $520 million was spent for a variety of services to children, including day care. Total social service grants in fiscal 1974 will probably be about $2.2 billion, of which a substantially increased proportion seems likely to be used by the states to subsidize day care.[21] Preliminary information on state plans indicates that perhaps 60 percent, or $1.3 billion, of these funds may be spent for day care in fiscal 1974.

The Department of Health, Education, and Welfare (HEW) issued new regulations in April 1973 covering these grants to states. The regulations require that the states establish advisory committees for day care services. The secretary of HEW is to establish standards for day care facilities. In-home care and day care centers may be used, but both have to be approved by the state as meeting the federal standards. Families with incomes up to 150 percent of state welfare standards are eligible for free day care, and families with incomes between 150 and 233 percent are eligible for day care on a sliding fee basis. Claims for day care have to be based on the fact that the parent or parents are working. The state standards for cash assistance for a family of four vary widely, but 150 percent of the average is approximately $4,760; and 233 percent is approximately $7,440. In other words, these regulations will permit many states to subsidize day care for families well into the middle-income ranges if they choose to do so.

In addition, some portion of the funds going to Head Start finance day care for low-income families. Head Start's primary mission is to provide compensatory education for preschool children in hopes of improving their ability to function satisfactorily when they reach school age, not to solve the problems of working mothers. Head Start began as a summer program, mostly to provide half-day nursery school for deprived children, but it has moved in the direction of full-year and full-day programs, with some of the funds being used to provide compensatory education in day care centers. Head Start gives grants to applicants who want to provide Head Start services. In fiscal 1974, 300,000 children will be served by full-year and summer programs and 20,000 children will be in experimental programs. The cost of the program is estimated to be $400 million in fiscal 1974. Of this, approximately a third is expected to go for day care.

21. See pp. 191–96.

In sum, total outlays for day care in the 1974 budget cannot be precisely estimated. The figure seems likely to run around $1.6 billion ($1.3 billion from social service grants to the states, $117 million under WIN, and roughly $130 million under Head Start).

In addition, indirect federal subsidies of demand for day care are provided in two ways. Mothers on welfare who are working are allowed to deduct necessary work expenses, including child care costs, from their income for the purpose of determining welfare benefits. Such a deduction is in effect a voucher for child care whose cost is shared between the state and federal governments, but the value of the voucher varies greatly from state to state and from one family to another.

The 1971 amendments to the individual income tax liberalized the indirect subsidies for day care by permitting families to increase their deductions for the cost of child care in computing their taxable income. Expenses of up to $400 a month for the care of a child under fifteen or a disabled person can be deducted. For child care outside the home, up to $200 a month can be deducted for one child, $300 for two, and $400 for three or more. Both parents must be working and have a combined income of not more than $18,000 to claim the full deduction. In the $18,000 to $27,000 income range, the amount that can be deducted declines by 50 cents for each additional $1 of income. This provision of the tax law became effective in 1972 and data on its impact are not available. However, the Treasury estimated when it was enacted that the revenue loss would be $145 million in calendar year 1972 and $152 million in 1973. This type of subsidy is of more value to middle-income families than to those with low incomes. At the time the bill was enacted, the Treasury estimated the distribution of the tax reduction by income class as shown in Table 4-12.

The current set of federal day care subsidies are complex and uneven in their effects—not unlike federal subsidies in housing and higher education. A minority of the poor—those with children enrolled in nonprofit day care centers subsidized by Head Start, WIN, or the social service grants to states—receive substantial benefits. But the subsidized centers have long waiting lists, do not exist in many neighborhoods, and serve only a small portion of low-income working mothers. Other low-income mothers make their own arrangements, some with varying amounts of subsidy from welfare, others with none. The only national program that provides entitlement to

Table 4-12. Estimated Distribution of Reduction in Income Tax Liability
Attributable to Liberalization of Child Care Deductions, by Income Class,
Calendar Years 1972 and 1973

	Cost of reduction (millions of dollars)	
Income class (dollars)	1972	1973
0–3,000	1	1
3,000–5,000	3	3
5,000–7,000	8	8
7,000–10,000	32	34
10,000–15,000	37	39
15,000–20,000	40	42
20,000–50,000	24	25
Total	145	152

Source: *Congressional Record*, Vol. 117, Pt. 35 (Dec. 9, 1971), p. 45858.

help pay for day care is the tax program, most of whose benefits go
to middle-income families.

Options for the Future

If ensuring good day care, especially for low-income families, comes
to be seen as a federal responsibility, there are strong arguments for
scrapping current programs in favor of a fairer, more comprehensive
program. At least two basic approaches might be used: increased
grants to state and local governments or nonprofit institutions to
make day care and related child development services available to
more people; a voucher program to help families buy day care services in the private market.

Advocates of the grants approach generally stress the need for institutional care—for more day care centers with well-trained staff and
educational or developmental programs and for public provision (or
at least strong public regulation) of the care. They doubt that the
private market will supply satisfactory care and fear that mothers will
fail to understand the importance of education for preschool children.
Advocates of the voucher approach believe most mothers can be relied on to choose good care for their children, if they have the money
to pay for it, and are skeptical of the merits of institutional care. They
point to the risk of creating a rigid day care bureaucracy—another
public school system—and to the potentially high costs of an institutional care system if standards were adopted prescribing high ratios of
staff to children and professional credentials and salaries for staff.

The cost of a voucher plan depends on who is entitled to aid, the value of the aid, and the extent to which eligible families use the vouchers to which they are entitled. Rough estimates of the cost of two voucher plans for day care are shown in Table 4-13. Both plans would provide vouchers worth a maximum of $1,750 for children under six and a maximum of $900 a year for children of six to twelve. The vouchers could be used to purchase full-day, part-day, after-school, or summer care from a variety of providers including public and private day care centers and private individuals. They could not be used to pay relatives living in the child's own household. Under the "low" plan the value of the subsidy would decline rather steeply as income rose; under the more expensive "high" plan the subsidy would decline less steeply and benefits would extend higher into the income distribution.

If the vouchers were available only to one-parent families, even the "high" program for all children under thirteen is estimated to cost only about $2.5 billion. This is about $1 billion more than estimates of the amount that might be spent for day care in fiscal 1974 under federal grants to the states for social services and WIN. Limiting the voucher program to one-parent families, however, would arouse strong opposition from married women in the labor force and would add to the perverse incentives already present in the welfare system to break up marriages. Extending the program to all families with children would cost about $8 billion for the "low" plan and $11 billion for the "high" plan. Since funds for the new programs would replace approximately $1.5 billion of existing child care expenditures, the

Table 4-13. Estimated Annual Cost of Alternative Day Care Voucher Plans
Billions of dollars

Eligible families	Low cost[a]	High cost[a]
One-parent families, child under six	1.2	1.3
One-parent families, child under thirteen	2.5	2.8
All families, child under six	4.7	5.9
All families, child under thirteen	8.0	11.0

Sources: Authors' estimates based on Elizabeth Waldman and Kathryn R. Gover, "Children of Women in the Labor Force, March 1970," U.S. Bureau of Labor Statistics (1971).

a. Both programs assume full voucher worth $1,750 for a child under six; $900 for a child between six and twelve. Families with incomes under $3,000 get full voucher. The value of the voucher falls more rapidly as income rises under the low program than under the high program. No benefits are available above these income levels; low plan, $10,800 with a child under six, $11,200 with a child of six to twelve; high plan, $15,200 with a child under six, $14,000 with a child of six to twelve.

added costs of the new program would be $6.5 billion and $9.5 billion respectively.[22]

Problems Not Solved by Child Care Vouchers

A national program of vouchers for day care would make it easier for low-income families to pay for child care, but would not ensure that children were well cared for and had their emotional and educational, as well as physical, needs attended to.

Use of the voucher approach assumes that mothers in general are able to make wise choices for their children if they have sufficient information about the options available and have some way of judging whether the choice they have made is good for their children or that something else might be better. At present, however, mothers must rely on word-of-mouth and informal impressions to evaluate the quality of care given. Federal funds for developing information networks in communities and improving measurement of the quality of care would be an important adjunct to a voucher program. Additional efforts could be made to raise the quality of care: special training for those taking care of other people's children; visiting nurses; educational television aimed at children in day care; and in-home instruction in the use of educational toys and materials.

Many people, however, see the voucher approach as inherently undesirable because it perpetuates child care arrangements that are largely informal, instead of setting up a new set of institutions, such as public developmental day care centers. This group argues that, even if mothers knew they wanted high quality institutional day care, it would not automatically come into existence just because there was a voucher system. Day care facilities are expensive, and there is a shortage of people with the training necessary to care for and teach small children. Hence, even with a voucher system, it would be important for the government to provide grants for the construction of day care centers and to subsidize the training of day care workers.

As an alternative to vouchers, the federal government could support day care by giving grants to state and local governments for the

22. These cost estimates depend, in part, on an assumption that 20–40 percent of the women with small children who are not now in the labor force would join the labor force if the new program were made available, the specific percentage depending on the age of the children. A more liberal assumption about labor force participation, raising the percentage of those entering the labor force (to a range of 35–40 percent), would increase the above cost estimates by about 20 percent.

operation of day care centers. These centers might be free like the public schools or they might charge a sliding scale of fees based on income. It would be easier to make sure that the centers met minimum standards in their staffing, facilities, nutrition, and educational program than to enforce such regulations under a voucher system. The cost per child of a publicly run day care network, however, would probably be high, and it is by no means clear that institutional care is preferred by mothers or demonstrably beneficial to children. The best policy may be a mixture: a voucher system plus public efforts to ensure that good quality institutional day care is available if mothers choose to use their vouchers to buy it.

5. Grants for Social Programs

UNDER THE TWO STRATEGIES DISCUSSED in Chapters 3 and 4 the federal government deals directly with the individual, affecting his cash income or helping him buy essential goods and services produced in the private sector. The next three chapters discuss the federal role in increasing publicly produced services, in some cases by providing them directly, but primarily by giving grants to state and local governments to help them produce more services or alter the nature of the services they produce.

When the federal government aids an individual the aid may fall anywhere along a spectrum from general to specific. The individual may receive a check to spend as he pleases, vouchers good only for food or medical care or—the most specific kind of aid—a bag of surplus flour. Similarly, federal aid to a state or local government may take the form of general revenue sharing with no strings attached, a block grant for a broad purpose such as elementary and secondary education, or a narrower "categorical" grant to support such very specific services as neighborhood health centers, education for the handicapped, or the training of nurses.

This chapter discusses federal grants to state and local governments (and in a few cases to private institutions, such as colleges and hospitals) to help them deliver a particular range of public services: the human or "social" services such as education, health care, manpower training, and urban development. A different range of public services—those dealing with the physical environment—are discussed in Chapter 6; Chapter 7 deals with general revenue sharing.

Grants for social programs are not an especially large item in the federal budget. They amounted to some $15 billion in fiscal 1973, or about 9 percent of total domestic spending. They deserve extensive discussion, however, because they represent a new and controversial role for the federal government (such grants were negligible ten years ago) and because the President's proposed budget for fiscal year 1974 makes more drastic changes in grants for social programs than in any other major area. The budget slashes *commitments* to spend on grants for social programs by about a third, from nearly $16 billion in fiscal years 1972 and 1973 to about $10 billion in 1974. This reduction in commitments does not immediately show up in *outlays*—the budget shows outlays for these programs dropping by only about $1 billion in 1974—but it will result in further reductions in outlays in subsequent years. Besides cutting funds for social programs, the 1974 budget reflects decisions both to reduce the number of grants and to give more discretion in the use of the money to state and local governments. The administration proposes to convert programs that account for about half of all social grant funds into four special revenue sharing programs, under which federal money would be provided to state and local governments in larger blocks and with fewer strings attached than is now the case, although there would still be some strings on the uses to which the funds were put.

The chapter opens with a discussion of the reasons for the federal government's assumption of responsibility in encouraging the delivery of specific social services. It examines some of the problems inherent in a strategy that emphasizes grants for social programs and suggests some criteria for choosing among various kinds of grants. This is followed by a brief description of the growth of social grants in the last decade and an examination of the administration's 1974 budget proposals. Subsequent sections discuss six areas in more detail (health services, social services, community action programs, elementary and secondary education, urban community development, and manpower training), comparing administration proposals in each area with one or more alternatives.

Why Grants for Social Programs?

As noted in Chapter 4, some goods and services normally produced in the private market are generally considered so essential to human well-being that there is a national interest in their distribution. One can make a case for the federal government's helping people buy these goods and services, and perhaps for federal efforts to regulate the market for them, to set standards, improve efficiency, or control prices. Such efforts, however, may not be sufficient to ensure an adequate supply. Even if everyone had health insurance, for example, there might be a shortage of doctors or other health care providers, especially in certain areas, and a reluctance to try out promising new forms of delivering services such as health maintenance organizations. Hence, a case can be made for federal efforts to break such bottlenecks; for example, by grants to increase the capacity of medical schools or to provide "seed money" to start new service-delivery organizations, especially in ghettos or in rural areas, where they are least likely to start without help.

A second range of services, such as law enforcement and elementary and secondary education, are by tradition produced by state and local governments rather than in the private market. There may be an equally strong national interest in the level, quality, and distribution of these services, but the mechanism by which the federal government expresses that interest must be aid to governments, not aid to individuals.

State and local governments vary greatly in their fiscal capacity to meet their citizens' needs for public services, but this in itself does not suggest a need for categorical grants. Rather, it suggests a need for the federal government to increase the resources of poorer state and local governments through revenue sharing without dictating how these resources are to be spent. The case for specifying, either broadly or narrowly, the nature of the activity to be supported rests on the belief that national priorities are different from state and local priorities— that even if they had greater resources state and local governments would fail to meet some important national needs.

State and local spending patterns might be expected to diverge from the national interest in three ways. *First,* state and local governments may spend too little on specific types of services thought to be of national importance, perhaps because the benefits of these services tend to spill over into other jurisdictions. An obvious example (discussed in Chapter 6) is control of water pollution. Without encouragement from some higher level of government, an upstream community can hardly be expected to spend substantial resources cleaning up its sewage for the benefit of downstream communities. Similarly, communities where there is a significant out-migration of young people may underinvest in education because many of the benefits could accrue to other communities. *Second,* states and localities may fail to meet the needs of some groups of citizens, especially those with little power and status in the community. Although a few states and localities have at times been more progressive than the national government, most have been relatively unresponsive to the needs of the poor and of minorities. Disadvantaged groups (for example, labor unions in the 1930s and blacks and the poor in the 1960s) have often turned to the federal government for help after failing to arouse state and local governments to awareness of their plight. The goal of providing more nearly equal opportunities for the disadvantaged—which was a growing national concern in the 1960s—cannot be met by relying on the highly unequal resources of state and local governments or on their willingness to provide the services that the disadvantaged require. *Third,* state and local governments may fail to finance risky or innovative ventures or to adopt new and more productive methods of delivering services that threaten an existing bureaucracy or overturn traditional ways of operating. This failure may reflect local reluctance to take chances on innovations that, even if successful, will largely benefit other communities, or it may simply reflect the stodginess of many state and local governments and their inability to attract administrators as able and imaginative as those attracted by the larger salaries and higher status of federal jobs.

Concern about bottlenecks in the supply of some essential private services and about the responsiveness of state and local governments to national needs provides the rationale for federal intervention in the delivery of social services. In theory the federal government could itself deliver the services about which it was concerned (as it does in the construction and operation of water resource projects along the nation's rivers). But another strategy has been followed. The federal government makes grants to state and local governments, and sometimes to private institutions, that pay part or all of the cost of providing services of a kind and in a way specified by federal guidelines and regulations. This is the social grant strategy.

Problems with a Social Grant Strategy

The most difficult questions to be answered in designing federal grants for social programs are how narrowly to specify the services to be provided and in what detail to regulate how the money is to be spent. On the one hand, since the purpose of a grant is to change the priorities that would otherwise have prevailed at the state and local level, there is a temptation to write very detailed regulations to ensure that the national purpose is actually being carried out. On the other hand, the country is large and diverse and detailed rules written in Washington may fail to reflect the realities of local situations, may inundate state and local officials with paperwork, and may actually prevent them from spending the money effectively. Moreover, there are limits to the federal government's ability to enforce detailed rules, especially when dealing with a large number of jurisdictions. For example, Title I of the Elementary and Secondary Education Act of 1965 (ESEA) makes grants to school districts to increase educational resources devoted to disadvantaged children. But how can the federal government ensure that such funds, while technically being spent in schools with large numbers of poor children, do not simply replace local funds in those schools so that the total spent on poor children is no higher than before? It does no good to compare spending in poor schools under a federal grant with spending in some earlier year, since rising teachers' salaries and other costs would have increased expenditures even without the grant. To meet this problem, regulations and standards have been written and rewritten by the Department of Health, Education, and Welfare (HEW). It is impossible to gauge precisely how successful they have been in making sure that the federal grant funds were actually an addition to the educational resources devoted to poor children. There has been some success but undoubtedly also some slippage.

In programs under which the federal government finances a new kind of service not previously undertaken by state and local governments, the federal funds clearly increase the total resources devoted to that particular purpose—legal services for the poor, manpower training, drug abuse clinics, and community action programs are examples. But when the federal grant constitutes only a modest fraction of the amounts already being spent by states and local governments, as in the case of education and law enforcement, it is difficult to ensure that the grants are not, in part at least, simply replacing state and local expenditures.

It is also more difficult than commonly supposed for the federal government to control the specific way in which the grant-financed services are used. In the urban renewal program, enacted in 1949, the federal government pays two-thirds of the cost of assembling and clearing land for renewal projects and makes grants and loans for redevelopment of the renewal area. It gradually became clear that urban renewal in all too many cases was displacing low-income residents to make way for commercial and high-income residential properties. To prevent this from happening (and for other reasons), federal policy makers sought to exercise significant control over the nature of local urban renewal plans. Regulations are voluminous, project applications must be submitted in great detail, and they are reviewed at great length. But as one analyst put it, "HUD has . . . over-regulated matters of detail and under-regulated matters of importance." In the reviewing process, a significant dissent by a HUD (Department of Housing and Urban Development) staff member "will send ripples through the entire program and since they operate under heavy time constraints and pressures to conform, the tendency is to prevent disruption and to sign whatever is put before them."[1] The large expansion in urban renewal funds during the 1960s also created pressure on federal administrators to approve local plans with few important changes so that unused funds would not accumulate and spoil the prospects for further appropriations. Finally, the number of professional staff members available to review local plans has always been far too small.

These same problems of enforcing federal policy arise, though perhaps to a lesser degree, in other grant programs. When complex planning and administrative issues are involved, federal control is difficult to achieve in any event, but it is made more difficult by the unwillingness of both Congress and the executive to provide the large number of federal personnel required to exercise such control. There are 15,400 school districts that receive funds under Title I of ESEA; in 1970 there were fifty professional personnel in the Office of Education administering all aspects of the program, only fifteen of whom were charged with dealing with the states on the complex problem of enforcing federal policy and regulations.

These problems are compounded by the tendency of grants to proliferate. As new problems are perceived, new grant programs are

---

1. Richard T. LeGates, "Can the Federal Welfare Bureaucracies Control Their Programs: The Case of HUD and Urban Renewal," Working Paper 172 (Institute of Urban and Regional Development, University of California, Berkeley, May 1972; processed), pp. 42, 15.

created, but old grants build a constituency that often keeps them alive even when the need for them may have passed or been outweighed by some newer concern. There has also been a tendency to provide separate grants to support the purchase of specific kinds of supplies or resources used in producing a public service rather than simply to finance the service itself. In the case of elementary and secondary education, for example, the federal government provides separate grants for library resources and for the purchase of equipment, and in higher education it makes separate grants to colleges and universities for undergraduate instructional equipment, for construction, and for libraries. The result of these various factors is a tendency for the number of separate grants to accumulate. While in any one situation a case may be made for a special federal grant to promote some new idea or innovation or meet some special need, the cumulation of individual grants increasingly involves the federal government in the detailed allocation of budgets in hundreds or thousands of recipient institutions.

By 1973 there were thirty-five separate categorical grant programs dealing with the delivery of health services and thirty-nine grants for child development and elementary and secondary education, fifteen of which dealt with vocational and adult education. There were four separate grants for public libraries and seven for special services to the aged. In the manpower training field the problem was not only the number of national grant programs—there were sixteen—but the fact that these grants were provided to a multiplicity of different sponsoring organizations in each community.

While the sheer number may not in itself be a serious problem, the proliferation of categorical grants has had several indirect effects which do create difficulties. Because there have been so many different programs, the funds in no one of them have even approached the level required to meet the need the program was intended to fill. Neighborhood health centers, community mental health clinics, model cities, Head Start programs, special services for the aging, work and training courses for welfare mothers, and a host of other grant programs have never had the resources to serve more than a small fraction of the people (or communities) who are by law eligible for their benefits.

Grant proliferation also tends to dissipate federal leverage. The federal government can exert influence over state and local decision making through the device of categorical grants when its efforts are concentrated in a reasonable number of areas, but by trying to push and pull state and local budget allocations in hundreds of directions at once, the various efforts to some extent neutralize each other, exhaust the limited capacity of local officials to administer complex programs, and generate mountains of unread reports.

In summary, grants for social programs represent a strategy by which the federal government can affect the delivery of certain public services at the state and local level to meet problems widely held to be a matter of national concern—increasing the level of services that provide important national benefits, providing more nearly equal opportunity for the disadvantaged, correcting maldistribution of public services, and encouraging reform and innovation in the way public services are delivered. The major difficulties encountered by the strategy stem from the tendency of categorical grant programs to proliferate in number as new ones are continually added while old ones seldom die. This proliferation defeats the very purpose of categorical grants. Funds are spread too thinly over too many programs; control over the use of the funds becomes increasingly difficult to exercise; red tape and delays abound.

Criteria for Pursuing a Social Grant Strategy

There is some danger that discussion about the social grant programs will degenerate into simplistic answers, in which each side falls back on generalized ideological arguments or slogans. An attempt to extricate the federal government from excessively detailed intervention in the provision of public services at the local level can go too far and sacrifice the very important federal goals of promoting innovation and helping to equalize opportunities. At the other extreme, defending programs whose detailed specifications go well beyond what is needed to pursue major national objectives will involve the federal government needlessly in the routine delivery of state and local public services.

There are no simple rules permitting a precise statement of the ideal degree of specificity and control the federal government should exercise in its grant programs, how much consolidation of categorical grants into larger blocks should be undertaken, and under what circumstances new categorical grants should be introduced. But consideration of the basic reasons for social grant programs, developed above, does suggest some criteria useful in dealing on a case-by-case basis with these problems as they arise.

As noted earlier, there are three matters for concern about the responsiveness of state and local governments to national needs. These provide three motives, often mixed in practice, for federal social grants: the desire to increase the *level* of specific public services or groups of services; the desire to *target* services on particular groups in the community; and the desire to promote *innovation* and reform in the delivery of public services. Concern about the responsiveness of the private market, discussed above, provides a fourth motive: the desire to break *bottlenecks* in the supply of privately produced essential services.

The appropriate design of a grant depends on which of the various motives is uppermost. The primary motive may be to increase the level of a service thought to be underfinanced by states and localities, especially to raise the level of spending in areas with low levels of spending. Raising spending on education in states with limited resources or helping states equalize educational expenditures among school districts would be an example. In such cases there is no need for the federal government to specify exactly who is to get the service or how it is to be produced. Its main concerns should be with devising a formula that channels the federal money into areas of high need and with making sure the federal funds do not simply replace state and local spending for the same purpose.

In the second case, where the national interest is served by "targeting"—that is, providing services to some particular group within a community—detailed specifications of the kind of public services to be provided may be unnecessary. The national interest in many grants for urban development—model cities, neighborhood facilities, urban rehabilitation, and the like—lies not so much in the particular mixture of services and projects in any given community as in the fair distribution of those services to low-income neighborhoods and in the establishment of institutional arrangements so that those in the neighborhood have a voice in decision making. To the extent that manpower training services are delivered as a public service by state and local governments (rather than through the provision of training vouchers to individuals), the aim of a categorical grant strategy lies more in ensuring that an appropriate share is made available for the disadvantaged than in controlling the kind of training programs offered. Similarly, the largest current federal program for support of elementary and secondary education has as its objective the provision of additional resources to educate children from disadvantaged backgrounds. Targeting, not program specification, is the central aim.

Federal support for encouraging innovation, on the other hand, must be fairly specific about the kind of service provided but need not continue as permanent financing of ongoing operations. The demonstration of new techniques of delivering services can provide local communities with opportunities for improving public services. Moreover, establishment of a new service usually creates a new client group and often brings together groups of interested professionals who can begin to exert pressure at the local level for the continuation of a new approach as categorical support tapers off. In some cases, channeling grant funds directly to governors and mayors can shift the location of decision making away from local bureaucracies oriented toward the status quo into more responsive hands. More generally, these kinds of categorical grants can be viewed as attempting to create a new set of opportunities or a lasting demand for improved services on the part of state and local communities, not as a permanent means of supporting ongoing services.

Grants whose primary objective is to break bottlenecks in the supply of essential services should also be temporary in nature, provided adequate funding is available to help individuals buy the services. For example, neighborhood health centers, originally sponsored by the Office of Economic Opportunity (OEO) and now by HEW grants, are a means of delivering a broad range of outpatient services, principally to poor families that are located in areas where there is a shortage of health services and that have little access to private physicians. If a reasonably comprehensive system of health insurance were made available to the poor, they could use that insurance to purchase services from neighborhood health centers, should they prefer to receive medical care in this fashion. The federal government may have to provide seed money to help these institutions get started and to encourage the formation of other kinds of institutions such as health maintenance organizations. But there would be no reason for the federal government to support these institutions with continuing grants or to make the decision that the poor must receive medical care in one particular way.

Finally, it is a generally useful rule, subject to exception, that grants be directed toward paying some part of the total cost of providing a service rather than toward the purchase of one particular resource used in producing that service. Grants for construction of facilities, as the next chapter points out in some detail, tend to encourage expenditures on capital investment that are excessive in relation to operating costs. The delivery of health services can be supported, for example, without tying the support to construction, to the purchase of equipment, or to any other single input. Whereas grants to local schools to increase educational outlays may well serve a national purpose, it is hard to defend one tying the grant to the purchase of books or school equipment. Technically, it is quite possible to design federal grants to support some fraction of the total costs of providing a service without confining the grant to a particular category of costs.[2]

Social Grants and the 1974 Budget Decisions

As shown in Table 5-1, federal expenditures on grants for social programs amounted to only about $1.3 billion in 1963 and grew almost twelvefold in the following decade. A small part of this growth came through the expansion of programs that were already on the books in 1963. Most of the growth, however, was attributable to new programs enacted in the 1960s. By 1973 spending for these new programs amounted to $11.1 billion, 70 percent of which was in four major areas: grants for elementary and secondary education, principally under ESEA; manpower training and public employment programs; urban development grants, about half of which are for the model cities program; and grants to the states for social services designed to reduce welfare dependency.

Each of these major categories includes a number (often a large number) of separate grants for specific purposes. In the case of health services, for example, one set of grants is made to support mental health efforts by state and local governments and nonprofit institutions. There are grants for construction of community mental health centers, for staffing of the centers, for special children's programs in

---

2. Because institutions delivering social services may sometimes have difficulty securing access to capital markets, it may be necessary for the federal government to guarantee loans for the construction of facilities.

the field of mental health, for special community drug-abuse projects, for statewide programs directed at drug abuse, for the staffing of clinics for alcoholics, and many others. Some grants are formula grants—that is, each state receives an amount determined by a formula set forth in law. Others are project grants, under which recipients apply for an individual grant, which is awarded or not on the basis of a review conducted by the administering federal agency. Even though project grants are not distributed by a legislative formula, federal agencies tend to use their own administratively determined formulas to set aside funds for each state or region in the country.

Table 5-1. Federal Grants for Social Programs, Fiscal Years 1963, 1973, and 1974

Millions of dollars

Program	1963	1973	1974
Total grants, all programs	1,285	14,852	13,963
"Old" programs, total	1,216	3,738	3,276
Vocational education and aid to impacted areas	377	952	373
Educational development and libraries	57	30	13
Health services	304	552	484
Manpower training and employment	134	350	379
Vocational rehabilitation	73	740	814
Agricultural extension	72	164	163
Urban renewal	199	950	1,050
"New" programs, total	18	10,141	10,116
Elementary and secondary education	...	2,325	2,855
Educational development and libraries	...	208	265
Health services	...	940	1,037
Manpower training and employment	...	2,505	2,065
Economic development	18	437	464
Grants to states for social services	...	2,364	1,800
Law enforcement assistance	...	474	701
Model cities and other grants of the Department of Housing and Urban Development	...	888	929
Other	51	973	571
Addendum: Programs principally directed to the poor[a]	100–200	7,885	...[b]

Sources: *The Budget of the United States Government*, and accompanying *Appendix* and *Special Analyses*, various fiscal years, and authors' estimates.

a. The major programs in this category are: Title I of the Elementary and Secondary Education Act; part of the health service grants; three-quarters of the manpower training and employment funds; community action programs of the Office of Economic Opportunity; and grants to states for social services.

b. The 1974 figure depends on how the various special revenue sharing programs, proposed in the 1974 budget in general terms, are drafted.

In its 1974 budget the administration proposes three major sets of actions with respect to the categorical social grants. First, it substantially reduces budget resources allocated to these programs. Second, it groups a number of them into four special revenue sharing programs: elementary and secondary education, manpower training, urban community development, and law enforcement assistance. Third, in one area, health, it eliminates several project grants, under which the federal government furnishes funds to individual projects, and converts them to state formula grants, under which the funds are allocated on a predetermined basis to the states, which assume responsibility for making the individual grants.

Only part of the expenditure savings from the budget reductions will be realized in 1974. Under each grant program the federal government enters into an agreement with state or local governments to make funds available for the purpose of the programs. On the basis of such agreements, or *commitments*, the state or local government can, in turn, make contracts or other arrangements to carry out the program. Actual cash expenditure of federal funds comes later, as the program or project proceeds and the federal government lives up to its earlier commitment to pay part or all of the costs. Expenditures may lag behind commitments for a long time, how long depending on the nature of the program.

Cutting back federal programs, therefore, first involves a reduction in the level of commitments; the expenditure savings are realized only gradually in subsequent fiscal years. Table 5-2 summarizes changes in the commitments for the social grant programs proposed in the 1974 budget. Because some of the budget cuts were begun in fiscal 1973, the best way of judging the size of reductions is to compare 1974 with the highest of the prior two years. This is done in the last column of the table. By this measurement, the programs were cut by $5.7 billion in fiscal 1974, a reduction of more than one-third.

Under the four special revenue sharing programs that the administration has proposed, total commitments in 1974 will be $3.7 billion lower than under the categorical grant programs they replace. In three of these areas—education, manpower training, and urban community development—the cuts were begun in fiscal 1973; peak commitments were reached in fiscal 1972. Special revenue sharing for urban community development is a unique case. Federal expenditures in this area will continue to rise, as commitments under the old programs are paid out gradually. But in contrast to the $2.5 billion and $2.4 billion of commitments made under the "old" categorical grant programs in fiscal years 1972 and 1973, no new commitments will be made in 1974. The administration proposes that the new special reve-

Table 5-2. Comparison of Program Commitments for Major Federal
Grants for Social Programs, Fiscal Years 1972 or 1973 and 1974[a]

Millions of dollars

Program	1972 or 1973[b]	1974	Change
Grants consolidated into special revenue sharing, total	**8,372**	**4,697**	**−3,675**
Elementary and secondary education	3,108	2,527	−581
Urban community development	2,555	0	−2,555
Manpower training	1,769	1,317	−452
Law enforcement assistance	940	853	−87
Major reductions in individual grants, total	**5,946**	**3,825**	**−2,121**
Health services	1,872	1,576	−296
Mental health, except drug abuse	475	393	−82
Health services planning and delivery[c]	1,240	1,058	−182
Disease control	157	125	−32
Educational development	176	105	−71
Miscellaneous grants for higher education	144	38	−106
Community libraries	59	0	−59
Grants to states for social services	2,513	2,000	−513
Community action	382	106	−276
Emergency employment assistance[d]	800	0	−800
Major increases in individual grants, total	**1,378**	**1,489**	**+111**
Emergency school assistance[e]	271	271	0
Drug abuse[e]	160	177	+17
Work Incentive Program	454	534	+80
Head Start	393	407	+14
Aid to developing colleges[e]	100	100	0
Total commitments, major programs	**15,696**	**10,011**	**−5,685**

	1972	1973	1974
Addendum: Total commitments, major programs	13,816	15,072	10,012

Sources: *The Budget of the United States Government, Fiscal Year 1974,* and accompanying *Appendix* and *Special Analyses;* and authors' estimates. Figures are rounded and may not add to totals.

a. A number of small categorical programs have not been included in this table.

b. Whichever year was larger.

c. Includes health service grants of the Office of Economic Opportunity.

d. Under the authorizing statute, commitments under the emergency employment program depend upon the level of unemployment. It is highly probable that commitments would automatically have dropped from 1973 to 1974, even with no specific action by the administration. Consequently the entry in the first column of the table for this program is an estimate of what commitments in 1974 would have been had the administration not eliminated the program.

e. There was a large increase in these programs between 1972 and 1973.

nue sharing grant come into effect in fiscal 1975 at a level of $2.3 billion. Most of that money ($1.7 billion) will have to be used by the recipient communities to pay off long-term commitments under the old categorical programs. In fiscal 1975 only $600 million will be available for new uses. Not until fiscal 1977 will the revenue sharing proposal provide as much new money to cities as was available under the old programs in fiscal 1973.

Most of the remaining categorical social grants—those that have not been proposed for inclusion in special revenue sharing—have been reduced fairly sharply. The $2.1 billion reduction in these programs arises from the elimination of a number of specific categorical grants within each major area and a cut in many others.

From a long-run standpoint, the important issues raised by the administration's budget for social grants do not primarily concern the restructuring of federal grant programs that the budget envisages. While not beyond debate, much of it seems quite sensible. Rather, the chief policy questions have to do with the level of funds for the restructured programs and the desirability of phasing out a number of existing grants without suggesting alternative means of dealing with the social problems that gave rise to them.

Health Services*

Administration Proposals

Many of the major grants for health services are being terminated or reduced. It is useful to think of these grants in two categories. First, there are grants under which the federal government shares the construction and operating costs of various kinds of public health services and assists state and local public health agencies in controlling communicable diseases. The administration approach seems to have been: reduce or eliminate most federal programs that support specific kinds of health services (except for the drug abuse program, which is expanded); provide continuing general support, at or slightly below prior levels, to state and local public health agencies for health services and disease control but increase state discretion as to the use of funds; and retain federal control over the programs that provide

*Prepared with the assistance of Karen Davis.

special health services for poor neighborhoods in inner cities and rural areas.

Under this approach the Hill-Burton grants for hospital construction were eliminated; grants for community mental health centers and alcoholism clinics will be phased out gradually as long-term agreements for federal support expire; and those grants for maternal and infant care under which the federal government currently selects the projects to support will be converted into state formula grants. On the other hand, the federal government will continue unchanged its project grant program for neighborhood health centers and other health services in poverty areas.

In the second category of health grants, those for planning, innovation, and development, a similar approach was followed. The $125 million regional medical program was terminated. Under this program the federal government supported, on an individual project basis, regional cooperative efforts (usually led by the major medical schools in a region) for such purposes as disseminating knowledge of up-to-date medical techniques and coordinating planning for the use of complex medical technology. On the other hand, the broad grants to state health agencies for planning their own public health programs were retained, after a slight cut, as were federal grants for research and development in health services.

Alternative Approaches

It is impossible to discuss the future of federal grants for health services except in the context of the availability of health insurance. If a federally supported health insurance program that covered the poor and near-poor fairly comprehensively were enacted, some of the current grants for support of various kinds of health services would be unnecessary. That is, an institution that provided treatment could charge for its services and people could use their insurance to pay the charges.

With the availability of such insurance, neighborhood health centers now supported by federal grants could look to patient charges for their financing. Similarly, community mental health centers, which now receive federal grants for construction and staffing, could derive part of their support from such charges. The latter institutions perform three functions. They provide an alternative and generally preferred means of caring for many of the long-term mentally ill who were previously confined to large state hospitals; they undertake community activities such as mental health education; and they provide mental health services to a broader segment of the population who do not need long-term intensive care. It is this third service for which they could recover charges from patients supported by health insurance. The other two functions, traditionally financed by state governments, would have to continue to be underwritten by public support.

Providing adequate financing to people for the purchase of health care, however, does not eliminate the need for federal intervention. Experience has amply demonstrated that the existing medical care system does not respond quickly to new demands placed upon it and that it leaves poor urban and rural areas without adequate health resources. Without specific action by the federal government, the introduction of a national health insurance program may accelerate the rise in medical prices and divert resources away from poor areas which already suffer from a shortage of health care. Two kinds of reforms are needed: first, federal developmental support for new types of medical care delivery which promise to use medical resources more effectively and distribute them more equitably; and second, federal incentives for health care personnel to locate in areas where such care is scarce and for an increase in the number of health professionals recruited from minority groups.

There are five major kinds of innovation in the delivery of health care which the federal government now supports through some type of separate grant. Neighborhood health centers (principally in inner cities) and community mental health centers have been mentioned. Grants are also made for projects to improve health service delivery in remote rural areas. Although the financing of their ongoing operations could be fully or partly borne by charges levied on patients under a comprehensive health insurance system, it is unlikely that new centers would spring up without federal developmental support. Health maintenance organizations (HMOs), which provide comprehensive medical services for a defined population in exchange for a fixed annual payment for each person served, are believed by many to offer a promising means of improving the efficiency and effectiveness of the health care system.[3] The administration proposes $60 million in de-

3. See Charles L. Schultze and others, *Setting National Priorities: The 1973 Budget* (Brookings Institution, 1972), pp. 232–34, for a discussion of HMOs.

velopmental grants in the 1974 budget, a sum it estimates will assist in the establishment or improvement of about 120 HMOs.

The Hill-Burton grant program has provided financial assistance for the construction of hospital bed facilities and, increasingly in recent years, for ambulatory and outpatient facilities at hospitals. This program is terminated in the 1974 budget. Its two basic objectives should be considered separately. More hospital beds are no longer needed; indeed, there are now too many in the United States. The occupancy rate in community hospitals has been declining since 1969 and is now below 80 percent. Not only does this excess capacity drive up the cost of medical care but it encourages hospital treatment of health problems that could be taken care of more efficiently and effectively on an outpatient basis—in doctors' offices, in clinics, or at home. There is, however, a need for expansion of outpatient and ambulatory care; it is often a better way of dealing with illness and is particularly important in poor sections of central cities, where there are few private physicians. But providing such support through construction grants is inefficient. Subsidizing construction leads to overinvestment in facilities and too little support for operation and maintenance.

Instead of these five separate grant programs—some supporting initial development, some ongoing services, and some capital construction—what is needed is a single broad grant program under which the federal government can furnish the seed money for the initiation and development of more effective means of delivering health care, according to the needs of particular areas and population groups. Under a federally supported health insurance system, the institutions developed should ultimately be required to meet the test of the marketplace. After the initial subsidized years they should make it on their own, at least in providing health care covered by insurance, financing the costs of such care (including the cost of capital) from fees. As time passes, the experience of different kinds of institutions should help the federal government judge which kinds of developmental grants to emphasize and which to reduce.

For all five of the areas concerned, the 1974 budget provides about $530 million in grants. Of that amount some $125 million represents the fiscal 1974 cost of carrying out long-term (eight-year) agreements to support community mental health centers; even though the administration proposes to phase this program out as the agreements expire, funds will have to be made available for a number of years to honor the agreements. Similarly, the total includes $135 million to carry out previous agreements on hospital construction under the terminated Hill-Burton program.

Under the alternative proposed here, the grants financing the delivery of ongoing services or the construction of facilities would be replaced with a new, flexible grant program for developmental purposes. With the need for expanding the availability of services in areas where they are inadequate and the acceleration of demands on the system resulting from a new health insurance system, total annual commitments of perhaps $500 million, to be reached by fiscal 1976, would be appropriate. Further expansion thereafter might be warranted depending on how successfully the new institutions meet the needs of the population they serve. The net additional cost of the new program would be about $250 million in fiscal 1976 and $225 million in 1978, over and above the expenditures projected by the administration.[4]

The development of new institutions for the improved delivery of health care would itself attract more physicians and allied health professionals into areas where such care is scarce, but several additional steps would contribute to this end.

Members of minority groups suffer particularly from lack of medical care, in part because many of them live in low-income areas and in part because of the shortage of medical personnel willing to serve inner city areas heavily populated by blacks and other minority groups. Federal efforts to increase the supply of medical personnel from minority groups would serve three purposes: providing members of these groups with greater professional opportunities; taking advantage of an underutilized resource—bright young people from minority groups—to increase the supply of medical personnel; and training people more likely to practice among minority groups. In a society where there were no distinctions of color or race, this last objective would be irrelevant. The problem of bringing additional health resources to the poor, whatever their race, would be the same. But until that point is reached, the availability of health care for minority groups may remain related to the availability of minority health personnel. Pursuit of these objectives would involve providing financial incentives for members of minority groups to attend medical and other

4. The relatively low net cost reflects the phasing in of the new programs as some of the old programs are phased out.

health professional schools, and perhaps financial incentives to medical schools to admit a greater number of students from minority backgrounds. This effort, however, would increase the supply of medical services to minority communities only after a fairly long period of time. There is also a need, particularly in this interim period, for supporting programs training minority paraprofessional personnel to work in community health organizations. Since the cost of such training should not be part of the charges levied on insured patients, separate financial support by the federal government would be necessary. At the present time the costs of many community health organizations are higher than would be justified by the provision of medical services only, because these organizations provide on-the-job training for community residents in paraprofessional skills—efforts that should be separately financed and expanded as the number of community-based organizations increases. The additional incentives needed to support the entry into medical and dental schools of an additional 1,000 minority group members each year and paying for the training of 10,000 paraprofessional personnel a year in community health organizations would require added budgetary expenses of about $60 million.

The regional medical program (RMP), which the administration proposes to terminate, is a planning and innovation-spreading effort. There are fifty-six regional cooperative arrangements supported by $125 million in annual federal grants. According to the administration, "There is little evidence that on a nationwide basis the RMP's have materially affected the health care delivery system."[5]

It is difficult to gauge the validity of this judgment. Initially, the RMPs were established to upgrade the treatment of heart malfunction and defects, cancer, strokes, and kidney disease; subsequently, they were broadened to deal with more general improvements in the health care system. Ideally, they were to provide a mechanism by which medical schools and other leading medical centers in an area could take the leadership in improving health care in their section of the country. Performance has varied, obviously, from one to another, and performance is exceedingly difficult to measure. Moreover, health care in the United States is a $77-billion-a-year industry. That it cannot be revolutionized through the expenditure of $125 million a year

5. *The Budget of the United States Government—Appendix, Fiscal Year 1974*, p. 383.

on RMPs is hardly surprising, and not in itself an indictment of the program.

The planning, innovation, and knowledge-dissemination functions of the RMPs have several characteristics: (1) unlike service delivery programs they cannot be supported by the marketplace, even with insurance; (2) medical schools and other health centers have no funds to support such efforts on their own—continuing support must come from public sources; (3) the major need for improvements in health service delivery varies substantially from area to area; and (4) the funds now devoted to RMPs are large in comparison with what states budget for health planning and with other federal funds available for health planning and development purposes.

It is unlikely that RMPs will be continued with state funds once federal support is withdrawn. The federal government has provided the means of launching these new organizations. Simply withdrawing its support will virtually ensure that most of them disappear, whatever their merits. One alternative to the administration's proposal for eliminating the program is to combine RMP funds with the $148 million in federal funds now available to states and local communities for planning and carrying out their own comprehensive health service projects, thereby allowing each state a choice between continuing to support RMPs and devising other mechanisms for accomplishing the same purpose. This would add some $125 million a year to the budget proposed by the administration.

All of the above discussion assumes the introduction of a national health insurance scheme, which would, among other things, provide reasonably comprehensive coverage with zero or low deductibles and coinsurance for the poor. If such a plan is not adopted, a strategy that included termination of service grants to neighborhood health centers would not be workable, since the centers would then have few sources of financial support. Similarly, the administration's plans to terminate the Hill-Burton program and to phase out support for community mental health centers would lead to serious consequences for the centers and for the expansion of ambulatory facilities in urban hospitals.

If there is no comprehensive insurance plan, therefore, a second alternative must be considered. This would include continuation and expansion of service grants for neighborhood health centers, roughly tripling the level of support by 1978 and making possible a substantial increase in coverage for the low-income population served by these centers; continuation of service grants for community mental health centers; expansion of the HMO development grants from the $60 million provided in the 1974 budget to $100 million in 1976 and $200 million in 1978; and conversion of the Hill-Burton construction grants into a new kind of grant costing $150 million a year and designed to encourage more ambulatory treatment in urban hospitals. Supporting health service delivery through construction grants has the disadvantages discussed earlier. As a substitute, the federal government could agree to pay a specified portion of the annual costs of any expansion in ambulatory care and outpatient treatment undertaken by hospitals serving areas with large concentrations of low-income people. Loan guarantees for construction would be made available as necessary. If these grants proved successful in substantially increasing the delivery of outpatient services, federal support could be increased in later years.

The education and training program for minority health personnel and the integration of RMP funds with state comprehensive health grants would also be incorporated in this alternative. Measured in terms of outlays this alternative would add $465 million in fiscal 1976 and $945 million in fiscal 1978 to the outlays projected by administration proposals. (This alternative costs more than the first one principally because, in that approach, health insurance would pay for some of the services financed by grants in the second alternative.)

Table 5-3 summarizes the added budgetary costs that would be incurred under the various approaches to health grants discussed in this section. The commitments that would be involved have been translated into their expenditure consequences.

Grants to the States for Social Services

Administration Proposals

In 1967 the basic law governing the public assistance program was amended to provide to the states federal grants covering 75 percent of the costs of social services designed to reduce the welfare rolls. In the language of the act, these services are defined as "services to a family or any member thereof for the purpose of preserving, rehabilitating, reuniting, or strengthening the family, and such other

Table 5-3. Federal Budget Outlays for Alternative Health Grant Programs,
Fiscal Years 1974, 1976, and 1978
Billions of dollars

Alternative	1974	1976	1978
1. Total outlays (assumes health insurance enacted)	**70**	**435**	**420**
New developmental grant for health services (net cost)[a]	0	250	225
Education and training of minority health personnel	20	60	65
Combine regional medical programs (RMPs) with state comprehensive health grants	50	125	130
2. Total outlays (assumes no health insurance)	**120**	**465**	**945**
Restore and expand service grants and redesign Hill-Burton (net costs)[a]	50	280	750
Education and training of minority health personnel	20	60	65
Combine RMPs with state comprehensive health grants	50	125	130

Source: Authors' estimates.
a. The net cost figures reflect a number of different factors: the new developmental grants replace some existing service grants; the expenditures under the administration's proposals decline over the next four years as community mental health center grants are phased out and outlays to pay off existing Hill-Burton commitments gradually recede; and as the new grants are introduced there will be some "doubling up" of expenditures to pay off commitments under prior service grants.

services as will assist members of a family to attain or retain capability for maximum self-support and personal independence."[6]

In effect this program has developed into something resembling a targeted special revenue sharing grant. It covers a broad range of social services but is directed at the specific groups in the population who are or might become welfare recipients—the aged, the disabled, and broken families with dependent children. It has grown very rapidly in recent years, which led the Congress to set a $2.5 billion ceiling on the program last year.

Under this program, states submit plans to the regional offices of HEW, specifying what services they intend to provide. State welfare offices can furnish the services either directly or through contracts with other state agencies, local governments, or nonprofit organizations.

Initially, use of the grants was delayed for three reasons: because HEW regulations were not in effect until 1970, because the various regional offices interpreted the law and regulations differently, and because it took the states some time to realize the potentialities of the

6. *Open-Ended Federal Matching of State Social Service Expenditure Authorized under the Public Assistance Titles of the Social Security Act*, Hearings before the Subcommittee on Fiscal Policy of the Joint Economic Committee, 92 Cong. 2 sess. (1972), p. 3.

new law, both in financing new services and in covering 75 percent of the costs of many services they were already providing. By 1972, expenditures had grown to $1.7 billion. California, Illinois, and New York, having recognized the possibilities of the program earlier than most states, were receiving a disproportionate amount of the funds. But other states learned fast. By July 1972 a preliminary tabulation of state plans submitted for fiscal 1973 indicated a requirement for $4.7 billion in federal outlays that year. Reacting to this rapid surge in outlays and the likelihood that future years would see even further increases, Congress, in an amendment to the 1972 general revenue sharing act, established the $2.5 billion ceiling. It also limited the maximum share that any state could receive to the ratio of its population to the national total.

Of the $1,653 million spent in 1972, $520 million went for services for children—day care, preschool programs, juvenile delinquency prevention, and the like. Some $300 million was devoted to locating housing, providing homemaker services for the aged, and carrying out similar home-related activities. Another $300 million went for medical treatment, family planning, and other health care services, and $160 million was used to help people find jobs. The remaining funds were spent for a variety of services such as marital counseling, compelling deserting fathers to make support payments, and legal services. In terms of population groups served, three-quarters of the grant funds are used for families with dependent children, and most of the remainder is used for services to the aged and disabled poor.

In its 1974 budget the administration proposed to cut the program back to $1.9 billion (even lower than the congressional $2.5 billion ceiling) by tightening up the regulations on the kinds of services and the population groups eligible for grant assistance. After much controversy it issued a new set of regulations in April 1973 which are more liberal than those apparently under consideration when the budget was drawn up. It is now likely that grants in 1974 will amount to $2.2 billion.[7]

Under the new regulations, persons who are on welfare or have recently been so are eligible for the services. Also identified is a group of potential welfare clients who may receive services so long as their

---

7. The grant total will be less than the $2.5 billion ceiling not because the regulations are so restrictive but because some states are choosing not to use up their share of the $2.5 billion.

income is not more than 150 percent of the state welfare standard. But only 10 percent of the grant funds may be used for this group of potential recipients, with several important exceptions. Day care services are exempt from the restriction; they may be provided free to those within the 150 percent income limit and, with a sliding scale of fees, to families with incomes up to 233 percent of each state's welfare standard. Family planning services, foster care for children, and certain other services are also exempt. On the basis of past experience and of plans submitted by the states for fiscal 1973, it is likely that a very large proportion of the funds—probably more than half—will be used for day care.

In thinking about the future of the program, there are several characteristics that are particularly important. First, because it supports such a wide range of services, with a generous 75 percent federal grant, states found it possible to use the program to support services that they or their local governments had been providing in any event. Three-quarters of the costs of an ongoing dropout-prevention program in the low-income schools of a particular district, for example, could be switched from local financing to financing by the state with funds received under the social service grants. The local funds thereby released could then be used for other purposes, such as teachers' pay increases or holding down property taxes. Some unknown fraction of the rapid growth in the social service grants has ended up not in providing additional services but in furnishing general financial assistance to state and local governments. This, of course, is bound to happen with many grant programs, particularly those that embrace a wide range of services. It is possible that the new regulations, which particularly encourage the provision of day care services, will result in more of the funds being used to expand the services provided rather than as substitutes for state funds in programs already in existence.

Second, restricting at least some of the services to those who are now or have recently been on welfare creates perverse incentives and sharpens inequities. A family with both parents and very low wages may not be eligible, whereas a one-parent family with the same income, or even with a higher one, is. Low income rather than family status ought to be the criterion of eligibility. Control of program size can be achieved by placing an overall ceiling on funds.

Finally, the formula enacted last year for the maximum amount available to each state—the ratio of its population to the total—is not logical for a program directed at providing social services to the poor. A distribution formula more closely tied to the incidence of poverty would be more appropriate.

Alternative Approaches

In addition to the administration's proposal for this program there are several alternatives that might be considered. Two are outlined briefly below.

One approach would be to convert the grants in an explicit way to a targeted social service revenue sharing program. The distributional formula among states could be changed to reflect the incidence of poverty. Eligibility provisions could be revised in a way to make the program available to the poor more generally instead of just to welfare recipients. Since a specific dollar amount would be given each state, control over total spending would not have to take the form of welfare-oriented eligibility restrictions. The program could be funded at the administration-proposed level of $2.2 billion. Alternatively, in view of the likelihood that this reduction of $300 million in program size would reduce social services to the poor in many localities, the $2.5 billion level in 1973 could be restored, and gradually increased in future years as wages and prices rose, to avoid reducing the real value of services offered. Fund allotments not used by some states could be redistributed among the others.

Another approach would be to split the program into two parts— day care and all other services. If a child care voucher program along the lines discussed in Chapter 4 was inaugurated, the day care part of this program could be replaced by the new initiative. If such a comprehensive program was not undertaken, it would still make sense to combine the day care services financed under the program, those provided by the Work Incentive Program (see pages 160–69), and the Head Start grants into a single child development and day care program. If it is assumed that $1 billion to $1.5 billion of the fiscal 1974 social service grants will be used for day care services, approximately another $1 billion would be left for other services, which could then be converted into the targeted special revenue sharing program described above.

Table 5-4 summarizes the cost of these alternatives. Since under the second alternative day care funds are being transferred to another

Table 5-4. Federal Budget Outlays for Alternative Social Service Grants, Fiscal Years 1974, 1976, and 1978

Millions of dollars

Alternative	1974	1976	1978
1. Administration proposal	2,200	2,300	2,445
		Additional cost	
2. Convert to explicit special revenue sharing, at 1973 levels of support	+300ª	+350	+360
3. Same as 1, but transfer day care portion to a separate day care program	+300ª	−900	−1,000
Amount transferred to day care	0	+1,250	+1,360

Source: Authors' estimates.

a. These estimates assume that any legislation which substantially revised this program, or transferred part of the funds to a new day care initiative, would be enacted too late in the session to have a major impact on 1974 outlays.

program, the budget reductions for the social service program do not represent cuts in the total federal budget. There is of course nothing sacrosanct about the funding levels shown in the table. The program could, for example, be increased above those levels if the provision of such social services was thought to warrant higher priority than other uses of budget funds.

Community Action Programs

The 1974 budget proposes abolition of the Office of Economic Opportunity. Established in 1965 as the agency to direct the attack on poverty, OEO made grants for a wide variety of services aimed at improving the health, earning power, and participation in community decisions of the poor. Over the past four years most of the operating programs supported by OEO have been transferred to other agencies: Head Start and neighborhood health centers to HEW; manpower programs to the Department of Labor. In the 1974 budget this process will be completed. In addition, the research program of OEO will be moved to other agencies. Throughout the period the community action program remained in OEO, eventually becoming the core of its operations, with a budget that reached $382 million in fiscal 1972. The 1974 budget proposes to abolish the community action program and to leave to the discretion of state or local governments decisions about whether to continue supporting the program in particular communities with their own resources.

Under the community action program the federal government provides grants to local community action agencies (CAAs) in poor urban and rural communities. The CAAs have three major functions: they organize, sponsor, and in some cases operate community programs for low-income residents—day care, manpower training, health clinics, and the like. (The grants to CAAs do not cover the costs of the projects they operate; those funds are drawn from federal, state, local, or private money disbursed under other programs.) The CAAs also provide a means for residents of low-income areas to participate in decisions about programs that affect their neighborhoods; the governing boards of the CAAs include a substantial representation of low-income neighborhood residents. Finally, as an adjunct to their other activities, they provide professional, semiprofessional, and clerical employment to residents of their neighborhoods. In 1972 the average size of the federal grant per CAA was $420,000, although the specific amount varied considerably from one community to another.

In the early stages of the antipoverty efforts, as the CAAs were getting under way, they became the focus of sharp political controversy. In many cities and rural areas, they were a new force, often sharply at odds with existing city or county officialdom. Usually the disagreements were less about the substance of the programs to be carried out than about who was to have the final voice in decisions about federal programs in the community. There were also problems about how CAA governing boards were to be selected—special neighborhood elections for the purpose often resulted in very low turnout.

In more recent years these problems have become less pronounced. With some exceptions, CAAs and local officials have worked out a modus vivendi under which the CAAs have retained an important but not unilateral power in decisions about the delivery of many social services in low-income neighborhoods. They have become in many areas an influential community organization lobbying for the interest of low-income sections of the city or county, analogous to other civic organizations in more affluent areas which have long had a weighty, if informal, voice in local government. And while the analogy can be carried too far, they also perform for today's minority groups part of the role, with both its virtues and its faults, that local political organizations carried out for the immigrants in city slums in an earlier era. Leadership of the CAAs, as with other voluntary organizations, has gravitated into the hands of local leaders who have a political or organizational flair and are willing to devote substantial time to community matters. In affluent neighborhoods federal financing is not necessary for community groups—influence and power flow to these groups without such financing. In poor neighborhoods this is not the case.

It is, of course, impossible to foretell the future of these organizations after the administration has eliminated federal support.[8] In some communities, state or local financial assistance will continue, probably at reduced levels. In many other areas the CAAs will expire. Some part of the functions they perform, in sponsoring, organizing, and operating other service programs, will have to be paid for (possibly out of social service grants) if those programs are to be continued. Presumably, these costs would eventually show up partly in the federal budget and partly in state and local budgets.

The performance of the CAAs and their relative importance as a means of providing social services to low-income neighborhoods vary tremendously from place to place. It is probably true that in many communities the cost of the CAAs and the size of the staff are high relative to the size of the programs they sponsor or operate. Yet they also provide professional and semiprofessional on-the-job training for a large number of people for whom such experience is hard to come by. And, as noted earlier, they now perform in low-income areas the role in influencing local decisions that other community organizations have traditionally carried out for more affluent groups. No other federal program supports these same objectives.

There is obviously no set of measures by which the effectiveness of the CAAs can be objectively measured. But in developing alternative budget strategies, continued support of the CAAs at approximately current levels is clearly an option to be considered. The rationale for continued support is particularly strong for a budget that otherwise moves in the direction of reducing federal control over the way in which grant-in-aid funds are used by state and local governments. Federal influence, exerted through specific grant programs, has often been the critical factor in channeling services to low-income residents

8. The OEO began cutting back grants in 1973, in order to phase out the programs gradually. But a federal district court recently ruled that OEO could not anticipate congressional decisions on the 1974 budget and must continue to fund the programs until Congress eliminated the funds.

or in securing for them a voice in decisions about grant-funded programs. Removal of that influence strengthens rather than weakens the case for federal support of community organizations that can bring their influence to bear toward the same ends.

Restoring support for the CAAs to the level reached in 1972 would add about $380 million to budget outlays. Maintenance of the real purchasing power of the CAA grants would require a gradual increase, to about $450 million by 1978.

Elementary and Secondary Education*

Administration Proposals

The 1974 budget proposes major modifications to and some reductions in current federal grant programs for elementary and secondary education. It substantially reduces, and makes some changes in, the aid to impacted areas program. It continues at roughly current levels the existing federal grant for compensatory education of disadvantaged children, and makes some modifications to the program. Finally, it groups about two dozen other categorical grants into one larger grant, removing most though not all of the federal specifications and controls on the use of funds. The three programs, collectively called "education special revenue sharing," would distribute a total of $2.8 billion in federal grants in 1974; their predecessors made available $3.1 billion in fiscal 1973 and $3.3 billion in fiscal 1972.

Of the $2.8 billion, $200 million will be earmarked for a substantially reduced impacted areas program. Under this program the federal government provided grants to communities for educating children whose parents were in one of two categories: either they lived and worked on tax-free federal property and sent their children to community public schools (Category A children), or they worked on tax-free federal property but lived on taxable private property (Category B children). In many cases Category B children lived and attended schools in relatively well-to-do suburban districts while the tax-exempt federal property on which their parents worked was located in another school district, often in the central city. The new revenue sharing program will make grants for Category A children, but none for Category B, thereby reducing the grants from $600

* Prepared with the assistance of Robert D. Reischauer.

million in fiscal 1972 and $440 million in fiscal 1973 to the $200 million level in fiscal 1974.

Of the remaining $2.6 billion, three-fifths (about $1.6 billion) will be used to continue, in modified form, the existing Title I of the Elementary and Secondary Education Act, which provides grants to school districts for compensatory education of disadvantaged children. The money would be allocated to each state according to a formula that takes into account the number of children between the ages of five and seventeen from low-income families and the state's educational expenditures per child. In turn, states are required to distribute this money first to "high need" school districts—those with large concentrations of poor children. If any money is left over, the state must allocate it among the remaining districts, providing money first to those with the next largest concentrations of poor children. To be eligible for funds, a school district must first provide equal educational resources from its own and from state funds to both rich and poor children, and then use the federal grant to provide additional services for the disadvantaged children. Moreover, three-quarters of the federal grant must be devoted to instruction in basic mathematics and language arts. This part of the special revenue sharing program retains many of the federal controls of the existing Title I program and adds a few new ones; the requirement about mathematics and language arts, for example, is new.

The remainder of the appropriation—approximately 35 percent of the total—is the only true revenue sharing, or block grant, aspect of the proposal. This portion replaces most of the current federal programs devoted to vocational education, education for the handicapped, equipment purchases, library support, the basic school lunch program, and a host of other small categorical aids, and it represents the major departure from existing practices. Restrictions would be eased, reporting requirements relaxed, and matching funds eliminated. This subgrant is distributed among the states according to the size of their school-age populations. While each state's allocation is tentatively earmarked for broad program areas—16 percent for educational programs for the handicapped, 43 percent for vocational education programs, and 41 percent for supporting services and materials—states would be free to spend the money within each of these areas as they saw fit as well as to shift money among the categories. For example, up to 30 percent of the funds earmarked for the handicapped or vocational education could be transferred to any other spending category of the program except aid to school districts with federally connected children. The supporting services and materials category is defined so broadly as to constitute general educational aid.

Alternative Proposals

The third element in the administration's approach—consolidation of a number of small special purpose grants into a broader grant—provides a modest annual program of general federal aid to elementary and secondary education, amounting in 1974 to about $1 billion. In considering future uses of incremental budget resources, one major alternative would be the substantial expansion and modification of this program, making it a vehicle for narrowing the disparities among states, and indirectly the wide disparities within states, in the provision of educational services.

The fiscal capacities of the fifty states and thousands of localities of the nation vary tremendously (see Chapter 7, below). To generate an equal amount of resources for public services, therefore, much higher tax rates must be imposed in poor jurisdictions than in wealthy ones. While this influences the levels of all public services provided by states and localities, its effect on the disparities in the quality of public education supplied by the nation's 17,000 school systems has received the most attention. Although the U.S. Supreme Court recently rejected the argument that the differences in educational spending resulting from the unequal distribution of taxing capacity violate the Constitution, the Court did point out that the system was badly in need of reform.[9]

While it can be argued that state governments have a responsibility, as well as the resources, to equalize the spending disparities among the school districts within their borders,[10] only the federal government can attempt to equalize educational resources among states. At present, spending varies from $563 per pupil in Alabama to almost three times that much in New York. As Table 5-5 illustrates, the spread in educational expenditures among the states arises from

9. *San Antonio Independent School District* v. *Rodriguez*, U.S. Supreme Court, 71-1332, opinion delivered March 21, 1973 (see section IV).

10. For this view, see Advisory Commission on Intergovernmental Relations, *Financing Schools and Property Tax Relief—A State Responsibility* (forthcoming).

Table 5-5. Disparities in Educational Expenditures Arising from Differences in Tax Effort and Personal Income among Selected States, School Year 1971-72

State	Actual expenditure per pupil[a] (dollars)	Tax effort: state and local school revenues as percentage of personal income	Personal income per pupil as percentage of national average[b]	Hypothetical expenditure per pupil if state's own tax effort was applied to U.S. average personal income per pupil[c] (dollars)
Ten highest states				
New York	1,513	4.9	144	1,078
Alaska	1,472	6.4	96	1,521
District of Columbia	1,284	3.3	167	838
New Jersey	1,280	4.7	129	1,009
Vermont	1,208	7.1	79	1,509
Connecticut	1,205	4.8	121	1,003
Michigan	1,132	5.6	96	1,175
Maryland	1,083	4.7	106	1,027
Delaware	1,082	4.7	105	1,034
Illinois	1,075	4.0	124	881
Ten lowest states				
West Virginia	726	4.1	76	923
South Carolina	725	4.2	70	979
Nebraska	714	3.5	95	752
Utah	707	4.9	65	1,056
Tennessee	684	3.8	77	864
Kentucky	668	3.4	81	798
Mississippi	655	3.7	63	929
Oklahoma	633	3.3	85	735
Arkansas	607	3.5	72	808
Alabama	563	3.2	71	749

Sources: Expenditures, enrollments, and sources of revenue from National Education Association–Research, *Estimates of School Statistics, 1972–73*, Research Report 1972-R12, Tables 11, 3, and 9 respectively; personal income from *Survey of Current Business*, Vol. 52 (August 1972), p. 25.

a. Expenditures include those financed by federal grants.
b. Based on attendance at public schools.
c. Existing federal grants were added to hypothetical state and local expenditures.

differences in both fiscal capacity and tax effort. With three exceptions, the ten states that spend the most had larger income per pupil enrolled in public shools than the national average; all of the ten states that spend the least had lower than average income. (The differences in income per pupil to some extent reflect the variation from state to state in the proportion of children attending private schools, but mainly reflect differences in per capita incomes.) If each state had the national average income per pupil but maintained its own tax effort, the disparities in educational expenditures would narrow but not disappear (see the last column of the table). The remaining differences are due to variations in tax effort.

It has become almost fashionable to downgrade the importance of education as a means of improving earning prospects or even of academic achievement and to deny a connection between additional budget dollars and better education. This is not the place to review the statistical and analytic controversies to which these views have given rise.[11] There is, nevertheless, a clear national interest in narrowing the wide differences in resources now devoted to education by state and local governments. On the average, people with more education do earn higher incomes than those with less education. Affluent communities do take pains to provide substantial funds for their schools, and affluent parents do demand expensive public school systems or send their children to private schools. In other words, those with income and education act as if education were important. The hiring, firing, promotion, and status rules in society tend to bear them out. However much these economic and social practices may overestimate the "true" value of education—and the evidence is mixed— equality of opportunity in today's society does imply equality of education. Moreover, many people would argue that local educational expenditures lead to significant national benefits over and above the benefits accruing to state and local taxpayers. As a consequence, the federal government has an interest in raising the general level of such expenditures beyond what state and local taxpayers provide.

A federal grant that provided an equal amount to each state for each school-age child could bring about some narrowing of disparities. But a more powerful equalizing formula would be one guaranteeing that states making equal educational tax efforts would command equal amounts of educational resources per child. Since no state could, or should, be required to reduce its educational spending, this would, in effect, provide every state with the equivalent fiscal capacity of the richest, New York. Each state's tax effort—taxes devoted to education as a percentage of the total personal income of the state's

---

11. For a recent statement of the iconoclastic view, see Christopher Jencks and others, *Inequality: A Reassessment of the Effect of Family and Schooling in America* (Basic Books, 1972), and also the reviews of Jencks in *Harvard Educational Review*, Vol. 43 (February 1973), pp. 37–164.

residents—would be calculated. The federal government would make a grant to each state sufficient to raise its educational resources to the amount that would be yielded by applying its tax effort to the New York State level of personal income. The only differences then remaining among the states would be differences in their willingness to tax themselves; variations caused by divergent fiscal capacities would be eliminated.

This approach represents an extreme—full equalization of fiscal capacities to the level of the richest state. New York would receive nothing and other relatively wealthy states very little. It would cost about $16 billion a year in 1974 and is unlikely to be enacted. A more moderate program, using the same approach, would aim not at full equalization, but at narrowing differences in fiscal capacity for education support. Under such a program the federal government would pay each state a grant equal to some percentage of the amount it spent on education out of state and local tax revenues. The percentage would be larger for low-income states than for high-income states. For example, the federal government could provide a grant equal to 20 percent of the tax receipts devoted to education in states with per capita incomes equal to the U.S. average, increasing the percentage to 40 percent in the poorest states and decreasing it to 10 percent in the richest.

The costs and educational consequences of such a program would depend partly on the extent to which states used the grants to increase educational expenditures rather than to reduce taxes.[12] Since the federal grant envisaged here is equivalent to a reduction in the "price" of education—state and local governments can buy more education for the same tax dollars—and since the use of the grant to reduce taxes in one year would cut the size of the grant the next, states would have some incentive to use the funds for added educational expenditures. Nevertheless, it is unlikely that all of the funds would be so used; a part would find its way into tax cuts, mainly in property taxes.

If the major purpose of such a grant is educational equalization, the federal government could incorporate a "maintenance-of-effort"

12. Because the federal grant under this scheme is a percentage of state and local tax resources devoted to education, use of federal grant money to reduce those taxes in one year will lead to a reduction in federal grants the next. Hence the more state and local governments use the federal grant to reduce taxes, the smaller will be the total size of the federal grant program.

provision in the program: as a condition of the grant each state, from its own tax resources, would have to devote at least as high a percentage of personal income to education as it did before the federal grant. In this way most of the grant funds would result in added educational expenditures.

Table 5-6 shows the costs in fiscal 1976 and the consequences of additional educational expenditures for programs of this type. The figures for alternative 1 show the results with no maintenance-of-effort provision and the assumption that 50 percent of the grant results in added expenditures. Alternative 2 estimates the costs of the same programs with a maintenance-of-effort provision sufficiently strong to ensure that 90 percent of the grants result in added educational expenditures. (The net costs to the federal government would be about $1 billion less than the figures shown in the table since this program would presumably absorb the $1 billion in general aid under the administration's revenue sharing program.)

A revenue sharing program for educational equalization would of

Table 5-6. Cost and Uses of Alternative Federal Grants for Educational Equalization, Fiscal Year 1976

Billions of dollars

Alternative and grant as percentage of educational expenditures[a]	*Federal cost*[b]	*Use*	
		Education	*Tax relief*
1. No maintenance-of-effort provision;[c] assumes added educational expenditures equal to 50 percent of the grant; grant equal to:			
20 percent of educational expenditures	10.0	5.0	5.0
30 percent of educational expenditures	14.0	7.0	7.0
50 percent of educational expenditures	21.5	10.7	10.7
2. Maintenance-of-effort provision;[c] assumes added educational expenditures equal to 90 percent of the grant; grant equal to:			
20 percent of educational expenditures	10.5	9.5	1.0
30 percent of educational expenditures	15.5	14.0	1.5
50 percent of educational expenditures	25.5	23.0	2.5

Source: Authors' estimates. These estimates assume a 7 to 8 percent annual growth in state and local expenditures between 1971 and 1976.

a. The grant is based on the percentage of taxes used for education in states with per capita incomes equal to the U.S. average, with the percentage increasing for states with per capita incomes below the U.S. average and decreasing for those with higher incomes.

b. The administration's special revenue sharing proposal for education contains $1 billion for broad-purpose grants that would be replaced by educational equalization grants. The net budget costs of the latter are thus $1 billion less than shown in the table.

c. A maintenance-of-effort provision requires that each state devote at least the same percentage of personal income to education as before the grant.

course do little to guarantee that wealth-related spending disparities among the school districts *within* each state were reduced. A state might use the federal grant to provide equal assistance per child to each district regardless of wealth. As a condition for receiving the grant, however, a federal stipulation concerning the tolerable range of spending disparities within each state could be imposed.

With a strong maintenance-of-effort provision a program of this sort would substantially raise the general level of educational expenditures. But unless the federal share of expenditures was very much lower in rich states than in poor states, it would do little to narrow differences in educational service. Rich states, precisely because they are rich, tend to spend a larger percentage of their income on education than do poor states. The smaller federal matching share in rich states is therefore applied against educational expenditures that are a higher fraction of income. As a consequence the two parts of the distribution formula tend to cancel out. Unless the shares for rich and poor states are widely different, there will be little narrowing of disparities. Securing legislation that absorbs substantial federal tax revenues and provides little for the populous wealthy states would be a most difficult political task.[13] One possible compromise would be the imposition of less stringent maintenance-of-effort provisions on richer states whose tax effort was already above average. In effect this approach would tend to raise educational expenditures in states with low incomes or low tax effort and to induce property tax reductions in wealthier states with high tax burdens.

There are many who would argue that narrowing the disparities in educational resources among states, and among school districts within states, is not enough. Children from poverty-stricken families and disadvantaged backgrounds need more educational help than other children if they are to have a fair chance in later life. As noted earlier, the compensatory education component of the administration's special revenue sharing program continues the current federal grants designed to provide school districts with extra resources for disadvantaged children. One use of additional budgetary funds would be the expansion of these compensatory education grants above the $1.6 billion level proposed in the 1974 budget.

Can extra money spent on schools at least partly make up for the

13. An analysis of alternative approaches to federal aid for educational equalization is contained in Robert D. Reischauer and Robert W. Hartman, *Reforming School Finance* (Brookings Institution, 1973), Chap. 6.

competitive disadvantages suffered by children whose home background prepares them less well for school than children from richer families? Unfortunately, the evidence is inconclusive. The several statistical studies that have attempted to determine how much difference the level of school expenditures makes on the educational achievements of deprived children show little relation between expenditures and achievement. But all of these studies have a number of weaknesses that make their essentially negative findings inconclusive. Other studies have identified some successful attempts, in individual schools, to overcome the handicaps of disadvantaged backgrounds.[14] All the successful efforts have required substantial extra spending per child—from $250 to $350 a year seems to be the minimum. But there were many other cases, in which equal sums were spent, without significant results. In short, it is fairly certain that compensatory education cannot work without substantial additional resources. What is not known is whether additional resources, widely applied, would generate widespread success.

At present the federal government's compensatory education program provides $1.6 billion to states under a formula that takes into account the number of children from families with less than $2,000 in income and from welfare families above that income level. The states then turn these funds over to school districts on the basis of the number of disadvantaged children in each district; within each district the funds must be used in schools with large numbers of such children in attendance. There are 7.9 million schoolchildren who meet the income and welfare criteria of the distribution formula. With a $1.6 billion program, this apparently means $200 of extra educational spending per disadvantaged child. In fact, however, the actual amounts made available per disadvantaged child are much lower than this. Some poor children are in schools that receive no additional money since they have only a small number of eligible children. In many schools that do receive additional funds, there are substantial numbers of children who are not disadvantaged. Despite monitoring and auditing by the federal government, some of the funds are merged with general school district budgets and are spread around to all schools. While it is impossible to make accurate estimates, the actual amount of added resources devoted to disadvantaged children probably amounts to $100–$150 per child each year,

14. Chapter 10 of *Setting National Priorities: The 1973 Budget* briefly summarized the evidence (pp. 355–58).

a 10–15 percent addition, on the average, to what would otherwise be spent on their education. Adjusted for inflation, the amount now provided per child by this compensatory education grant has not increased much since the program was begun in 1965.

As noted, the successful local compensatory education programs required $250–$350 per pupil in additional expenditures (which is not to say that the provision of such sums will itself be a sufficient condition for success). If the inevitable slippage in the program is taken into account (that is, some funds will necessarily be applied to other than disadvantaged children), providing extra resources of this amount would cost about $4.1 billion in 1976, some $2 billion higher than the level projected for that year under the administration's proposals:

Effective support level	*Cost* *(billions of dollars)*
$300 per child	4.1
$400 per child	5.5
Less: cost of compensatory component of educational special revenue sharing	−1.8

Programs for compensatory education and narrowing disparities in educational expenditures tackle different aspects of the equal opportunities problem. The first is designed to enable jurisdictions of differing financial capacity to spend equal amounts on education. The second proceeds on the theory that, for the disadvantaged, equal opportunity requires unequal spending. The two programs are not in conflict. They can be pursued singly or together. Both are addressed to matters of general national concern; both could absorb large budgetary sums. But neither requires detailed federal intervention in the specific kinds of educational services required. The program for narrowing disparities targets resources to different jurisdictions, which is solely a matter of the distribution formula. The compensatory program requires more federal regulation, because it seeks to target resources on particular groups of students within particular jurisdictions.

Urban Community Development*

Administration Proposals

The urban special revenue sharing proposal offered by the administration, under the Better Communities Act proposed in 1973, is in-

* Prepared with the assistance of Robert D. Reischauer.

tended to replace seven categorical grant programs that now provide assistance to urban areas for community development purposes. To date, under these programs the federal government has concentrated its resources on projects in relatively few communities at any one time. It has required detailed applications and reporting on these projects and has played an active role in supervising and modifying individual projects so as to conform to HUD's notions of the national interest.

In budgetary commitments, the urban renewal and model cities grants are the largest of the programs to be incorporated into the new revenue sharing proposal ($1,454 million and $645 million, respectively, in fiscal 1973). The existing grants for sewer and water facilities, open-land purchases, and neighborhood facilities, as well as loans for urban rehabilitation and public facilities, with total commitments of $270 million in 1973, would also be consolidated into the new program. The administration is asking for $2.3 billion in appropriations for urban special revenue sharing, which is about equivalent to the 1973 level of commitments under all the existing programs it will replace. But distribution of the new funds would not begin until fiscal 1975.

Three-quarters of the new block grants would be directly distributed to cities with populations of over 50,000 and to large metropolitan counties according to a formula based on population, the number of people with incomes below the poverty line, and overcrowded housing conditions. The poverty component of the formula is given double weight. The remainder of the funds (after 5 percent has been set aside for uses determined by the secretary of HUD) goes to governors, who must distribute half the money they receive to metropolitan governments according to a formula but may spend the rest where they see fit.

Since the programs being terminated were all project grants (that is, communities submitted applications for individual projects which were approved, modified, or rejected on a case-by-case basis), the money was spread very unevenly across the metropolitan areas of the country in any one year. Distributing federal aid for community development by means of a formula will result in a more even distribution of money among metropolitan areas, but large lump-sum commitments for major projects will not be available. Recipient governments will be able to use the block grants for many types of community development activity, including all the purposes for which the seven existing grants or loans are now made. The matching requirements, application procedures, and planning and reporting regulations that accompanied the old programs will no longer be imposed.

To avoid large reductions in the grant funds available to particular cities under the new grant, as compared with the sums they had been receiving under the old programs, the Better Communities Act contains a complex set of "hold-harmless" provisions. These provisions guarantee that regardless of what the distribution formula implies every community will receive in the first year of the new program at least as much as its annual average for the past five years under the old programs combined. The guarantee will gradually phase out over five years, at the end of which time the new formula will completely govern the distribution of funds. Thus in the first year of the program the amounts going to most communities will be governed by the "hold-harmless" provisions, but when the new formula is fully in effect, the distribution of grants will be substantially different.

Table 5-7 compares the relative distribution of federal community development funds under the existing programs with the distribution implied by the Better Communities Act. The Northeast, which has benefited greatly under the urban renewal and model cities programs, would receive a far smaller fraction of the total while the West would receive a substantial increase. The nation's three largest cities would gain. Many of the cities that have proved particularly adept at securing community development grants, such as Baltimore or Tulsa, however, would find themselves with a significantly smaller fraction of the total federal effort after the hold-harmless provisions expired. Dallas, Phoenix, and the other cities, which for philosophical or other reasons have not been active participants in existing community development programs, would gain considerably under the Better Communities Act. Of more significance than the winners and losers among specific governments is the shift in community development decision-making power implied by the Better Communities Act. Urban counties and states, most of which have not heretofore played an active role in community development programs, would exercise control over 40 percent of the money. Those jurisdictions presumably would spread the urban county allocations among the metropolitan communities of less than 50,000 persons, while the states would have broader discretion in distributing their resources. Although the federal government would deal directly with far fewer recipients of community development funds than it has in the past, the total number of

Table 5-7. Distribution of $2.3 Billion According to the Better Communities Act Formula, and Prior Program Experience, by Region and Selected Governments
Millions of dollars

Region or government	Prior program experience[a]	Better Communities Act[b]
United States, total	2,300	2,300
Region		
Northeast	738	619
North Central	530	518
South	661	639
West	345	453
Type of government		
Cities of over 1 million	316	338
Cities of 500,000 to 1 million	341	236
Cities of 150,000 to 500,000	491	288
Urban counties[e]	85	425
State (discretionary funds)[d]	...	567
Selected local governments		
New York City	107	149
Chicago	50	61
Los Angeles	46	48
Baltimore	39	18
San Francisco	33	12
Minneapolis	20	6
Tulsa	15	5
Wichita	15	4
Dallas	3	14
Phoenix	1	9
Omaha	1	5
Miami	2	9
El Paso	1	8

Source: Unpublished data from the Department of Housing and Urban Development. Figures may not add to totals because of rounding.

a. Derived from the average of grants and loans received by each community during the five fiscal years ending in 1972 from the seven programs consolidated under the Better Communities Act. Special adjustments are made in certain cases for communities that did not participate in some of the programs in the early part of the period. For comparative purposes these figures have been inflated so that they add to $2.3 billion.

b. Estimated distribution of funds after all "hold-harmless" provisions (discussed in the text) have lapsed. Based on preliminary figures that do not take account of the changes in metropolitan areas announced by the Office of Management and Budget on April 27, 1973.

c. Counties in metropolitan areas with population exceeding 200,000, exclusive of cities within the county of over 50,000 inhabitants.

d. Fifty percent of the state discretionary funds under the Better Communities Act would have to be passed on to local governments in metropolitan areas. The remainder could be distributed to any local governments in the state.

municipalities benefiting from federal community development money might increase substantially.

The prospect for passage of an urban special revenue sharing program to replace existing categorical grants in this area is brighter than that for the other block grant proposals. Last year the Senate passed such a program as part of the omnibus Housing and Urban Development Act of 1972. The concerned subcommittees in the House seemed willing to accept the plan, but the bill was never voted on by the full House. The program worked out by congressional committees last year, however, required that HUD approve applications of big cities to use the funds made available by formula. In other words, it was more like a consolidation and simplification of existing grants than an automatic revenue sharing program. The relevant interest groups on the whole have been willing to support the concept of block grants for community development if sufficient funding for such a program is guaranteed. Mayors have been anxious to get more control over community development grants, which are now often made to specialized local agencies that may have closer relations with HUD than with local political forces. The final factor that augurs well for the political prospects of the proposal is that the administration, having impounded the funds needed for new commitments under the existing categorical grants, is giving the recipients a choice between revenue sharing and nothing.

Three major issues are raised by the administration's urban revenue sharing proposal. The first of these has to do with the amount of funds provided. As an earlier section of this chapter briefly explained, new grant commitments under the seven existing programs have already been curtailed and will drop to zero in fiscal 1974. Since many of those programs involve large-scale projects, under which federal expenditures are paid out gradually over many years as work is completed, spending under previous commitments will continue at a high though gradually declining level for some time. In 1974, urban communities will have no money for new projects, and even in 1975, $1.7 billion of the $2.3 billion provided in the President's proposal will have to be used by recipients to pay for work being completed under old commitments, leaving only $560 million for discretionary use. Not until fiscal 1978 will the full $2.3 billion in grants under urban special revenue sharing be available for commitment to new projects (Table 5-8). The apparent reason for this schedule is the administration's desire to avoid a "doubling up" of federal expenditures during the transition to the new program. Under the new program, funds will be disbursed in full to recipient governments each year. If, therefore, the entire $2.3 billion had been made available to

Table 5-8. Federal Funds Available for New Commitments and Federal Expenditures under the Administration's Urban Special Revenue Sharing Proposal and Predecessor Programs, Fiscal Years 1972–77[a]

Millions of dollars

Description	1972	1973	1974	1975	1976	1977
Funds available for new commitments	2,471	2,379	0	560	1,700	2,200
Predecessor programs	2,471	2,379	0	0	0	0
Available under special revenue sharing	...	...	...	560	1,700	2,200
Federal expenditures	1,987	1,804	1,906	2,300	2,300	2,300
Used to liquidate predecessor programs	1,987	1,804	1,906	1,740	600	100
Available for other uses	0	0	0	560	1,700	2,200

Sources: Same as Table 5-2.

a. See the text for a discussion of the urban revenue sharing proposal of the administration as presented in the 1974 budget documents.

communities for discretionary use in fiscal 1974, total federal spending on the program would have been $4.3 billion—$2.0 billion to pay off the continuing work on prior grants and $2.3 billion in disbursements to communities under the new program. Avoidance of this "doubling up" led to the requirement that communities first use the special revenue sharing money to pay for ongoing work under the old program, leaving only the residual funds for new projects. The consequence of this decision will be a sharp dip, extending over many years, in funds available to mayors to make new commitments. Correspondingly, if mayors commit the new grant funds for projects that take a long time to complete, the flow of local spending for community development purposes will decline in the immediate future.

A second issue concerns the "lumpy" nature of community development activities. Major projects for urban rehabilitation are not one-year affairs. Long-term plans for land acquisition, relocation of residents, construction, and development are involved. Because of the inevitable uncertainties in planning, frequent modifications in development activities are necessary. Nevertheless, if publicly controlled development is to proceed, funds for more than a year ahead must be committed. Under the existing urban grants, particularly urban renewal and the various facilities programs, federal grant commitments in any one year tended to be concentrated on a limited number of communities, even though when averaged over a number of years the grants have been much more broadly distributed. Concentration of grants made it possible to provide individual communities with the larger lump-sum commitments needed for long-term development. Under the new program, each year's funds will be widely dispersed among a large number of communities. Theoretically, local officials, to the extent that they could count on a continuing stream of appropriations by the Congress, might be able to make long-term commitments for the future use of those funds. In practice, however, legal and financial obstacles would probably make this impossible. As a consequence, it is quite likely that funds under the new program will be used for smaller projects and for financing ongoing services, at the expense of major urban rehabilitation programs. While there is no a priori reason to assume that this is undesirable, the change will clearly alter the nature of the federal impact on urban development.

The third issue is related to control over the use of funds. There are two aspects of this problem. As an earlier section of this chapter pointed out, the national goals to which federal urban development grants are addressed do not require detailed federal specification of precisely what projects or services are to be undertaken in each local community. From this standpoint, the existing programs are unnecessarily restrictive of communities and the administration's proposals introduce a very desirable degree of flexibility. But national goals imply strong concern about targeting—there is a national interest in ensuring that a substantial portion of these federal grants be used for the benefit of residents of low-income neighborhoods. Consolidating the various programs and converting from project to formula grants, as in the administration's proposals, will in effect remove federal control over targeting. In many central cities, the growing political power of minority groups may be sufficient to enforce appropriate targeting. But in a large number of communities this may not be the case. Moreover, current federal grants, used for large-scale demolition and reconstruction, are hedged about with specific protections for residents, such as provision of housing for people of low and moderate incomes in urban renewal projects and requirements that displaced residents be helped to find decent housing elsewhere. While enforcement of these facets of urban renewal and other grants has been spotty, they have undoubtedly turned the course of development projects in a healthy direction. A broad formula grant, as proposed by the administration, even if accompanied by appropriate statutory language, could substantially reduce the effect of these safeguards.

Alternative Approaches

The first major problem discussed above—the sharp dip in discretionary funds available to local communities under the administration's proposal—could be overcome without causing a "doubling up" of federal cash outlays in the transition years. Starting in 1974, the urban revenue sharing grant could make available $2.3 billion in commitment authority, under the rules and distributional formula proposed by the administration. But communities would not be required to pay old commitments out of the new money—these would be paid by the federal government, as is now the case. However, having provided the $2.3 billion in new commitment authority, the federal government would then stipulate a maximum rate at which it would furnish cash to pay off commitments made under the new grant. At present, given the type of projects undertaken with the seven existing grants, there is a long lag between commitments and cash outlays. Stipulating a gradual cash payout of the new commitments therefore should not cause local communities any hardship. They could immediately undertake new projects and programs, subject only to managing the resulting cash flow so as not to exceed the stipulated maximum.

The budgetary cost of this modification would range from zero, if the stipulated relationship of cash flow to project commitments was set at the average relationship under existing programs, to some positive amount, if the cash flow was assumed to speed up in the new program (which is likely). For purposes of budgetary estimation we have assumed some moderate doubling up, amounting to $600 million in fiscal 1974 and $1 billion in 1975, which will decline to zero by 1978 as the transition to the new program is completed.

A much more fundamental restructuring of the proposed special revenue sharing program would be in order if the second and third problems discussed above were given great weight. An alternative attempting to deal with those problems while retaining much of the flexibility of the administration's proposal could be constructed as follows:

1. Seventy-five percent of the funds for urban community development would be made available for all the purposes now allowed in the administration's proposal, on a guaranteed four-year basis. The administration, for example, contemplates $2.3 billion a year, which over four years amounts to $9.2 billion. Under the alternative proposal, 75

percent of this, or $6.9 billion, would be appropriated in the first year and remain available over the four-year period. By this means, communities would be able to make large lump-sum commitments. The remaining 25 percent would be subject to annual appropriation, which the Congress could increase or decrease as it saw fit.

2. Communities would be free to commit the 75 percent for projects or programs at whatever pace met their objectives. But, as suggested above, to avoid the "doubling up" problem the federal government would stipulate the maximum cash flow which could be claimed each year to pay off those commitments.

3. The program would include several specifications on the use of funds. In each community, a certain proportion would have to be used for programs and projects in low-income areas of the city, this proportion being higher than the ratio of the residents of those areas to the total population of the community; and in all projects involving demolition of housing and community facilities in low-income areas, equivalent housing and facilities would have to be provided for displaced residents.

Under the existing categorical urban grants, the federal government approves each project separately. Targeting restrictions are, in theory at least, enforceable. But enforcing the targeting restrictions in a formula block grant will not be so easy. Communities could use the federal funds, for example, to replace projects and programs previously carried out in the target areas with local money and devote the funds thereby saved to tax reductions or to expenditures in other parts of the community. Regulations will have to be written establishing criteria and calling for the submission of data to minimize the diversion of targeted funds.

Even with such regulations, enforcement will be difficult. One possible, if somewhat novel, means of enforcement would be through an appeals process. Instead of poring over thousands of project applications, as is now the case, federal technical experts could form the staff of an "administrative appeals" body. Groups of citizens who believed that the targeting and safeguards were not being met, according to the law and published regulations, could appeal to the administrative body, which would judge the evidence, make appropriate findings, and, where relevant, require communities to conform their uses of funds to the law and regulations. To minimize frivolous cases, the law could require that an appeal be based on a petition signed by some substantial portion of the citizens of an affected area.

There is a wide range of levels at which the urban community development programs could be funded, and the funds could be made available in a number of ways—through a continuation of existing categorical grants, adoption of the administration's proposal, or enactment of the modified program discussed above. Changing the administration's program to take care of the "doubling up" problem without the sharp dip in commitments now contemplated would add up to $1 billion to budget expenditures in the next few years. To emphasize the use of future incremental budget resources for federal aid to urban developmental projects, in either targeted or nontargeted ways, the program could be increased sharply. Raising the program from $2.3 billion to $5.0 billion by 1978, for example, would increase the annual developmental grants under the administration's program from $17 to $37 per capita in Detroit, from $25 to $54 in Jackson, Mississippi, and from $8 to $17 in a wealthy area like Montgomery County, Maryland. Table 5-9 shows the expenditure consequences of some alternative possibilities. (Budget expenditures, under the maximum cash flow procedure, would tend to grow more slowly than grant commitments.)

Table 5-9. Federal Budget Outlays under Alternative Urban Community Development Programs, Fiscal Years 1974, 1976, and 1978
Billions of dollars

Alternative	1974	1976	1978[a]
1. Administration proposal	1.9	2.3	2.3
	Additional cost		
2. Begin $2.3 billion program in 1974 and use maximum cash flow technique[b]	0.6	1.0	0.0
3. Increase program to $5 billion commitment level by 1978[c]	0.6	0.9	1.6
4. Increase program to $7.5 billion commitment level by 1978[b]	0.6	1.5	3.7

Source: Same as Table 5-2.
a. Under alternatives 3 and 4, budget outlays would continue to increase for several years after 1978.
b. In 1975 additional expenditures would be $1.0 billion.
c. Assumes use of maximum cash flow limitations.

Manpower Training*

In fiscal 1972 the federal government committed $2 billion to its major manpower training and work support activities. Funds for these programs were reduced slightly in fiscal 1973, to $1.7 billion, and will rise in fiscal 1974 to $1.9 billion. Some major changes in emphasis have been made, and a large number of the component programs will be consolidated, through administrative action, into a manpower special revenue sharing fund.

For purposes of evaluation the various manpower training programs can conveniently be divided into three groups: (1) general manpower training and job placement programs; (2) the separate program of training and placement for welfare recipients; and (3) federally supported temporary jobs for disadvantaged young people.

General Manpower Training

The original Manpower Development and Training Act of 1962 (MDTA) was launched in a period of high unemployment. Its sponsors feared that general economic recovery, while reducing the overall unemployment rate, would pass many workers by. Automation, technological change, and industrial relocation were seen as making the skills of many workers obsolete and creating a demand, largely unmet, for workers with newer skills. Training workers in new skills and for new jobs would make it possible for them to find employment and would enable employers to fill job vacancies, thereby easing the upward pressure on wages and prices that would otherwise accompany a return to economic prosperity. In its early years, the typical trainee sought by the MDTA programs was a blue-collar worker with a high school education and a strong attachment to the labor force who was facing extended unemployment and needed training to improve his skills or to learn new ones.

Two developments in the 1960s shifted the emphasis of the program. As economic recovery proceeded, the overall unemployment rate was gradually reduced. Unemployment among adult (twenty-five to sixty-four) male workers fell to a very low level (less than 2 percent by 1968). The earlier fears of automation-induced joblessness among these workers receded. Simultaneously, the country turned its atten-

* Prepared with the assistance of Michael Timpane.

tion to the problems of poverty and to the "hard-core" unemployed—those without long experience at one job, suffering educational and cultural disadvantages, many of them black and victims of the additional sting of racial discrimination in job seeking. The Economic Opportunity Act of 1964 provided funds for manpower training programs for disadvantaged workers, and the training programs under MDTA also began to shift their efforts toward this group. By 1971, about 60 percent of the MDTA participants were the disadvantaged.

At present, four major types of general training activities are carried out by the federal government. Under the MDTA *institutional* programs, unemployed and underemployed persons (mostly poor) receive formal education and training in skills in the classroom. Funds are apportioned to states by a formula based on the size of the labor force, the unemployment level, and other job-related factors. These funds are granted to local project sponsors by the Labor Department and constitute 90–100 percent of the support of specific training projects. Trainees take job-preparation courses, usually for a year or less, while drawing modest training allowances if they are heads of households or deprived youths.

A second program, MDTA *on-the-job training*, is run by state employment service offices with federal funds. These offices negotiate contracts with public and private employers in each state to cover the cost of on-the-job training for persons who could not, in the judgment of the employment service, otherwise obtain full-time employment. In 1967 a third element was added, the national *JOBS* (Job Opportunities in the Business Sector) program, jointly administered by the Department of Labor and the National Alliance of Businessmen, representing a number of relatively large business firms. Partly through subsidies and partly through unsubsidized arrangements, national firms agree to hire, train, and upgrade disadvantaged workers.

Several specialized programs are also conducted. One provides subsidies to government agencies to hire and train disadvantaged workers for public service careers. Another provides jobs in conservation activities in rural areas. And under the concentrated employment program, the Labor Department seeks to concentrate and coordinate its manpower services in some eighty areas where large numbers of disadvantaged persons live. In these areas enrollees receive the whole range of services—testing, basic education, training, counseling, and placement.

The *Job Corps* is a national training program sponsored by the federal government for severely disadvantaged young people. Established in 1964, it was originally a residential program, under which the trainees lived at the Job Corps center. Later, some of the centers were converted, partially or fully, to nonresidential training schools. The initial costs were very high (over $8,000 per enrollee in 1967), but they have since declined year by year. In 1972 some 23,000 man-years of training were provided by the Job Corps.

The performance of the various training programs must be considered in the context of national employment policies. From the viewpoint of the trainees, the purpose of the programs is to increase the likelihood of finding and keeping a job and to provide the skills for better-paying jobs. But by itself, this objective would merely mean reshuffling the existing number of good jobs—the success of program trainees would be at the expense of other workers.[15] Manpower training programs therefore have to be viewed in the light of overall labor market and general economic policies aimed at creating a larger number of decent jobs.

Except in periods of general recession, as Chapter 3 pointed out, the problem of disadvantaged workers is not so much lengthy unemployment as sporadic employment with bouts of unemployment between jobs. Such workers have limited access to the steady better-paying jobs with career opportunities that are available to most of the labor force. The problem is greatest for young workers, particularly blacks, and for women, especially mothers receiving Aid to Families with Dependent Children (AFDC). For white men unemployment is a very limited problem except in isolated pockets of economic distress—during periods of general prosperity the unemployment rate for this group drops below 2 percent. For black men the problem is greater, but less than for black youths.

The prospects for disadvantaged workers improve in periods of sustained prosperity. Employers are increasingly short of skilled and semiskilled labor. Job vacancies rise, and all along the line workers have a better chance of moving up. Some severely disadvantaged workers, unemployed or working at unrewarding jobs, are able to

15. Some argue that even this would be a desirable outcome. Insofar as disadvantaged and minority workers are concerned, such a process would at least put them on equal footing with other groups. In practice, however, if additional good jobs are not available, those displaced by successful trainees are likely to be themselves disadvantaged.

transfer to steadier high-paying work. The pool of labor available to fill the casual, dirty, low-paying jobs in society—dishwashers, porters, maids, busboys, casual laborers—begins to shrink. If prosperity continues long enough, these jobs have to be upgraded, with better wages and working conditions, and those who use the services they provide have to pay higher prices.

This "natural" process of upgrading, however, takes time and is often inefficient. Unfilled job vacancies multiply, wages are bid up rapidly, and inflation sets in. Ideally, federal manpower training programs should accelerate the upgrading process and increase its efficiency. By providing the disadvantaged with skills and job counseling the programs can help them move out of casual low-paying work into the better jobs which prosperity creates and, by enabling employers to fill job vacancies more speedily, reduce inflationary pressures. This is not to say that training alone is sufficient. Mothers with small children may need child care services, and many workers require extensive job counseling and placement efforts.

In sum, what government manpower training programs seek to achieve by upgrading the salable skills of disadvantaged workers could also be done by sustained economic prosperity, which forces private employers to upgrade workers. The major objective of manpower training programs is to make the upgrading process more efficient and thereby both improve the chances of disadvantaged workers and reduce the inflation that goes with high employment.

To judge how well the manpower training programs perform this function, it would be necessary not only to evaluate the outcome of the program for those who were actually trained, but also to consider what impact the programs had on the labor market process through which workers, particularly disadvantaged workers, are hired and upgraded in periods of prosperity. The latter aspect is virtually impossible to gauge. During the years of high prosperity and tight labor markets (1968–69), some 300,000 to 400,000 people were served each year by the general manpower training programs. In a labor force of 80 million people, with a labor turnover of perhaps 20 million a year, the effect of these programs cannot be identified.

The manpower training programs have usually been evaluated on a more limited basis by comparing their costs with the increased earnings they produce for enrollees, through higher wages and greater employment. The evaluations that have been done suffer from many problems—particularly from their inability to follow trainees for a sufficiently long period after leaving a program and the impossibility of determining the extent to which successful trainees displace other disadvantaged workers.

Within these limitations, the major studies of the MDTA programs, both institutional and on-the-job, indicate that they have been neither a disaster nor a roaring success. The higher earnings of trainees upon graduation (relative to those in similar circumstances who were not in the program) would, if sustained for a period of years, exceed the costs of the program. Both advantaged and disadvantaged workers shared in the gains, but the earnings of the latter group after completing the program, though increased, still tended to average below the poverty level. In these studies, on-the-job training programs generally seemed to show better results than institutional training. But an important part of the gains from the program seems to have been due to the immediate employment effects of counseling and job placement services, rather than to permanently higher earnings from training in skills; there is some evidence that after a period of time the wages of workers who have not been in the program catch up with the wages of those who have.

The JOBS program has not been evaluated. One large survey showed that in 1968 the average annual income of participants rose from $1,500 to $2,600 in the first year after placement.[16] But as JOBS was designed to hire the unemployed, this is not surprising. Since 1968 was a year of high employment, many of these workers would have found jobs anyway—how much better off they were under the JOBS program is not known. Moreover, the program was conceived to meet the unemployment problems of disadvantaged workers, which persist even in a period of high prosperity. It was only beginning to operate when the economy fell into a recession. Firms have been unable or unwilling to fulfill JOBS quotas and contracts, placements have sometimes been bogus or inappropriate, and there is reason to fear that JOBS employees who are earning somewhat more are doing so at the expense of unsubsidized fellow workers. How JOBS might work in a period of sustained prosperity cannot be predicted from experience.

16. *Studies in Public Welfare: The Effectiveness of Manpower Training Programs: A Review of Research on the Impact on the Poor*, a Staff Study prepared for the use of the Subcommittee on Fiscal Policy of the Joint Economic Committee, 92 Cong. 2 sess. (1972), p. 59.

The early evaluations of the Job Corps stood in some contrast to those of MDTA. Working in a novel, experimental format with limited groups of "hard-core" young people, the Job Corps compiled an early record of astonishing costs, high attrition rates, modest educational gains, and visible economic benefits only for those trainees who stayed on for most or all of the program. Unlike MDTA, however, the Job Corps record seems to be improving with time. Better screening and counseling services, together with general economies of operation, have sustained the reported educational and economic benefits and lowered costs. Attrition remains a serious problem. While no study has yet established a high rate of economic return for the Job Corps investment, those who have recently studied the program are not ready to declare it a failure. Moreover, the costs of the Job Corps may have been overstated since the computations did not take into account the savings from other income transfers, which would have been paid out had these youths not been in the Job Corps. Finally, the Job Corps, unlike the other programs, is focused entirely on the neediest, most disadvantaged young workers. For this limited group, the Job Corps approach may be the only way to help.

From their beginning in 1962, the training programs contained a modest component—the Community Work and Training program, and later, the Work Experience and Training program—aimed specifically at *welfare recipients*. As the 1960s progressed, however, the problem was transformed from one of minor to one of major social significance, as the national welfare system grew swiftly despite economic prosperity and falling unemployment rates. In 1967 this concern with welfare growth led to the creation of the Work Incentive Program (WIN), which went beyond its predecessors in offering the recipients, mainly AFDC mothers, an incentive to accept training and employment. Before WIN, income from work was deducted dollar-for-dollar from relief payments; under WIN, the worker retains "$30 plus one-third" of every month's earnings. In addition, the program has tried to cope with the welfare recipients' need for individual attention and support both during and after the training. It has expanded day care services for mothers, increased its counseling and placement services, and provided subsidies for employers to hire WIN trainees. In 1972, Congress made WIN registration mandatory for welfare heads of household. Funds for the program have grown sharply, from $117 million in fiscal 1969 to $293 million in 1973, and, unlike other manpower programs, a further expansion to $534 million is proposed for 1974.

The gross statistics on the WIN program suggest that it has a limited usefulness. Through 1971 the number of welfare recipients placed in jobs by WIN was insignificant—about 7 percent of those who were referred to the program. The new mandatory registration (enforced by the threat of losing welfare benefits), subsidization of private jobs, and expansion of child care and supportive services were seen as means of improving this performance. And there has been some improvement. WIN registered almost 600,000 "employables" during the first half of fiscal 1973, and it placed 60,000 registrants in jobs in the same period. But most of the jobs were low paying, and this limited progress was achieved at great cost. Costs per recipient for child care, support, and job subsidies have multiplied several times since 1971 and account for most of the rise in overall program costs. Moreover, much of WIN's short-run job placement program may have resulted from its professed "creaming" of the best of the new registrants and from the recent upturn in employment. Some of the recent progress, however, may also be due to more effective job training in WIN.

Claims that WIN reduces the cost of welfare programs have not been substantiated. There is evidence that in states with high welfare benefits WIN's primary result is to draw some working heads of low-income households back onto welfare, through which they can obtain free child care and supportive services and modestly increased income.[17]

Once the existing reservoir of mandatory registrants is processed through the program this year and next, WIN will be concerned chiefly with the smaller universe of new welfare registrants, who fall into three groups. A large number, experience shows, remain on welfare a relatively short time, since they find jobs on their own or leave welfare for reasons not associated with employment. WIN may help some of these find better jobs than they otherwise would. Some new registrants have preschool children or health problems and will, under current rules, be excused from mandatory participation in the program. Of the remainder, an indeterminate but relatively small number, who would have remained on welfare for a long time, may find em-

17. See, for example, Gary L. Appel, *Effects of a Financial Incentive on AFDC Employment: Michigan's Experience between July 1969 and July 1970* (Minneapolis: Institute for Interdisciplinary Studies, 1972).

ployment with the help of the panoply of training and supportive services offered by WIN.

Under the Neighborhood Youth Corps (NYC), three programs for young people are carried out. *Summer jobs* are provided for over half a million disadvantaged young people, a majority of whom are blacks in inner cities. An NYC *in-school* part-time employment program provides work experience and earnings to 120,000 youths, while another 50,000 high school dropouts are given work experience (and a small amount of training) in the NYC *out-of-school* program.

In improving the later employability and carnings of enrollees, the NYC programs have not been strikingly successful. Many of the jobs that NYC sponsors do not offer significant training opportunities, although they often provide a familiarization with work that public schools are said to lack. But since these programs are not principally training programs, they must be judged by other criteria. The summer program, with low bureaucratic overhead, provides a substantial income transfer to half a million poor youths in the inner city. The in-school program gives part-time work and some pocket money to youths, many of whom have far fewer opportunities for such work than the rest of the school-age population, and to some extent keeps in-school youth from competing with recent graduates for entry-level jobs.

In sum, of the large array of manpower programs, two are national in scope. The Job Corps is administered by the Labor Department, either directly or through contracts with private firms. The JOBS program, as explained earlier, is chiefly directed toward placing workers with larger national business firms. The other programs are principally carried on through federal grants to sponsors in local communities. In many communities there are not only many different programs, but also several sponsors for each program, leading to a bewildering menu of training, placement, and work support programs.

In recent years the Labor Department has sought to decentralize the operations of its manpower training services. At the state level and in metropolitan areas, Cooperative Area Manpower Planning Systems (CAMPS) have been set up in an attempt to generate state and local manpower planning efforts. CAMPS advisory committees have been created at state and local levels to help governors and mayors plan manpower policies in their areas. The manpower revenue sharing proposals of the administration, discussed below, would turn over much of the responsibility for manpower training decisions to governors and mayors, relying on CAMPS for the necessary planning and coordination at the state and local level.

Administration Proposals

The President's manpower budget for 1974 has three major characteristics:

1. As noted earlier, WIN will be expanded rapidly, from $117 million in fiscal 1969 and $293 million in fiscal 1973 to $534 million in 1974. A significant part of the added funds will be used to increase child care services, the lack of which has proved a bottleneck.

2. Funds for the other programs (measured in terms of commitments) will be reduced from $1.8 billion in 1972 to $1.4 billion in 1973 and to $1.3 billion in 1974.

3. Except for WIN, federal manpower training activities will be converted, through administrative action rather than legislation, into a special revenue sharing program.

Since 1969 the administration, in one form or the other, has advocated the special revenue sharing approach to manpower training. Initially, consolidation was proposed through administrative action; opposition by the Congress led to the abandonment of the proposal. In 1971 and 1972 legislative action was proposed, but Congress did not accept it. In the 1974 budget the administration has returned to the concept of achieving manpower special revenue sharing by administrative measures.

While details of this year's proposal were not available at the time of writing, its essentials are known. The $1.3 billion of manpower training funds would be divided into two parts. The Labor Department would retain one-fourth for research and development, for program supervision, and for the two national programs (JOBS and Job Corps) which would be continued but at a reduced level. The remaining three-fourths would be divided among states and localities according to a formula. Governors and mayors would be free to allocate those funds among the various manpower programs now in existence, to reduce or eliminate some, to increase others, or to devise different kinds of manpower services as they saw the need. The CAMPS advisory committees would be relied on to assist governors and mayors in planning the use of their manpower funds.

A good deal of local discretion to choose trainees and the kinds of skills to be taught already exists within each program. The results have been mixed. However, the effects of granting state and local officials greatly increased discretion in the use of manpower funds cannot be predicted. State and local officials are less likely to be able to assess the changing national labor market and to adapt their training program accordingly. Local union interests may be successful in preventing the manpower programs from training people in skills that they wish to restrict to their members. Yet the federal government has not always been successful in the past in coordinating its manpower training programs with national labor market conditions or in resisting pressures to minimize training in certain skills; and the existing multiplicity of programs resulted more from uncoordinated bureaucratic enterprise than from legislative categorization. In the earlier years of the training programs, before there were federal requirements about allocating substantial sums to the disadvantaged, local choices did not allocate funds in this direction. But times have changed and the past cannot automatically be projected into the future. In essence, there is no reason to believe that decentralization to state and local officials will somehow sharply improve the operations of the manpower training programs. On the other hand, the programs will probably not collapse because of decentralization. Although there will be somewhat less red tape, in some localities the poor will probably get less attention than they do now, and improvement in the coordination of manpower and other national economic policies will be more difficult to achieve.

Alternative Approaches

There are basically two aspects of decentralization in manpower training policy: decentralization of decisions about the kinds of services to be offered and who should provide them; and decentralization of decisions about who should receive the subsidized services. In the first set of decisions, there is fundamentally no reason why decentralization should not go far beyond state and local officials. Why not let the individual, with help and counseling, decide what services he needs and wants and from whom he will get them? The second set of decisions—who should be entitled to the subsidized services—is more properly a matter of national concern, since it essentially involves problems of equal opportunity and national labor markets. This approach was used successfully after World War II in the job-training component of the GI bill. And the same approach, for college-level training, has been incorporated in the newly enacted federal Basic Opportunity Grant program (discussed in Chapter 4).

A manpower voucher program could be designed as an alternative to continuation of the present federally directed manpower training programs or to special revenue sharing. It would replace the current MDTA, JOBS, and Job Corps programs as well as the smaller specialized programs. The Neighborhood Youth Corps, which serves more to transfer income than to provide training, would not be replaced and should be considered separately. The manpower voucher could be modeled after the Basic Opportunity Grant program already enacted for student aid in higher education. Each high school graduate whose family's income was below $11,000 could be offered either a basic grant to attend a college or university or a job-training voucher worth twice as much as the basic grant, but for one year only. Eligibility for using the voucher could continue through the age of twenty-four, by which time most potential beneficiaries would have gained education or job experience *or* have fallen into the more profound personal predicaments that other social programs are better able to handle. This manpower voucher could be used to purchase training at licensed public and private training institutions or to subsidize on-the-job training provided by public or private employers, upon whom might then rest an obligation to employ the trainee for some period of time after the training subsidy expired.

About half of the 4 million persons who graduate from or drop out of high school each year would be eligible because of low family income. Of these, perhaps 800,000 will attend postsecondary institutions under the Basic Grant program or with other financial assistance. If 50 percent of the remainder chose to leave the labor force to go into the armed services or to enter the job market directly, only 600,000 young people would be likely to take the voucher option. At an average entitlement of $1,500 per person, the annual cost would be $900 million. For the first few years, the annual price tag might be somewhat higher as those who had recently left school and were under the age limit took advantage of the new benefit.

For those over twenty-four and already in the labor market or reentering it, one could construct a companion but more modest *re*training grant that would allow for some shorter-term or less intensive training with eligibility occurring when annual income dropped below, say, $5,000. In any given year there might be 5 million wage earners between twenty-four and sixty-five who were unemployed or at work earning less than $5,000 a year and not on welfare. If each year 20 percent of those eligible used a training grant of $500, the annual cost would be another $500 million. In addition, for heads of household who chose to take institutional rather than on-the-job training, a small living allowance of $100 a month might be made available for a period not to exceed six months. This would add perhaps $200 million a year to program costs. (Alternatively, a tougher policy could offer training programs principally at night or on a part-time basis, thereby avoiding the expense of living allowances.)

Finally, in situations where the government felt a special responsibility to provide more intensive retraining opportunities, the size of the voucher and the living allowances could be increased. Such enriched programs could be made available as part of a reconversion program in communities hard hit by defense cutbacks, as an element in readjustment assistance for workers suffering severely from import competition, or as programs of the Job Corps type for severely disadvantaged youths. The added cost of such enrichment would depend on the nature of the reconversion program and the eligibility standards.

Because a manpower voucher program would replace many of the current manpower training programs, its net budgetary costs would be less than the gross costs cited above. A voucher program, with the eligibility provisions spelled out above for the young and for older low-income workers, would cost about $1.6 billion a year, minus $800 million, which the administration estimates would be spent in 1974 on the programs displaced by vouchers. Net costs would therefore be about $800 million a year.

If a voucher program was adopted, provision would have to be made for counseling and job placement services, particularly for the severely disadvantaged, who would need such help in selecting appropriate training opportunities. The vocational education programs of the public school systems might participate in the counseling and placement process. The federal government currently makes available $400 million a year to state employment services for placement and counseling activities. This might be increased to ensure the availability of adequate services.

A voucher system would have many advantages. It could greatly extend the range of training opportunities. Under the current programs, enrollees are often limited to choosing among the relatively few training courses that have been set up under a federally sponsored grant. With vouchers, a wide range of both public and private institutions could offer courses, accepting the voucher in payment. Present programs are also inequitable. Because of limited funds, training opportunities must be rationed, and persons in like circumstances are treated differently. This is true both among the various training programs and between academic (college) and nonacademic (job training) opportunities. The new federal student aid grants already provide some opportunities for the nonacademically inclined person who simply wants good vocational preparation (provided it can be obtained in some academic guise), but such opportunities should be extended to all.

The voucher approach is not without its problems, however. As in the case of government provision of assistance in other fields, such as health insurance, housing allowances, and day care, some government regulation or certification of suppliers will be necessary if trainees are to be protected against fraud and abuse. Firms might seek windfall profits by setting up on-the-job training programs with no real content. Private firms might spring up, offering worthless training courses; public and nonprofit institutions might do the same. Some check on this would come from competition, from counseling, and from neighborhood word-of-mouth information. But on top of this the federal government—perhaps through delegation to state and local agencies —would have to provide standards. The red tape and inefficiencies of such intervention, however, would probably be less than under the current system in which the federal government is directly responsible for supporting inidividual training programs. Finally, a gradual transition to the new program would be advisable, to avoid the abuses and supply shortages that would probably accompany its immediate extension to all eligible recipients.

WIN might also be given a new direction. As an earlier section pointed out, expectations that this program will sharply reduce welfare rolls are unlikely to be realized. Costs for each successfully placed trainee are huge. In its 1974 budget the administration plans to devote $243 million of the $534 million allocated to WIN to child care, counseling, job placement, and other supportive services. The other

$290 million will be used for training and job subsidies. As an alternative, the various supportive services could be continued, and most of the training funds could be used—with a gradual transition—for a voucher program, coordinated with the voucher systems described above. The costs of such a voucher system are hard to estimate, but they are unlikely to be higher, and indeed might be lower, than current WIN expenditures.[18]

The future of the Neighborhood Youth Corps under manpower revenue sharing is uncertain; it will depend on how state and local agencies decide to allocate manpower revenue sharing grants among the different programs. If NYC shared proportionately in the 25 percent reduction in commitments for manpower training programs incorporated in the 1974 budget, the program would decline from $500 million in fiscal 1972 to about $375 million in fiscal 1974. If a manpower voucher program was adopted in place of revenue sharing, separate funding of NYC could continue, more or less along current lines. How large the program should be depends on how one evaluates its merits as a means of modest income support and work experience for disadvantaged young people. Several steps might be taken: funds for the in-school and summer programs could be restored to the fiscal 1972 level and increased beyond that to allow for the inflation that has occurred. With these funds the NYC could make summer jobs available to about half a million disadvantaged youths and continue its modest program of part-time jobs for in-school and out-of-school youth. At the same time, if a comprehensive manpower voucher system was enacted, reduction or elimination of the out-of-school program could be considered. The budgetary cost of the first action would be approximately offset by the savings from the second.

Table 5-10 summarizes the expenditure consequences of the alternative manpower programs outlined here, computed in terms of changes related to the administration's budget.

Conclusions

The administration's proposals for the future of the social grant programs have two major characteristics. First, the total budgetary resources devoted to these programs would be reduced; second, in a

18. If a large-scale child care system, along the lines discussed in Chapter 4, was adopted, the $117 million for child care in WIN could be eliminated.

Table 5-10. Net Federal Cost of Alternative Manpower Training Programs,
Fiscal Years 1974, 1976, and 1978[a]

Millions of dollars

Alternative	*1974*	*1976*	*1978*
1. Manpower voucher program, total	500	1,000	1,075
Gross costs	500	1,800	1,925
Reduction in existing grants	...	−800	−850
2. Restore Neighborhood Youth Corps (NYC) summer and in-school programs to 1972 level and eliminate NYC out-of-school program	——No net cost——		
3. Revise Work Incentive Program; provide services but rely on voucher for training	——No net cost——		

Source: Authors' estimates.
a. Cost in terms of changes from the administration's program as presented in the 1974 budget documents.

number of areas grants would be consolidated into large blocks, restrictions and regulations on the use of grant funds would be lessened, and state and local governments would be given greater discretion in spending the money.

The alternative approaches discussed in this chapter have several features. In most, though not all, cases, they would require additional budgetary funds. Most of them have major distributional objectives: narrowing disparities among jurisdictions (educational equalization) or directing services toward particular groups (compensatory education, targeted urban development grants, manpower training vouchers, health service developmental grants). Like the administration's proposals, they generally look to less federal control over what kinds of services are delivered but, unlike some of the administration measures, retain controls over who gets the services. In several cases—for instance, health services and manpower training—the alternative approaches outlined here provide even greater decentralization of decision making than the administration proposes, since they rely on voucher or insurance systems which give individual recipients, rather than state and local governments, control over the specific kinds of services to be purchased.

6. Investing in the Physical Environment

THE FEDERAL GOVERNMENT will spend $15 billion in fiscal 1974 on activities designed to affect the physical environment (see Table 6-1). Outlays for various forms of transportation, principally highways and aviation, account for 60 percent of this total. Construction and operation of inland waterway projects—flood control, navigation, irrigation, and hydroelectric power—consume 19 percent. Expenditures for the control of pollution, primarily grants to municipalities for the construction of waste treatment plants, add another 14 percent, and recreation expenditures about 5 percent.

About half of the federal expenditures in this area are grants-in-aid to states or local governments, for investment in highways, airports, urban mass transportation, and municipal waste treatment plants. The other half mainly supports direct federal activities, for construction and operation of dams, levees, and other waterway projects, national park sites, and airways navigation and control facilities; for the operations of the Coast Guard; and for paying the federal costs of regulating air and water pollution. A small but growing federal operating subsidy is paid to Amtrak, the quasi-public corporation that under the Rail Passenger Service Act of 1970 took over the operation of passenger trains on the nation's railroads.

These activities are aimed at a number of different national objec-

Table 6-1. Federal Expenditures on the Physical Environment, by Program, Selected Fiscal Years, 1950–74

Millions of dollars

Program	1950	1960	1965	1970	Estimate 1973	Estimate 1974
Transportation, total	1,152	4,001	5,615	6,921	8,708	8,984
Highway	497	3,106	4,026	4,700	5,180	5,079
Urban mass transit	...	...	11	106	460	661
Air	159	508	795	1,187	1,684	1,810
Water	447	509	728	909	1,200	1,282
Other	49	−122	55	19	184	152
Other, total	876	1,409	2,197	2,834	5,030	5,794
Environmental protection	0	40	134	350	1,148	2,128
Water resources	831	1,264	1,848	1,980	3,065	2,795
Recreation	45	105	215	370	641	701
Water and sewer facilities[a]	0	0	0	134	176	170
Physical environment, total	2,028	5,410	7,812	9,755	13,738	14,778

Sources: Derived from *The Budget of the United States Government*, and accompanying *Appendix* and *Special Analyses*, various years.

a. Programs of the U.S. Department of Agriculture and the U.S. Department of Housing and Urban Development.

tives and are supported in many different ways by the federal government, but they have a common characteristic—the federal government is directly involved in the construction or operation of major physical systems. And this characteristic gives rise to certain problems peculiar to this category of federal activities.

The Rationale for Federal Involvement

In the categorical social programs, federal involvement in the provision of services at the state and local level stems principally from national concern about a fair distribution of services, equality of opportunity, and support for innovative systems of delivery. While not completely absent, these considerations play a much smaller role in the fields of transportation and physical environment. Federal activities in the latter area are primarily the result of concern about "spillovers." By their very nature, transportation networks, environmental control, and waterway development cannot be left to the unaided and uncoordinated actions of industry or state and local governments.

Interstate and intercity transportation networks provide benefits that extend far beyond the communities in which they are physically located. Left to their own devices, states and localities would undoubtedly invest too little in highways and airports, many of whose benefits accrue to citizens of other communities. Federal programs of grants-in-aid for these purposes were undertaken both to achieve a desirable level of investment and to impose some centralized planning on national transportation networks. In several cases the nature of the facility demands a single national system—the air-navigation and traffic-control system that the federal government constructs and operates is an obvious example.

Environmental pollution is no respecter of state or local boundaries. Regulation of air and water pollution by private industry has gradually been shifted from state to federal control. Public investment in this area is required chiefly for the construction of municipal waste treatment plants. Upstream communities, on their own, inevitably underinvest in treatment facilities, since their citizens would be paying taxes to provide cleaner water mainly for the benefit of those living downstream. In addition to regulating pollution discharges, therefore, the federal government provides grants-in-aid for the construction of such plants.

Waterway development also affects citizens living in many different political jurisdictions. Navigation, irrigation, hydroelectric power, and flood control projects provide benefits along whole river basins and need to be planned, constructed, and operated in that context. Individual states or communities in a river basin could, in theory, join together in a regional authority to undertake these activities. But it was decided long ago that, rather than provide grants-in-aid to some regional collection of state and local governments, the federal government would construct and operate major waterway developments itself.

In 1962, the federal government began for the first time to provide grants-in-aid to local communities for subsidizing investment in *public mass transportation*—subways, bus lines, and the like. The rationale for a federal program cannot be based on spillover effects—at least in the sense that it is for intercity transportation, pollution control, or waterway projects. The benefits of urban mass transit are usually confined to the citizens of the metropolitan areas in which the systems are located. A number of reasons have been cited for the federal role in this activity. First, the fragmented nature of local governments in metropolitan areas, which may contain anywhere from dozens to hundreds of separate jurisdictions, makes it very difficult to plan and finance mass transit systems—a federal role is needed.[1] Second, the generally accepted role of the federal government in dealing with air pollution problems may warrant a federal subsidy to improve mass transit systems as a means of reducing the use of automobiles and the pollution they cause. Third, improved mass transit may open up greater employment opportunities for disadvantaged inner-city residents, who do not have automobiles for commuting to work.

The major reason, however, for the mass transit subsidy program—which has been repeatedly renewed and enlarged in the past ten years—is the belief on the part of the Congress and the executive that the decline in the patronage of mass transit systems since the Second World War threatens the viability of central cities, that this threat is a matter of national concern, that financially hard-pressed cities cannot afford to make major investments in these systems, and that therefore federal grant assistance is warranted.

While not the only ones, these are the major areas of the civilian budget that involve the federal government in the construction or operation of large physical systems. This chapter examines some of the important problems of program design and emphasis which have to be faced in developing a federal budget strategy for this area during the next five years.

Some Basic Problems

As it is now carried out, federal support for transportation and environmental systems brings with it a number of problems. First, there is the problem of perverse incentives. The federal government makes grants to communities to cover a large part of the cost of constructing and purchasing equipment for mass transit systems and municipal waste treatment plants, but does not subsidize the operation of these systems. Inefficiency and ineffectiveness are the inevitable results. The decisions of operators of mass transit systems are biased toward facilities with heavy capital but low operating costs (for example, rapid rail systems rather than bus lines). Repair and maintenance, for which the transit system pays all the costs, are neglected, while capital equip-

---

1. Where the metropolitan area lies entirely within a single state, however, this justification for federal, rather than state, intervention has much less force.

ment, which federal grants support, is replaced prematurely. Similarly, after waste treatment plants are constructed with federal money, local budgets fail to include sufficient funds to operate and maintain them effectively.[2]

Direct federal investments are made in very expensive waterway developments, which confer sizable benefits on those who do business or live in their vicinity. These beneficiaries pay only a small fraction of project costs—the general taxpayer foots most of the bill. Even though the benefits of many projects are less than the costs, they are far greater than the charges to beneficiaries. As a consequence local groups urge their congressmen to support uneconomic federal waterways projects, and the log-rolling process in Congress ensures that year after year the "pork-barrel" river and harbor bill contains far more projects than are proposed in the budget.

The second problem is the categorical nature of some of the grant programs, which arises principally in connection with the various federal grants for urban transportation. The issue is, should money now allocated to urban areas for interstate and other highways from the federal Highway Trust Fund be available for supporting mass transportation at the discretion of local officials? Ideological labels tend to get confused in this controversy—that is, many of those who question special revenue sharing because it is free of federal controls at the same time vigorously support the right of urban communities to choose whether they will use grants from the Highway Trust Fund for highways or for mass transit.

A third major problem, not peculiar to the programs in this category, is the appropriate level of federal support. Congress and the administration differ sharply over the level of federal grants for waste treatment facilities. Congress has authorized $11 billion in grants during fiscal years 1973 and 1974, but the administration plans to use only half that amount. Similarly, the administration, following a precedent set by its predecessor, has been giving the states substantially lower highway grants than Congress has authorized. And finally, the 1974 budget contemplates a major reduction in federal spending

2. There are other incentive problems in the federal government's current approach to controlling air and water pollution, particularly in its regulation of industry. These problems were discussed in Charles L. Schultze and others, *Setting National Priorities: The 1972 Budget* and *The 1973 Budget* (Brookings Institution, 1971 and 1972). The discussion in this book concentrates on the incentive problem in the grant program for construction of waste treatment plants.

on waterways, which, as noted above, are a favorite area for congressional additions to the budget.

The remainder of this chapter examines these problems and offers some alternative proposals for this federal role in three specific areas: urban transportation, treatment of municipal wastes, and investment in waterways projects.

Urban Transportation

The federal government's support for urban transportation has about tripled in the past fifteen years. As Table 6-2 shows, the bulk of that support is for urban highway construction; assistance for mass transit, introduced in the mid-1960s, grew slowly for a while but is now approaching $1 billion a year.

Federal grants for the construction of highways come from the Highway Trust Fund, which is fed by federal taxes on gasoline, oil, tires, tubes, trucks, and buses. Basically, two kinds of federal assistance are available: grants covering 90 percent of the costs of constructing the 42,500-mile Interstate Highway System and grants that pay 70 percent of the costs for other highway and highway-related investments. Urban areas receive a share of both kinds of grants, but they are made to state governments, whose highway departments have a major voice in the location and design of federally aided highways. Until recently, highways in urban areas were not distinguished from

Table 6-2. Federal Financial Commitments for Urban Transportation, by Use of Funds, Selected Fiscal Years, 1960–74

Millions of dollars

Use of funds	1960	1965	1970	1973	1974
Urban highways, total	1,080	1,587	1,934	2,045	2,100
Interstate	880	1,357	1,682	1,400	1,300
Other	200	230	252	645	800
Mass transit, total	...	60	160	980	1,000
Capital grants[a]	...	60	133	864	872
Other, including research and development	...	...	27	116	128
Total	...	1,647	2,094	3,025	3,100

Sources: *The Budget of the United States Government—Appendix*, various years; except interstate for 1960–70, which are from U.S. Department of Transportation, Office of the Assistant Secretary for Policy and International Affairs, *1972 National Transportation Report: Present Status, Future Alternatives* (1972), Table III-18; and for 1973 and 1974, which are authors' estimates based on recent trends and the nature of projects to be completed.

a. Some years include small amounts of loans.

other highways in the legislation authorizing federal highway grants.[3] In 1972, however, both the House and Senate highway bills explicitly provided for a separate urban highway grant, to which the administration has proposed to devote $800 million in fiscal 1974. In addition, since some of the interstate system routes are located in urban areas, these are eligible for the 90 percent grants.

Grants for *urban mass transit* are made directly to urban governments. In fiscal 1974 this program will receive $1 billion. Almost $900 million of this will be used for capital grants for new facilities, with the remainder for planning, research and development, technical studies, and training grants. Under the capital grant program the federal government pays two-thirds of the "net project costs" for new transit facilities. The funds must be rationed since they are not sufficient to make grants covering all the investment required for the nation's urban mass transit systems. Net project costs represent the part of new transit facility costs that fare-box revenues cannot "reasonably" be expected to repay. In the proposals submitted to the federal government, revenues from fares are virtually never projected to cover more than operating expenses; in practice, therefore, the federal government pays two-thirds of the full cost of facilities when it makes a mass transit grant.

Urban mass transportation falls into three major types: bus lines, rapid rail transit, and rail commuter lines. Rapid rail transit refers to rail facilities within cities, usually subways in the center of the city with above-ground extensions in outlying areas. There are only ten major systems now in operation in the United States, New York's subway system being the largest and San Francisco's Bay Area Rapid Transit System (BART) the newest. There are sixteen rail commuter services, most of them owned by railroads and operated on long-existing railroad rights of way.

Last year the Senate and House passed highway and public transportation bills that, in different ways, would have made important changes in the federal urban transportation program. Because of disagreements between the two houses, no legislation was enacted. This year the Congress is again considering these bills, together with a set of recommendations from the administration. Three major issues arising

---

3. Specific provision was made for modest amounts (about $210 million a year) for urban extensions of state primary and secondary highways.

from the federal government's role in this area reflect the three basic problems outlined earlier in this chapter.

1. Should urban mass transit facilities for both rail and bus systems be eligible for grants from the new urban segment of the Highway Trust Fund (whose revenues come solely from taxes on highway users)? In similar vein, should federal grants reserved for controversial urban segments of the Interstate Highway System, now blocked by local opposition to freeways, be made available for mass transit facilities or other transportation uses?

2. Should the federal government continue to subsidize only the capital costs of urban mass transit, or should it extend such assistance to operating costs?

3. What should be the level of federal support for urban transportation? Is it reasonable to expect that greatly increased federal grants for expanded mass transit would arrest and reverse the decline in transit ridership, and reduce the congestion and air pollution that afflict many central cities?

Financing Mass Transit from the Highway Trust Fund

The separate highway bills passed by the House and Senate last year and again in early 1973 diverged on the question of using the Highway Trust Fund for the support of urban mass transit projects. The Senate bill made all types of mass transit facilities eligible for grants from the Highway Trust Fund; the House, however, limited the use of the funds to highway-related mass transit projects, such as the construction of special bus lanes, and explicitly prohibited the use of the funds for the purchase of buses or for rapid rail or commuter rail transit facilities.

The argument, pressed hard by highway interests, for excluding rail transit from eligibility for Highway Trust Fund money is that the receipts for the fund come from gasoline and related taxes paid by highway users and that since this money represents "charges" for the use of the highways constructed under the program, they should be used only for highway-related purposes. This argument is hard to justify. In the first place, gasoline taxes are just that—taxes; only very roughly do they serve as a price or charge for costs incurred in the use of specific highways, and the gasoline taxes paid by citizens of urban areas are only remotely related to the amount of highway construction undertaken there. Second, it makes little sense for the federal government to decide what kind of transportation to support in local areas on the basis of a financing arrangement instituted seventeen years ago. Highway Trust Fund revenues are now running well ahead of highway expenditures ($6.0 billion versus $4.5 billion in fiscal 1974). To expand highway-related expenditures to match these revenues simply because the taxes are funneled through a trust fund is surely not the way to strike a balance among different kinds of transportation.

There are, indeed, legitimate questions about the effectiveness of subsidies to rail transit as a solution to the problems of congestion and air pollution in large cities. And as later discussion in this chapter points out, the current federal programs for mass transit subsidies, which bias local decisions toward inefficient concentration on heavy capital-using investments, need fundamental restructuring. But excluding assistance to rail transit from the urban transportation component of the Highway Trust Fund is not the way to deal with these questions.

The same problem arises, in a somewhat more complicated way, for the remaining urban segments of the Interstate Highway System. Under the Federal Aid Highway Act of 1956, the federal government undertook to pay 90 percent of the cost of constructing the 42,500-mile interstate system.[4] At that time the cost of the system was estimated as $26 billion, the completion date as 1972. Now the estimated cost of the system is $76 billion—three times the original estimate—and the scheduled completion date is in the early 1980s. Part of the rise in costs reflects general inflation, but the largest part represents a real increase in highway costs caused by changes in design, rapidly rising land prices along rights of way, and initial underestimates of highway costs in urban areas.

By September 1972, 37,500 miles of the system were either completed or under construction—30,500 miles in rural areas and 7,000 miles in urban communities. Of the remaining mileage, approximately 1,000 miles are scheduled for urban areas and 4,000 for rural areas. Some of the urban segments are freeways designed principally to bring commuters downtown; others are links in the interstate system. While the remaining urban mileage is small compared with the total 42,500 miles in the system, it accounts for some of the most expensive and controversial segments. About 140 miles of urban and 69 miles of rural construction are being held up by vigorous local controversy. Opposition to urban freeways has grown sharply, on grounds that

4. The 1956 legislation authorized 41,000 miles; 1,500 miles have since been added to the system.

they disrupt local neighborhoods, intensify downtown congestion, and increase air pollution by encouraging more commuter automobile traffic. Most of the routes in question are very costly because of the high value of land and improvements they would displace. The estimated average cost of the 209 miles of controversial urban and rural interstate segments is $20 million a mile. In some urban areas the cost is huge: one 2.9-mile segment in Washington, D.C., would cost $84 million a mile; a Chicago segment would cost $46 million a mile, and a 22-mile stretch in the Boston area would require a total of $500 million.

The administration has proposed, as part of the pending highway bill, that, in response to a joint request made by a state and the local governments concerned, the secretary of transportation may withdraw controversial segments from the interstate system, and make the federal share of the cost of constructing them available for other highways or for urban mass transit within the area. (The secretary could not approve withdrawals of linking segments critical to the interconnections of the interstate system.) The federal share of the cost of the controversial 209 miles would amount to $3.5 billion, two-thirds of this within urban areas. Even if this provision were adopted, not all of these segments would be withdrawn. But subject to agreement between state highway departments and local officials, a substantial sum of money could become available to urban areas for flexible use, either for mass transit investments or for improvements on highways other than those of the interstate system.

One major ciriticism of this proposal is that it would penalize areas that have gone ahead rapidly with their interstate highway program and reward those that have delayed. But aside from portions of the system that are critical for connecting it, there appears to be no national interest in the construction of urban freeways, especially in view of the opposition of the affected areas. While flexible use of the funds designated for these freeways should, perhaps, have been granted some time ago, the failure to do so then seems a poor reason not to do so now.

The Problem of Perverse Incentives in Mass Transit Subsidies

The present federal program pays two-thirds of the capital cost of urban mass transportation projects. Four major kinds of grants are made: (1) for purchase of buses and other improvements to bus lines;

(2) for purchase of cars and other facilities on commuter and rapid rail transit lines; (3) for development of completely new rapid rail systems or major extensions of existing lines, such as San Francisco's BART and Washington's Metro; and (4) for municipal takeover of privately owned transit companies, principally bus lines. Table 6-3 shows the distribution of grants among these major purposes from the inception of the program in 1965 through December 1970.

These capital grants are made by the Department of Transportation on a case-by-case basis, after reviewing applications for assistance from individual communities. Funds from the urban component of the Highway Trust Fund, if they are made available for this use, will flow out to urban communities on a formula basis (as is the case with all grants from the fund), although the specific projects will still be subject to at least pro forma review by the federal government. The two forms of assistance, however, share one characteristic: the grants they provide may be used only for investment in facilities; they cannot be used to cover operating costs.

As noted above, providing assistance for mass transit in the form of capital grants biases local decisions toward the choice of projects with a high ratio of capital costs to operating costs, often at a heavy cost in efficiency. This happens in two ways.

In the case of existing mass transit systems—for example, bus lines —as vehicles reach a certain age, a decision must be made to spend

Table 6-3. Federal Capital Grants for Mass Transit, by Purpose, from 1965 through December 1970[a]

Millions of dollars

Purpose	Total project cost	Federal grant
Purchase of buses and other bus-related facilities	180	112
Municipal takeover of private lines	87	58
Development of major new rail transit facilities	597	327
Purchase of equipment or other improvements on existing commuter and rapid rail transit systems	309	178
Miscellaneous[b]	92	61
Total	1,265	735

Source: U.S. Department of Transportation, Urban Mass Transportation Administration, *Approvals of Capital Grants and Loans and Technical Studies Grants*, UPA-1 (1971). Figures may not add to totals because of rounding.

a. The grant program was initiated by the Urban Mass Transportation Act of 1964; the first grants were approved in 1965.

b. Includes fare boxes, two-way radios, ferry boats, and others for which the category could not be determined.

operating funds to maintain and repair them or capital funds to replace them. If the federal government is paying two-thirds of the cost of new equipment, but nothing toward repair and maintenance, local transit officials will naturally replace buses very quickly, long before they should be scrapped. The total costs of providing mass transit will rise sharply, and a large part of the subsidy will serve not to benefit riders but to cover the costs of inefficient decisions. One recent study[5] of Chicago and Cleveland bus operations concluded that the federal policy of making mass transit grants only for capital investment caused inefficiencies that wasted some 23 percent of the grant—that is, it stimulated wasteful decisions to replace buses much too soon, which absorbed 23 percent of the subsidy in the form of unnecessary costs.

Even more important, the present capital grant technique favors the development of rapid rail transit systems. Compared to other forms of mass transportation, the capital costs of new rapid rail transit systems are very high relative to operating costs, and since the former are subsidized while the latter are not, the federal grant program encourages development of new systems. Except where rights of way are available along existing rail beds or median strips of freeways, constructing underground or grade-separated routes for rapid rail through urban areas is very costly. Once constructed, these routes, unlike bus routes, are fixed in position and cannot be adapted to changing traffic and residential patterns. They require large investments in facilities operated seven days a week, 24 hours a day, to meet rush-hour traffic problems that exist only about 20 hours in a 168-hour week. Only along very high-density routes are their average costs per passenger as low as or lower than those of other forms of urban transportation.

The BART system in San Francisco exemplifies the problem. The annual cost of paying interest on and amortizing the capital investment of this system amounts to about $78 million. With an annual expected passenger volume of 60 million to 70 million, this amounts to a capital cost of $1.10 to $1.30 per passenger trip, or a round-trip cost of $2.20 to $2.60 for capital facilities. (Operating costs, another $0.65 per trip, are expected to be covered by fare-box revenues.) These capital costs are borne by local and federal taxpayer subsidies, and are not

5. William B. Tye, "The Capital Grant as a Subsidy Device: The Case Study of Urban Mass Transportation," in *The Economics of Federal Subsidy Programs*, A Compendium of Papers submitted to the Subcommittee on Priorities and Economy in Government of the Joint Economic Committee, 93 Cong. 1 sess. (1973), Pt. 6, pp. 796–826.

covered by the fare charged to users. Taxpayer subsidies exceeding $2.00 per round trip are an expensive way of dealing with commuter transportation problems.

Construction of BART was well along before the federal government's urban mass transportation appropriations had become very large. As a consequence the federal share of capital costs was small (about 10 percent); most of the subsidy is borne by local property taxpayers. The federal government, however, did put up two-thirds of the cost of two major extensions of the Boston subway, of a 16-mile extension of the Long Island Railroad, and of a 15-mile extension of the Chicago rapid transit. The $3 billion Metro system in Washington, D.C., will be heavily supported by federal grants, and the citizens of Atlanta recently approved a $1.4 billion rapid transit system that will be eligible for federal subsidy.

Needed is a federal subsidy technique that does not encourage over-investment in capital facilities or tip the scales in favor of rapid rail transit development when that is not the most appropriate mode of transportation. There have been numerous suggestions that the federal government subsidize the *operating* expenses of urban mass transit systems. In 1972 the Senate (but not the House) passed an amendment to the Urban Mass Transportation Act under which the federal government would pay two-thirds of any state and local subsidies made to cover the operating expenses of urban mass transit systems. In 1970 the revenues of eleven out of fourteen major commuter rail lines in the United States failed to cover even operating expenses, much less capital costs. All but two of the rapid rail lines had operating deficits, as did one-third of all the urban bus lines. And for all three of these types of transportation systems, the frequency and size of operating deficits have increased sharply in the past two decades.

A simple subsidy of operating deficits, however, is no answer. An open-ended federal subsidy that made up some percentage of operating costs or covered a given fraction of operating deficits would be an invitation to inefficiency and excessive wage increases. The federal government could not, in the long run, stand ready simply to bear a large fraction of any increases in cost. It would soon find itself playing a large regulatory role, specifying labor relations and operating policies for hundreds of subsidized transit operators, a role for which it is ill-equipped.

But there are alternatives. The federal government could pay local communities a fixed amount per passenger trip, or a fixed percentage of passenger revenues (that is, a negative sales tax). Such a subsidy could replace the current project grants for capital investment and would not bias decisions toward capital-intensive investments and undermaintenance. Since mass transit companies, public or private, need to estimate revenues well into the future in order to plan and borrow funds for investment, the federal government would have to enter into long-term commitments about the payment of such subsidies.

If made available in this new form, funds now devoted to federal capital subsidies for urban mass transit could have a surprisingly large impact on transit operations. In 1970 the total passenger revenues of urban commuter rail, rapid rail, and bus lines amounted to $1.8 billion. Federal capital grants for urban mass transit now amount to about $900 million a year. If the urban segment of the Highway Trust Fund were also opened up for mass transit investments and if, for example, one-half of the funds were used for that purpose (rather than for highways), another $400 million would be available, bringing the total up to $1.3 billion. At 1970 levels of passenger patronage, fares could be reduced by an average of 75 percent on every urban mass transit system in the country without exceeding the $1.3 billion current annual level of support. This amounts to a federal subsidy of 45 cents per round trip for every rider. While most analyses of the demand for mass transit indicate that the increase in ridership generated by lower fares is relatively modest, some would occur. As a consequence, the $1.3 billion would have to be spread over a larger number of riders, leading to a smaller reduction of fares. But even after generous allowance for this fact, the current $1.3 billion level of mass transit grants would make possible a 50 percent fare reduction. Or, viewed another way, the initial 75 percent reduction could be maintained with an additional outlay of only $400 million, bringing the total subsidy up to $1.7 billion.

The new subsidy need not be used solely for fare reduction—it could finance improvements in speed, comfort, or frequency of service. And the fare reductions or service improvements would not be uniform for all systems. The new form of subsidy would be less generous than the current program toward the very expensive, capital-intensive systems like BART. (Presumably, communities that wished to construct such systems would have to put up a larger amount of local taxpayers' money than is now the case.) Compared to the current program, the new subsidy would be more generous to bus lines or other, less capital-intensive forms of public transportation.

This general approach has a number of variations, depending principally on whether a flat subsidy per passenger or a subsidy proportional to fare is undertaken. Each version would have different consequences, and any final plan would have to consider the pros and cons of each.

A subsidy based on a flat amount per passenger trip would cover a larger share of costs for short trips than for long ones. It would also represent a larger percentage of costs for low-cost modes of public transportation than for high-cost ones. Short trips on bus systems would benefit most under this approach. As a consequence it would foster fare reductions and service improvements of a kind particularly beneficial to inner-city residents. A subsidy based on a percentage of fare-box revenues would tend to be most generous to longer trips and high-cost modes. Thus it would be most likely to benefit suburban commuters using rapid rail transit, and most suited to promoting competition with automobiles. Since both objectives are being sought —improving the transportation system for inner-city residents and diverting suburban commuters from automobiles to mass transit—a subsidy scheme that combined the two approaches might be desirable. One-half of the subsidy could be made available as a flat amount per passenger and one-half as a percentage of fare-box revenues.

One illustrative program might be as follows:

1. The current $900 million urban mass transportation grant program and the $800 million urban segment of the Highway Trust Fund would be combined into a new urban transportation program. This would make $1.7 billion available.

2. The federal government would stand ready to pay local communities a subsidy for mass transportation, half on a per-passenger basis and half on the basis of a percentage of revenue. Long-term (perhaps ten-year) commitments would be made.

3. The size of the mass transit subsidy would be so calculated that if every community took advantage of it some $1.3 billion of the $1.7 billion would be used.

4. The remainder of the fund would be available for urban highway investment. In addition, any community that so chose could use its mass transit subsidy entitlement for highway purposes.

There are a number of other ways in which such a program could be designed. The central point, however, is that mass transit grants should be provided by means that neither encourage excessively capital-intensive systems nor reward inefficiency by subsidizing operating deficits.

How Large Should Mass Transit Subsidies Be?

The foregoing dealt with the question of what *form* the mass transit subsidies should take. It did not deal with the *size* of the subsidy program. In the case of mass transit, this depends on how effective the subsidy is in achieving the national objectives for which it was undertaken. As noted earlier in this chapter, subsidies to mass transit may be justified as a means of relieving the congestion and reducing the pollution that unrestricted use of automobiles inflicts on crowded city streets. They may also be viewed as a way of equalizing opportunities for poor inner-city residents through the provision of cheap and speedy public transportation between home and work.

The two objectives often conflict. Since the poor are less likely to drive to work, a program aimed at reducing the number of cars on the street must be directed toward inducing the relatively well-off suburban commuter to take the subway or the bus. Radial lines, operating with a limited number of downtown stops, achieving high speeds, and accompanied by inexpensive suburban feeder bus service, would come closest to meeting this objective. As *Setting National Priorities: The 1971 Budget* pointed out, most of the new rapid rail transit lines now being constructed or planned under federal grants have these characteristics, and involve very large subsidies for middle-income suburbanites who live near the transit stops. The $2.20 to $2.60 subsidy provided by the taxpayer for the average round trip on BART implies, for example, a $600 a year subsidy to the typical middle-income commuter from the suburbs. A system directed toward the poorer working residents of the city would feature cheap and frequent crosstown bus service, carrying central city residents to their places of work. For poor older people, a mass transportation subsidy for cheap "jitney" service, either on schedule or on limited "to-order" call, would be most effective.

Since the mass transit subsidies that are concentrated principally on middle-income suburban commuters cannot be justified on income distribution grounds, provision of federal funds must hinge on their success in diverting commuters from automobiles to mass transportation, thereby promoting more efficient use of city streets while reducing congestion and air pollution. What evidence is available, however, indicates that subsidies for the price or quality of public transportation, if unaccompanied by penalties or restrictions on travel by car, is unlikely to shift large numbers of people to mass transit.

The use of automobiles for commuting downtown has several characteristics. On the one hand, most people who use cars for this purpose would own one in any event, so that the extra cost of driving to work is relatively modest, Combined with the convenience of door-to-door transportation, this gives the automobile a distinct advantage over public transportation for the individual user. One study conducted in Chicago in the early 1960s concluded that the price of public transportation would have to be negative—that is, people would have to be paid to take public transit—in order to induce at least 50 percent of commuters by car to switch to buses or subways.[6] Surveys of commuters traveling on new rapid rail transit lines have shown that in most (though not all) cases these commuters had switched from buses or streetcars rather than from automobiles.[7] Moreover, while many commuters living near new rapid transit lines would switch from cars, thereby relieving congestion initially, the lower congestion would then induce other commuters who had been riding buses or traveling in car pools to take their own automobiles to work, causing congestion and pollution to rise toward earlier levels.

The other characteristic of car travel is the substantial cost it levies that is not borne by the car owner himself. Each automobile added to the daily traffic stream slightly increases the congestion on the streets and thereby slows down the average speed of all other drivers. In congested conditions each car imposes "delay costs" on all other drivers using the same streets at the same time. A study of traffic in downtown London showed that the cost of automobile travel in highly congested areas, taking into account these delay costs, was approximately $1.00 a mile.[8] And these estimates do not include the cost of damage from air pollution that automobile travel causes. In

6. Leon N. Moses and Harold F. Williamson, "Value of Time, Choice of Mode, and the Subsidy Issue in Urban Transportation," *Journal of Political Economy*, Vol. 71 (June 1963), p. 262.

7. J. R. Meyer and M. Wohl, *The Urban Transportation Problem* (Harvard University Press, 1965), pp. 99–100.

8. In congested traffic (speeds of eight to ten miles an hour), delay costs were estimated to be about 83 cents a mile at 1964 prices. This would be equivalent to about $1.10 at 1974 prices. *Road Pricing: The Economic and Technical Possibilities*, Report of a Panel set up by the Ministry of Transport (London: Her Majesty's Stationery Office, 1964), p. 3.

other words, while the individual car owner finds driving to work relatively cheap and convenient, it is much more costly for society. But since it is the driver, not society, who decides whether or not to drive, excessive use of cars and clogging of downtown streets result. If drivers were charged the true costs of driving, mass transit would suddenly appear far more attractive.

This analysis implies that subsidies that reduce the price of public transportation are themselves unlikely to divert much traffic from automobiles unless they are accompanied by charges on drivers in congested areas that cover the full social cost of their trips. In theory, tolls that varied by location and by time of day, based on the degree of congestion and pollution, would be the ideal means of regulating automobile traffic. Various electronic and radar systems that would record the passage of individual cars and bill the owners accordingly have been suggested as the means of achieving this goal. At present, these are still impractical. But research and development funds could profitably be spent on the design of such systems. In the interim the only feasible device for charging drivers the full social costs of their use of downtown streets appears to be the imposition of stiff fees on all parking spaces during daytime hours. Provision could be made (through the issuance of special stickers or licenses) for residents of downtown areas. While parking fees are an imperfect means of dealing with the problem, they may be the only way, at the present time, of providing the incentives required to achieve a balanced transportation system in urban areas. In any event, restrictions on car use will almost certainly prove necessary in most central cities if they are to meet congressionally imposed air pollution standards by the 1975 deadline.

A federal grant program that made available transit subsidies of the type described above, *on condition* that recipient communities acted to levy stiff parking fees or took other actions to restrict the use of automobiles in congested areas during peak hours, might be successful in reducing both congestion and air pollution. For the reasons spelled out earlier, subsidies alone, even if they reduced fares to zero, are not likely to achieve this result.

What would be the budgetary cost of a conditional subsidy program, combining reductions in transit fares and improvements in service with charges on car use in congested areas? For a federal subsidy program that reduced average transit fares by 50 percent from the current level, the total budgetary cost would depend on how many

Table 6-4. Annual Cost to the Federal Government of a Conditional Transit Subsidy, by Various Levels of Automobile Diversion[a]

Percentage of urban car trips diverted to public transportation		Cost to federal government (billions of dollars)
Work trips	Other urban trips	
0	0	0.9
20	5	1.5
40	10	2.0
60	15	2.5

Source: Authors' estimates.

a. Assumes a federal subsidy program that reduces average transit fares by 50 percent from the current level, on condition that recipient communities impose high parking fees or other restrictions that discourage automobile use.

automobile passengers were diverted to mass transit. Table 6-4 gives estimates, which are necessarily very rough, of the size of federal budgetary costs at various assumed levels of such diversion.

Since about $1.3 billion is available in federal funds for mass transit grants,[9] the added cost of providing a subsidy equivalent to a 50 percent fare reduction would not be huge, even if the subsidy, in combination with parking fees, diverted 60 percent of commuter automobile traffic to mass transit. The cost of the program, on those relatively extreme assumptions, would still amount to only $2.5 billion annually, a net addition to the current program of only $1.2 billion.

Many urban public transportation systems, as a result of several decades of declining patronage, are now operating at far less than capacity. Some increase in ridership could occur without substantial expansion of capacity. But large diversion of commuters from automobiles to mass transit would require significant investment by local transit authorities, public and private. Even with long-term federal commitments for annual subsidies, borrowing the necessary funds in the private market might be very difficult, in view of the past financial problems of transit companies. As a consequence the federal government might find it necessary to provide some kind of loan guarantees. With federal subsidy commitments along the lines spelled out earlier, however, there is no justification for interest subsidies or grants as a means of providing capital. Such devices would simply reintroduce

9. As noted above, this assumes that the $800 million urban segment of the Highway Trust Fund will be made available for both highway and mass transit purposes and that one-half of the funds will be used for mass transit.

the problems that plague the present program. The capital costs of the necessary transit expansion should not be separately subsidized.

Grants for Constructing Waste Treatment Plants*

A major budgetary issue, and a source of controversy between the administration and the Congress, revolves around the level of federal grants for the construction of municipal waste treatment works. In October 1972 the Congress passed, over the President's veto, the Federal Water Pollution Control Act Amendments of 1972, which provided $18 billion in funds for waste treatment—$5 billion for fiscal 1973, $6 billion for 1974, and $7 billion for 1975. The act also raised from 55 percent to 75 percent the share of these municipal construction costs paid by the federal government. In addition, the bill provided money for federal reimbursement to local communities that had constructed waste treatment plants since 1956 without federal grants.

For fiscal years 1973 and 1974 the administration has proposed to make available $5.4 billion in new construction grants, while the Congress provided $11 billion for those two years. (The grants will not result immediately in cash outlays; these will take place gradually as actual construction occurs.) The basic budgetary issue between the Congress and the administration concerns the desirability and feasibility of providing grants at the full level provided by last year's water pollution control bill.[10]

Two considerations dominate the evaluation of this issue. The first has to do, again, with incentives. A federal policy that subsidizes 75 percent of the costs of constructing waste treatment plants but provides no incentives or other mechanisms to ensure that they are appropriately maintained and operated will lead to disappointing pollution control results. The second consideration involves the questions of how much investment is required in municipal waste treatment

* Prepared with the assistance of Ivars Gutmanis, National Planning Association.

10. The administration is also making $1.9 billion available for reimbursement to states and communities on previously constructed facilities. In a recent court case involving the city of New York contesting the government's withholding of waste treatment funds, the court held that the Environmental Protection Agency must *allot* each state its pro-rata share of the full congressional authorization. But under the budgetary procedures that govern this program, allotment of funds simply gives a state the right to apply for federal approval of grants in an amount equal to its full share. This decision is being appealed, and it is still unclear whether the federal government will be required to approve and issue grants in that amount, once the applications have been received. *City of New York* v. *Ruckelshaus*, U.S.D.C., District of Columbia (decided May 8, 1973).

plants and how rapidly construction can be expanded to meet that requirement without bringing about sharp increases in costs.

Construction versus Operation and Maintenance

It does little good to pour money into construction of plants if, once built, they are operated inefficiently or below capacity. This has been a major problem. In a 1970 survey of sixty-nine municipal waste treatment plants, the General Accounting Office found that forty had operational, mechanical, or structural problems, and that twenty-eight bypassed some sewage wastes into streams without treatment.[11] In many instances municipal treatment plants operate at far less than rated capacity because of failure to provide necessary maintenance, repair, or upgrading on time.

It is expensive to maintain and operate plants effectively. While 75 percent of construction costs are borne by the federal government, operating costs are fully supported by local taxpayers. And since a large part of the benefits of effective operations—cleaner water—accrues to those who live downstream, outside the taxing jurisdiction of the community that runs the plant, the motivation for incurring the necessary operating costs is weakened. Last year's volume of *Setting National Priorities* suggested that this problem could be alleviated by levying a charge on all communities per unit of polluting wastes discharged into the waterways.[12] This would make effective operation of a municipal treatment plant profitable; every reduction in pollutant discharges would save the city money. Since a federal levy on financially hard-pressed city governments, even for purposes of pollution control, might evoke cries of outrage, the money so collected could be placed in a special fund and returned to municipal governments by a formula in which payments were in inverse relationship to per capita pollution in each municipality. This would provide a double incentive for effective pollution control by municipal governments—first, to minimize the federal effluent charge, and second, to maximize the grant from the special fund.

This proposal would not, of course, do away with the need for fed-

11. Testimony of Elmer B. Staats in *Water Pollution Control Legislation—1971* (*Oversight of Existing Programs*), Hearings before the House Committee on Public Works, 92 Cong. 1 sess. (1971), p. 8.

12. This "effluent charge" would be part of a broader system of charges applicable also to the discharge of industrial pollutants.

eral assistance in the construction of plants. The appropriate level of construction grant assistance would still present a policy issue.

Varying Estimates of Waste Treatment Plant Construction "Requirements"

For several years the Environmental Protection Agency (EPA) has attempted to estimate, by several alternative techniques, the need for municipal waste treatment plant construction. In 1971 EPA conducted a survey of all communities whose population was over 10,000, asking for their waste treatment construction plans covering the fiscal years 1972 through 1976. These plans represented the construction that communities estimated they would have to undertake to meet federal and state water pollution control regulations. In general these regulations require that all municipalities process their waste through secondary waste treatment plants, which remove about 85 to 90 percent of the major damaging water pollutants. The communities' construction plans surveyed by EPA included construction of completely new plants, as well as expansion, improvement, and replacement of existing ones. After reviewing the responses and making estimates for construction by smaller communities not included in the survey, EPA in early 1972 arrived at a figure of $18.1 billion as the "needed" construction over the coming five years.[13]

At about the same time, EPA also prepared an alternative estimate of "need." This was based not on a survey of communities, but on an economic and engineering cost model, in which EPA projected the cost of construction needed to meet current federal and state pollution control regulations, and allowed for such factors as population growth, replacement of deteriorating facilities, and inflation in construction costs. For the five-year period 1972–76, this alternative technique produced estimated construction requirements of $14.4 billion,[14] a more conservative figure than the survey estimate of $18.1 billion.

As noted earlier, the 1972 act increased the federal share of construction costs to 75 percent. Applied to the $18 billion survey estimate of construction needs, a 75 percent federal share would require $2.7 billion in new construction grants each year for five years. The 1974 budget proposals of the administration, which make provision for

13. U.S. Environmental Protection Agency, *The Economics of Clean Water* (1972), Vol. 1, p. 114.
14. Ibid., pp. 119–27.

new construction grants of $5.4 billion in the two-year period 1973 and 1974, match this figure, and adding the state and local share would produce a total of $3.6 billion a year for construction.

The Congress, on the other hand, authorized federal grants of $5 billion, $6 billion, and $7 billion a year for the fiscal years 1973, 1974, and 1975, a total of $18 billion over the *three*-year period. With a 75 percent federal share, this implies a total construction figure of $24 billion. Given the timing of the grants, the congressional program would average $7.3 billion a year for the first two years, about twice the $3.6 billion a year in the administration's program.

Several factors probably influenced the congressional choice of a higher grant program. The 1972 act made the construction of sewage collection systems eligible, under certain conditions, for federal grants. The inclusion of these systems was designed to attack the problem of separating storm sewers from sanitary sewers, which are combined in most areas. During heavy storms the volume of water in the system outruns the capacity of waste treatment plants and raw sewage is dumped directly into the watercourse. Little is known about the most effective ways of dealing with this problem; constructing additional sewers to separate the two systems is only one approach. The costs of attacking the problem nationwide are very uncertain, and estimates range from $15 billion to $45 billion.

The $24 billion of total construction implied in the congressional authorization could have been derived by taking the administration's $18 billion "needs" estimate, adding $6 billion for collection systems, and compressing the five-year program into three years. (To meet the recent congressionally imposed deadline that all municipalities provide secondary treatment of their wastes by July 1, 1977, construction of the needed plants would have to begin during the next three years.) Starting with the $24 billion for the total construction program, to be gotten under way within three years, the Congress then provided federal funds to cover 75 percent of the costs. Quite apart from questions of relative priorities in the federal budget, how desirable and how feasible would it be to accelerate waste treatment construction at the pace implied in the congressional authorizations?

The Rate of Expansion in Construction Capacity

One of the central questions is how fast work on waste treatment plants, which entails heavy industrial construction and specialized knowledge, can expand without bringing on sharp cost increases and inefficiencies. While there is no unequivocal answer to this question, Table 6-5 provides some indirect evidence. It shows the rate at which federally assisted waste treatment plants have been constructed in recent years, and compares this with what is contemplated in the administration and the congressional programs. The table also shows the annual rate of increase in construction costs for waste treatment plants during this period and the rate of expansion in the real value of construction starts.

Over the seven-year period 1965–71, the real value of construction starts rose at an annual average rate of 22 percent. Near the end of the period construction costs began to increase sharply, partly as a result of general inflation, but probably also because of the rapid growth in the demand for the services of firms capable of such construction. Even the administration's program contemplates a very sharp rise in the annual rate of construction, and carrying out the congressional program would require a huge increase. For comparison purposes a third projection is shown which assumes a very optimistic 30 percent annual

Table 6-5. Federally Assisted Construction Starts for Waste Treatment Plants, Calendar Years 1965–71, and Projections for Fiscal Years 1973–74

| Year | Value of starts (millions of current dollars) | Percentage increase from prior year | | |
		Value of starts	Construction prices	Real value of construction
Actual (calendar years)				
1965	365	...	...	...
1966	490	34.1	3.9	30.2
1967	397	−18.9	2.9	−21.8
1968	671	69.0	2.8	66.2
1969	937	39.6	7.3	32.3
1970	1,361	45.2	7.8	37.4
1971	1,700	24.9	15.0	9.9
Projections (fiscal year 1973–74 average)				
Administration program	3,600	...	...	...
Congressional program	7,300	...	...	...
Program with 30 percent annual increase in construction capability[a]	4,000	...	...	...

Sources: Actual data: U.S. Environmental Protection Agency, *The Economics of Clean Water* (1972), Vol. 1, Table 12, p. 136. Projections: authors' estimates based on *The Budget of the United States Government—Appendix, Fiscal Year 1974*, the Federal Water Pollution Control Act Amendments of 1972, and, for the third projection, the assumptions explained in the text.

a. Assumes a 7.5 percent annual increase in construction costs. This projection has a one-half year slippage in the program since fiscal year 1973 was almost half over before congressional action was completed and the funds were allocated.

increase in construction capability, along with a 7½ percent annual increase in construction costs.[15] The administration's program, therefore, appears to contemplate construction at a level slightly below that which would be made possible by a very rapid expansion in construction capability. The congressional program, on the other hand, would call for a much faster rate of expansion, implying a continuing growth in capacity of about 65 percent a year.

The congressionally authorized program of waste treatment plant construction is designed to ensure that every municipality has secondary waste treatment works in operation by July 1, 1977. And indeed, the deadline will be breached if construction proceeds at a slower rate than that envisioned in the congressional authorization. But construction of plants is not the magic answer to the control of municipally generated pollution. A construction schedule that overtaxes the capacity of the industry to expand, and the lack of a mechanism to enforce effective operation of completed plants, might well produce a rapid rise in costs and a series of poorly run and underutilized facilities rather than an effective answer to pollution problems.

Water Resource Projects

In each of the three fiscal years 1972 through 1974, the federal government will spend between $2.6 billion and $3.1 billion for constructing and operating major water resource projects (see Table 6-6). In the period 1964–70 outlays for these programs grew very slowly, and all the growth stemmed from increases in operating costs and the construction of steam power plants for the Tennessee Valley Authority (TVA) and of power transmission lines. Construction of projects devoted entirely to water resources was reduced. In the next three years outlays for all types of programs rose very sharply, from $2.0 billion in 1970 to $3.1 billion in 1973. And according to the administration's budget, outlays would have risen to $3.4 billion in 1974 had action not been taken to pare the programs by $600 million.

The federal government carries out four primary kinds of activities in this area:

15. Since fiscal 1973 was almost half over before congressional action was complete and the administration allocated funds, this projection provides for a half-year slippage in the program. This has the effect of increasing the projected construction outlays.

1. *Navigation projects.* It dredges channels, constructs locks and dams, and otherwise modifies natural watercourses to make them navigable for barge traffic. No charges are levied on barge operators for the costs of these activities.

2. *Irrigation projects.* It provides the dams and canals necessary to divert river water into irrigation ditches. Farmers are charged for the water, but at prices far below the economic cost of the projects.

3. *Flood control.* It constructs levees, dams, and other works needed to reduce flood damage along waterways. It does not, however, regulate private investment in flood plains, and therefore has little voice in determining whether it makes sense to protect investments that should never have been made in the first place. Local communities are charged a relatively small fraction of project costs, principally through contributions of land and easements along the stream banks.

4. *Power projects.* It constructs dams to produce hydroelectric power and sells the power at a price that covers costs, except that the interest rate charged against the power project does not fully reflect

Table 6-6. **Federal Outlays for Major Water Resource Projects, Selected Fiscal Years, 1964–74**

Millions of dollars

				Estimate	
Type of project or program	*1964*	*1970*	*1972*	*1973*	*1974*
Construction					
Flood control	438	355	536	669	592
Irrigation	125	88	108	176	152
Navigation	237	189	251	281	234
Multiple purpose dams	390	346	566	551	530
Subtotal	1,190	978	1,461	1,677	1,508
Transmission facilities and Tennessee Valley Authority power plants	207	450	630	513	535
Total construction	1,397	1,428	2,091	2,190	2,043
Operation, maintenance, and other[a]	376	552	571	875	751
Total outlays	1,773	1,980	2,662	3,065	2,795
Plus: administration cuts	...	...	...	121	594
Equals: "unconstrained" budget	...	...	...	3,186	3,389

Sources: Construction, *Special Analyses, Budget of the United States Government, Fiscal Year 1974*, p. 259, *Special Analyses . . . 1972*, p. 260, and *The Budget of the United States Government, Fiscal Year 1966*, p. 423; other data, *The Budget of the United States Government* and *Appendix*, relevant years. Figures may not add to totals because of rounding.

a. Principally operation and maintenance by the Corps of Engineers and the Bureau of Reclamation, but small amounts of Federal Power Commission outlays are also included.

the cost of capital. In the area served by TVA, the government is the principal electricity supplier and constructs steam power plants to supplement its hydroelectric power.

These activities generate two additional kinds of expenses. Having constructed the various projects outlined above, the federal government also operates them. As projects are completed, total expenditures for operations and maintenance grow steadily (by 100 percent over the last ten years). Similarly, as government hydroelectric projects are connected into large regionwide power pools, which are increasingly typical of modern power systems, substantial and growing federal investments in transmission lines become necessary.

While outlays for these programs constitute a relatively modest proportion of the total budget, they are nevertheless very large sums. With the exception of AT&T, no firm in the nation has an annual investment budget as large as the federal government's $2 billion yearly outlay for water resource construction.

More than most other federal activities, investments in water resource projects are made, purportedly at least, on the basis of their direct economic benefits. Yet a number of weaknesses in the decision-making process have led outside observers to doubt the justification for many of them. Three central problems are at issue. The first is economic. The calculations tend to overstate benefits and understate costs. The other two are political. Since individuals and groups who could well afford to pay for them benefit from projects that are provided at greatly reduced costs, they have a strong motivation to lobby for the authorization of uneconomic projects. Furthermore, the procedure by which Congress appropriates funds for these projects tends to encourage overinvestment and excessive spending. These problems were discussed at some length in *Setting National Priorities: The 1971 Budget*,[16] and will be summarized only briefly here.

Economic Benefits and Costs

Before any project is recommended by the administration and authorized by the Congress, calculations are made to determine if it yields a return on the government's investment at least equal to an appropriate interest rate. Until a few years ago the interest rate used in these calculations was substantially below the rate that the govern-

16. Charles L. Schultze with others (Brookings Institution, 1970).

ment paid on its own securities. At a time when the government was paying 5 to 6 percent, the interest rate used in the calculations approximated 3 percent. This meant that many projects yielding a very low economic return were accepted. One study of 147 Corps of Engineers projects started between 1946 and 1962 showed that, even on the basis of the dubious definition of benefits used in justifying the projects, three out of five yielded returns of less than 5½ percent.[17] Another examination of six irrigation projects of the Bureau of Reclamation indicated that only one yielded a return greater than 5 percent and three showed a loss.

Several years ago a new policy was adopted requiring that all projects show a return at least equal to the current yield on long-term government securities. Under that policy the interest rate currently used for evaluation of projects is 5.5 percent.[18] But the policy applies only to newly authorized projects. A number of major projects were authorized by the Congress before the new interest rate criteria came into being but have not yet been started. Although many of them would not yield net benefits high enough to qualify under the new policy, they remain eligible for congressional appropriations and the initiation of construction.

Even more important than the problem of the rate of return on these projects is the dubious measurement of economic benefits often employed in justifying them. In the case of irrigation projects, the value of additional crops grown on irrigated acreage is treated as an economic benefit even though in most years the Department of Agriculture is simultaneously spending large sums to induce other farmers to plant fewer crops. The economic benefits of navigation projects are measured by comparing the transportation rates paid by shippers using the waterway with current rail or truck rates. But rail and truck rates often have little relationship to costs, and such a comparison usually overstates the cost savings of water-borne transportation. In the case of flood control, economic benefits are measured as the costs of the flood damage to private investments located in flood plains that

17. Reported by Robert H. Haveman, *Water Resource Investment and the Public Interest: An Analysis of Federal Expenditures in Ten Southern States* (Vanderbilt University Press, 1965), Chap. 5.

18. For projects authorized before 1968, the rate is 3.25 percent. The rate used to evaluate the Corps of Engineers projects is equal to the market yield on long-term government bonds at the beginning of the fiscal year. However, the rate cannot be increased by more than 0.25 percent annually.

would have occurred without the project. But in all too many cases, the flood plains should never have been developed intensively to begin with—the protection simply encourages uneconomic investments there. What is needed is not an open-ended policy of protecting any and all such investments, but a national policy of regulating investments in flood plain lands, through zoning and other devices.

In general, the economic criteria used to evaluate water resource projects tend to understate costs by the use of a low interest rate charge and to overstate benefits by an uncritical acceptance of immediate effects as a valid measure of national economic gains. Even after correction for deficiencies, many projects still provide benefits that outweigh costs sufficiently to warrant their undertaking. Many others, however, do not.

Subsidized Beneficiaries

Most water resource projects, except those providing electric power, charge the beneficiaries only a small fraction of the cost. While the situation varies from case to case, beneficiaries of these projects are usually not the poor or moderate-income groups. The benefits of flood control generally show up in appreciated land values. Where low- or moderate-income homeowners are being protected, this windfall might not be a serious problem. But an increasing number of flood control projects are designed to open up for development lands on which there is still little construction, and thus land developers and speculators are the major beneficiaries. Moreover, on many flood plain lands it is chiefly commercial and industrial investments that are protected—and again, many of them should never have been made in the first place. But having taken a calculated risk in investing in a flood-prone area on cheap land, the investors persuade the government to undertake flood protection and reap the benefits of increased land prices.

Navigation projects provide subsidized transportation to some localities in competition with others having no such advantages. While part of the benefits of low-cost transportation are shared widely by all who buy the products so transported, some clearly accrue to those who, either through luck or foresight, own land and businesses in the favored locations. And one project spawns another, as disgruntled business firms along one watercourse see their more fortunate competitors become the beneficiaries of massive federal investments, and quite naturally seek the same favored treatment.

As a general proposition, the imposition on beneficiaries of federal charges covering a substantial fraction of the costs of water resource projects would have at least two advantages: willingness to pay the charges would be a solid indication of the economic feasibility of the project; and the payment of such charges would relieve the general taxpayer of subsidizing well-to-do land owners and business firms. While there are some valid economic reasons not to charge beneficiaries the full costs of large-scale projects, the advantages of doing so, in terms of greater equity and lessening pressure for uneconomic projects, probably outweigh the disadvantages. Moreover, levying a charge on beneficiaries that covers a significant fraction of costs would change the political incentives. Projects whose costs exceeded their benefits would be seen as such by the beneficiaries themselves, since they would be bearing the costs. As a consequence the widespread practice of lobbying for uneconomic projects would be sharply curtailed, and many projects that might be initiated under current policy would fall by the wayside.

Congressional Procedures

The procedure by which Congress appropriates funds for water resource projects lends itself to the inclusion of questionable projects in the budget. Most of these projects take many years to construct. When Congress appropriates funds to start a new project, however, it does not appropriate the funds necessary to complete it; rather, each year Congress appropriates enough to cover the construction costs for that year. In the first year of a project, those costs are particularly small—the Tennessee-Tombigbee waterway project, with a total estimated cost of $465 million, was started with an appropriation of $1 million in fiscal 1971. As a consequence, by adding only a very small amount to the budget, sufficient for the modest first-year costs, the Congress can add many projects, whose ultimate costs are very large, to the President's budget recommendations. Once started, a project is most unlikely to be terminated before completion.

In the ten years from 1961 to 1970, various presidents requested 282 new construction projects for the Corps of Engineers at a total cost of $4.1 billion. The Congress in that same period appropriated funds for

552 new starts whose total construction costs were $8.6 billion—more than twice what had been requested. Yet in no one year did the appropriations required to begin any of the new projects amount to more than a few million dollars. And by slightly reducing the appropriations for construction work on projects begun in earlier years, Congress each year appeared to be cutting the President's budget while it was actually doubling the eventual amount of construction. The practice continued at an accelerated pace in the appropriations for fiscal year 1973 enacted last year. The President asked for thirteen new starts at a total cost of $452 million; the Congress appropriated money for thirty-seven new starts at a total cost of $1,146 million— two and one-half times the requested amount. Yet the appropriations required for the first year of construction on all the congressional additions amounted to only $7 million.

Revising congressional procedures to require that the full costs of the project be appropriated in the year the project is started would confront the Congress with the budgetary consequences of its actions. A $100 million project could no longer be launched on a $1 million appropriation. This "full-funding" technique has been proposed to the Congress in past years, but it has always been resisted vigorously, and successfully.

Future Budgets for Water Resources

In the 1974 budget the administration requested only five new starts with an ultimate cost of $69 million. In addition, it proposed to stretch out and delay the pace of construction in ongoing projects to ensure reductions in budget expenditures. As Table 6-6 shows, the administration estimates that its actions would reduce 1974 expenditures $594 million below the level to which they would have otherwise increased. This estimated reduction seems a bit generous, in the sense that the increase projected before the action to reduce spending was taken seems out of line with recent experience. Nevertheless, significant cuts were made. For the short run, major reductions can be achieved only by stretching out construction of ongoing projects. And this may increase total project costs, since there is an optimum pace of construction that minimizes costs. In the long run, control over new starts is the only way to effect savings.

If new starts for future years are proposed at a level no higher than the average submitted by the administration in the past decade (adjusted for inflation), and—more to the point—if the Congress does not exceed that total, the level of construction outlays by 1977 could be reduced from the $2.0 billion programmed in the 1974 budget to perhaps $1.5 billion. If, in addition, policies for levying reasonable charges against beneficiaries were adopted, an even greater reduction in net budget costs could result. A small part of this would stem from the collection of the charges themselves, but most of it would occur because, under such policies, many projects would no longer be desired by the beneficiaries themselves.

Table 6-7. Federal Outlays, Fiscal Years 1970 and 1973, and Budgetary Alternatives, 1974, 1976, and 1978, for Investment in the Physical Environment

Billions of dollars

			Projected		
Description	1970	1973	1974	1976	1978
Total outlays before administration cuts	9.8	14.5	16.7	21.1	24.5
Administration cuts	...	−0.8	−1.9	−3.9	−4.9
Total, after cuts	9.8	13.7	14.8	17.2	19.6
Alternatives					
1. Revise urban transportation grant program	...	...	0	Up to 1.2	Up to 1.5
2. Increase federal highway and urban mass transit to match receipts of the Highway Trust Fund	...	...	0	1.1	1.6
3. Provide new starts for water resources construction at the average level recommended by the administration during past 10 years	...	...	0	−0.2	−0.4
4. Substantially raise charges to beneficiaries for water resource budgets	...	...	0	−0.1	−0.2
5. Provide waste treatment grants at congressionally authorized level	...	...	+0.3	+3.0	+4.0

Sources: Derived from *The Budget of the United States Government*, and accompanying *Appendix* and *Special Analyses*, relevant years, and projections by authors.

Summary of Alternatives

Table 6-7 shows the budgetary consequences of pursuing the various alternatives discussed in this chapter. The first line projects the budget for investment in the physical environment *before* the cuts the administration proposes. Those cuts are then shown separately. Finally, the budgetary implications of the alternatives outlined in the chapter are projected. All the data are shown as actual outlays, which in most cases follow the making of grants or letting of contracts after a lag of one or more years.

7. General Revenue Sharing

UNDER A REVENUE SHARING strategy a portion of federal tax receipts are disbursed by means of a predetermined formula to state and local governments, with few strings attached. Washington's role is that of collecting taxes and distributing the receipts to lower levels of government; it is not involved in designing, administering, or regulating the specific public services on which the money is spent. These tasks are left to the recipients of the money.

Two types of revenue sharing may be encompassed by this strategy: *general revenue sharing*, under which the recipient units of governments are free to use their grants as they see fit, and *special revenue sharing*, or block grants, under which the recipients must spend their grants on programs in a broad functional area, such as education or urban development. Besides allowing the recipients a great deal of discretion as to how to use their grants, the two types of revenue sharing have certain other characteristics in common. First, the distribution of money is automatic: the recipient unit of government need not apply for the grant, and the amount it receives depends solely on the way in which the demographic and socioeconomic characteristics of the state or locality fit the distribution formula. Second, red tape—rules, regulations, restrictions, and reporting requirements— are kept to a minimum. Third, the recipients are not required to provide matching funds or to maintain prescribed levels of expenditures.

Note. This chapter was prepared with the assistance of Robert D. Reischauer.

266

There is no neat line of demarcation between categorical grants and various forms of special revenue sharing. The four special revenue sharing proposals of the Nixon administration retain many detailed specifications of how the funds are to be used that make these programs like a series of modifications to the existing grants for social programs. For that reason they were discussed with the other social grant programs in Chapter 5. In theory, it is possible to design a general revenue sharing program that literally has no federal controls or a special revenue sharing grant that contains only a loose designation of some broad functional area of spending. In practice, of course, the matter of "no strings attached" is relative. The general revenue sharing program enacted last year, for example, contains a number of restrictions and regulations that distinguish it somewhat from simple cash grants without strings to states and localities.

Few major domestic initiatives have received broader bipartisan support than the federal government's initial foray into the revenue sharing strategy—the State and Local Fiscal Assistance Act of 1972. Evidently the prospect of "less red tape" had great appeal. Furthermore, revenue sharing was seen as a way of getting at certain problems that lay beyond the established federal strategies. Various proponents hoped for various results. Some viewed revenue sharing as the solution for general fiscal problems confronting state and local governments. Others welcomed revenue sharing as a means of reducing the direct involvement of the federal government in domestic problems. Still others hoped that revenue sharing would redistribute resources among states and localities so as to enable the poorer ones to raise the level of public services they provided.

Broad Objectives

During the years leading up to enactment, the major rationale given for pursuing a revenue sharing strategy was that it offered an all-purpose means of overcoming a number of very different general fiscal problems afflicting state and local governments. Although short-run economic conditions have changed considerably since the initial years, revenue sharing is still seen in part as a vehicle for fiscal reform.

Solving Fiscal Problems

A task force established by President Johnson in 1964 first proposed revenue sharing as a method of alleviating what was then seen as a growing fiscal imbalance in the federal system. In their judgment, the resources needed by states and localities to provide adequately the public services for which these units had traditionally been responsible were likely to grow more rapidly than the ability of these governments to raise revenues. At the same time, with continued economic prosperity, the progressive nature of the federal tax system would generate revenues at a pace far faster than that needed to maintain and even expand existing federal programs. A surplus, or "fiscal dividend" as it was called, would develop, which, unless disposed of, could become a drag on the nation's economy. Although tax cuts could be counted on to absorb this fiscal dividend, revenue sharing was seen by the task force members as a preferable alternative. The task force suggested that the gap between state and local needs and revenues be filled by distributing to the states 2 percent of the federal personal income tax base each year; revenue sharing thus was to be a way of channeling federal surpluses into an expansion of much needed state and local public services.

The fiscal dividend, however, was devoured first by the expanding war in Southeast Asia and then by a combination of federal tax cuts and growth in domestic federal spending. As part of this growth, federal grants to state and local governments rose sharply, from $8 billion in 1962 to $36 billion in 1972. But the bulk of the additional grant funds was directed toward the federally dominated, though state administered, transfer programs such as public assistance, Medicaid, and food stamps and toward such new public services as manpower training, model cities, and community action programs. A much smaller part of the growth was used to support the traditional state and local functions—education, law enforcement, sanitation, and the like. In effect, what happened was that the federal government directed the use of federal resources toward a set of nationally determined and newly chosen goals rather than providing those resources to state and local governments for additional expansion of the more traditional public services. This development can be interpreted as a rejection by the President and the Congress of revenue sharing as a strategy for dealing with the fiscal imbalance in the federal system. Instead, reliance was placed on other strategies—cash transfers, helping people buy essentials, and categorical grants—as the preferred means of using the fiscal dividend.

By 1970 it became clear that the problem of fiscal drag had at least temporarily disappeared. Rising expenditures and tax cuts left little fiscal dividend to be distributed. But at about the same time the fiscal problem of state and local governments appeared to be getting worse. Many observers became convinced that the tax base on which state and local governments depended for their revenues was not expanding fast enough to furnish those governments with the revenue needed to meet their responsibilities. They were being asked not only to finance growth in their traditional programs but also to find funds to pay their share of the costs of new federal initiatives. Revenue sharing then attracted new attention as a potential means of providing the additional revenues. President Nixon expressed this view when first unveiling his general revenue sharing program in the 1971 State of the Union Message: "All across America today, States and cities are confronted with a financial crisis. . . . Most are caught between the prospects of bankruptcy on the one hand and adding to an already crushing tax burden on the other."

In retrospect, the fears of spreading municipal bankruptcy, chronic state budget deficits, and continuing program cutbacks were exaggerated. The fiscal tribulation of states and localities during the 1970 to 1972 period stemmed largely from the cyclical downturn in the economy. The recession increased the demand for state and local services. Rising unemployment forced many onto the welfare rolls, and falling incomes caused more citizens to shun expensive private services in favor of their cheaper public counterparts, such as municipal hospitals and public colleges. While the demand for state and local services was increased by the recession, the downturn in the economy also undercut the revenues of these governments. During this three-year period, the revenues of state and local governments fell about $11 billion below what they would have been had the economy been running at full employment. To compensate for this increased demand and revenue shortfall, states and localities were forced to raise their tax rates and impose new taxes. Between 1969 and 1971 state sales taxes were enacted or raised twenty times, state personal income taxes were raised thirty times, and corporation income taxes went up thirty-six times.

Pressure was also exerted on state and local finances from another source. Unionization, political and racial forces, and a widespread feeling that public employees were underpaid combined to push up wages and fringe benefits in the public sector even faster than those

in the private sector. The costs of goods and services purchased by
states and localities also rose rapidly during this period, and the cost
of borrowing reached its highest level in decades, but rising wages
played the largest role in pushing up the costs of providing state and
local services.

As the economy began to pick up in 1972, the general fiscal crisis
that many had predicted as the chronic condition of state and local
governments began to abate. While the aggregate figures on state and
local budgets published by the Department of Commerce are an inadequate measure of the fiscal health of these governments, the data
for fiscal 1972, which revealed an aggregate general government surplus of $3.7 billion, made it clear that a dramatic change had taken
place. By the year's end, almost one-third of the state governments
expected to end their fiscal years with substantial surpluses—California $850 million, New York $75 million, Arkansas $100 million,
Florida $300 million, and so on. A few large cities were rumored to
have modest surpluses also.

Projections of the aggregate fiscal outlook for the next decade suggest that the cyclical crisis of the past three years did not foreshadow
a long-run imbalance. Rather, the balance that appeared in 1972
should continue for some years. If the relative size of existing federal
grant programs is maintained and an expanding economy leads to
relatively full employment, states and localities *in the aggregate*
should be able to maintain and improve the public services they now
provide. Even without higher tax rates, the increase in their revenues
should slightly outpace the increased expenditures necessitated by
population growth, inflation, and a moderate improvement in service
levels. Table 7-1 projects state and local budgets on these assumptions.

The reasons for this projected improvement are fairly easy to iso-
late. They were discussed in *Setting National Priorities, 1972*[1] and need
only be summarized here.

In the first place, the population groups served by many major state
and local programs will not increase as rapidly in the 1970s as they
did in the 1960s. Whereas the number of children attending public
elementary and secondary schools increased 27 percent in the last
decade, the recent decline in the birthrate has caused a leveling off;
the number of school children should drop by 2 percent by 1980, re-

1. Charles L. Schultze and others, *Setting National Priorities: The 1972 Budget*
(Brookings Institution, 1971).

Table 7-1. State and Local Expenditures, by Function, and Revenue, by Source, Fiscal Years 1971, 1975, and 1978

Billions of dollars

	Expenditure		
Description	1971 (actual)	1975 (estimate)	1978 (estimate)
Expenditure and function			
General expenditure	150.7	206.3	259.4
Local schools	41.8	56.1	68.3
Higher education and other education except local schools	17.6	26.6	36.7
Public welfare	18.2	27.2	36.4
Highways	18.1	20.8	23.7
Hospitals and health	11.2	16.6	21.9
Basic urban services[a]	19.9	27.3	34.5
Administration and other[b]	23.8	31.6	37.7
Utility deficit	1.4	1.8	2.2
Debt retirement and additions to liquid assets[c]	11.6	18.0	22.4
Contributions to retirement systems	5.2	7.1	9.0
Total	168.9	233.2	293.0
Source of revenue			
Taxes	95.0	140.3	173.8
Property	37.9	53.8	64.9
Individual income	11.9	23.5	33.2
Corporation income	3.4	5.7	7.3
Sales	33.2	46.3	55.6
Other	8.6	11.0	12.7
Federal grants-in-aid	26.1	43.2	53.9
Fees and charges	16.9	23.7	30.5
New debt issued	12.2	27.4	31.7
Miscellaneous[d]	7.4	10.8	13.3
Total	157.6	245.5	303.3

Sources: 1971, U.S. Bureau of the Census, *Governmental Finances in 1970–71*, GF71–No. 5 (1972); 1975, 1978, authors' estimates. Figures may not add to totals because of rounding.

a. Includes fire protection, police protection, correction, sewerage and other sanitation, parks and recreation, housing and urban renewal, and transportation and terminals.

b. Includes administration and general control, general public buildings, interest on general debt, employment services, and miscellaneous functions.

c. Excludes assets of social insurance funds.

d. Includes special assessments, sales of property, interest earnings, profits from liquor stores, and other miscellaneous earnings.

ducing the pressure for expanded school budgets. Similarly, barring a drastic change in the definition of eligibility, welfare rolls cannot expand as fast as they have in the past because today the welfare system is much closer to serving all of the eligible population. Of course, benefit levels could be raised significantly, and the working poor, most of whom are not now eligible, could be encompassed by some new program. But such changes are likely to occur only if the federal government assumes all the costs of the public assistance programs.

Second, several recent federal initiatives should give states and localities some fiscal relief. Under the social security amendments of 1972, for example, the existing welfare programs for the aged, disabled, and blind will be replaced by a federal supplemental security income program. This could relieve states of about a $1 billion responsibility each year. In the area of higher education, the recently enacted program of aid to college students could allow the states to raise tuition at public universities, thus shifting some of the burden for maintaining these institutions onto the federal government and the families of richer students.

Third, the rate of increase of public employee compensation is likely to moderate during the 1970s. After a decade of rapid improvement in wages, pensions, and other fringe benefits, public employee wages in a large number of areas now match or exceed those of comparable jobs in the private sector, and job security, pension plans, vacations, and other fringe benefits tend to be more generous. Wage increases will continue but are less likely to exceed the rise in private wages and salaries, as they have in the last eight years.

Fourth, the revenue structure of states and localities has gradually been shifting toward taxes that are more responsive to economic growth. Personal and corporation income taxes constituted only one-tenth of the tax revenue of states and localities in 1960; by 1972, just under one-fifth came from such sources.

Finally, the general revenue sharing program, even if not expanded further, will give these governments roughly $6 billion a year, which they can use for support of general government programs.

Some notes of caution should be introduced at this juncture. Surpluses of the magnitude shown in Table 7-1 will in reality never appear in state or local budgets. They will be eaten up by tax reductions or expenditures on new programs. Pollution control, day care, early childhood education, and school finance reform are just a few of the candidates that could easily absorb any "spare change" in the pockets of states and localities. Moreover, if the federal government dismantles existing grant-in-aid programs and does not replace them with equally generous special revenue sharing distributions, states and local governments will have to accept an added burden if they decide to continue the specific programs now funded from these grants-in-

Table 7-2. Amount and Growth of Federal, State, and Local Taxes, and Percentage
of Personal Income, Selected Fiscal Years, 1960–72

	Federal			State and local		
Fiscal year	Amount (millions of dollars)	Ratio to 1960 level	Percentage of personal income	Amount (millions of dollars)	Ratio to 1960 level	Percentage of personal income
1960	96.1	1.0	24.0	40.0	1.0	10.0
1965	123.7	1.3	23.0	58.6	1.5	10.9
1967	150.1	1.6	23.9	70.1	1.8	11.1
1970	190.3	2.0	23.6	100.1	2.5	12.4
1972ᵃ	227.2	2.4	24.3	124.7	3.1	13.3

Sources: U.S. Department of Commerce, Bureau of Economic Analysis, *Survey of Current Business*, various issues, Tables 1.9, 3.1, 3.3.

a. Preliminary estimate by authors based on Bureau of Economic Analysis data.

aid. Finally, much of the growth in fiscal capacity will probably occur in jurisdictions that already have adequate public services. Deteriorating cities and poor rural areas may still be hard pressed to provide even minimal levels of public services. On balance, however, the case for an expanded revenue sharing strategy cannot rest on a projected overall shortage of state and local revenues to meet the growth in existing programs.

An alternative fiscal rationale for general revenue sharing has recently emerged—to provide relief to state and local taxpayers. In his statement accompanying the signing of the general revenue sharing bill in Philadelphia in 1972, President Nixon put tax relief at the top of the list of possible effects of the new program: "In many States and localities, it will mean lower property taxes or lower sales taxes or lower income taxes than would otherwise have been the case. Revenue sharing can provide desperately needed tax relief for millions of Americans."[2]

Compared with the growth of federal taxes, the increase in state and local revenues has been substantial: between 1960 and 1972 these receipts more than trebled. As a fraction of personal income, state and local taxes went up by a third (Table 7-2). The political cost of this increase, however, was considerable. A widespread revolt against property tax increases manifested itself in the rejection of school budgets and bond issues; governors who had supported raising sales and in-

2. "Statement by the President Upon Signing the Bill Providing State and Local Fiscal Assistance," *Weekly Compilation of Presidential Documents*, Vol. 8 (Oct. 23, 1972), p. 1535.

come taxes were defeated in their bids for reelection almost without exception. Relieving the "crushing burden" of state and local taxes thus engendered a good deal of public support. The fiscal rationale for revenue sharing had not necessarily weakened, but it had shifted considerably since the mid-1960s—from a tool for providing increased public services to a method of providing tax relief at the state and local level.

Redistributing Income and Resources

In addition to its fiscal objectives, revenue sharing has been seen as a means of affecting the distribution of income and public services. Two different kinds of redistribution are involved: a redistribution of income among individuals through a shift in the kind of taxes they pay and a redistribution of public services so as to favor poorer states and local governments.

One kind of redistribution has to do with the tax system. Despite its numerous loopholes and special preferences, the federal tax system, which would raise the money needed for revenue sharing, is slightly progressive—the higher a taxpayer's income, the greater the share taken by federal taxes. State and local taxes, on the other hand, are generally regressive or at best proportional—the poor pay the same or possibly a higher share of their income in state and local taxes than do the rich. To the extent that revenue sharing substitutes federal for state and local taxes as a way of financing state and local services, the total tax system becomes somewhat more progressive, relieving some of the tax burden for lower-income groups and increasing it for upper-income groups. Redistribution would be greatest if the federal income tax were increased to pay for revenue sharing, balanced by an equal decrease in the less progressive of state and local taxes, especially sales levies.

Another possible redistributional objective involves the way in which shared funds are distributed among state and local units of government. Although the earlier sections of this chapter suggested that there does not appear to be an imbalance between the *aggregate* resources and responsibilities of state and local governments, there is a problem of imbalance in the distribution of these resources.

States and localities differ tremendously both in their ability to raise revenues and in their needs for public services. As the first column in Table 7-3 indicates, per capita income, which offers a crude measure of a jurisdiction's ability to raise revenues, varies widely among the states—the lowest (Mississippi) is about half the highest (New York). Fiscal capacities, as measured by the yield of an average system of taxes and charges, are even more varied (second column of Table 7-3). Some states in which per capita income is not very high have the ability to levy special taxes on extractive natural resource industries—copper and other minerals in Wyoming, oil in Louisiana. States such as Florida and Nevada, with large tourist industries, gain from sales and amusement taxes paid by visitors.

The disparities that exist within any one state are even greater; wealthy suburbs often have five or ten times the per capita tax base of poorer communities only a few miles away. Thus to generate an equivalent level of per capita spending on public services, poor jurisdictions would have to impose much higher tax rates than rich ones. This disparity is further complicated by the fact that equal spending may not guarantee equivalent levels of public services because the needs for and costs of such services vary tremendously from state to state or from community to community. Most often the areas with the greatest needs are those that are least able to raise necessary revenue. For example, if the fraction of the population living in poverty is used as a

Table 7-3. Relative Per Capita Income and Fiscal Capacity, Highest and Lowest States, 1971

Relative per capita income[a]		*Relative fiscal capacity*	
State	*Ratio of per capita income to U.S. average*	*State*	*Index of fiscal capacity*
Highest		*Highest*	
New York	1.20	Nevada	1.72
Connecticut	1.20	Alaska	1.70
Alaska	1.17	Wyoming	1.46
Nevada	1.16	California	1.20
New Jersey	1.16	New York	1.15
Lowest		*Lowest*	
Mississippi	0.67	South Carolina	0.71
Arkansas	0.74	Mississippi	0.73
Alabama	0.74	Alabama	0.74
South Carolina	0.76	West Virginia	0.76
Louisiana	0.78	Arkansas	0.78

Sources: *Survey of Current Business*, Vol. 52 (August 1972), p. 25; and Allen D. Manvel, unpublished material for Brookings project, Monitoring Revenue Sharing.
a. Excludes District of Columbia.

crude guide to a state's relative need for expenditures on welfare, the five poorest states have three times as much "need" as the five richest states. Similarly, central cities with deteriorating tax bases often have problems of crime, pollution, hard-to-educate children, and decayed housing that wealthier suburbs do not have to contend with at all.

In sum, public services and tax rates vary significantly from state to state and from locality to locality. Very often the areas with the highest taxes provide the least adequate services.

Federal and, to a lesser extent, state grants have been used to moderate this problem. For example, state aid to school districts is usually related inversely to the size of the tax base of the district; the fraction of each state's share of welfare expenditures paid by federal grants is higher for states with lower average incomes. Similarly, a great number of federal programs are designed to help only jurisdictions with specific problems—urban renewal, model cities, public housing grants, youth employment grants, and so forth. Some states (for example, New York) have also instituted programs of general urban aid to help cities with their special problems. In the Minneapolis–St. Paul region a metropolitan tax sharing scheme has been instituted. But such programs are relatively small. Most state and local services must be financed from the existing tax base without any compensation for the area's relative ability to raise revenue or its need for services.

Revenue sharing is intended to moderate the variation that now exists in state and local tax rates and public service levels. To do this the distribution formula has to include such elements as the fiscal capacity of recipient jurisdictions, their need for public services, and possibly the relative cost of providing such services. To the extent that revenue sharing displaces the federal grant-in-aid programs that now allot a disproportionate share of their funds to poorer or needier jurisdictions, its redistributive effect will be muted. It is worth noting that the redistributive goal of revenue sharing can be thwarted if states and localities use the receipts to reduce their most progressive taxes or spend their grants on programs and projects that disproportionately benefit their wealthiest citizens.

Decentralizing Power

A third broad objective that has been advocated for revenue sharing is decentralization. According to this view, revenue sharing is needed to restructure—or revitalize—the federal system. Supposedly the proliferation and expansion during the past decade of federal programs, particularly the categorical grants, has shifted too much of the decision making about public programs to Washington. There are three different, though related, aspects of this argument—the problem of power, the problem of effectiveness, and the problem of priorities.

In the view of the administration, federal bureaucrats and lawmakers make decisions that would best be left to state and local officials. Often the federal agencies administering grant programs deal directly with their counterparts in state and local bureaucracies, further undercutting the authority and budgetary control of governors, mayors, and elected legislatures.[3] Judgments about the details of local programs— where facilities are located, the specific kinds of services to be provided, who is eligible and who is not—are made in Washington rather than in the communities themselves and by the elected officials close to the problems. Though conceding that some programs must be national in scope and directed by the federal government, this view holds that the balance has shifted too far in that direction. Feeling that they have little say about their government, citizens have become frustrated, alienated, and cynical. A revenue sharing strategy, it is argued, will remedy the situation by shifting decision-making power and budgetary control back to states and localities, which are pictured as more attuned to local needs, more responsive to local pressure, and better able to deal with the actual problems of individual communities.

The second aspect of this rationale for revenue sharing deals with the related problem of program effectiveness and efficiency. No matter how capable the federal government is of administering any particular grant program effectively, the proliferation of categorical grants over the past ten years has enmeshed it so deeply in trying to control the delivery of hundreds of individual programs at the local level that it has become tied up in red tape and confusion. Continuing changes in the laws, regulations, and appropriations governing these programs have made it difficult for state and local governments to plan their own budgets and programs. And the very complexities of the grant-in-aid system rewards grantsmanship rather than need. Chapter 5 discussed

---

3. For an example, see Jerome T. Murphy, "Grease the Squeaky Wheel: A Report on the Implementation of Title V of the Elementary and Secondary Education Act of 1965, *Grants to Strengthen State Departments of Education*" (Harvard Graduate School of Education, 1973; processed).

the problem of grant proliferation and suggested various means of dealing with it while still retaining certain aspects of the categorical grant approach. Concentrating future budgetary increase on the general revenue sharing strategy would deal with the problem in a more radical way by avoiding many of the federal controls on the use of grant funds.

Finally there is the problem of priorities. General revenue sharing is not simply an alternative means of accomplishing the same goals as other federal programs. It emphasizes different objectives. Depending on precisely how it is designed, it might result in some reduction of state and local taxes, some increase in the general level of services typically provided by state and local governments, and some narrowing of fiscal disparities among those governments, so that they can provide more nearly comparable services. Categorical grants and other federal domestic programs have different goals. They aim at delivering the kinds of public services that most states and localities, left to their own devices, would not provide at all or provide at a lower level, even with the additional revenues available. Hence, the emphasis given to revenue sharing over other strategies—particularly categorical grants—must depend not merely on judgments about the distribution of decision-making power in a federal system and the relative efficiency with which public services are delivered, but also on judgments about what combination of national goals it is important to pursue in a total federal budget that necessarily commands limited resources.

The Existing Program

The disparate rationales for pursuing a revenue sharing strategy imply different sorts of programs, each with its own method of distributing the revenues and its own set of broad restrictions and incentives. Some of the broad objectives are antithetical to others. Clearly it would be difficult to pursue major tax relief and a large increase in spending simultaneously. If the prime objective of revenue sharing is to increase the general level of state and local services, an attempt should be made to minimize the amount of the grant that recipient units of government divert into tax relief. One means of doing so is to base the distribution of shared revenues on each jurisdiction's tax effort. The distribution formula, for example, might include the ratio of tax collections to personal income in the jurisdiction. A state or local government that used one year's revenue sharing funds to reduce taxes would find its revenue sharing allotment smaller in the next year (provided other jurisdictions did not do the same). Many needy jurisdictions, however, precisely because they are poor, find it difficult to take as high a percentage of their citizens' incomes in taxes as do richer jurisdictions. They would be penalized under such a distribution formula. Yet if the objective of revenue sharing is to eliminate disparities among governments in service levels, it is precisely these poorer jurisdictions that should receive disproportionate allotments of funds.[4] By contrast, if the primary goal of revenue sharing is to revitalize state and local government, the distribution of resources should not necessarily be skewed in the direction of jurisdictions that are poor or have high tax efforts. Rather, the formula under the "revitalize" assumption should reward those that are potentially the most responsive to public wishes. But there is no objective and politically acceptable means by which the federal government can rank state and local governments on this basis.

The general revenue sharing program enacted last year reflects the conflict among the various rationales for revenue sharing. Its complex distribution formula also reflects political realities; it is a compromise among the interests of many different kinds of jurisdictions—rich versus poor, cities versus states, suburbs versus central cities.

The existing general revenue sharing program calls for the distribution of approximately $6 billion a year for the next five years to the nation's general-purpose governments. The money is first allocated among the states. Each state as an area is allotted the amount available to it under either the original Senate version or the original House version of the general revenue sharing plan, whichever is greater.[5] Under the Senate's distribution formula the revenue is divided among the states according to their total populations, relative incomes, and tax efforts (that is, the ratio of total taxes collected to personal income); the House version of the formula includes, in addition, urbanized population and state income tax collections. One-third of each state's allotment is given to the state government to use

4. One could define effort in a progressive manner (for example, the square of the ratio of tax receipts to personal income).

5. For 1972 each state area's allotment was reduced by about 8.4 percent so as to keep the total within the appropriated limit of $5.3 billion.

as it sees fit. The remaining two-thirds is divided among the county areas of the state on the basis of each county's population, tax effort, and relative income. The county governments, townships, and municipalities receive portions of this allotment equal to each one's share of the aggregate tax receipts (other than for schools) collected by these units within a county area.[6] The amount designated for the municipalities of the area is apportioned among them on the basis of their populations, tax efforts, and relative incomes. A similar distribution method is used to divide up the township's share. All told, more than 38,000 units of government—states, counties, municipalities, townships, Indian tribes, and Alaskan native villages—receive revenue sharing checks from the Department of the Treasury. Four-fifths of these jurisdictions have fewer than 2,500 inhabitants. The smallest recipient of revenue sharing is California's one-member Cortina Rancheria Indian tribe.

To one degree or another all the objectives mentioned in the previous section are pursued by the general revenue sharing program. The conflicting nature of these goals means that the program's effectiveness in achieving any of the objectives is partly offset by its attempt to achieve the others. The redistributional objective is pursued by allowing the relative income factor to play an important part in determining the distribution of resources. States and local governments whose residents have below-average incomes usually receive larger grants, both in absolute terms and as a percentage of personal income. In general, the southern states benefit most (Table 7-4). Yet because of other components of the distribution formula, the state of New York receives more, on a per capita basis, than three of the five states with the lowest per capita incomes. At the local level, the redistributional effect of the revenue sharing program is further muted, since the tax-effort factor often offsets the relative income factor. Poor, rural counties, precisely because they are poor, tend to have tax levies for purposes other than schools that are only a small fraction of personal income, and hence are penalized by the tax-effort term in the

6. A few state governments, including Delaware, West Virginia, and Kentucky, currently receive more than one-third of the revenue sharing funds coming into the state because of the provision in the law that revenue sharing entitlements in excess of the sum of 50 percent of a township's or municipality's adjusted tax revenues and its intergovernmental receipts will be added to the entitlement of the county government; should the county government's amount then exceed the 50 percent limitation, the excess goes to the state government.

Table 7-4. Per Capita Personal Income and Revenue Sharing Grants, Five Richest
and Five Poorest States and County Areas, 1972

Dollars per capita

State	State		Three richest counties in state		Three poorest counties in state	
State	Personal income	Revenue sharing grant	Personal income	Revenue sharing grant	Personal income	Revenue sharing grant
Richest states						
Connecticut	3,885	22.16	4,209	14.33	3,265	12.31
Alaska	3,725	21.63	4,525	19.28	3,112	16.48
New Jersey	3,674	23.22	4,344	10.97	3,005	16.34
California	3,614	27.16	4,432	17.36	2,434	27.11
New York	3,608	32.28	4,573	13.58	2,292	29.73
Poorest states						
Mississippi	1,925	39.85	2,575	23.02	1,113	32.53
Arkansas	2,142	28.36	2,723	18.33	1,392	17.74
South Carolina	2,303	27.59	2,685	18.72	1,384	14.36
Alabama	2,317	26.28	2,852	20.19	1,215	16.37
Louisiana	2,330	33.65	2,825	24.42	1,189	25.33

Sources: State population and personal income, U.S. Department of the Treasury, Office of Revenue Sharing, "Data Used for Interstate Allocation" (computer tabulation); county population and personal income, Office of Revenue Sharing, "Data Elements, Entitlement Period 1" (1973; processed); revenue sharing grants, calculated from Office of Revenue Sharing, "3rd Payment, Entitlement Period 3" (1973; processed). (Adjustments were made for California and Connecticut on the basis of additional information.)

formula. In four of the ten states listed in Table 7-4, the three poorest counties on average receive smaller per capita revenue sharing grants than the three richest, and in two more the amounts are approximately the same. In the poorest counties, however, the revenue sharing grant usually constitutes a larger percentage of personal income than it does in the richest counties.

The limits placed on the maximum and minimum amounts that any jurisdiction may receive also reduce the redistributional impact of the revenue sharing program. The stipulation that no local unit of government obtain more than 145 percent of the average per capita grant to local governments in the state where that unit is located penalizes numerous local governments. The rule affects the largest cities in twelve states (Boston, St. Louis, Norfolk, Philadelphia, Baltimore, Hartford, Wilmington, Louisville, Detroit, Newark, Cleveland, and Providence), and it is felt in a few impoverished rural counties as well. Conversely, the guarantee that no unit of local government will receive less than 20 percent of the statewide average per capita grant ensures that significant revenue sharing funds flow into even very rich jurisdictions such as Hewlett Bay Park Village, New York, or low-tax jurisdictions such as the townships of the plains states.

The probable effect of the distribution formula on the use of revenue sharing funds is hard to project. Including tax effort in the formula encourages states and localities to increase expenditures rather than cut taxes. However, there are many other factors in the formula, and for most jurisdictions revenue sharing is only a small fraction of total revenues collected. A state or local government that uses funds to cut taxes may be penalized by only a small reduction in future revenue sharing grants if a number of other local governments in the state are doing the same thing.

Under the law, state governments may use their revenue sharing allotments for any expenditures they wish to make or for reducing taxes. Localities are required to spend their grants on the "priority" expenditure categories—public safety, environmental protection, public transportation, health, recreation, libraries, social services for the poor or aged, financial administration, and ordinary and necessary capital expenditures. But the force of this restriction will probably be very limited.[7] In practice, local governments can use money from revenue sharing to replace their own funds that would otherwise be used to support the priority categories. The freed local resources can then be used to reduce local taxes or to increase expenditures on items not on the priority list.

At its current level, general revenue sharing amounts to less than 5 percent of the collective expenditures of the recipient units of government. This is obviously not enough to bring about a drastic change in state or local governmental behavior or lead to a revitalization of the federal system. It can be argued, however, that some changes in the structure of local government are being affected by the restriction of revenue sharing to general-purpose governments and that an expansion of the revenue sharing strategy would reinforce this influence. School districts and special service districts, which have proliferated in recent years, are not eligible for revenue sharing funds. Some ob-

7. In March 1973 a federal district court ruled that Atlanta violated the revenue sharing act when it put $4.5 million of its revenue sharing money in its general fund to pay firemen's salaries, and then transferred an equivalent amount from the general fund to the water and sewer fund in order to reduce water and sewer rates in accordance with a city resolution stipulating that its revenue sharing allotment be used for tax relief. Similar tax relief uses in other localities have not been challenged in the courts. Charges that revenue sharing caused switching from one use to another, however, could be proved only in the first year of the program when budgets had already been made up without expectation of the revenue sharing grant.

servers think that such single-purpose governmental entities are less visible and less responsive to popular pressure than units of government that bear general responsibilities. The exclusion of single-purpose districts from the revenue sharing program may provide an impetus for merging these special entities with general-purpose bodies.

Many of the incentives built into the revenue sharing program could have important repercussions. Some of these effects were intended. For example, the state income tax factor contained in the House's interstate distribution formula may lead some states to rely more heavily on income taxes than sales taxes for their revenues. On the other hand, some of the repercussions of the general revenue sharing program may come as a surprise. In parts of the nation the skeletal governments that were left in the graveyard of fiscal federalism may come back to life. For example, eleven midwestern and plains states have nearly 13,000 township governments, of which the overwhelming majority in recent years have spent little, taxed less, and generally been of minor importance. Partly because of the guarantee that all local government units receive a revenue sharing grant equal to at least 20 percent of the per capita state average, more than $80 million a year will be pumped into these townships, an amount equivalent to more than one-third of their tax revenue in 1971. The revenue sharing program also may result in local governments' relying less heavily on user charges and fees. Whereas taxes are counted in the distribution formula, user revenues are disregarded. Replacing sanitation, sewerage, or municipal utility charges with increased property taxes would therefore raise a jursidiction's revenue sharing allotment. In the opinion of most observers, fees and charges are now underutilized, so this would be a step in the wrong direction. Finally, in some states the distribution of the revenue sharing money—two-thirds to local governments and one-third to state governments— might significantly alter the state-local fiscal balance that has evolved over the past century. In places where the state traditionally has assumed much of the fiscal responsibility for supporting public services, the infusion of money to the local governments, particularly if the current program should be expanded, would represent a major increase in discretionary budget authority. For example, in Delaware the recipient local government units will get under the current program grants approaching one-third of their current tax receipts, while the state will receive an amount under 3 percent of its tax revenue.

It is far too early to analyze how recipients of revenue sharing are

using their grants.[8] Many state governments appear to be devoting
sizable fractions of their allotments to increasing aid to school districts, to holding down state taxes, and to providing direct property
tax relief for the elderly. At the level of local government, it appears
that many recipients are saving their checks for use in fiscal year 1974.
The spotty surveys that have been undertaken indicate that a large
portion of the money being spent is going into capital goods. In part
this is because the first $8.3 billion distributed represented a lump-
sum retroactive payment for the last half of fiscal 1972 as well as the
regular fiscal 1973 allotment. Since few governments had counted on
receiving revenue sharing funds, their fiscal 1973 budgets were already
balanced, and the revenue sharing checks were a windfall. Rather
than expand old or initiate new services late in the fiscal year, construction or the purchase of capital equipment was seen as a logical
alternative. It is possible that the "temporary" nature of the revenue
sharing program may be influencing the uses to which the money is
put. Some local officials have expressed the fear that if they expand
services and the program is terminated after five years, there will be
public pressure to continue the services but no corresponding willingness to raise taxes. On the assumption that the program will continue,
however, revenue sharing funds will eventually become an integral
part of state and local budgets. It will be difficult, if not impossible, to
distinguish the uses to which they are put from the use of state and
local revenues generally.

The Likely Outcome

What effect the current revenue sharing program will have is still
unsettled. If the tax-effort factor in the distribution formula has a
strong influence on state-local decisions, the proportion of funds used
for state and local tax cuts will be low, but, as explained earlier,

8. Some preliminary indication is provided by Advisory Commission on Intergovernmental Relations, "Revenue Sharing: View from the Field," ACIR Information Bulletin
73-3 (March 1973); "Preliminary Results of November 1972 Survey of Federal Grants,"
Senate Subcommittee on Intergovernmental Relations of the Committee on Government Operations (March 1, 1973; processed); *Public Management*, Vol. 55 (January
1973), which devotes the entire issue to revenue sharing; and "Revenue-Sharing Bo-
nanza—Latest Plans of Cities, States," *U.S. News and World Report* (March 5, 1973),
pp. 24–26. More thorough evaluations will be forthcoming from the Brookings Institution's project on Monitoring Revenue Sharing, the Office of Revenue Sharing of the U.S.
Department of the Treasury, and the U.S. General Accounting Office.

this would reduce the redistributional effects of the program. The reverse emphasis might of course have the reverse effect—redistribution prevailing over local tax effort. Further restriction on the kinds of units eligible to receive the funds might alter the program's effect on the federal structure but would encounter substantial political opposition and possibly produce a number of unintended results. Although these elements of the program are under federal control and can be varied to emphasize different objectives, Washington cannot fully determine how state and local governments will respond to the receipt of revenue sharing funds. To a large extent, the impact of the program will be in their hands.

Four possible outcomes are shown schematically in Table 7-5. (In all cases tax and expenditure changes, up or down, refer to changes from levels that would have existed in the absence of revenue sharing.)

Case 1 assumes that federal taxes are not increased and therefore that general revenue sharing is financed by a reduction in other federal programs. It also assumes that state and local governments use the funds to increase expenditures rather than cut taxes. In this case, total public expenditures remain unchanged, and the progressiveness of the tax system as a whole remains unaffected. Disparities among state and local governments in the levels of public services are narrowed, while state and local governments take a larger part, relative to the federal government, in determining expenditure priorities.

Case 2 also assumes no change in federal taxes and therefore that revenue sharing is at the expense of other federal programs. Unlike case 1, however, it assumes that state and local governments use the funds to reduce taxes, keeping expenditures unchanged. As a result, the overall level of public expenditures and taxes decline—the expenditure reduction taking place at the federal level and the tax reduction at the state and local level. The whole tax system—federal, state, and local—would be somewhat more progressive.

Case 3 assumes that federal taxes are raised to finance general revenue sharing (or that a federal tax cut that otherwise would have taken place is forgone). Other federal programs are unchanged, while state and local governments use the proceeds of revenue sharing to increase their expenditures. As a result, total public expenditures and total taxes increase, with the tax increase taking place at the federal level and the expenditure increase at the state and local level. Fiscal disparities among state and local governments are narrowed.

Table 7-5. Alternative Results of General Revenue Sharing on the Level and Composition of Public Expenditures and Taxes[a]

Case	Alternative outcome				Results
	Federal taxes	Expenditures on other federal programs	State and local taxes	Expenditures on state and local programs	
1	0	−	0	+	Unchanged total level of public expenditures and taxation; shift of decisions over budget allocation from federal to lower levels of government; narrowing of state and local fiscal disparities.
2	0	−	−	0	Reduced level of total public expenditures and taxation; expenditure reduction at federal level; tax reductions at lower levels of government.
3	+	0	0	+	Increased level of total public expenditures and taxation; higher state and local expenditures supported by higher federal taxes; narrowing of state and local fiscal disparities.
4	+	0	−	0	Unchanged level of total public expenditures and taxation; increase in federal taxes balanced by cut in state and local taxes, leading to a somewhat more progressive overall tax system.
Likely	slight +	large −	partly −	partly +	Combination of above results, with major impact a mixture of cases 1 and 2.

a. 0, no change; −, reduction; +, increase.

Case 4 also assumes that federal taxes are increased to finance revenue sharing but that state and local governments use the proceeds to reduce their own taxes. The net result is an unchanged total level of public expenditures and taxes but an improvement in the overall tax structure toward a more progressive system.

Impossible as it may be to predict the actual outcome, some mixture of all four cases seems likely. The addition of revenue sharing to the panoply of existing federal programs may lower the probability that the increase in federal revenues accompanying economic growth will be used for a federal tax cut. But the major source of financing for revenue sharing is likely to be a slower rate of increase in other federal programs. State and local governments will probably use revenue sharing funds both to avoid future tax increases and to raise the rate of increase in their expenditures. As a consequence, some combination of all of the various outcomes is likely: a modest shift in the locus of decision making from federal to lower levels of government; some narrowing of disparities in state and local provision of public services; and a slight movement in the direction of a more progressive tax system. And finally, if the effect of revenue sharing in reducing state and local taxes is greater than its effect in raising federal taxes, total revenues and expenditures of the public sector will decline—and vice versa.

Expanding the Program

In future federal budget strategies, revenue sharing is easily expandable. The level of appropriations could be increased without taking on the political problem of modifying the distribution formula. Alternatively, at the price of substantial political controversy, expansion could be accompanied by modifications in the formula to emphasize tax effort, to distribute more of the additional funds to one form of government (for instance, central cities) than to others, or to increase the redistributional effects. With the projected 1976 level of state and local revenues as a benchmark, each additional 1 percent of the revenues contributed by revenue sharing would cost the federal government $1.5 billion.

Compensatory Public Services for the Poor

An expansion of general revenue sharing could be designed to focus on the peculiar problems of jurisdictions containing large concentrations of low-income families. In general, low-income families require more in the way of traditional public services as well as expensive, specialized services. For example, for equivalent levels of safety, cleanliness, and educational attainment, more would have to be spent in a slum than in a typical suburb for police protection, sanitation, and schools—not to mention the added resources needed for day care, welfare, drug treatment and health clinics, and public recreation facilities. The added burden that poor families place on public services is compounded by their inability to contribute appreciably to the support of these services through taxes. Middle- and upper-income residents of jurisdictions with large numbers of poor people therefore bear the cost of supporting the public services required by those who are unable to pay. Faced with the situation, middle- and upper-income families have tended to segregate themselves in exclusive suburban jurisdictions. Zoning and building requirements have been imposed to exclude those who would be a fiscal drain on the community.

A revenue sharing program that compensated states and localities for the cost of providing public services for their low-income residents would alleviate this problem. The amount any jurisdiction received would be equivalent to some fraction of that government's per capita expenditures (financed from its own resources) on public services, multiplied by its number of low-income residents. Such a program would concentrate money in central cities and rural areas. Wealthy suburbs would receive little if anything from such a grant, except as they began to admit low-income residents in larger numbers than they now do. Presumably a compensatory public service revenue sharing program would reduce the reluctance of suburbs to accept low-income housing and would thereby help break up the concentrations of persons with excessive public service needs in a few jurisdictions.

The cost of such a program and its precise distribution among various jurisdictions would depend on two characteristics: the definition of "low-income" residents and the fraction of per capita expenditures reimbursed under the grant formula. Table 7-6 shows the distribution of funds under a program making grants to any jurisdiction

Table 7-6. Distribution of $5 Billion of General Revenue Sharing Grants under a Compensatory Public Service Formula, Selected States

State	Total grant (millions of dollars)	Grant per capita (dollars)	Grant per poor person (dollars)
States with largest per capita grants			
Mississippi	111.1	50	145
Louisiana	162.1	44	174
Alaska	12.9	43	363
New Mexico	42.3	42	186
District of Columbia	27.6	37	224
Median state			
Nevada	11.7	24	268
States with lowest per capita grants			
Indiana	85.7	17	174
New Jersey	114.1	16	199
Ohio	166.3	16	160
Connecticut	44.1	15	208
New Hampshire	10.3	14	158

Source: Authors' estimates, based on the formula described in the text.

equal to one- third of its per capita expenditures times the number of residents whose incomes were below the poverty line (using 1970 census data for the calculation).[9] The total cost to the federal government would be $5 billion. The program could be made more or less generous by changing both the fraction of expenditures covered and the definition of low income. Each 10-percentage-point change in the fraction of per capita expenditures covered would change program costs by about $1.5 billion.

9. How such a program would distribute money within a state can be shown by what might happen, for instance, in New Jersey. The problem-ridden city of Newark would receive roughly $23 per capita, relatively wealthy neighboring Bergen County would receive only $5 per capita, and the relatively poor rural Cumberland County would receive about $10 per capita.

8. The Rising Cost of Defense

THIS YEAR'S DEFENSE BUDGET suggests remarkably little change in the peacetime defense posture of the United States. Against the backdrop of dramatic breakthroughs in international relations and a consequent diminution of the prospects for conflict, the defense posture reflects an essentially standpat position on force levels and defense policy, and its cost continues to go up.

In part, this is a matter of timing. The cease-fire in Vietnam, for example, came after the budget was prepared. Although progress in the negotiations during the fall of 1972 pointed strongly to an early end of direct American involvement, it may have been tactically difficult to submit a budget based on that assumption. In addition, views differ about when the President's initiatives toward Moscow and Peking and current arms control negotiations can safely begin to affect force planning, and to what extent. Besides, given the long periods necessary to design and build new weapon systems, the size and complexity of the defense organization, and the domestic and international political considerations involved, new conceptions of the international order do not automatically lead to revisions in force levels and spending.

Still, the fact remains that a year of major progress in the President's quest for international peace has been followed by a substantial increase in the defense budget. In contrast to the emphasis on savings and on eliminating less effective programs in the domestic side of the budget, initiatives to streamline defense forces and make them more efficient are few. Cuts have been made in strategic defense programs as a result of agreements at the strategic arms limitation talks (SALT) and actions have been initiated to close a number of excess military bases. Apart from these programs, not a single area of the defense budget shows significant dollar savings, either this year or in the future.

Summary of the Defense Budget

In total, the President proposes that the United States spend $79 billion in fiscal 1974 for defense purposes—not counting $1.5 billion for military programs in the Atomic Energy Commission budget.[1] This represents 6 percent of gross national product, and hence the sixth successive yearly decline in the proportionate claim of defense on the nation's resources.

Requested defense expenditures, however, are $4.2 billion higher than in fiscal 1973. Similarly, the $85 billion requested in total obligational authority for the Defense Department is $4.1 billion more than in fiscal 1973. Expected pay and price increases account for virtually all this rise in funding requests. However, when the reduction in the cost of the Vietnam war is taken into account, the fiscal 1974 budget provides for an increase in *real* spending on non-Vietnam or peacetime military forces of $2.3 billion in outlays and $3.4 billion in total obligational authority. In effect, this year's peace dividend is to be used for military rather than civilian purposes. (Before fiscal 1974, savings in defense spending made possible by the troop withdrawals from Vietnam can be viewed as having gone to civilian programs.) Financial comparisons of total military expenditures, baseline (or peacetime) force expenditures, and incremental expenditures for Vietnam are shown in Table 8-1.

The force structure implications of the 1974 budget can be summarized as follows:

1. The budget shows "national defense outlays" as $81 billion, including the total appropriation of $2.4 billion for the Atomic Energy Commission. While the military component of the AEC budget ($1.5 billion) is an integral part of national security costs, we are not in a position to assess the programs involved; consequently, all our estimates of defense costs exclude them. Nor does this discussion consider such appropriations as those for veterans' benefits or interest on the national debt, which are related to past expenditures on national security but not to current or future defense forces.

For strategic forces, the continuation of programs to modernize all three offensive components—sea-based missiles, land-based missiles, and bombers. In general, offensive force levels remain virtually unchanged, while capabilities, as reflected in survivability and number of warheads, steadily increase. Defensive programs, on the other hand, are being cut back, a shift made possible in part by the 1972 strategic arms limitation agreement with the USSR.

For baseline general purpose forces, stabilized force levels and a small decline in manpower. The process of improving capabilities by modernizing weapons will continue, with primary emphasis on ships and tactical aircraft. Major new weapon systems for ground forces are now being developed, but their main fiscal impact will not be felt until the second half of the decade.

In addition, the budget contains funding requests for residual operations and military assistance in Vietnam, both of which will be

Table 8-1. Financial Summary of the Department of Defense Budget, Selected Fiscal Years, 1964–74

Billions of dollars

Description	1964	1968	1972	1973	1974
In current dollars					
Total outlays	50.8	78.0	76.0	74.8	79.0
Baseline force	50.8	58.0	68.7	68.9	74.9
Vietnam additions	...	20.0	7.2	5.9	4.1
Total outlays as percentage of gross national product	8.3	9.4	6.9	6.2	6.0
Total obligational authority	50.7	75.6	77.7	80.9	85.0
Baseline force	50.7	56.3	70.7	74.7	82.1
Vietnam additions	...	19.3	7.0	6.2	2.9
In 1974 dollars[a]					
Total outlays	84.5	111.8	84.9	78.7	79.0
Baseline force	84.5	84.1	76.9	72.6	74.9
Vietnam additions	...	27.7	8.0	6.1	4.1
Total obligational authority	84.5	109.0	86.8	85.1	85.0
Baseline force	84.5	82.4	79.1	78.7	82.1
Vietnam additions	...	26.6	7.7	6.4	2.9

Sources: U.S. Department of Defense, News Release 44-73, Jan. 27, 1973; Department of Defense, unpublished computer tabulation (1973). Also see note a below. Figures may not add to totals because of rounding.

a. Estimates of constant dollar costs differ from those used by the Department of Defense in that retired pay is calculated by multiplying the number of retirees in each year by the average cost of retiree benefits in fiscal year 1974, rather than by "straightlining" fiscal 1974 costs for all previous years. Retirees' data for this calculation are from *The Budget of the United States Government—Appendix, Fiscal Year 1974*, p. 274; *Department of Defense Appropriations for 1973*, Hearings before a Subcommittee of the House Committee on Appropriations, 92 Cong. 2 sess. (1972), Pt. 6, p. 1125; and Department of Defense, News Release 44-73, Table 1.

reduced substantially as a result of the cease-fire. Possible savings, however, could be partly absorbed by economic assistance in the post-war reconstruction of Vietnam.

The Structure of Forces

Comparison of present force levels and costs with those in selected prior years highlights the changes taking place in the defense structure and their fiscal and military significance.

As is evident from Table 8-2, force levels have fluctuated widely over the past decade. Furthermore, forces are now substantially different—in both composition and capability—from what they were in the early 1960s. In particular:

• The Vietnam war bulge has been eliminated. Since 1968, military manpower on active duty has been reduced by almost 40 percent (from 3.5 million to 2.2 million) and sharp cuts have been made in most types of general purpose forces.

• Present forces are considerably smaller than they were in 1964 (the last pre-Vietnam year). There have been reductions of one-fifth in the number of army divisions, close to one-half in the number of aircraft carriers and other naval vessels, and 17 percent—about 450,000 men—in military manpower on active duty. On the other hand, the Department of Defense continues to employ about the same number of civilians.

• Strategic forces have been drastically revamped since 1961. In effect, a large part of the bomber force has been replaced by land- and sea-based missile systems. The number of defensive forces (including manned interceptors and surface-to-air-missile batteries) have been cut by two-thirds.

• There has been a steady increase since 1961 in the firepower of ground force weapons, the capability of tactical aircraft, the mission effectiveness of Navy ships, and amphibious assault capacity. In general, U.S. forces are more mobile and sustainable in combat than they were a decade ago and have better command and control capabilities. For example, the total lift capacity of tactical air forces is almost double what it was in 1961, even though the number of aircraft is about the same. The aircraft capacity of the average carrier (as measured by A-4 aircraft equivalents) is up by 25 percent. And air cargo capacity

Table 8-2. Structure of U.S. Military Forces, Selected Fiscal Years, 1961–74[a]

					Estimate	
Description	*1961*	*1964*	*1968*	*1972*	*1973*	*1974*
Personnel (thousands)						
Active duty military	2,484	2,685	3,547	2,322	2,288	2,233
Reserve military[b]	1,086	1,048	1,001	979	970	994
Civilian	1,042	1,035	1,287	1,050	1,012	1,013
Offensive strategic forces						
Land-based missiles	28	854	1,054	1,054	1,054	1,054
Sea-based missiles	80	336	656	656	656	656
Strategic bomber squadrons[e]	125	88	40	30	30	28
Total offensive warheads[d]	4,800	5,400	4,500	5,300	6,800	8,100
Defensive strategic forces						
Manned interceptor squadrons[e]	75	64	48	27	27	27
Surface-to-air missile batteries[f]	216	159	135	68	63	63
General purpose ground forces						
Army divisions	14	16⅓	18	13	13	13
Marine divisions	3	3	4	3	3	3
General purpose tactical air forces[g]						
Air Force squadrons	61	73	85	74	72	70
Navy squadrons	84	85	78	66	68	69
Marine Corps squadrons	28	28	27	27	28	27
Aircraft (all services)[h]	2,840	3,000	3,010	2,760	2,790	2,790
Lift capacity of aircraft (millions of pounds)[i]	40.3	52.1	65.6	72.5	75.1	74.5
Naval general purpose forces[j]						
Aircraft carriers[k]	24	24	23	17	16	15
Other active vessels[l]	868	873	912	596	529	467
Average age, all vessels (years)	12.9	15.2	17.5	15.1	14.5	13.3
Airlift forces						
Strategic airlift squadrons	31	32	30	17	17	17
Strategic airlift capacity[m]	23.5	28.5	35.1	39.4	43.1	43.1

Sources: Department of Defense, News Releases 44-73, January 29, 1973, and 72-71, January 29, 1971; U.S. Department of the Navy, "Historical Data—Active Fleet Levels" (unpublished tabulation, February 1, 1973); *The Budget of the United States Government, Fiscal Year 1970*, p. 75, . . . *Fiscal Year 1974*, p. 79, and . . . *Appendix—Fiscal Year 1974*, p. 270; Department of Defense, *Annual Report for Fiscal Year 1962*, Tables 18, 24, and *Annual Report for Fiscal Year 1964*, Table 2; *Annual Defense Department Report, FY 1973*, Statement of Secretary of Defense Melvin R. Laird before the Senate Armed Services Committee on the FY 1973 Defense Budget and FY 1973–1977 Program (February 15, 1972), Table 4; *Fiscal Year 1972 Authorization for Military Procurement, Research and Development, Construction and Real Estate Acquisition for the Safeguard ABM and Reserve Strengths*, Hearings before the Senate Committee on Armed Services, 92 Cong. 1 sess. (1971), Pt. 5, p. 3529; unpublished data from the Department of Defense. Also see notes below.

a. All figures are for the end of the fiscal year.

b. Reservists in paid status.

c. Includes medium-range bombers based overseas and, in 1968–74, B-52s converted for use in Southeast Asia.

has nearly doubled since 1961, despite a cut of 50 percent in the number of strategic airlift squadrons.

Defense budgets have not consistently paralleled these changes in force levels. As Table 8-3 shows, the present budget for peacetime forces is somewhat less, in dollars of constant purchasing power, than in the early 1960s. However, the cost reduction is smaller than might be expected in view of the size of the reductions in force levels. Within the budget totals, moreover, significant contrasts emerge. Today's strategic forces cost much less than did comparable forces in either 1962 or 1964, principally because present systems were funded largely in the late fifties and early sixties. The new phase of strategic force modernization in which the United States is now engaged will push these costs higher over the balance of this decade. On the other hand, today's general purpose forces cost more than those maintained before the Vietnam war, even though their number has been greatly reduced. Moreover, the budget for general purpose forces is also likely to rise in the future as a result of manpower costs and current modernization programs.

The Structure of Costs

We have, in short, been moving toward a defense structure costing progressively more per organizational, or force, unit—a tendency that profoundly influences the evolution of the U.S. defense posture. Four developments have contributed to this result: the rising price of de-

Notes to Table 8-2, continued

d. Authors' estimates based on force loadings derived from information appearing in various congressional hearings and International Institute for Strategic Studies, *The Military Balance*, various years. Cruise missiles on submarines, medium-range ballistic missiles, and tactical nuclear weapons are excluded.

e. Active Air Force and Air National Guard units.

f. Active Army and National Guard batteries and Air Force (Bomarc) squadrons. These figures include some units considered to be, and funded as, general purpose forces; for example, eight Hawk batteries in Florida.

g. Number of fighter/attack squadrons: Estimates are based on material from sources cited above, various other Department of Defense publications, and unpublished data from the Departments of the Navy and the Air Force.

h. Unit equipment.

i. Aggregate lift capacity of unit equipment aircraft is equal to maximum take-off weight less empty weight of aircraft, in millions of pounds. Lift capacity can be used either to extend range or enlarge payload and hence is a good index of overall capabilities.

j. All data are derived from unpublished Department of the Navy sources.

k. Includes antisubmarine warfare carriers.

l. Excludes aircraft carriers and strategic forces.

m. Units in millions of pounds, maximum payload. Authors' estimates based on force levels and unit capabilities listed in John W. R. Taylor (ed.), *Jane's All The World's Aircraft* (McGraw-Hill), various years; *Aviation Week and Space Technology*, Vol. 96 (March 13, 1972), p. 95; and unpublished data from the U.S. Air Force.

Table 8-3. Distribution of Department of Defense Budget, by Category, Selected
Fiscal Years, 1962–74

Total obligational authority in billions of dollars

					Estimate	
Category	1962	1964	1968	1972	1973	1974
In current dollars						
Strategic nuclear forces	17.1	16.0	14.4	16.3	16.6	18.0
Baseline general purpose forces	32.2	33.5	39.8	50.5	53.7	58.8
Retired pay	0.9	1.2	2.1	3.9	4.4	5.3
Subtotal	50.2	50.7	56.3	70.7	74.7	82.1
Vietnam additions	...	...	19.3	7.0	6.2	2.9
Total	50.2	50.7	75.6	77.7	80.9	85.0
In 1974 dollars[a]						
Strategic nuclear forces	28.3	26.1	20.7	18.0	17.4	18.0
Baseline general purpose forces	56.6	56.3	58.3	56.6	56.4	58.8
Retired pay	1.6	2.1	3.3	4.5	4.9	5.3
Subtotal	86.5	84.5	82.3	79.1	78.7	82.1
Vietnam additions	...	...	26.6	7.7	6.4	2.9
Total	86.5	84.5	108.9	86.8	85.1	85.0

Sources: Data for 1962–72 are derived from Department of Defense, unpublished computer tabulation (1973). The costs of strategic nuclear forces are the sum of the strategic forces program, half of the intelligence and communications program, one-tenth of the National Guard and Reserve program, four-tenths of the research and development program, and a percentage of the three support programs—central supply and maintenance, training, medical, and other general personnel activities (excluding retired pay), and administration—which varied each year in direct proportion to the ratio of operating costs between strategic and all other forces. The costs of baseline general purpose forces were taken as Department of Defense total obligational authority less the cost of strategic forces, Vietnam, and retired pay. These estimates differ from those given in *Setting National Priorities: The 1973 Budget* because of methodological refinements and the correction of errors. Data for 1973 and 1974 are derived by the authors according to the methodology used for budget projections (see Chap. 9). Figures may not add to totals because of rounding.

a. Estimates of constant dollar costs of prior year authorizations differ from those used by the Department of Defense in that retired pay is calculated by multiplying the number of retirees in each stated year by the average cost of retiree benefits in fiscal year 1974, rather than by using the total fiscal 1974 costs for all previous years.

fense manpower (military and civilian), the growing ratio of manpower to force levels, the growing burden of retired pay, and the increasing sophistication and cost of weapon systems. While these developments are interrelated and have overlapping effects, each is worth examining separately so as to demonstrate its influence on recent defense budgets.

Price of Defense Manpower

Military and civilian pay increases have been the most important single determinant of changes in recent defense budgets. In fiscal 1974 alone the Defense Department baseline payroll will go up by $1.5 billion, despite a reduction of some 50,000 in manpower. This continues a trend that began in 1969, following legislation to make federal salaries—military and civilian—competitive with those in the private sector. It resulted in "catch-up" pay increases in fiscal 1969 and fiscal 1970, and in subsequent annual increases equivalent to those in the private sector. Under the provisions of this legislation, military and civilian pay increases include an allowance for imputed growth in productivity equal to the gain experienced in the private sector, as well as adjustments necessary to compensate for inflation. This link to productivity in the private sector means that even if the number of people employed by the Department of Defense remains unchanged and even if there is no inflation in the economy, defense manpower costs will continue to rise.

The 1971 amendments to the Selective Service Act increased military pay and allowances further to provide the incentives needed to create an all-volunteer service. Pay increases under this legislation went predominantly to enlisted men—those just entering the service and others in the lowest grades. Military pay in these categories, which had been disproportionately low, was increased by roughly 60 percent. Pay and allowances in other categories were increased by much less, but probably by more than was needed to attract the necessary number and quality of volunteers. Except for those aimed to attract reservists and a relatively small number of specialists, no additional pay incentives have been proposed for fiscal 1974 to encourage enlistments, suggesting that the cost of moving to an all-volunteer service has been almost entirely paid.

A higher grade structure now characterizes both military and civilian personnel, and this too has increased average pay in the Department of Defense. The sharp cut in total personnel that occurred after 1968 was probably a major cause of this grade escalation since reductions tend to affect persons with the fewest years of service. The continuing introduction of more sophisticated weapon systems requiring more highly skilled operating and maintenance personnel may also work in this direction. In any event, now that levels of defense manpower are stabilized and issues of grade structure have been subjected to closer scrutiny within the administration, the trend toward a higher structure has ended and, in fact, is being reversed; but this process, unless forcefully pushed, will take a long time.

The combined impact of these factors has been to increase average military pay by 113 percent, and average defense civilian pay by 66 percent, since 1968. The relative importance of each factor in contributing to this result is estimated as follows:[2]

Components of pay increase,
fiscal 1968–74

Source of increase	Percentage increase in active military pay	Percentage increase in Defense Department civilian pay
Comparability with private sector		
To achieve comparability (catch-up)	11	8
To maintain comparability	77	49
Volunteer service—incentive pay	15	0
Higher grade structure	10	9
Total percentage increase	113	66

Thus considerations of equity and public policy have drastically increased the price of defense manpower. The legislative decision to make federal pay comparable with that in the private sector accounted for about three-fourths of this increase; special pay incentives to spur enlistments and the escalation in grade structure accounted about equally for the balance. It is evident, therefore, that the price of defense manpower would have risen substantially with or without the all-volunteer service. It is also evident that as a result of all these factors a system characterized by persistent underpayment of personnel has been replaced by one based on competitive market forces. The element of the "free good" in defense manpower—and hence in the defense budget—has been eliminated. And the cost has run high. If the price of defense manpower since 1968 had increased at the same rate as pay in the private sector, the 1974 defense budget would be approximately $6 billion lower than it is.

2. These factors interact with each other. The effect of this interaction has been arbitrarily allocated among the factors in proportion to their size.

Military pay as used in these calculations does not include allowances, such as those for quarters and subsistence, which rose much more slowly during this period. Because allowances are excluded, percentage increases in military pay are somewhat overstated for purposes of comparison with percentage increases in civilian pay. Since there are different views of the monetary value of military allowances and fringe benefits, the amount of this overstatement cannot be estimated with precision.

The figures in the table may not add to totals because of rounding.

Use of Manpower

Defense manpower, as noted earlier, has been declining proportionately less than force levels, but by how much less and to what effect? One way of quantifying this phenomenon is to estimate the number of men—military and civilian—that can be associated with major force units and to compare the results for different years. This highly aggregated measure is shown in Table 8-4. The widely divergent trends shown for the four military components should not be overemphasized since factors unique to each component are in part responsible for the divergence. Furthermore, the methodology is too simplified for use as a decision-making tool. Nonetheless, it serves to highlight an important emerging problem in defense costs: on the average, the total number of military and civilian personnel presumably needed to man, train, direct, and sustain each combat unit has risen sharply since fiscal 1964.

A number of factors account for this marked structural change.

Table 8-4. Military and Civilian Defense Manpower per Combat Unit, 1964 and 1974

| | Number of men per unit (June 30)[a] | | |
Type of unit	1964	1974 estimate	Percentage increase, 1964–74
Military			
Air Force strategic units[b]	135	136	0.7
Army divisions	51,306	55,385	8.0
Navy ships[c]	502	723	44.0
Tactical aircraft[d]	86	123	43.0
Civilian			
Air Force strategic units[b]	33[e]	61	84.8
Army divisions	18,616[e]	26,538	42.6
Navy ships[e]	220[e]	424	92.7
Tactical aircraft[d]	44[e]	59	34.1

Sources: Manpower: 1974, derived from Department of Defense, *Military Manpower Requirements Report for FY 1974* (1973), pp. 99–102; 1964, derived from unpublished data from the Department of Defense. Units: unpublished data from the Department of Defense.

a. The sum of the number of men assigned directly to appropriate combat categories plus an apportionment of manpower assigned to support categories. (The categories are those used in the Department of Defense's *Fiscal Guidance*.) Men assigned to auxiliary forces (for example, intelligence and security, or communications) are not apportioned and are not included in these totals.

b. The number of strategic bombers and missiles, and manned interceptors assigned to continental air defense, authorized for operational active-duty squadrons.

c. Excludes strategic submarines and their tenders, and attack aircraft carriers. The crews for these vessels are included in other manpower categories.

d. The number of aircraft authorized for operational active-duty squadrons: Navy, Air Force, and Marine Corps.

e. Because of data inadequacies, the distribution of civilian manpower in 1964 was assumed to be the same as the distribution in 1974.

The most notable are the effects on manpower of providing greater firepower and mobility through more advanced technology, the legacy of a large support establishment built for the Vietnam war, and the many personnel decisions that determine the balance between combat and support forces. While the number expected to be on the front lines has decreased, the number supporting each of these men (by maintaining equipment or evacuating casualties, for example) has increased, causing a rise in total manpower per combat unit. In part, the change reflects the expanding use of technology to enhance firepower and reduce the number of men exposed to enemy fire, in an effort to increase combat effectiveness and reduce casualties. In part, the trend reflects the growing complexity of military organizations and of the structure needed to keep them in a state of readiness. What has been happening to the organization of military power has some parallels in private industry, where the ratio of indirect to direct costs tends to rise as capital investment increases. The point here is not to evaluate the merits of what has happened, but to emphasize that at the very time the price of military manpower is rising sharply, it is being used more, rather than less, intensively. Thus the change in the use of defense manpower has reinforced, rather than partly offset, the effect of higher pay on the defense budget.

Retired Pay Obligations

Over $5 billion, or 6 percent, of the 1974 defense budget is slated for the payment of benefits to those who have retired from the military service. Ten years ago this obligation consumed $1.2 billion, or 2.4 percent of the defense budget. Since then the obligation has risen more than four times, both because the number of military retirees has more than doubled and because the pay base on which their benefits are calculated has grown so rapidly. Since both these trends remain in effect, the cost of this obligation is sure to grow further. In addition, the 1974 budget includes a proposal to raise benefits for those already retired by recomputing the pay base on which these benefits are calculated. By the end of the decade, retired pay could account for 7.2 percent of the defense budget.

Cost of Weapon Systems

The marked upward trend in the unit cost of weapon systems from one generation to the next is well established. For example, the average real cost of producing a fighter in the early 1960s was five times greater than during the Korean war; bomber costs increased seventeen times in the same period and the cost of a transport nearly seven times.[3] This trend has continued to the present. The F-14 fighter now being purchased by the Navy costs five times as much in dollars of constant purchasing power, and the Air Force's F-15 almost three times as much, as the F-4 included in the 1964 budget. Similarly, today's attack submarine and the new army tank will cost approximately 50 percent more, after adjusting for inflation, than their counterparts cost in the 1964 budget. Much of this increase stems from the higher performance constantly demanded of each new system and the increasing technological complexity needed to achieve it.

What is noteworthy for present purposes is that this spectacular growth in the unit cost of weapon systems has not caused total procurement costs to rise and in this sense has not pushed up the size of the defense budget.[4] Data for almost two decades show that total military investment (taken to be represented by funding authority for procurement; research, development, testing, and evaluation; family housing; and construction) has on the whole been fairly stable. These data, showing trends in baseline military capital investment, adjusted for inflation and excluding incremental expenditures on the Vietnam war, are as follows:

	Average annual total obligational authority in billions of 1974 dollars		
Period (*fiscal years*)	*Strategic* *forces*	*General purpose* *forces*	*Total*
1956–60	15.0	16.9	31.9
1961–64	13.2	22.5	35.7
1965–69	5.9	25.0	30.9
1970–73	6.0	22.4	28.4
1974	5.5	24.6	30.1

3. The "flyaway" cost of the first F-4s, introduced in 1961, was $3.5 million, while an F-86 of Korean war vintage was $690,000. A B-50 bomber cost less than $2 million in 1950; a B-58 in the late 1950s, $35 million. A C-119 transport cost $1.4 million in 1950; a C-141, $9.8 million in the early 1960s. All figures are in constant fiscal 1974 dollars and are based on data in *CVAN-70 Aircraft Carrier*, Joint Hearings before the Joint Senate-House Armed Services Subcommittee of the Senate and House Armed Services Committees, 91 Cong. 2 sess. (1970), p. 111.

4. Weapons of less complex design could, of course, have reduced the defense budget both by reducing procurement costs (if the same number of units had been procured) and by avoiding the increase in manpower required to service more complex weapons.

A declining trend in investment in strategic forces and a rising trend in investment in general purpose forces are evident. During the period 1961–64, when the two trends converged, a temporary bulge in total investment appears. Apparently, as the defense budget came under pressure in the 1960s—because of the rise in the cost of weapon systems and because of Vietnam—military planners had to choose between strategic force and general purpose force investment. When fiscal pressures intensified because of the rising cost of manpower, beginning in 1969, decision making shifted toward accepting a stretch-out of modernization[5] and a gradual reduction in the number of weapon systems.

In sum, for all the reasons outlined above, manpower-related, rather than procurement, costs have come to dominate the defense budget. The rapidity and extent to which this has happened are shown by the following data:

	Average annual percentage distribution of baseline defense outlays		
Period (fiscal years)	*Active pay and allowances*	*Retired pay*	*Total pay and allowances*
1956–60	40.7	1.4	42.1
1961–68	42.6	2.7	45.3
1969–72	48.2	5.0	53.2
1973–74	51.6	6.8	58.4

Little respite is in sight. If the current defense posture is not altered substantially—that is, if manpower stays near current levels, pay legislation is not revised, and current programs for weapon systems are carried out—it is estimated that total pay and allowances will account for 54 percent of the defense budget by 1980. Thus the structural change in defense costs that has been evident since 1969 is likely to continue well into the future.

5. A recent General Accounting Office report showed an average 34 percent slippage in the date of initial operational capability (IOC) of forty-nine systems under development. Of course, slippage occurs for many reasons other than limits on available funds. Moreover, additional slippage and modernization stretch-outs probably occur after the IOC has been attained. Comptroller General of the United States, *Acquisition of Major Weapon Systems, Department of Defense*, Report to the Congress (July 17, 1972), p. 46.

Policy Issues

It is evident from the foregoing that the defense budget has been squeezed between the rising unit cost of defense and fiscal constraints on total defense spending. The changes in military planning criteria initiated by President Nixon in 1971, which led to reductions in force levels, was one response. Generally, however, forces were reduced across the board, and schedules for replacing weapon systems were lengthened, largely in response to fiscal expediency rather than as part of a deliberate policy trade-off between weapon capabilities and force level requirements. Efforts seem to have been concentrated on striking a balance in the short term between existing requirements and available funds. Less attention has been paid to devising ways of using manpower more efficiently or simplifying the design of weapon systems. And for the most part, no changes have been made in the assessment of U.S. interests abroad, and of the forces necessary to protect them.

In all likelihood the problem posed by tighter budgets and higher unit costs will worsen and call for more far-reaching forms of adjustment. What policy issues will such adjustments raise? What choices will be available for managing them? And what will be their domestic and foreign consequences?

Three broad alternative courses of action can be envisaged:

• One possibility would be to leave the defense posture relatively unchanged and accept higher constant dollar total costs. In practice, this course of action would probably mean that the defense budget would increase by almost as much as the rate of increase in GNP, thus leaving little if any margin for shifts in national spending priorities between military and civilian programs. Even after accepting increases in defense spending in this range, the United States might be in danger of pricing itself out of its strategies. In other words, it might be unable to maintain the forces needed to carry out existing foreign and defense policies.

• Another possibility might be adoption of the goal of constraining defense costs without cutting back on the missions that U.S. military forces are designed to achieve. In practice, this course of action would seek to achieve present objectives through greater efficiency and the acceptance of such security risks as might result from reductions in readiness, a slower pace of weapon modernization, and narrower operating margins to deal with contingencies.

• A third possibility is that fiscal pressures and competing domestic requirements might dictate substantial cutbacks in defense spending, which in turn would require comparable reductions in force levels and missions. Logically, these reductions should derive from a reassessment of foreign interests and of the forces needed to protect them, but equally they could develop as a result of a series of unrelated decisions based principally on fiscal expediency and bureaucratic log-rolling.

These alternatives should be considered in any event, even in the absence of budgetary stringency or cost pressures, as part of the continuing search for greater efficiency, as part of a continuing review of requirements in response to shifting international circumstances, or as part of the nation's continuing review of its priorities. The point here is to emphasize that fiscal and cost pressures will increase the urgency of such reassessments and may in themselves force the direction and pace of change.

There are numerous variations in any of these approaches, and together they imply a wide range in the size, composition, and cost of defense forces. Making a choice among these alternatives, moreover, should be based on a clear idea of U.S. needs well into the future. The defense posture consists of weapon systems that require a long lead time to develop and procure, of manpower whose training entails costly investment, and of forward deployments that are the product of political alignments and defense policies developed over many years. Furthermore, changes that can result in savings over the longer term frequently involve initial one-time costs. Equally significant, the more sudden the change, the greater is the danger of disproportionate foreign political reactions and of unnecessary waste in the management of programs.

The next three chapters are designed to clarify the security, political, and fiscal issues that must be considered in choosing among the three approaches described above. Chapter 9 outlines the major features and force decisions of the 1974 defense budget and projects their financial implications through 1980. Chapter 10 examines the issues of foreign policy and manpower policy that bear on the consideration of alternative defense strategies and budgets. Finally, Chapter 11 outlines alternative defense postures and budgets, principally to answer, as specifically as possible, the question, How would each of these broad alternative courses of action, and the defense budgets associated with them, affect national security?

9. Changes and Trends in the Defense Budget

THIS CHAPTER DISCUSSES the main decisions about procurement and force levels reflected in the 1974 budget and how they will affect the composition and cost of U.S. military forces through the remainder of the decade. It projects defense budgets for each fiscal year through 1980. These projections, shown in tabular form at the end of the chapter, can be summarized briefly:

• The trend in defense costs is strongly upward. By 1978 current defense policies would require funding authorization of $93.4 billion in constant 1974 dollars. This would represent an increase of over $11 billion, or 14 percent, in the cost of the *baseline* force.

• Defense costs stated in current dollars would rise much more sharply because of pay and price increases for military goods and services necessary to compensate for inflation. By 1978 the current dollar defense budget could reach $104 billion, or almost 25 percent more than in fiscal 1974.

• Modernization programs (in large measure for strategic forces) and manpower-related costs would account about equally for this increase.

• Retired pay alone will reach $6.4 billion in constant dollars by

305

fiscal 1978, absorbing close to 7 percent of the defense budget. Even so, the trend will still be upward.

• Defense would account for almost 6 percent of projected gross national product (GNP), approximately the same proportion as in fiscal 1974. If current policies are carried forward, therefore, military spending over the next four years could not be expected to yield to domestic needs in competing for shares of the increase of national output.

A note of warning must be emphasized. The projections should not be taken as predictions of future defense budgets. They lack such precision not simply because of limitations in estimating procedures but because actual budgets will depend on decisions about defense policy, which change from year to year. Furthermore, the projections are based on the 1974 defense budget as presented to the Congress by the administration and therefore do not take into account the congressional review, which in recent years has resulted in roughly a 4 percent reduction of the requests. Instead of predicting actual budgets, these projections are meant to measure what would happen in the future if current decisions on force levels, weapon acquisition programs, and manpower policies were left unchanged. They serve, therefore, to highlight the need to review current defense policies in terms of their longer-range budgetary implications.

The nature of these projections can be clarified further by drawing attention to the static and dynamic elements they contain. Static elements predominate in the sense that they affect factors accounting for the major part of the budget. In the absence of official policies or programs to the contrary, the projections assume the following as constant: the number of major combat units; readiness levels (as reflected in training, maintenance, and deployment policies); and total research and development expenditures. Together these assumptions mean that civilian and military manpower will remain virtually the same throughout the period and that there will be no significant improvement in the efficiency with which it is used.

Dynamic elements include the following: analysis of the projected cost and production schedule of current major weapon programs; the phasing out of Vietnam war costs and the merging of residual military support to Vietnam into the military assistance program; changes in retired pay resulting from predictable increases in the number of retirees; an allowance to cover the cost of future requests for new weapon programs, principally during the second half of the decade; and an allowance for growth in the real cost of new weapons.[1]

The projections are based on an analysis of the four primary military components: strategic, ground combat, naval, and tactical air forces. The last three are referred to as general purpose forces. Cost data on a fifth category—airlift and sealift forces—will be shown but not discussed separately, since the funds involved are relatively small and significant change is not in prospect.

The amounts specified as the cost of each of these components include direct costs as well as an apportionment of indirect operating expenses, such as intelligence and communications, training, logistical support, and administration. While the resulting figures are necessarily approximations, they provide a better indication of the full costs of each major military component than the breakdown shown in more widely used presentations of the defense budget, and they lend themselves more readily than other cost breakdowns to comparisons between the primary military components in terms of their respective claims on defense resources.

Strategic Forces*

Strategic nuclear forces are the cornerstone of U.S. military power, and budgetary appropriations for them are the subject of comparatively wide public and congressional discussion. Yet strategic forces are not the major factor in the defense budget: in fiscal 1974 they account for about one-fifth of total defense expenditures.

Strategic *offensive* forces consist of bombers, land-based missiles, and sea-based missiles. Each element has an independent capability of absorbing an all-out Soviet attack and retaining enough destructive

---

1. The allowance for new weapon programs totals $6.2 billion, or 6 percent of estimated expenditures on major weapon programs. Estimates of cost growth have been related chiefly to the degree of technological advance incorporated in weapon systems under development or procurement. They are based on (1) a General Accounting Office survey of 116 major weapon systems being developed or procured; see Comptroller General of the United States, *Cost Growth in Major Weapon Systems* (1973); and (2) a RAND study of aircraft missile and sensor systems developed in the 1960s; see Robert Perry and others, *System Acquisition Strategies*, R-733-PR/ARPA (Santa Monica: RAND Corp., June 1971). Total growth in cost associated with obligations made during the period 1974–80 is projected to be $19.4 billion, or 20 percent of estimated expenditures on major weapon programs and 15 percent of total procurement. However, only three-fourths ($14 billion) of this estimated growth is expected to appear in budgets before fiscal 1981.

*Prepared with the assistance of Alton H. Quanbeck.

power to inflict unacceptable damage in retaliation. This redundant deterrent is called the "triad," and represents the outgrowth of policy and procurement decisions made fifteen years ago. Strategic *defensive* forces include air and ballistic missile defenses and early warning systems.

United States strategic planning is influenced by projections of Soviet strategic capabilities and objectives, and presumably the reverse is true for the USSR. From 1965 to 1972, as the USSR rapidly built up its strategic force levels and approached a position of parity with the United States, the suspicion that the Soviet Union was aiming for superiority threatened to accelerate an already formidable arms race. The landmark U.S.–Soviet arms limitation agreements reached in 1972 as a result of the strategic arms limitation talks (SALT) and the follow-on discussions that began in March 1973 represent an important step forward in bringing the instabilities in this situation under control. This is the principal new development that should enter into appraisals of current U.S. strategic programs.

The significance of the accords stems from two factors: (1) they establish the principle that the safety of each country lies in mutual vulnerability rather than in defense—that is, on each having secure retaliatory capabilities—and (2) they increase each side's understanding of the other's intentions regarding its future strategic forces. The second round negotiations now under way are aimed at further reducing uncertainties by controlling the qualitative characteristics of weapons and by placing quantitative restraints on forces not limited in the first round. Thus SALT can contribute to the security of both countries by helping to avoid overreactions, inhibiting the introduction of weapons that threaten to upset the balance, and generally slowing the arms race.

Realization of these potentialities is by no means assured. The first SALT agreements leave both sides wide latitude to pursue programs whose aims are qualitative improvements in forces and hedges against a breakdown of the agreements. Thus it has been reported that the USSR is now developing three new types of land-based missiles and has recently begun to deploy an extended range submarine-launched missile. Similarly, the United States has ongoing major research programs in ballistic missile defenses and in several areas of offensive technology. Whether and how rapidly the two countries can move toward further arms limitation depend on a number of military, political, and bureaucratic considerations. Nevertheless, the fact that SALT agreements now exist and that follow-on discussions have begun means that planners in both countries will have to take arms control consequences specifically into account in deciding on strategic programs. This is a matter of considerable significance—for security, for foreign policy, and for the defense budget.

Decisions in the 1974 Budget

Despite SALT, the budget provides for a marked increase in spending for strategic forces, in 1974 and in subsequent years. There are three reasons for this seeming paradox. First, the United States is in the midst of modernizing all three offensive systems that make up the triad; these programs were initiated several years ago and are not prohibited by the SALT accords. Second, the administration believes that continuation (and sometimes acceleration) of these modernization programs provides both bargaining chips in current negotiations with the USSR and hedges against Soviet technological breakthroughs. And third, a large portion of the immediate budgetary savings from SALT—that is, the savings from eliminating all but one Safeguard antiballistic missile (ABM) site—were reflected in cuts made in last year's budget.

Total spending authority for strategic forces—including investment, operating, and indirect costs—is estimated to be $18.0 billion, a real increase of $500 million from fiscal 1973. Large expenditures are requested to carry out modernization programs for *each* element of the triad, and as a result the number of U.S. nuclear warheads is increasing at a faster rate than at any time in history. The largest increase in spending is for Trident, the new sea-based missile system. On the other hand, budget requests for defensive systems are down and there are some indications that air defense as well as missile defense is being deemphasized. As shown in Table 9-1, however, defensive systems continue to account for one-fourth of total strategic costs.

These are the major decisions on strategic force programs reflected in the 1974 budget:

For sea-based systems, another dramatic spending increase, from $0.8 billion to $1.7 billion, on the accelerated Trident program. This system is scheduled to be introduced into service in 1978. The Navy seems to have slowed development of the Trident I missile so that it will become available at the same time as the new submarine. Avail-

Table 9-1. Allocation of the Strategic Forces Budget by Component, Fiscal Year 1974

Component	Cost (billions of dollars)	Percent of total
Offensive systems, total	13.4	74
Bombers	5.6	31
Sea-based strategic missiles	4.7	26
Land-based strategic missiles	3.1	17
Defensive systems, total	4.6	26
Air defense	3.2	18
Ballistic missile defense	1.3	7
Civil defense	0.1	1
Total offensive and defensive	18.0	100

Sources: Estimated from material in U.S. Department of Defense, "Program Acquisition Costs by Weapon System: Department of Defense Budget for Fiscal Year 1974" (1973; processed), and from material appearing in various authorization and appropriation hearings before House and Senate committees on the Department of Defense budget for fiscal 1973. Indirect costs are allocated among components in proportion to direct operating costs.

ability of the missile at an earlier date had been scheduled, in case unexpected developments in Soviet antisubmarine warfare technology made it desirable to use a longer-range missile on existing Poseidon submarines before the new Trident submarines became operational.

Budget requests to complete the Poseidon program total nearly one-half billion dollars. The program will modify thirty-one of the forty-one Polaris submarines to enable them to carry missiles with multiple independently targetable reentry vehicles (MIRVs). With this year's request, funding for the thirty-one submarines will have been completed; requests in future years will be relatively small and principally for spares.

For land-based missiles, approximately $800 million for improvements to the Minuteman missile force, including reduced but still sizable funds to improve Minuteman's prelaunch survivability and its command and control system. The largest part is for the program to replace the 550 single warhead Minuteman I missiles with advanced versions (Minuteman III), each carrying three independently targetable warheads. This program will be completed in fiscal 1975. But the Air Force has repeatedly recommended that the Minuteman II force (450 missiles) also be converted to a MIRV configuration—bringing the total Minuteman III force to 1,000 missiles—at a cost of almost $2 billion. Before the presentation of the 1974 budget, the Defense Department had not publicly endorsed this recommendation. The

1974 budget, however, includes $23 million to begin procurement of these additional MIRV missiles, although the Defense Report indicates that a firm decision on the program has not yet been made.[2]

As a result of the SALT agreement, the budget requests funds to complete only one Safeguard site. A second Safeguard site, designed to defend the national capital, is also permitted under the SALT agreement, but apparently is now seen as unnecessary. Nevertheless, nearly half a billion dollars is earmarked for research and development on ABM systems, and close to half that amount is designated for research on the Safeguard system, which is scheduled to be operational before mid-1975.

For bombers, almost $500 million for continued development of the B-1, the new strategic bomber. A decision on whether to procure the B-1 is to be made in 1975; if the program is approved, it could enter into service in fiscal 1979. The 1974 budget also contains funds to complete the program to provide a new air-to-surface short-range attack missile (SRAM) for the late model B-52s and FB-111s. As they are introduced into operational squadrons, these weapons are sharply increasing the number of U.S. offensive warheads. Two older-model B-52 squadrons will be retired, at an annual saving that could reach $150 million a year, but all the remaining bomber squadrons apparently will be kept in service. Funds have been requested to modify the older B-52s, thereby permitting them to operate through the end of the decade.

For air defense, approximately $200 million for the new airborne warning and control system (AWACS). Spending on AWACS, almost entirely for research and development, is at about the same level as in fiscal 1973. No further reductions have been made in the air defense force structure; however, restraint in the announced objectives of the program suggest that it is being deemphasized and that the pace and scope of other previously planned modernization programs—those for surface-to-air missiles and manned interceptor aircraft—are now being reconsidered.

Altogether, investment in major new strategic systems for which

2. The secretary of defense said: "To protect the option to deploy more than 550 *Minuteman* IIIs, if that should prove to be necessary in the future, another $23 million has been requested for long leadtime items." *Annual Defense Department Report, Fiscal Year 1974, Statement of Secretary of Defense Elliot L. Richardson before the Senate Armed Services Committee on the FY 1974 Defense Budget and FY 1974–1978 Program* (March 28, 1973), p. 57. (Hereinafter referred to as Defense Report.)

procurement or development expenditures are now being made could eventually amount to $58 billion, of which $21 billion has been funded in previous budgets, $4.5 billion is requested in the 1974 budget, and almost $33 billion would be required in the future. These costs are shown in Table 9-2. It is evident that programs to modernize existing land-based and sea-based systems—the Minuteman, SRAM, and Poseidon programs—are well on their way to completion. Less evident is the fact that the SALT accords made it possible to avert the huge cost of an ABM system: the twelve-site Safeguard program contemplated in the 1973 budget would eventually have involved additional expenditures of at least $8 billion. Over the rest of the decade, the level of strategic investments will be dominated by the Trident and B-1 programs and significantly affected by decisions on whether to convert the balance of the Minuteman force to MIRV missiles and on whether, and to what extent, it is necessary to modernize air defenses.

Table 9-2. Estimated Modernization Costs of Major Strategic Programs
Total obligational authority in billions of 1974 dollars

	Modernization costs[a]			
Program	*Through fiscal year 1973*	*Fiscal year 1974*	*Beyond fiscal year 1974*	*Total*
Land-based missiles	**10.9**	**1.4**	**5.5**	**17.8**
Minuteman[b]	4.8	0.8	3.0	8.6
Ballistic missile defense[c]	6.1	0.6	2.5	9.2
Sea-based missiles	**6.8**	**2.2**	**11.3**	**20.3**
Poseidon	5.7	0.5	0.3	6.5
Trident[d]	1.1	1.7	11.0	13.8
Bombers	**2.5**	**0.7**	**12.0**	**15.2**
B-1[e]	1.2	0.5	9.8	11.5
Air-to-surface missiles[f]	1.3	0.2	2.2	3.7
Air defense[g]	**0.9**	**0.2**	**3.8**	**4.9**
Total	21.1	4.5	32.6	58.2

Sources: Same as Table 9-1.

a. Includes research and development, procurement, ship construction, and military construction expenditures. Past investment includes only that associated with the system as constituted at present; for example, Sentinel antiballistic missile system costs are excluded.

b. Assumes all Minutemen (1,000) are modified to carry multiple independently targetable reentry vehicles (MIRVs).

c. One-site Safeguard plus continued development of site defense of Minuteman (SDM).

d. Assumes that 10 submarines with 24 missiles each (plus spares, and so forth) will be bought.

e. Assumes 210 aircraft (unit equipment).

f. Short-range attack missiles (SRAM) and subsonic cruise armed decoys (SCAD).

g. Assumes 42 airborne warning and control systems, improved manned interceptors for 7 squadrons, and over-the-horizon radar. No funds for surface-to-air missiles are included.

Furthermore, two decisions reflected in the 1974 budget could result in very large costs in the more distant future, although the requests themselves are small. One is for $15 million to continue development of a new kind of strategic missile for submarines, the cruise missile. The second is for $6 million to initiate development of a new mobile land-based ballistic missile, the first indication of plans for a successor to Minuteman. Neither program is prohibited by the present SALT accords but constraints on the deployment of such weapons presumably will be considered in the current negotiations.

These decisions, taken as a whole, serve to illustrate the salient feature of the current strategic force posture: despite the SALT agreements and the cutback in objectives from superiority to sufficiency, force planning continues to call for the maintenance of the triad and modernization of each of its elements at a rapid pace.

Strategic Force Financial Projections

With no change in policy, decisions in the 1974 budget imply that spending on strategic programs, in dollars of constant purchasing power, will increase by more than 20 percent during the next few years. Total strategic costs would reach $20 billion a year by 1976 and close to $22 billion annually near the end of the decade. This projection, shown in Table 9-3, rests on the following assumptions about specific programs:

• Continuation of the Trident program at its present pace, with four submarines in service by the end of 1980. Development of the 6,000-mile-range Trident II missile will begin in fiscal 1978.

• Procurement of the B-1 bomber beginning in fiscal 1976 and reaching $2 billion a year by the late 1970s. A new tanker for the bomber force will be developed by the end of the decade.

• Conversion of the entire Minuteman missile force to MIRV missiles.

• Procurement of forty-two AWACS, principally to replace existing ground radar and control systems; introduction of a new air defense interceptor (probably a version of the F-15) in the late 1970s.

• Maintenance of current spending levels on ABM research and development.

• An allowance averaging $900 million a year for cost growth, as-associated principally with the development of Trident, the B-1, and AWACS.

Table 9-3. Projected Costs of Strategic Forces, by Category, Fiscal Years 1973–80[a]
Total obligational authority in billions of 1974 dollars

Category	1973	1974	1975	1976	1977	1978	1979	1980
Major system acquisition[b]	4.2	4.5	5.0	6.2	6.2	6.0	6.0	5.9
Other investment[c]	4.8	5.0	5.0	5.1	5.3	5.6	5.6	5.5
Direct operating costs[d]	3.7	3.7	3.6	3.6	3.6	3.6	3.6	3.6
Indirect operating costs[e]	4.8	4.8	4.6	4.6	4.6	4.7	4.7	4.7
Subtotal	17.5	18.0	18.2	19.5	19.7	19.9	19.9	19.7
Allowance for cost growth	...	...	0.3	0.6	1.2	1.3	1.5	1.6
Allowance for new initiatives	...	...	...	...	0.1	0.2	0.4	0.4
Total	17.5	18.0	18.5	20.1	21.0	21.4	21.8	21.7

Sources: Derived by authors from data in the documents listed in Tables 8-1, 8-2, 8-4, and 9-1 above. See discussion in text. Figures may not add to totals because of rounding.
a. Excludes incremental costs of the war in Vietnam.
b. Includes research and development, procurement, and military construction costs directly associated with major systems.
c. Research and development, procurement, and military construction traceable to strategic forces other than that covered in note b.
d. Includes military personnel and operations and maintenance appropriations for active forces funded in program I of the Five Year Defense Program (FYDP), plus all military personnel and operations and maintenance appropriations for reserve strategic forces.
e. A share of indirect operating costs such as communications, training, logistical support, and administration (programs III, VII, VIII, and IX of the FYDP) proportionate to the direct operating costs of strategic forces. Also includes civil defense appropriations.

• An allowance averaging $200 million a year to cover the cost of future requests for new weapons. Candidates include procurement of the new surface-to-air missile (SAM-D) for strategic air defense, accelerated acquisition of a new tanker for the B-1, and development of mobile land-based missiles.

These projections make no allowance for program and budget reductions that could result from a second-round SALT agreement or from an improvement in U.S.–Soviet understanding coincident with continued arms control discussions. On the other hand, they also make no allowance for the consequences of either a stalemate in the discussions or an abrogation of the first SALT agreement. Either of the latter contingencies could lead to an acceleration of present programs, a resumption of ABM deployments, and the decision to procure new types of strategic weapons, such as the strategic cruise missile or the mobile land-based missile, all of which would result in steadily rising budgets for strategic forces well into the 1980s.

Baseline General Purpose Forces

The United States maintains general purpose forces, both active and reserve, to deter conventional and tactical nuclear attack in a wide range of contingencies and, should deterrence fail, to protect the United States and its interests overseas. While there is no fear of an attack against the United States with conventional forces, this administration believes, as did all its post–World War II predecessors, that U.S. security requires a strategy of forward defense. Hence the United States stations substantial forces abroad to supplement those of its allies and designs its general purpose forces so that they are capable of rapid worldwide deployment. Furthermore, in the administration's view, U.S.–Soviet nuclear parity means that strong conventional forces, because they give the United States the option of defense against aggression without recourse to nuclear weapons, "are more important, rather than less important, to the deterrence of war."[3]

Budget requests for baseline or peacetime general purpose forces are estimated to total $55 billion, or almost two-thirds of the defense budget. Generally speaking, the 1974 budget provides for qualitative improvements in these forces, principally through the acquisition of new weapons, but only minor changes in their structure. Continuing emphasis is being placed on upgrading the readiness and combat capabilities of reserve components.

Ground Combat Forces

The 1974 budget provides for a small reduction in manpower and a modest increase in procurement for active ground forces, and additional investments for equipping and modernizing ground force reserves. There are no indications of a change in planning contingencies that would affect the size and composition of these forces.

Active ground forces consist of thirteen Army divisions, three Marine divisions, and support forces. Reserve components consist of eight National Guard divisions, one Marine division, and a variety of other combat and support units. Of the sixteen active divisions, six and one-third are stationed abroad (four and one-third in Western Europe, one in Korea, and one on Okinawa). Roughly one-third of ground force manpower is deployed overseas.

Decisions in the 1974 Budget

Manpower-related expenditures account for approximately three-fourths of the total cost of ground forces. Hence, even more than for

3. Defense Report, p. 5.

the other military components, decisions on the size and use of manpower are the main determinants of the cost of ground forces. In fiscal 1974, Army manpower will probably decline from 825,000 to about 790,000, or by 4 percent, mostly as a result of the cutback in support functions made possible by the U.S. withdrawal from Vietnam, including the closing of excess military bases.[4] The return of ground forces to a peacetime footing, therefore, will reduce support forces more than combat forces, but the ratio is still high by pre-Vietnam war standards.[5]

Procurement and modernization issues are far less important for ground forces than for other components. If strategic systems are excluded, Army procurement is mostly for equipment having a relatively low unit cost and for consumables such as ammunition. The cost of major ongoing procurement programs shown in the budget is about $600 million, principally for the M-60 series tank, antitank missiles, and other missiles.

A number of major development programs are now under way that focus on the longer-term modernization of armored and mechanized forces, surface-to-air missile capabilities, and helicopters. If all are eventually approved, these programs could cost approximately $11 billion during their acquisition period (Table 9-4). Procurement of these weapons would add close to $1 billion a year to the ground force budget by the end of the decade.

The $4.4 billion budget request for all reserve components—$400 million higher than in 1973—implies another substantial expansion in expenditures on ground forces, which claim at least half the total budget for these components. Equipment valued at $800 million will be issued to Army reserve units, part of a $4 billion total over the past five years. Practically all of this equipment came from excess stocks of the active forces, which were larger than usual because of the phasing out of the Vietnam war. Continuation of the program to upgrade weapons in the hands of reserve units, however, will probably require increasing procurement of new equipment rather than acquisition of excess stocks from the active forces, and will therefore be more of a drain on the budget in the future.

4. The budget shows a reduction in Army end strength from 825,000 to 804,000 based on a residual force in South Vietnam that includes about 11,000 Army personnel. With the end of U.S. involvement we assume that an additional number at least equal to this residual force will be deactivated in 1974.

5. See discussion in Chapter 10.

Table 9-4. Estimated Cost of Programs to Modernize Ground Combat Forces

Total obligational authority in millions of current dollars

Program description	Research and development cost through fiscal year 1973	Budget request, fiscal year 1974	Costs beyond fiscal year 1974[a]	
			Research and development	Procurement
Surface-to-air missile (SAM-D)	630	190	490	3,700
Battle tank (XM1)	20	50	380	2,600
Utility tactical transport aircraft system (UTTAS), a transport helicopter	80	110	210	1,550
Advanced attack helicopter (AAH)	20	50	350	1,380
Mechanized infantry combat vehicle (MICV), an armored personnel carrier	20	10	20	200
Total	770	410	1,450	9,430

Source: Unpublished data from U.S. Department of the Army (1973).

a. Estimated total costs through program completion as scheduled at present.

Future Shape of Ground Forces and Their Cost

These programs imply the maintenance of ground forces at about their present size but an increase in their firepower and mobility. Their size and composition will be based predominantly on requirements for a war in Europe, although some Army and Marine divisions will continue to be specially trained and equipped for Asian contingencies. The expanding investments in the readiness and capabilities of reserve components apparently will continue to be viewed as a hedge against the contingency of a protracted war in Europe rather than as a substitute in some measure for active forces.

Costs, in 1974 dollars, are likely to increase gradually over the remainder of the decade, from $22 billion in fiscal 1974 to over $24 billion in fiscal 1980 (Table 9-5). The chief assumption leading to this projection is that no further reductions will be made in ground force manpower beyond the amount estimated for fiscal 1974. On the other hand, it is also assumed that additional pay incentives to underwrite the all-volunteer service will not be required. In that event, constant dollar costs will rise principally because of greater expenditures for new weapon systems and, less significantly, because of increased investments for guard and reserve forces.

Table 9-5. Projected Costs of Ground Combat Forces, by Category, Fiscal Years 1973–80[a]

Total obligational authority in billions of 1974 dollars

Category	1973	1974	1975	1976	1977	1978	1979	1980
Major system acquisition[b]	0.8	1.1	1.3	1.5	1.7	1.9	2.0	2.0
Other investment[c]	3.4	3.9	4.0	4.1	4.2	4.3	4.4	4.5
Direct operating costs[d]	8.2	8.7	8.7	8.7	8.7	8.7	8.7	8.7
Indirect operating costs[e]	9.3	8.4	8.4	8.4	8.4	8.4	8.4	8.4
Subtotal	21.7	22.1	22.4	22.7	23.0	23.3	23.5	23.6
Allowance for cost growth	...	...	...	0.1	0.4	0.5	0.6	0.6
Allowance for new initiatives	...	...	...	...	...	0.1	0.2	0.3
Total	21.7	22.1	22.4	22.8	23.4	23.9	24.3	24.5

Sources: Same as Table 9-3.

a. Excludes incremental costs of the war in Vietnam.

b. Includes research and development, procurement, and military construction costs directly associated with major systems.

c. Includes research and development, procurement, and military construction traceable to ground combat forces other than that covered in note b.

d. Includes military personnel and operations and maintenance appropriations for active forces funded in program II of the Five Year Defense Program (FYDP) plus all military personnel and operations and maintenance appropriations for reserve ground combat forces.

e. A share of indirect operating costs such as communications, training, logistical support, and administration (programs III, VII, VIII, and IX of the FYDP) proportionate to the direct operating costs of ground combat forces.

Naval General Purpose Forces*

There are few surprises in this year's expenditures for naval general purpose forces. The 1974 budget provides for sustaining a high level of new ship construction and for a real increase of approximately $400 million in the total cost of naval forces. Two recent trends will continue: (1) the number of ships will decline, as the number of new ships entering service will be less than the number of older ships, mostly from World War II, that are retired; and (2) the fleet will be newer and increasingly composed of more capable ships.

Decisions in the 1974 Budget

Since there is a long lead time in shipbuilding, the Navy's current procurement programs will largely determine its budgets for the rest of this decade and the structure of its forces in the 1980s. This year's major program requests can be summarized as follows:

For carriers, almost $700 million to complete funding of the fourth nuclear carrier, CVN-70, which was authorized last year and is to be delivered in 1981. With this ship, the Navy will have 12 carriers of

* Prepared with the assistance of Arnold M. Kuzmack.

post–World War II design in the early 1980s, which, in view of the age distribution of present carriers and the availability of shipbuilding capacity, will be the maximum force level for the future. To maintain that level, moreover, a new carrier would have to be authorized every other year through virtually the balance of this century.[6] In fiscal 1974 the Navy plans to retire 2 of its 7 World War II carriers and to commission a new nuclear-powered aircraft carrier, the *Nimitz*, resulting in a drop from 16 to 15 in the carrier force level. Thus the inevitable reduction to a force level of 12 carriers is being postponed for as long as possible.

For new destroyers, a request of almost $600 million for DD-963 escorts. These ships are designed primarily to protect aircraft carriers, although they can be used to defend other naval forces and merchant vessels against submarines as well. The total program calls for the construction of 30 vessels, of which 16 had been authorized before fiscal 1973. This year's request would complete funding of 7 more of these vessels, and fund long lead-time procurement for the last 7 DD-963s in the program.

For nuclear-powered attack submarines, over $900 million for 5 submarines and advance procurement funds for 5 more submarines planned for fiscal 1975. These submarines are designed principally to attack enemy submarines. Before this year's request, 80 nuclear-powered attack submarines were either in service, under construction, or authorized. In 1968, the Defense Department indicated that requirements might total 66 submarines, but in 1970, Navy statements referred to a goal of 105 submarines to be reached by building 5 a year. More recent statements do not discuss plans for the future.

For antisubmarine warfare (ASW) aircraft, continuation of Navy procurement to modernize both its sea-based and land-based systems. Approximately $500 million is requested to complete procurement of 45 carrier-based ASW aircraft (S-3A). The total program calls for building 199 aircraft, of which 48 have previously been authorized. In the case of land-based ASW aircraft (P-3C), the Navy is continuing the procurement rate Congress authorized in fiscal 1973, when it cut the budget request from 24 to 12 aircraft.

For new types of combat ships, deferral of most procurement fund-

6. See discussion of the carrier obsolescence problem in Charles L. Schultze and others, *Setting National Priorities: The 1973 Budget* (Brookings Institution, 1972), pp. 121–24.

ing for two major programs, the sea control ship (SCS) and the patrol frigate (PF). This may reflect doubts about these programs, delays in their development schedule, or simply no leeway for moving from development to the more costly procurement phase in a Navy shipbuilding budget that was already high as a result of increased funding for the new aircraft carrier and the Trident strategic submarine program.

Future Shape of the Navy

What do these programs suggest about the composition and functions of naval general purpose forces in the early 1980s?

In composition, naval general purpose forces are not likely to be substantially different from what they are now. With the exception of large cruisers, all the major types of ships now in service will be well represented, along with a few new ones. The total number of ships will be close to the present level, with the decline evident since 1968 coming to an end in the mid-1970s and then being reversed. Aircraft carriers, about 12 in number, will continue to be the dominant element in the fleet. Approximately 220 escort ships will be in service, causing an increase of approximately two-thirds in the ratio of escorts to aircraft carriers. Capabilities for antisubmarine warfare will have been greatly expanded; in addition to new escort ships, there will be over 100 nuclear-powered attack submarines and more capable ASW aircraft in service. On the other hand, a continued decline in the number of auxiliary vessels (oilers and cargo, ammunition, and repair ships) may make the Navy more dependent on replenishment and repair facilities abroad, even though political trends indicate that such arrangements may well be less reliable in the future. The Navy may seek to mitigate this problem by engaging U.S. merchant ships under long-term contract.

Naval general purpose forces in the 1980s will be designed, as they are now, for two principal missions: to launch air attacks and carry out amphibious operations against land targets (projection mission), and to keep sea lanes open in time of war by protecting ships from enemy attack (sea control mission).

Successful completion of the first mission depends on aircraft carriers, since they are the primary vehicle for projecting U.S. power from the sea. In practice, carriers probably would not be used at all, or at most in ancillary operations, against land targets in a war with the

USSR, chiefly because of the limited range of their strike aircraft and because, when in confined areas such as the Mediterranean, they would be vulnerable to attack by Soviet land-based aircraft, submarines, and possibly missiles launched from surface ships.[7] Thus the United States is likely to need fewer carriers for the projection mission in the 1980s, although the extent of the reduction depends primarily on the degree to which the United States continues to maintain forces to assist allied nations, mainly in Asia, in conflicts not involving the USSR.

Forces needed for the sea control mission in the 1980s depend on (1) the projected size and composition of the Soviet Navy, the only force capable of threatening U.S. shipping on a broad scale; and (2) on planning criteria for fighting a war with the USSR, notably the assumed length of a conventional war with the USSR. In practice, requirements for the sea control mission derive from planning for a protracted NATO (North Atlantic Treaty Organization) war in Europe and the need in such a contingency for maintaining lines of communication between the United States and Western Europe.

The primary threat to Western sea lanes would be from Soviet submarines. At present, the Soviet Navy operates about 270 torpedo attack and cruise missile submarines, down more than 40 percent from a peak in the late 1950s of nearly 500. On the assumptions that the Soviet Union will retire all submarines by the time they are twenty years old and that submarine construction continues at the rate of the past five years, this force will become still smaller—between 200 and 230 by 1980, and perhaps 170 by 1985. On the other hand, individual submarines in the present force are more capable than their predecessors. Each carries more torpedoes, they have greater range and improved sensors, and about one-fourth have cruise missiles. Soviet submarines are noisier than their American counterparts, however, and their operational capabilities in the Atlantic are hampered by their restricted access to the open sea. Most new Soviet submarines are nuclear-powered; in 1980 about three-fourths of the Soviet fleet will be nuclear.

The principal forces the United States would use to combat the submarine threat to Western shipping are escort ships, attack sub-

7. Considerations affecting the vulnerability of aircraft carriers are discussed in Charles L. Schultze and others, *Setting National Priorities: The 1972 Budget* (Brookings Institution, 1971), pp. 71–81.

marines, ASW aircraft, and mines—all of which are being modernized. Carriers could also be used to defend shipping in the Atlantic, but the efficiency of using them in this role is a matter of dispute. A carrier's ASW aircraft could be used against Soviet submarines and its fighter aircraft could be brought into play in the event that Soviet land-based aircraft were used to attack shipping in the Atlantic.[8] On the other hand, a case can be made that in an Atlantic campaign U.S. land-based aircraft and other ASW forces would be more effective and less costly for these purposes.

In any event, requirements for Navy general purpose forces to carry out the sea control mission will hinge principally on assumptions about the length of the war. If it is relatively short—say, less than three months—logistic support would come primarily from prepositioned U.S. stockpiles and from European sources; hence shipping requirements across the Atlantic would be relatively small. A more protracted war would mean a continuing requirement to move large quantities of matériel by sea. In general, U.S. naval forces in being in the early 1980s will have been designed for a relatively protracted war in Europe.

A third important function of naval forces is to provide a U.S. "presence" in peacetime or in time of crisis, in order to express U.S. interest in an area and to exert U.S. influence on the terms of settlement in possible disputes. While this mission may well be the one most likely to be needed in the future, it can be satisfied by the forces for the other two missions and therefore does not add to force requirements.

Financial Projections

In recent years the Navy has been able to initiate substantial new programs without great sacrifice in its carrier strike forces and without incurring major real increases in its baseline budget principally because the cost of new programs has been partly offset by savings in operating costs as ships from World War II were retired. Apart from the possibility of retiring older carriers more rapidly, this source of savings is now virtually exhausted. Choices may therefore be more difficult in the future, all the more so because the new ships, which will soon be replacing retired ships on a one-for-one basis, generally have more sophisticated equipment and higher operating costs.

8. The Soviet Navy has about 300 medium-range strike aircraft equipped with cruise missiles. It is arguable whether, in view of their range and weaponry, these forces are likely to be used to attack shipping in the Atlantic.

Indeed, current programs and policies indicate a gradual rise in the cost of Navy general purpose forces over the balance of the decade. As shown in Table 9-6, the costs of these forces are projected to increase from $15.6 billion in 1973 to $16.5 billion in 1980, in dollars of constant purchasing power. The following specific assumptions underlie this projection:

• Completion of current procurement programs.

• Annual procurement of ten patrol frigates and two sea control ships by fiscal 1976.

• Authorization of two additional aircraft carriers, that is, one every three years. This is one carrier less than would be strictly necessary to maintain a twelve-carrier force in the 1980s.

• A growth in the cost of existing weapon programs averaging $500 million a year, associated principally with shipbuilding programs.

• An average allowance of $350 million a year for the initiation of new weapon programs during the second half of the decade. Candidates include a tactical cruise missile submarine, the surface effects ship (a vessel that rides on a cushion of air), and auxiliary ships.

• Maintenance of current manpower levels.

Table 9-6. Projected Costs of Naval General Purpose Forces, by Category, Fiscal Years 1973–80ᵃ

Total obligational authority in billions of 1974 dollars

Category	1973	1974	1975	1976	1977	1978	1979	1980
Major system acquisition[b]	3.1	3.6	3.4	3.9	3.4	2.6	2.7	2.7
Other investment[c]	3.7	2.9	2.8	2.9	3.0	3.0	3.0	3.1
Direct operating costs[d]	4.2	4.5	4.4	4.3	4.4	4.5	4.6	4.7
Indirect operating costs[e]	4.6	5.0	4.8	4.6	4.6	4.7	4.8	4.9
Subtotal	15.6	16.0	15.4	15.7	15.4	14.8	15.1	15.4
Allowance for cost growth	...	...	0.1	0.5	0.8	0.8	0.8	0.5
Allowance for new initiatives	...	...	...	0.2	0.5	0.5	0.6	0.6
Total	15.6	16.0	15.5	16.4	16.7	16.1	16.5	16.5

Sources: Same as Table 9-3.
a. Excludes incremental costs of the war in Vietnam.
b. Includes research and development, procurement, and military construction costs directly associated with major systems.
c. Includes research and development, procurement, and military construction traceable to naval general purpose forces other than that covered in note b.
d. Includes military personnel and operations and maintenance appropriations for active forces funded in program II of the Five Year Defense Program (FYDP) plus all military personnel and operations and maintenance appropriations for reserve naval forces.
e. A share of indirect operating costs such as communications, training, logistical support, and administration (programs III, VII, VIII, and IX of the FYDP) proportionate to the direct operating costs of naval general purpose forces.

Tactical Air Forces*

The cost of supporting the baseline level of tactical air forces in fiscal 1974 is estimated to be $16.5 billion, up $1.6 billion from last year. Force levels are unchanged at twenty-one Air Force, fourteen Navy, and three Marine air wings.

The investment portion of the tactical air force budget will continue to be dominated by two aircraft, the Air Force F-15 and the Navy F-14. Both are long-range, high-performance fighters now in the procurement phase. The F-14 is expected to become operational in fiscal 1974, the F-15 in fiscal 1975. Together, they will account for nearly one-third of the funds devoted to acquiring new tactical air weapons during the 1970s. Their high unit cost and the heavy claim they make on available procurement funds will probably lead to a continuing decline in the total active aircraft inventory. Each year the Air Force, Navy, and Marine Corps lose over a thousand aircraft of all types to ordinary peacetime wear and tear. Yet in fiscal 1974, only 418 new aircraft will be procured and projections envisage an average no higher for the rest of the 1970s. This net loss will reduce the total aircraft inventory by approximately 4 percent in 1974—not enough to require changes in the authorized number of squadrons or the aircraft strength of each squadron, because the aircraft inventory had been swollen by procurement for the Vietnam war, and because some of the planes being retired, such as auxiliary aircraft, no longer fit into present force plans and are not being replaced. A decline of this magnitude, however, cannot be sustained for too long before requiring a reduction in force levels.

Despite the attention usually given to procurement decisions, three-fifths of the total cost of tactical air forces consists of operating expenses—for personnel, maintenance of equipment and facilities, and consumables. At the same time, however, operating costs are sensitive to the complexity of the new aircraft being introduced. High-performance, multipurpose aircraft are much more costly to operate—as well as more costly to procure—than aircraft designed for a single kind of battlefield mission.

Decisions in the 1974 Budget

As is the case with naval forces, the long lead time for developing and building new weapon systems means that current procurement

* Prepared with the assistance of William D. White.

programs will determine the structure of tactical air forces ten years from now. Hence, in considering these programs, two related sets of issues should be kept in mind. First, what missions will U.S. tactical air forces have to perform in the years ahead? Second, should they be performed by specialized or multipurpose aircraft?[9] The following budget requests merit special attention because of their cost or force structure implications.

For the F-15 fighter, over $1.1 billion to procure 77 aircraft and to continue development of the aircraft, engine, and avionics. The program is proceeding on schedule toward procurement of 729 planes (enough to equip six operational wings by 1980) at a total cost of $8.4 billion. So far, costs have gone up by less than 10 percent since development was initiated, an unusually good record, if it holds, for a high technology weapon system. Nonetheless, as matters now stand the acquisition cost of each F-15 will average $11.5 million, or about three times the cost of the aircraft it is replacing, the F-4 fighter, and a further increase in F-15 costs is nearly certain.

Production of the F-15 may be continued well beyond the announced program. The plane is now justified as a long-range air superiority fighter that will be able to counter new Soviet designs either over the battlefield or deep within enemy territory; for this purpose it will replace the F-4 on a one-for-one basis. The multipurpose F-4 now constitutes two-thirds (fourteen air wings) of Air Force tactical fighter strength. When the present F-15 program is completed, the Air Force may wish to replace more F-4s, which by then will be a twenty-year-old design, with F-15s. In addition, the Air Force will probably develop a reconnaissance model of the F-15 to replace its F-4 counterpart. If only half the present number of F-4s were replaced in these ways, the F-15 program would continue well into the 1980s and involve a cost of at least $15 billion (in 1974 dollars). In peacetime, costs of this magnitude could not be sustained without cutting heavily into other programs. Hence the actual size of the F-15 program will depend on the number of air wings maintained in service and on the extent to which military planners decide to use relatively low-cost, specialized planes, such as the A-10 or the lightweight fighter (LWF), for some missions rather than to rely on the F-15, as they have on the F-4, to do everything.

9. These issues and their implications for force levels and budgets are discussed in *Setting National Priorities: The 1973 Budget*, pp. 132–43.

For the F-14 fighter, over $600 million for procurement of 48 air-craft (the same number as in fiscal 1973) and for continuing develop-ment. Until recently, the Navy program called for procurement of 301 aircraft (122 production aircraft have been funded through fiscal 1973, plus 12 for research and development) at a total cost of $5.4 billion, but it is in trouble because of the increase in costs. Depending on what elements of cost are included and how much more cost growth is as-sumed, the acquisition cost of each F-14 system (including the Phoe-nix missiles only it can carry) will reach between $24 million and $27 million, or twice the estimate made in 1969, and the total cost of com-pleting the 301-plane program will be $8 billion.

These problems are accentuated by controversy surrounding the role of the aircraft carrier, whose defense will be the primary mission of the F-14s. If the aircraft and its new missile perform as specified, the system should be a great improvement over the F-4 in defending carriers. Whether this improvement is worth the cost, however, de-pends on the usefulness of the carrier in a war with the USSR, par-ticularly on whether carriers would be used against land targets in such a conflict. For protection of sea lanes and for use against adver-saries other than the USSR, the F-4 will be adequate for many years to come.

What then are the possible outcomes of the F-14 program? If addi-tional price increases are not granted, the program will end at 122 op-erational aircraft, at a total cost of $3.3 billion. This number would permit one squadron to be placed aboard each of six carriers, pre-sumably those deployed in the European theater. Or the program might be set at 220 aircraft, deleting the aircraft previously planned for Marine air wings.[10] With 220 aircraft, one F-14 squadron could initially be placed on each carrier in the force, but gradual attrition would ultimately require a reduction of F-14 squadrons and deploy-ments. This program would cost about $6.0 billion. At the other ex-treme, and on the assumption that price difficulties with the contractor are settled, the Navy might press for eventually buying enough F-14s

10. The program to buy 301 F-14s included 50 to 80 aircraft for the Marine Corps. However, the 1974 budget request indicated that the Marine Corps was planning to pur-chase an advanced version of the F-4 instead of the F-14. This position has again changed. Marine Corps Commandant General Cushman recently testified that the Marines have decided to buy F-14s. Moreover, a report in *Aviation Week and Space Technology* (June 4, 1973), p. 13, suggests that this change will increase the total program to 385 aircraft in-stead of restoring the program to the previous figure of 301.

to replace all F-4s (and its RA-5C reconnaissance aircraft) on the twelve carriers it expects to maintain in the 1980s. The program would then increase to 800 aircraft at a total cost of at least $15 billion.

For the A-10 (formerly the A-X), approximately $150 million for continued development and advance procurement of long lead-time items for the first 26 aircraft. This low-cost plane is specially designed for the close support of ground troops.

The program has proceeded on schedule and calls for eventual procurement of approximately 730 aircraft at a cost of $1.7 billion. Nonetheless, controversy over how the close-support role should be carried out is by no means over and interservice rivalry is still a factor. The Army continues to compete; its Cheyenne helicopter gunship program is dead, but it is now proceeding with the development of a lower-cost replacement (the advanced attack helicopter, AAH). The Marine Corps is completing procurement of the Harrier vertical or short takeoff and landing (V/STOL) aircraft, and may seek an improved design after the present program is completed in 1975. The Air Force itself seems to have doubts; some spokesmen have expressed preference for more of the already operational A-7, despite its higher cost, on the grounds that it is more versatile than the specialized A-10.

Equally significant, the effects of the A-10 on force levels seems to be an open question. Apparently the Air Force wishes to develop an improved close-support capability without sacrificing its capability to perform deep-penetration missions. Hence it recommends that the A-10 squadrons be added to force levels and not replace existing squadrons of F-4s or A-7s, which would increase rather than reduce future costs.

For the lightweight fighter (LWF), additional money to develop prototypes of two different designs. This program to develop a low-cost fighter designed to achieve air superiority over the battlefield is being carried out in low key. Should the program survive and reach the procurement stage, the aircraft could serve as a replacement for some portion of the present F-4 fighter strength. In that event, the program would have considerable budgetary significance since the LWF would provide a low-cost alternative to the F-15. At its present pace, however, the program is not likely to produce a prototype until 1976, if at all.

For the advanced medium short takeoff and landing transport (AMST), continued funding for research and development. While this new transport is being developed as a tactical aircraft, which suggests a capability to operate from marginal airfields near the battle area, it will be large enough to fly intermediate-range missions as well. Thus it may end up as an expensive multipurpose replacement for present C-130s, rather than a lower-cost, smaller, and truly tactical transport. If the AMST reaches the procurement stage—which in any case could not be before the last part of the seventies—the program could reach 1,000 aircraft and cost $6 billion to $8 billion.

Future Shape of Tactical Air Forces

Taken as a group, these procurement programs suggest that U.S. tactical air forces in the 1980s will be similar to today's forces—in size, composition, and doctrine. They will be designed principally for a protracted NATO war with the USSR. (Long-range interdiction missions would be relatively unimportant to the outcome of a short, intense war.) Force levels are likely to be fairly stable, with a reduction of two Navy air wings (corresponding to the eventual reduction to twelve carriers) possibly offset by the addition of two A-10 air wings to the Air Force. Multipurpose aircraft with a long-range attack capability will predominate. In the early 1980s some 2,300 aircraft, or roughly 80 percent of authorized tactical air strength, will be in this category. Consequently, the capability to perform deep-penetration missions against sophisticated opposition will remain unimpaired.

One factor that might alter this structure is a shift in the direction of specialized, lower-cost aircraft, either because of a change in planning criteria for a NATO war or because of fiscal pressures. If the A-10 is used as a replacement for, rather than an addition to, existing multipurpose aircraft, its introduction would be a move in this direction. A more significant development would be the procurement of a lightweight fighter, but this now seems less likely.

Technology could also alter this structure substantially, although it would take much longer. For example, the continued development of laser-guided bombs would so increase the accuracy of air-delivered munitions that fewer sorties would be required to destroy a given target. The extent to which this development could affect force level requirements will depend on the pace of technological advance in air defense. Or again, a continued advance in the functions that drone aircraft can perform could dramatically affect the future structure of tactical air forces.

Financial Projections

These budgetary decisions, together with our estimate of the direction of current policies, imply that expenditures on tactical air forces for the rest of this decade will remain fairly stable averaging $16.6 billion a year. These financial projections, shown in Table 9-7, are based on the following specific assumptions:

• Constant force levels.

• Completion of the present programs for the F-15 and A-10, and purchase of 301 F 14s.

• Development of reconnaissance versions of the F-15 and F-14, and initial procurement of the new tactical transport (AMST) near the end of the decade.

• Continued development, but no procurement, of the LWF.

• Continued modernization of reserve tactical air forces, mainly through gradual transfer from the active forces of F-4s, which are more costly to operate and maintain than the older aircraft they will replace.

• An allowance averaging $400 million a year for future requests for new weapon programs. Candidates include an all-weather version

Table 9-7. Projected Costs of Tactical Air Forces, by Category, Fiscal Years 1973–80[a]
Total obligational authority in billions of 1974 dollars

Category	1973	1974	1975	1976	1977	1978	1979	1980
Major system acquisition[b]	3.5	3.9	4.1	3.8	3.4	3.2	2.3	2.3
Other investment[c]	2.3	3.0	3.2	3.3	3.3	3.3	3.3	3.3
Direct operating costs[d]	4.9	4.9	4.8	4.8	4.9	5.0	5.0	5.2
Indirect operating costs[e]	4.2	4.7	4.4	4.3	4.3	4.4	4.5	4.6
Subtotal	14.9	16.5	16.5	16.2	15.9	15.9	15.1	15.4
Allowance for cost growth	...	...	0.1	0.1	0.4	0.5	0.4	0.3
Allowance for new initiatives	...	...	0.1	0.1	0.3	0.6	0.8	0.8
Total	14.9	16.5	16.7	16.4	16.6	17.0	16.3	16.5

Sources: Same as Table 9-3.
a. Excludes incremental costs of the war in Vietnam.
b. Includes research and development, procurement, and military construction costs directly associated with major systems.
c. Includes research and development, procurement, and military construction traceable to tactical air forces other than that covered in note b.
d. Includes military personnel and operations and maintenance appropriations for active forces funded in program II of the Five Year Defense Program (FYDP) plus all military personnel and operations and maintenance appropriations for reserve tactical air forces.
e. A share of indirect support costs such as communications, training, logistical support, and administration (programs III, VII, VIII, and IX of the FYDP) proportionate to the direct operating costs of tactical air forces.

of the A-10, a Navy V/STOL aircraft for the sea control ship, and expanded procurement of the F-14 and F-15.

• An allowance averaging $250 million a year for cost growth, associated principally with the F-15 and A-10.

These projections imply a continued decline in total aircraft inventory, though not in the authorized number of combat squadrons, over the balance of this decade, a trend that may be a source of savings in operating costs paralleling the experience of the Navy in retiring older ships. Eventually, however, and even in the absence of changes in planning requirements, fiscal constraints may force military planners to choose between maintaining their present emphasis on multipurpose aircraft and accepting a reduction in force levels, and moving more rapidly toward specialized aircraft of lower unit costs while retaining something close to present force levels.

Residual Costs of the Vietnam War

The signing of the cease-fire agreements in 1973 brought to an end a costly phase in the history of U.S. involvement in Southeast Asia. Total expenditures on the war in Vietnam came to $112 billion ($145 billion in 1974 dollars). These figures, shown in Table 9-8, are official Department of Defense estimates of incremental costs—that is, expenditures over and above what would have been spent in peacetime.

Table 9-8. Incremental Cost of the War in Vietnam, Fiscal Years 1965–74
Outlays in billions of dollars

Fiscal year	Current dollars	1974 dollars
1965	0.1	0.1
1966	5.8	8.7
1967	18.4	25.9
1968	20.0	27.7
1969	21.5	28.5
1970	17.4	22.0
1971	11.5	13.8
1972	7.2	8.0
1973 estimate	5.9	6.1
Subtotal	107.8	140.8
1974 estimate	4.1	4.1
Total	111.9	144.9

Source: Department of Defense, unpublished computer tabulation (1973).

Residual expenditures for Vietnam are to continue in fiscal 1974. The budget includes requests for $2.9 billion in obligational authority and $4.1 billion in outlays for Vietnam. In part, the difference between these two figures is accounted for by the fact that outlays tend to exceed obligational authority when a program is declining. An additional factor contributing to the difference is the acceleration of the flow of military assistance in the fourth quarter of 1972 to get equipment and supplies to Vietnam before restrictions in the truce documents went into effect. To do this the United States borrowed matériel such as airplanes, helicopters, and tanks from its own forces and from those of allies (for example, Iran, Taiwan, and the Republic of Korea). These items will be procured in fiscal 1974, partly from the fiscal 1973 authorizations for Vietnam, for repayment to the lenders. Procurement of airplanes and helicopters for these purposes alone will account for approximately $400 million. If this explanation is correct, the request for obligational authority is more relevant to the discussion of Vietnam requirements in fiscal 1974 than the request for outlays.

Department of Defense officials have stated that the budget request was prepared before the cease-fire was signed and would be revised in light of subsequent developments in Vietnam. Specifically, the request for $2.9 billion in budget authority assumed the continued presence of a small number of U.S. troops in Vietnam and a moderate level of U.S. air operations comparable to that maintained in 1972 before the North Vietnamese Easter offensive. Of the $2.9 billion, $1 billion was to support U.S. forces in Southeast Asia. The remaining $1.9 billion was for military assistance to allied forces in South Vietnam and possibly in Laos—about half for procurement of equipment and supplies and half in support of operations. How will each of these components of Vietnam costs be affected as a result of the cease-fire?

Support of U.S. Forces in Southeast Asia

With U.S. forces now withdrawn from Vietnam, incremental costs in this category would be associated with Air Force units in Thailand and Guam (about 50,000 men) and Navy ships off the coast of Vietnam (about 15,000 men). Since almost all of these men are part of the baseline force, incremental costs would be restricted to such items as pay and other personnel bonuses for duty in a war zone, costs associated with a long logistical pipeline and with shorter tours of duty, and possibly higher than normal expenditure on ordnance, fuel, and repair parts for continued operations in Cambodia. If these forces are not reduced or withdrawn in fiscal 1974, incremental costs are estimated to be about $500 million instead of the $1 billion now included in the budget for these purposes. Should the United States resume the air war in Vietnam or Laos on even a moderate scale, these incremental costs could quickly rise.

Military Assistance: Equipment and Ammunition

Approximately $950 million has been requested for this category of military assistance. Unless large-scale fighting erupts, this amount will not be needed. The South Vietnamese probably entered the cease-fire period fully equipped. Requirements for replacing worn-out equipment, which is permitted under the cease-fire agreement,[11] would be small in the first year or so. An approximation of future annual needs can be based on the following calculation: South Vietnam has the equivalent of approximately twenty infantry divisions, each of which has about the same equipment, excluding tanks, as a U.S. infantry division. On the assumption that, because of poor maintenance and some battle attrition, South Vietnamese divisions will have to replace equipment twice as fast as a U.S. infantry division in peacetime, requirements might come to $200 million a year at the outside. In the case of its air force, South Vietnam at present probably has more aircraft than it can operate. First-year costs for replacement and spares would be very low, if there were any at all; eventually they might reach $100 million a year. There may be an additional requirement to supply military equipment to Laos, but the amount in almost any circumstances would be relatively small.

Military Assistance: Operating Costs

The remaining $950 million requested in the budget is for support of South Vietnamese regular forces, militia, and police (for food, fuel, other consumables, repair parts, construction, and pay) and for pay-

11. The cease-fire agreement permits "periodic replacement of armaments, munitions and war material which have been destroyed, damaged, worn out or used up after the cease-fire, on the basis of piece-for-piece." "Agreement on Ending the War and Restoring Peace in Vietnam," Article 7, in U.S. Department of State, News Release, "Documentation on Viet-Nam Agreement" (Jan. 24, 1973; processed), p. 34.

ing about 8,000 American civilian technicians under contract to the U.S. government to train the Vietnamese in the use and maintenance of military equipment. As long as the United States assumes responsibility for supporting these forces, the cease-fire in itself would not eliminate requirements for this category of military assistance. Perhaps $500 million a year could be saved, however, if fighting does not escalate beyond present levels. Additional savings would depend on reductions in the number of South Vietnamese forces or on increased South Vietnamese self-reliance.

In sum, if present U.S. programs for Vietnam were adjusted solely for the effect of the cease-fire, the residual cost of Vietnam in the fiscal 1974 Department of Defense budget might be reduced from $2.9 billion to about $1.1 billion. Should large-scale fighting resume, most of the possibilities for reducing expenditures would disappear.

As against these possible savings, the President has stated that he would recommend programs to help in the reconstruction of both South and North Vietnam and that this would not be at the expense of domestic programs. As yet there are no indications of how large these reconstruction programs might be, beyond President Nixon's indication during the course of the Paris peace negotiations that the United States might contemplate a five-year reconstruction program for all of Indochina amounting to $7.5 billion.

Insofar as South Vietnam is concerned, the administration has recommended an economic reconstruction program of approximately $500 million funded under the Foreign Assistance Act and not in the Department of Defense budget.

Finally, what might happen to residual Vietnam costs beyond fiscal 1974 if the cease-fire proves to be a transition to political stability and economic reconstruction in Southeast Asia? In that event, the present administration posture would permit further sizable reductions in military assistance to South Vietnam and the removal of part or all of the U.S. forces now in Thailand. American programs in Korea following the 1953 cease-fire there provide at least an indication of possible trends after fiscal 1974 in the level of U.S. assistance to Vietnam. During the period 1953–61 U.S. military and economic assistance to Korea averaged $450 million a year, which in 1974 dollars would come to an average annual program of about $700 million, higher at the beginning of the period and declining thereafter.

Financial Implications of the 1974 Defense Posture

A summary of the preceding projections is shown in Table 9-9. Total defense costs, in dollars of constant purchasing power, are expected to rise steadily through 1980. The defense budget, including al-

Table 9-9. Projected Department of Defense Total Obligational Authority, by Mission Category, and Outlays, Fiscal Years 1974–80

Mission category	1974	1975	1976	1977	1978	1979	1980
Total obligational authority in billions of 1974 dollars							
Strategic forces	18.0	18.5	20.1	21.0	21.4	21.8	21.7
Ground combat forces	22.1	22.4	22.8	23.4	23.9	24.3	24.5
Navy general purpose forces	16.0	15.5	16.4	16.7	16.1	16.5	16.5
Tactical air forces	16.5	16.7	16.4	16.6	17.0	16.3	16.5
Airlift and sealift forces	1.7	1.7	1.7	1.7	1.7	1.7	1.7
Family housing	1.2	1.2	1.2	1.2	1.2	1.2	1.2
Military assistance[a]	1.3	1.5	1.4	1.3	1.2	1.1	1.0
Subtotal	76.8	77.5	80.0	81.9	82.5	82.9	83.1
Incremental cost of the war in Vietnam	2.9	...	...	...	...	...	...
Retired pay[b]	5.3	5.6	5.9	6.1	6.4	6.7	7.0
Allowance for real pay increases[c]	...	1.1	2.2	3.3	4.5	5.8	7.2
Total	85.0	84.2	88.1	91.3	93.4	95.4	97.3
Total obligational authority in billions of current dollars							
Allowance for pay increases due to inflation[d]	...	1.0	2.1	3.2	4.3	5.6	6.9
Allowance for price increases[e]	...	1.5	3.1	4.8	6.5	8.2	9.9
Total	85.0	86.7	93.3	99.3	104.2	109.2	114.1
Outlays in billions of current dollars							
Total[f]	79.0	81.7	89.3	96.3	102.2	108.2	113.1

Source: Authors' estimates.

a. The military assistance program is assumed to decline gradually for the rest of the decade, as the Korean program is completed and as some present recipients of foreign military sales credits—such as Israel—move to commercial terms. The increase in fiscal 1975 occurs because it includes $300 million for deliveries of military equipment to South Vietnam which was formerly included in Vietnam war costs.

b. The cost of retired pay in constant dollars is calculated, in each year, by multiplying the projected average number of retirees by the average level of benefits in fiscal 1974.

c. Assumes real pay increases of 3 percent a year corresponding to the average increase in productivity in the private sector.

d. The following rates of increase were used in these calculations: military payroll, 3.3 percent per year; civilian payroll, 2.5 percent per year; retired pay, 2.5 percent per year cost of living allowance, plus 7.2 percent pay-related increase per year for new retirees.

e. The following rates of increase were used in these calculations: military construction and family housing: 4.5 percent in fiscal 1975, 4.2 percent in fiscal 1976, and 4.1 percent per year thereafter; research and development: 4.0 percent in fiscal 1975, and 3.8 percent per year thereafter; procurement, nonpay portions of military personnel and operations and maintenance appropriations, real cost growth, and new initiatives: 3.0 percent in fiscal 1975 and 2.7 percent per year thereafter.

f. Outlays in current dollars are estimated for each year by adding to outlays for the previous year the projected increase in total obligational authority plus an allowance of $1 billion a year to close part of the gap between funds authorized and funds spent by fiscal 1980. This gap, amounting to $6 billion in fiscal 1974, is assumed to be reduced to $1 billion in fiscal 1980. Outlays for 1975 rise less rapidly than would be expected because they reflect the presumed savings in Vietnam costs. Should requests for Vietnam be reduced substantially in fiscal 1974, the reductions would be restricted to outlays for that year alone. Outlays shown for subsequent years would not be affected.

lowances for pay increases and inflation, could reach $114 billion in current dollars by 1980.

Should this projection be characterized as conservative, exaggerated, or middle range? As a projection of current policies it probably falls in the middle range. For example, the eruption of fighting in Vietnam, leading to increased tension in Asia, or reversals in East-West negotiations could rapidly generate funding requests substantially higher than those now projected. On the other hand, a successful transition to peace in Vietnam and substantial progress in East-West negotiations on arms control could spur large reductions in force levels and budgets.

As a prediction of what will happen, however, the projection is probably on the high side. Given continuing fiscal pressure, the indicated trend in defense spending probably would result, sooner or later, in executive branch initiatives to reduce forces and manpower and to stretch out modernization programs, or in congressionally imposed restrictions on available funds. The issues then become how large these reductions should be and how they can be made safely or with least risk. The next two chapters discuss these issues, outlining some of the major factors underlying alternative defense budgets and indicating how they might be integrated into coordinated defense postures corresponding to alternative spending levels.

10. Defense Budget Issues

IN THE MID-1930s the U.S. defense budget amounted to $900 million, equivalent to perhaps $7 billion at today's prices and pay scales. This sum financed a powerful navy (oriented principally to the contingency of war with Japan), a small air force, and ground forces that amounted to little more than a nucleus for mobilization. Fewer than 300,000 men were in the active armed services and 150,000 civilians were employed in defense agencies—about one-seventh of the present totals. As a whole, the U.S. defense posture of that time reflected disillusion, in the aftermath of World War I, about America's capacity to influence events in Europe and the wisdom of doing so.

A complete turnabout took place as a consequence of World War II and the widespread political and economic disorganization that immediately followed. Nuclear weapons and long-range delivery systems in themselves made a profound difference. Their existence in the hands of a potential adversary posed a threat to the continental United States for the first time in more than a century and brought hitherto unknown complexities to the problem of creating an international structure sufficiently stable to avoid a world military catastrophe. More generally, the United States came to define the protection of its security interests in terms of a forward defense strategy and active involvement in the affairs of Europe and Asia. Deterrence of war, it was believed, required the peacetime deployment of sizable U.S. forces in these areas and the maintenance of large backup forces at home.

Almost three decades of peace in Western Europe, on the one hand, and U.S. involvement in two wars in Asia, on the other hand, have brought about surprisingly few changes in the broad concepts underlying this defense posture. Substantial shifts in tactics have occurred during the period, notably in the degree of reliance to be placed on nuclear as opposed to conventional forces. But the concept of a forward defense strategy and its main military force underpinnings continue to be operative today.

This chapter discusses how forces are allocated under this strategy and how alternative force requirements might affect U.S. security, foreign policy, and defense costs. Three major policy areas are examined: strategic force requirements, which relate directly to the deterrence of an attack on the continental United States; general purpose force requirements, which relate to U.S. security through their effect on the military balance in Europe, the Middle East, and Asia; and manpower policies, which can significantly affect defense costs independently of foreign policy and military strategy.

Strategic Forces and the Question of Sufficiency*

Selective protests notwithstanding, there seems to be a broad consensus within the executive and legislative branches that strategic planning should be based on the assumptions (1) that the USSR has reached a position of strategic parity with the United States and (2) that regaining strategic superiority would not be practical for the United States and would not contribute to U.S. security. Hence, the administration's goal of strategic sufficiency commands widespread support. The same is true, although to a lesser extent, for the principal tenet of the administration's strategic doctrine—that deterrence depends on the maintenance of secure retaliatory capabilities. In this case support results partly from the view that the alternative doctrine of relying on impregnable defenses against strategic attack is at present neither technically nor financially feasible. There is even fairly general agreement on how much is needed militarily to achieve suffi-

---

* Material in this section is drawn from Alton H. Quanbeck and Barry M. Blechman, *Strategic Forces: Issues for the Mid-Seventies* (Brookings Institution, 1973). This staff paper provides a comprehensive analysis of the major strategic policy issues, their background, and their budgetary significance. See also Charles L. Schultze and others, *Setting National Priorities: The 1973 Budget* (Brookings Institution, 1972), pp. 93–109.

ciency; that is, on how many and what kinds of forces provide a secure retaliatory capability against present Soviet strategic forces.

Controversy within the government over strategic forces, therefore, rests less on broad differences over the goals of strategic doctrine than on how these goals should be achieved. Three questions are of central importance:

• What forces are required as a hedge against unforeseen developments, such as a breakthrough in Soviet technological capability, a reversal of the trend in U.S.–Soviet relations toward détente, or a breakdown in the strategic arms limitation talks (SALT) and abrogation of the existing agreements?

• What forces are required for political reasons, such as deterring the Soviet Union and China from hostile foreign policy initiatives, maintaining the confidence of allies, and generally underwriting the U.S. position in foreign affairs?

• What forces are required for "bargaining chips" to encourage progress in U.S.–Soviet arms limitation negotiations?

One's view of much of the fiscal 1974 strategic force budget depends on the position taken on each of these questions. The same is true for major weapon development programs now being funded—programs that will shape the nation's strategic posture and dictate the cost of strategic forces for the next fifteen to twenty years. Consequently, this section examines the major strategic programs in terms of how they would be affected by alternative positions on these three questions—in other words, by alternative criteria for strategic sufficiency.

The Trident Program

Sea-based missile systems, the least vulnerable element of the triad (see Chapter 9), will be the keystone of the U.S. strategic deterrent for the indefinite future. At some point a follow-on system will be necessary to replace the present Polaris/Poseidon submarines, the newest of which will be twenty years old (the retirement age for planning purposes) by 1987. Hence, the issues raised by the Trident strategic submarine and missile program are not whether but rather how fast and in what numbers it should be built and what its characteristics should be.

In 1972, the administration, with the support of the Congress, accelerated the Trident program, advancing the date on which the system was to enter service from the early 1980s to 1978. It did so principally for two reasons: (1) to induce the Russians to agree to the inclusion of submarine-launched ballistic missiles in the first SALT accord; and (2) to allay concern at home and among U.S. allies that the strategic balance was shifting in favor of the USSR. Apparent success in the first purpose has led the Defense Department to continue emphasizing the accelerated program as an important bargaining chip in the second-stage SALT negotiations.

If these political factors were not considered dominant, the Trident program could be carried out at a more moderate pace and at a significantly lower cost over the balance of this decade without jeopardizing U.S. security. Savings would be possible from two sources:

• Stretching out the pace of modernization (assuming constant force levels) would make longer use of existing systems possible. Furthermore, a more moderately paced program would avoid the waste inherent in concurrent development and procurement of a complex system. Development would be more orderly and contracting procedures more effective. On the other hand, if the present pace of development is maintained, the real cost of building ten submarines—the present program—is likely to be significantly more than $13.5 billion, the cost estimate announced in 1972 and the most recent one available.

• Moving directly to development of the Trident II missile, which has a range of 6,000 nautical miles, instead of first developing the 4,500-mile-range Trident I missile would also save money. The latter was originally justified for possible use in existing Poseidon submarines should the USSR appear on the verge of a breakthrough in anti-submarine warfare (ASW) technology during the brief period before the Trident submarine became available. Slippage in the Trident I missile program's schedule, so that it will now be available at about the same time as the new submarine, indicates that this consideration is no longer believed important. A decision to slow down the submarine program, therefore, could also lead logically to a parallel decision to skip development of the Trident I missile and move directly to development of the longer-range Trident II missile. This eventually could save at least $2.5 billion—the estimated total cost of developing one generation of these missiles.

Estimates taking both factors into account are that, if it was decided to revert to the earlier schedule, bringing the first Trident into service in the early 1980s, the strategic force budget would be reduced by an average of $1.0 billion a year for the rest of this decade. Perhaps half of this cost reduction would represent a deferral of costs into the 1980s and half would be savings from greater production efficiency in building the submarine and from avoiding the cost of building the Trident I missile.

Strategic Bomber Force Levels

With the scheduled reduction of two B-52 squadrons in fiscal 1974, the strategic bomber force will decline to 438 planes deployed in operational squadrons. Nearly 60 percent of this force—255 aircraft—will consist of newer B-52s, the G and H models built between 1958 and 1962. These planes are now the core of the strategic bomber force, and their effective service life should extend into the 1980s. They are being equipped with new air-to-surface short-range attack missiles (SRAMs) and will eventually be equipped with subsonic cruise armed decoys (SCADs) to improve their penetration capability. Also, measures have been taken to increase their chance of escaping destruction on the ground in the event of concentrated missile attacks launched from Soviet submarines. About 40 percent of these aircraft are kept on constant ground alert and could therefore be expected to survive any preemptive attack. The on-alert part of the strategic bomber force alone is considered capable of destroying a large enough portion of the USSR's population and industry to deter a Soviet first strike.

The remainder of the bomber force will consist of 117 older B-52s—D models built in the late 1950s—and 66 FB-111s, first introduced into the force in 1971. Whether to continue to operate the older part of the B-52 force and the FB-111s constitutes a significant budgetary issue. These planes add little to U.S. strategic capabilities and are expensive to operate. The older B-52s are not considered worth equipping with new missiles, and the FB-111s, although very new, are severely limited in range and payload. Furthermore, these bombers require an equivalent number of tanker aircraft to operate effectively, which adds considerably to total operating costs. It is estimated that if the older B-52s, the FB-111s, and their tankers were gradually phased out of the active force over the next few years and placed in storage, possible savings could average $1.2 billion a year over the balance of the decade.

Arguments against this course of action focus on two factors: first, that the United States should not reduce its bomber force without persuading the USSR, through SALT, to make an equivalent reduction of its strategic forces; and second, that the possibility of using the older B-52 bombers for conventional bombing, as in the Vietnam war, justifies keeping them in operation.

The B-1 Program

If the United States is to maintain indefinitely a bomber force as an independent element in its strategic deterrent, it will be necessary to introduce a follow-on bomber to the B-52 sometime in the 1980s. Concern about the B-1, which is now the sole candidate, centers on the possibility that it will provide only marginal improvements in capability at very high cost. A danger exists that in 1975—the date of the scheduled procurement decision—the B-1 will be chosen simply because it is the only option available.

One alternative would be to postpone decisions on any new bomber until the second-round SALT discussions shed more light on future requirements.

Another alternative would be to postpone a decision for two or three years and invest now in the parallel development of a different kind of strategic aircraft: a standoff bomber carrying long-range cruise missiles. Research and development costs would be relatively low, since this kind of bomber could be based on aircraft designs already in use, such as that of the Boeing 747 or the Lockheed C-5A, and could use missile systems already being developed, such as the Air Force's SCAD. Procurement costs would also be lower than those of the B-1; since the new bomber would not have to penetrate Soviet air defenses, it would not need as much sophisticated electronic equipment as the B-1 and would not have to be acquired in as large numbers. Finally, operating costs would be lower because tankers would not be needed.

To pursue this option probably would require additional research and development expenditures during the next several years, since experimental work on the B-1, though slowed down, would not be discontinued unless work on the concept of a standoff bomber proved it to be preferable. The relatively small additional investment required might be worthwhile to permit an informed choice in the mid-1970s. Should a standoff bomber prove to be the more desirable system, its cost in the 1970s might average approximately $600 million a year less than that of the B-1 program.

ICBM Force Levels

Budgetary issues relating to land-based intercontinental ballistic missiles (ICBMs) arise, in part, from real doubts as to their ultimate survivability. Should the United States continue to spend money on programs designed to make the ICBM a credible deterrent for the indefinite future? Or should such investments be avoided on the ground that they are not likely to contribute enough to deterrence to justify their cost? The administration has moved toward the first course of action, but with some equivocation. It has carried forward the MIRV (multiple independently targetable reentry vehicle) and the Silo Upgrade programs for the 550 Minuteman I missiles and has requested initial, though still small, funding to extend these measures to the 450 Minuteman II missiles. One Safeguard antiballistic missile (ABM) site is being completed, and the fiscal 1974 budget request includes funding for a high level of ABM research and development. On the other hand, by negotiating the SALT agreement, the administration has avoided building the full Safeguard system. It also has decided against other costly programs seeking to make ICBM sites less vulnerable, and apparently it has not made a final decision on converting Minuteman II missiles to MIRVs.

A lower-cost alternative still consistent with continuing the triad would be to maintain ICBMs at reduced force levels. The 550 Minuteman/MIRV missiles, which will be fully funded in fiscal 1974, will have enough destructive potential to serve as an independent deterrent for many years to come, and continuing research and development on ABM technology could provide some insurance for their future capability. But instead of investing additional funds to convert them to MIRVs, the United States could phase out the Minuteman II missiles. This course of action would save approximately $500 million a year ($300 million a year from avoiding the cost of a Minuteman II/MIRV program and $200 million in direct and indirect operating costs). Arguments against this course of action would be: (1) the possible loss of a bargaining chip at SALT; and (2) concern over the political repercussions of a deteriorating U.S. position in numerical force comparisons with the USSR.

How Much Air Defense?

The administration seems to have adopted far more modest objectives for strategic air defense than heretofore.[1] These new objectives are to defend Washington, D.C., from air attack, to defend generally against small air attacks (with a few days' warning), and to restrict unauthorized penetration of U.S. air space. Apparently, the administration no longer plans to build forces to defend military and key urban-industrial targets against major air attacks—a change in planning criteria that should lead to substantial savings in the future. For example, plans to buy the new surface-to-air missile (SAM-D) as a strategic defensive system have evidently been dropped, which will save $2.3 billion. Moreover, procurement of a new manned interceptor for air defense seems to have been postponed for at least a few years.

A program designed strictly for these newly reduced objectives could probably be carried out with even smaller force levels and slower-paced modernization programs than are now contemplated. A more modest program would call for: (1) phasing out the present force of surface-to-air missiles in the next several years; (2) deactivating the seven active Air Force interceptor squadrons and further postponing purchase of a new interceptor; and (3) reducing projected procurement of the airborne warning and control system from forty-two to twenty units. Savings from such a cutback in the air defense program would average $900 million a year from fiscal years 1974 through 1980.

Abandoning the Triad

Beyond the kind of issues outlined above, judgments also differ on the number of independent systems necessary to provide confidence in U.S. strategic retaliatory capabilities. Maintenance of the triad is founded on the view that the unique capabilities inherent in three different and independent systems are desirable from a military perspective because (1) they provide a high-confidence hedge against a technological breakthrough in defenses against, or unforeseen operational failures in, any one system, and (2) they complicate Soviet strategic planning. If the United States were prepared to reduce the level of

---

1. See, for example, the definition of air defense objectives in U.S. Department of Defense, *Military Manpower Requirements Report for FY 1974* (1973), p. 18.

confidence that this type of redundancy provides, further cuts in strategic forces could be contemplated.

One alternative would be to base strategic planning on a "dyad" consisting of sea-based missiles and bombers. All programs to protect or modernize ICBMs would be abandoned, and the land-based missile force as a whole would be phased out; this would be done gradually—say, by 1980—to diminish unfavorable political consequences. This approach would mean canceling the Minuteman/ MIRV program, the one-site Safeguard ABM program, and most ABM research and development programs. Annual savings from these actions would average $2.0 billion for the rest of the decade. Judgments about the possible military consequences of this course of action depend on estimates of not only the benefits of redundancy but also the potential vulnerability of land-based missiles. Judgments about the probable political consequences depend on how much weight is attached to numerical force comparisons as an element in the conduct of foreign policy.

A more drastic alternative would be to move toward reliance on a sea-based system alone, gradually phasing out all other offensive programs as the Trident became available. Additional savings might average about $3 billion a year. With reduction to a single system, uncertainty about both military and political consequences becomes very large; this course of action therefore has implications that are fundamentally different and potentially involve much greater risks than those of previously outlined measures.

Issues and Budgets: A Summing Up

Spending on strategic forces can be reduced in three ways: by cutting offensive forces, by slowing weapon modernization, or by reducing air defenses. Spending less would imply that the United States was giving up some military or political capabilities: redundancy in retaliatory forces, flexibility in war-fighting capabilities, political potentialities related to force levels, or bargaining chips in U.S.–Soviet arms control negotiations. Hence, the desirability of the reductions depends ultimately on subjective judgments of how much, if at all, these capabilities are in fact affected and on the dollar value attached to any changes in these capabilities.

Differing positions on the major strategic programs discussed above reflect differences in these kinds of judgments. At the risk of over-simplification, these positions can be grouped into four alternative strategic postures: maintaining the current strategic force, which is as ambitious a posture as seems likely in view of the fiscal and foreign policy considerations discussed in earlier chapters; a less costly triad; a dyad composed of submarines and bombers; and a sea-based system only. Average annual costs (in 1974 dollars) for each of these postures range from $13 billion to $20 billion over the balance of this decade. The composition and projected cost of each set of strategic forces, shown in Table 10-1, are summarized below.

Alternative 1 is a projection of the administration program—maintenance of the triad with extensive modernization of each element. This posture constitutes a high-confidence strategic deterrent that emphasizes political considerations and the need to negotiate with the USSR on further arms reductions from a position of strength.

The estimated cost of this program, as described in Chapter 9, will rise steadily throughout this decade, averaging $20.2 billion a year in 1974 dollars.

Alternative 2, a lower-cost triad, maintains all the major precepts of current strategic planning but places much less weight than alternative 1 on political factors and bargaining chip considerations. It calls for: (1) the unilateral elimination of the relatively less effective components of present U.S. strategic forces (the older B-52 bombers

Table 10-1. The Cost of Alternative Strategic Postures, Fiscal Years 1974, 1977, and 1980

Total obligational authority in billions of 1974 dollars

Alternative	*1974*	*1977*	*1980*	*Annual average, 1974–80*
1. The present posture[a]	18.0	21.0	21.7	20.2
2. A less expensive triad[b]	16.4	15.8	17.6	16.2
3. A dyad—bombers and sea-based missiles[c]	16.0	13.6	15.9	14.4
4. A sea-based force[d]	16.9	12.6	10.5	13.0

Source: Authors' estimates. All cost estimates include an allowance for indirect operating expenses such as training, medical care, and administration.

a. Projection of the cost of carrying out present strategic programs. See Chapter 9, pp. 307–15, for details.

b. Differs from alternative 1 in a slower development pace for Trident; slower development of a new strategic bomber, including a choice between the B-1 and a standoff bomber; phase-out of older model B-52s and FB-111 bombers; selected reductions in air defense (see text); and curtailment of the Minuteman/MIRV program at 550 missiles.

c. Differs from alternative 1 in all the measures listed for alternative 2 plus phasing out all land-based missiles and antiballistic missile systems by fiscal 1980.

d. Differs from alternative 1 in stopping all modernization programs for offensive weapons except Trident and gradually phasing out all strategic bombers, land-based missiles, and antiballistic missile systems by fiscal 1980; and selective reductions in air defenses (see text).

and the FB-111 bombers); (2) slowing down the submarine and bomber modernization programs and halting the Minuteman/MIRV program at the level of 550 missiles; and (3) a reduction in air defense programs consistent with very modest air defense objectives. This alternative might be said to involve some reduction of confidence in the U.S. retaliatory capability, but in view of present redundancies the reduction and the political consequences are likely to be small, if not negligible.

The average annual cost of this alternative is estimated to be $16.2 billion, or $4 billion less than that of alternative 1. Annual savings would reach this level fairly soon.

Alternative 3, a dyad composed of submarines and bombers, is based on the assumption that land-based ICBMs will ultimately become vulnerable and that, in any event, two independent strategic systems provide a sufficient hedge against the unforeseen. Thus, in addition to the reductions in alternative 2, programs to improve the survivability of land-based missiles are canceled and existing missiles phased out before the end of the decade. A small ABM research program is maintained to keep up with technology.

The disadvantage is that the United States would be giving the USSR a three-to-one advantage in the number of missile launchers. Although this difference does not affect U.S. retaliatory capabilities or eliminate U.S. superiority in the number of warheads, its political consequences are less certain. If the USSR did not on its own make commensurate reductions in its missile launchers, the United States would be under pressure to insist on a change in the SALT agreement that would permit an increase in the number of U.S. sea-based missiles in the 1980s. These considerations suggest that existing land-based missiles be phased out in stages and that the United States observe the Soviet reaction at each stage before proceeding to the next.

The average annual cost of this alternative is estimated to be $14.4 billion over the period 1974-80, or $5.8 billion less than that of alternative 1. Savings peak after a few years.

Alternative 4, reliance on a sea-based system alone, rests on the judgment that a large, sophisticated sea-based force alone can provide sufficient confidence in U.S. strategic retaliatory capabilities for the indefinite future. Far more than in alternative 3, this course of action attaches relatively little weight to the three military risks that redundancy in strategic systems seeks to minimize: (1) the possibility of a Soviet breakthrough in antisubmarine warfare technology; (2) an unforeseen failure in any one system; and (3) a breakdown in communications that would make it impossible to use any one system during an enemy attack. The political uncertainties, in terms of allied and Soviet reactions, are great.

Under this alternative, the Trident program is continued at its present accelerated pace, and provision might be made to increase submarine force levels in the 1980s. On the other hand, the B-1 and the ICBM programs are canceled and existing bomber and land-based missile forces are phased out gradually as Trident submarines come into service. The program also calls for a modest research program on ABM technology and maintenance of air defenses for surveillance and early warning only.

The average annual cost of this alternative over the period 1974–80 is estimated to be $13 billion, with costs declining steadily over the period. At the end of the decade, costs stabilize at approximately $10 billion a year.

General Purpose Forces: Regional Alternatives

Whereas strategic forces are founded on requirements for the defense of U.S. territory, the size and disposition of general purpose forces are not. The United States, by virtue of geography and the absence of a military threat from bordering countries—to say nothing of its strategic deterrent—needs very few conventional forces to defend its sovereign territory. A core defense force, for example, might consist of a handful of ground units dispersed among bases on both coasts and in Alaska and Hawaii, naval forces for control of contiguous waters, and a tactical air arm for surveillance and protection against unauthorized overflights. In addition, providing a hedge against uncertainties would call for research and development expenditures to keep up with advances in military technology and the maintenance of a mobilization base. General purpose forces on this scale would not be much different from those the United States maintained in the 1930s, except for the navy that the United States then maintained to meet a Japanese naval threat that is, of course, nonexistent today.

General purpose forces since the end of World War II have been much larger than these core defense forces because of a belief that the security of the United States is linked to the security of other nations; in other words, that conflict elsewhere in the world could ultimately involve the United States or adversely affect its security in other ways. The fact that the United States became involved in four wars in little more than half a century can be taken as confirmation or a result of that belief, depending on one's point of view.

By this reasoning, a U.S. contribution to the security of other nations adds to the security of the United States in three ways:

• By preventing Soviet expansion in Western Europe and the Middle East and Chinese expansion in Asia; by deterring Soviet or Chinese resort to force in these areas and reducing the chances of miscalculation; and by maintaining a military balance conducive to effective East-West negotiations.

• By giving Western European countries and Japan confidence in their own security, thus encouraging economic and political connections among the industrial countries that make it possible for them to prosecute positive programs to improve the general welfare, including that of the developing world.

• By reducing the incentives for Germany and Japan to rely on their own armed strength for their security and perhaps to build independent nuclear forces in the process—a development that would virtually eliminate the possibility of creating a less dangerous East-West relationship and immensely complicate the problem of avoiding nuclear catastrophe.

In pursuit of these objectives, U.S. postwar military force planning progressively moved toward a strategy of deterring conflict by participating in alliances in Europe and Asia, maintaining sizable U.S. forces in those areas in peacetime, and keeping even larger forces at home to back up these commitments.

This expanded view of national security enjoyed widespread support for at least two decades following World War II, partly because the early postwar weakness of Western Europe and Japan combined with the aggressive posture of the USSR gave it compelling logic—a logic that was sustained by these countries' remembrance of World War II. However, the recent moves toward détente with the USSR and China, the growing economic power of Western Europe and Japan, and the disillusionment over Vietnam have clouded the issues linking events abroad to U.S. force requirements. Divergent views center on four questions. Is the risk of military pressure by either the USSR or China real enough to justify the maintenance of large U.S. conventional forces in peacetime? Are U.S. interests in Western Europe, Asia, and elsewhere worth the cost of participating in the defense of these areas? Can U.S. military forces overseas and backup forces at home effectively contribute to the promotion of these interests? In any event, do not Western European countries and Japan now have the capability to provide for their own defense, particularly if they see U.S. nuclear forces as their protection against possible Soviet or Chinese nuclear threats or attacks?

This definition of national security issues omits trade, investment, and other economic considerations, an omission that may seem surprising at a time when doubts about future U.S. oil and other raw material supplies and concern about the balance of payments are receiving a great deal of public attention. Foreign economic relations are, of course, important to the U.S. economy, but probably less so than for any industrial country except the USSR. For example, foreign trade for the United States amounts to less than 5 percent of its gross national product. Furthermore, the United States has the resources and technical resiliency to adjust to interruptions of its imports of specific raw materials, although such adjustments in the case of an interruption of oil supplies could involve substantial costs, including those resulting from temporary shortages. Indeed, foreign economic relations are probably important to the United States more because of their potential effect on political and security relations with other countries than because of their effect on the U.S. economy. More fundamentally, however, it would be neither necessary nor efficient to maintain large peacetime forces solely to assure the flow of raw materials. The cost of maintaining military forces larger than those strictly necessary for deterrence and defense would almost certainly far exceed the cost of assuring adequate supplies of raw materials by other than military means (such as stockpiling; investing in higher-cost supplies, standby productive capacity, and other forms of diversification; and the development of substitutes).

This section examines requirements for general purpose forces in light of alternative views of national security interests and of the best means of protecting them. It does so by first outlining the justification for existing forces and their disposition abroad; then examining the relation of U.S. forces to the military balance in Europe, the Middle East, and Asia; and finally presenting alternative views of U.S. security interests, the forces and budgets they would require, and the consequences they might entail.

Justification for Existing Forces

This year's official statements on military strategy and foreign policy indicate very little change in the administration's formulation of national security requirements. The main features may be summarized as follows:

• Strategic parity with the Soviet Union enhances the importance of general purpose forces as a stabilizing factor in situations involving great power interests.

• Although the threat posed by the USSR and China is somewhat ameliorated, "it is clear that we will continue to have fundamental differences with both of these nations, and these differences cannot be ignored."[2]

• Both the USSR and China are continuing to increase their military capabilities and the United States will fall into a position of inferiority if it does not improve its own. "The military balance, at this crucial juncture in world affairs, is very delicately poised."[3]

• Finally, the United States must maintain its commitments to its allies, not "to play the role of world policeman" but "to contribute to . . . a stable international structure. . . . Without a firm belief in the steadfastness of U.S. commitments and in the continuing capabilities of U.S. forces to support our interests around the globe, we and our allies cannot ensure our security nor continue negotiations with the basic confidence needed to develop new relationships."[4]

Thus the main postulates underlying a forward defense strategy are seen as still valid.

Military requirements for the defense of Western Europe, to which the United States is linked "through basic historical, political, and economic ties,"[5] continue to take priority over requirements for the defense of other areas and are the major determinant of the size and

2. *Annual Defense Department Report, Fiscal Year 1974, Statement of Secretary of Defense Elliot L. Richardson before the Senate Armed Services Committee on the FY 1974 Defense Budget and FY 1974–1978 Program* (March 28, 1973), p. 2.
3. Ibid., p. 3.
4. Ibid.
5. Ibid., p. 23.

composition of U.S. general purpose forces. These requirements are part of a strategy devised in common by the NATO countries, a strategy that has "evolved over the years to meet changing conditions and realities."[6] In the administration's view, U.S. forces stationed in Western Europe are a critical part of that strategy; they are for military as well as political reasons essential to a credible conventional defense posture in Western Europe. Hence, it is argued, they should not be reduced except as part of an agreement with the USSR involving mutual force reductions. Moreover, all U.S. forces stationed at home are viewed as potentially deployable during a war in Europe.

The administration's statements about U.S. forces supporting Asian commitments contain subtle ambiguities and indications of change which, taken together, point to a declining U.S. military role in the area. *For the near term*, the United States will "maintain some well equipped forces overseas for deterrence, or for an appropriate response if deterrence fails. . . . *In the longer term*, effective security in Asia will depend in large measure upon the developing interrelationships among the four major powers whose interests converge in the region—Japan, China, the Soviet Union, and the United States."[7]

In addition, as indicated above, two key political judgments cut across the administration's assessment of general purpose force requirements. First is the conviction that the United States can achieve useful results in bargaining with the USSR and China only if it can speak from a position of military strength. In other words, strong general purpose forces must be maintained to underwrite the continuing movement from an era of confrontation to an era of negotiation. Second is a belief that, because even moderate changes in U.S. force levels and deployments abroad can significantly affect the confidence of allies and the calculations of potential adversaries, any changes should take place gradually and be managed with care.

In exploring the basis for possible changes in force levels and dispositions, it is important to understand how U.S. forces fit into the military balance in the areas abroad where the United States has major commitments or interests. The present geographic distribution of U.S. general purpose forces, which results from these considerations, is estimated in Table 10-2. The estimate is based principally on official

6. Ibid.
7. Ibid., pp. 24, 25. Emphasis added.

Table 10-2. Possible Distribution of Proposed General Purpose Forces, by Geographic Contingency, End of Fiscal Year 1974

Type of force	European contingencies		Asian contingencies		Worldwide contingencies and strategic reserve, based in U.S.[a]	Total
	Based in Europe	Based in U.S.	Based in the Pacific[b]	Based in continental U.S.		
Active army divisions[e]	4⅓	3⅔	2[b]	...	3	13
Marine division airwings[g]	...	1	1	1[d]	...	3
National guard and reserve divisions	...	3[e]	...	...	6[f]	9
Navy carrier task forces	1	5	1	8	...	15
Air Force fighter/attack squadrons	21	4	11	...	34	70
Air National Guard and reserve fighter/attack squadrons	...	22	...	...	6	28
Total active-duty military manpower[g]	300,000	630,000	280,000	370,000	650,000	2,230,000

Source: Authors' estimates, derived primarily from U.S. Department of Defense, *Military Manpower Requirements Report for FY 1974* (1973).
a. Including about 40,000 personnel in various other places, primarily in the Western Hemisphere.
b. Includes one division stationed in Hawaii.
c. A small fraction of Marine division forces are deployed forward on ships.
d. Located on the West Coast.
e. Armored or mechanized.
f. Infantry divisions equipped for Asian contingencies but deployable to Europe if required.
g. Estimated distribution of all active-duty manpower including an allocation of administrative personnel and other supporting functions; all strategic forces manpower are included in the strategic reserve.

policy statements and information on the way in which forces are deployed, equipped, and trained.

Too much should not be made of such force allocations. For example, the ground combat divisions shown as earmarked for European contingencies consist of eight armored or mechanized Army divisions committed to the North Atlantic Treaty Organization (NATO) by present agreements, as well as one Marine division located on the east coast of the United States and oriented to Europe. Should a conflict appear imminent or actually break out, however, all divisions based in the United States, including those designated, equipped, or trained for Asian contingencies, presumably would be employed in the European theater. Divisions actually deployed in the Pacific (Korea, Okinawa, and Hawaii) would probably be the last to be used in Europe and might in fact be kept where they were in an effort to deter a simultaneous crisis in Asia. Similarly, in the event of a large-scale conflict in Asia all forces in the United States, including those committed to NATO, might be sent to the Pacific, but the divisions in Europe would be the last to be moved, if they were moved at all.

The Military Balance in Europe*

The predominant justification for existing U.S. general purpose forces is the contribution they now make to a credible NATO deterrent posture in Western Europe, which is founded on their ability to fight a war in Europe should deterrence fail. In this connection the central region of Europe is critical, the objective there being to prevent attacking forces from penetrating far into Germany. At a minimum, NATO forces must be able to contain attacking forces long enough to allow time for negotiations to end the conflict.

Measuring what is necessary to accomplish this mission involves more than a simple comparison of manpower and units. For example, the total number of divisions in the Soviet army cannot be compared on a one-for-one basis with forward deployed NATO divisions since Soviet units are very different in size, equipment, and capability. Also, less than half the divisions in the Soviet army are full-strength, combat-ready units; the rest would require from thirty to ninety days to

* Material in this section on comparative military capabilities in Europe and their implications for structuring U.S. general purpose forces is based on a Brookings defense analysis staff study on the U.S. military role in NATO being carried out by Richard D. Lawrence and Jeffrey Record.

be brought to combat readiness. Furthermore, the Soviet Union needs to maintain forces in the Far East, which significantly limits the number of units it could mobilize from within its borders for an invasion of Western Europe.[8] And how many Eastern European divisions the USSR can count on for such an enterprise remains an open question. All too often analysts lump all Warsaw Pact units together even though it is evident from examining the situation in each country that the contribution of Eastern European divisions to a Soviet offensive against NATO's central front would be limited.

Even so, NATO's ability to thwart a sudden, deliberate, well-coordinated Soviet attack continues to be hotly argued. Many experts flatly deny that NATO could. Others, emphasizing the preponderance of its economic and manpower resources, take the opposite position. But even in the highly improbable contingency of deliberate Soviet attack, the skeptics are influenced as much by doubts about the way NATO forces are organized and their readiness as by fears that Warsaw Pact forces would have overwhelming numerical superiority.

In general, NATO's requirements for successful forward defense are defined in terms of (1) maintaining sufficient forward deployed forces to contain an initial attack, whether premeditated or stemming from miscalculation or accident; (2) maintaining a mobilization and reinforcement capability sufficient to offset the Warsaw Pact's buildup potential; and (3) sustaining NATO forces in combat for as long as the Warsaw Pact can sustain its forces in combat.

A comparison of the military balance in the central region, drawn up with these requirements in mind, is shown in Table 10-3. Three features of this comparison merit emphasis. The forces estimated for each side include only those projected to be available on the basis of politically realistic assumptions and after taking readiness factors into account. Thus, with the exception of territorial forces, all French ground units and all French tactical air units are for purposes of analysis included in NATO's defensive forces, even though France is not technically part of the NATO military organization; on the other hand, only about one-fourth of Eastern European forces are included in the total the Warsaw Pact is estimated to have available for an

---

8. The Soviet buildup of forces in the Far East during the second half of the 1960s was accomplished in part by drawing on forces within the USSR. While the number of Soviet divisions deployed in Eastern Europe was actually increased during this period as a result of the invasion of Czechoslovakia, backup forces for Soviet western deployments were reduced.

Table 10-3. Comparison of NATO and Warsaw Pact Forces in the Central Region on M-Day and Thirty and Sixty Days Later[a]

Thousands

Force	M-Day	M + 30[b]	M + 60[b]
Ground combat troops[e]			
Total NATO	365.0	555.0	585.0
U.S.	90.0	130.0	160.0
Total Warsaw Pact	500.0	775.0	910.0
USSR	355.0	625.0	760.0
Total deployed military manpower[d]			
Total NATO	660.0	1,045.0	1,105.0
U.S.	200.0	285.0	345.0
Total Warsaw Pact	670.0	1,030.0	1,210.0
USSR	470.0	830.0	1,010.0
Medium tanks[e]			
Total NATO	6.7	7.7	8.2
U.S.	1.2	1.9	2.3
Total Warsaw Pact	11.3	16.8	19.2
USSR	7.9	13.4	15.8
Tactical aircraft[f]			
Total NATO[g]	2.7	3.7	4.9
U.S.	0.6[h]	1.5[i]	2.7[j]
Total Warsaw Pact	4.3	5.5	7.2
USSR	3.7[k]	4.9	6.6[l]

Sources: Authors' estimates, based on data in T. N. Dupuy and Wendell Blanchard, *The Almanac of World Military Power* (2d ed., T. N. Dupuy Associates, 1972), and International Institute for Strategic Studies, *The Military Balance, 1972–1973* (IISS, 1972).

a. M-Day, defined as the day each side begins its military buildup, is assumed to be the same for both sides. If Warsaw Pact forces began a buildup earlier without being detected by NATO, the alignment of force projections would be altered.

NATO countries assumed to contribute to the defense of the central front are: Belgium, the Netherlands, Great Britain, Canada, West Germany, France, and the United States.

Pact forces, in addition to those of the USSR, are calculated on the basis of political assessments and readiness factors; they include all of East Germany's six divisions, three of the thirteen Polish divisions, and six of the ten Czechoslovakian divisions. Forces from Hungary, Romania, and Bulgaria are ruled out entirely. All Pact ground forces appearing in the table represent only those considered available for offensive operations against Western Europe.

b. Forces available on M-Day and through M + 60 are judged to be as follows. M-day non–U.S. NATO forces consist of the active armies of Belgium, the Netherlands, and West Germany, and the British, Canadian, and French contingents stationed in West Germany. By M + 30 the buildup consists of three division equivalents of West German territorial forces, five French divisions, one reserve division from the Netherlands, and one reserve division from Belgium. The buildup of U.S.-based divisions is assumed as follows: plus two and two-thirds by M + 30 and two more by M + 60 (assumes one Marine division for use in the central region). For the USSR, post-M-Day transfers of divisions to the central region from Russia are as follows: plus twenty-four divisions by M + 30 and twelve more divisions by M + 60. Divisions now in the Far East are not moved to the central region.

c. Combat troops on both sides were estimated by applying the following combat–support ratios to deployed divisions: for non-U.S. NATO divisions, 60:40; for U.S. divisions, roughly 50:50; and for Eastern European and Soviet divisions, 75:25.

d. Equals deployed combat troops plus deployed support troops.

e. Tanks at M-Day include: medium tanks of Belgian, Dutch, and West German armies, thirty-two Canadian medium tanks, estimated tank strength of British and French contingents in West Germany, and medium tanks in four and one-third U.S. divisions in West Germany. Added by M + 30: remainder of medium tanks in French First Army, plus medium tanks in two and two-thirds more U.S. divisions. Added by M + 60: medium tanks in another two U.S. divisions (one armored and one Marine Corps).

f. Does not include light bombers, reconnaissance and transport aircraft, or attack helicopters.

invasion of the central region (as distinguished from the larger Eastern European forces that would be available for defensive purposes). Second, instead of a division count, which is misleading, the number of combat troops, as well as the total number of troops participating in the mobilization in the central region, are estimated for each side. And finally, the contributions by the United States and the Soviet Union to their respective alliances is specified.

It is assumed in this comparison that neither side will be able to draw on all its military resources, including manpower, in the first few months following mobilization. Constraints are severe for both. The USSR is not likely to draw on its sizable forces in the Soviet Far East for two reasons: Soviet commanders would be cautious about stripping defenses there and they would be hampered by the inadequacies of the Trans-Siberian Railroad. For the United States, time is a problem in organizing and transporting forces across the Atlantic. For all practical purposes the main forces considered in this military comparison are: for NATO, the active forces (brought to full strength) of Western European countries committed to the forward defense of the central region, plus active forces from the United States earmarked for NATO and assumed to be deployable to the Continent within sixty days of the start of mobilization; and for the USSR, its active units now in Eastern Europe and those stationed in the western half of Russia, including the necessary reserves to man these divisions at full strength. Newly recruited manpower would be available on both sides only after the first two months of mobilization and thus could not significantly affect the military outcome in the early stages of the war.

What do these military comparisons imply for NATO? In strictly numerical terms, the balance is promising rather than ominous in its implications for a successful defense of Western Europe. Established military doctrine holds that, as a rule of thumb, the Warsaw Pact

---

Notes to Table 10-3, continued

g. The entire tactical air strength of the participating European NATO countries, including France, is assumed to be available on M-Day.

h. M-Day strength equals 500 aircraft now on the Continent plus 120 with the Sixth Fleet.

i. By M + 30 the following aircraft will be added: 240 from four carriers in the Atlantic, 400 from the United States, 130 from Asian deployments, and 120 assigned to one Marine air wing.

j. Added by M + 60: 800 aircraft taken from U.S. reserve formations, 120 more from active U.S. Air Force, 180 from three additional carriers, 120 from a second Marine air wing.

k. Includes two-thirds of the combat aircraft assigned to the Soviet Tactical Air Force (TAF) and one third of the aircraft in the Soviet Air Defense Command (ADC).

l. Added by M + 60: another one-sixth of ADC tactical combat aircraft plus another one-sixth of TAF aircraft.

countries, as the presumed attacker, should muster something close to a three-to-one numerical advantage in ground combat forces, at the theater level, to have a reasonably good chance of overrunning the NATO center.

Forces immediately available to the Warsaw Pact command in the central region, together with reinforcements during the first two months of mobilization, fall substantially short of achieving this superiority. Only the participation of all the Czechoslovakian and Polish divisions in an attack, which is unlikely, could measurably affect this conclusion. In the second two months, the Warsaw Pact advantage might increase moderately. Beyond that, NATO probably would begin to overcome its early inferiority in ground strength as, first, Western European forces and, subsequently, U.S. units were mobilized, trained, and deployed. Although the Warsaw Pact countries would have a numerical advantage in tanks and tactical aircraft, NATO would be stronger in antitank weapons. Moreover, the qualitative superiority of NATO's weapons would be pronounced. Its aircraft generally can deliver larger quantities of ordnance on ground targets. American aircraft have new, highly accurate bombs and rockets based on a technology the Soviet Union has not yet demonstrated. And helicopters have made U.S. ground forces more mobile and therefore more effective in ground combat.

Possible NATO weaknesses, therefore, stem not from numerical imbalance but from the way the two potentially opposing forces are organized and deployed. NATO forces are structured for a protracted war: its ground forces arc heavy in support units designed to sustain divisions in combat for long periods; its tactical air forces include a large proportion of expensive, long-range, multipurpose aircraft that, in addition to providing support for troops on the battlefield, aim at achieving air superiority as a prerequisite for interdicting lines of communication and destroying industrial facilities deep in enemy territory; and its naval forces are structured to project power ashore from carriers (of marginal value in Central Europe) and to keep Atlantic sea lanes open to sustain a logistical pipeline between the United States and Western Europe.

On the other hand, Soviet forces, which are the model for Eastern European forces, are geared for highly mobile offensive operations aimed at achieving a quick victory. Soviet military strategy, should a major war break out, is to overrun Western Europe before NATO can mobilize and bring to bear its superior manpower and economic resources. This strategy is manifested both in Soviet military doctrine and by the structure of Soviet forces. About three-fourths of Soviet divisional manpower is assigned to combat functions and only one-fourth to support functions. The ratio of tanks (inherently offensive weapons) to men in a Soviet armored division is twice that of a U.S. armored division. Soviet tactical air doctrine emphasizes air defense and close support of ground troops; thus, Soviet aircraft sacrifice range, cost less, and can be procured in greater numbers. In short, Soviet forces are optimized to achieve victory in probably thirty and certainly no more than sixty days. Consequently, their capacity to sustain a longer war would be seriously hampered by distinctly inferior logistic and support capabilities.

This difference between Soviet and NATO forces raises a number of important questions about the role, structure, and size of U.S. forces.

For one, are the U.S. forces committed to the defense of Western Europe effectively organized for that role? It is evident that without these forces a successful conventional NATO defense would not now be conceivable. As indicated in Table 10-3, U.S. forces in the central region account for approximately one-fourth of NATO ground combat troops and tanks and one-third of NATO tactical air power. Furthermore, active ground forces in the United States are the most important single source of reinforcements available to NATO in the relatively early stages of a war. But do the U.S. military resources now deployed in Western Europe provide maximum defensive capability in the period that matters most—the first thirty to sixty days of conflict—or are they too oriented to a long war to function successfully in a shorter conflict? Similarly, could forces in the United States earmarked for NATO actually be deployed in Europe during this early critical period?

Second, how valid is the rationale for the remainder of U.S. general purpose forces—the ground forces that could not be deployed in Europe until long after conflict had been initiated, the naval forces maintained to keep Atlantic sea lanes open indefinitely, and tactical air forces designed for deep penetration missions? Such forces would have little bearing on the outcome of a relatively short, conventional war in Europe. They must be viewed either as required to fight a major war in Asia or (and this is more likely) as providing a hedge against the possibility that a war in Europe would be contained at conventional levels in its initial phase, and continue for an indefinite period thereafter, with neither side being forced to negotiate or use nuclear weapons.

The Military Balance in the Middle East

The United States has maintained a military presence in the Middle East for more than a quarter of a century, but the relative importance of the various interests underlying that presence has shifted perceptibly during that period.

First are the interests that stem from NATO. In 1948 the United States deployed forces in the Mediterranean to counter Soviet military pressure against Greece, Turkey, and Iran. When NATO was formed, these forces, together with those of allies in the area, took responsibility for the protection of NATO's southern flank and for initiating diversionary military action from the Mediterranean should war break out in Central Europe.

Second, these forces serve as a counterpoise to Soviet forces in the Mediterranean. They are meant to reassure and protect countries friendly though not formally allied to the United States, deter resort to force by others, and contribute to stability in the region, uneasy though it is. More recently, the possible importance of U.S. naval forces in the area as a means of assuring access to oil has received increasing attention.

Third, the United States has maintained military facilities in the area to strengthen its strategic position relative to that of the USSR. These include a submarine base in Spain, radar sites in Turkey, and communication facilities elsewhere. All have greatly diminished in military significance because of advances in technology; this trend continues.

Whatever the situation in the past, the U.S.–Soviet military balance in the area is now determined principally by the naval forces deployed by the two powers in the Mediterranean.[9]

9. This discussion of U.S. and Soviet naval forces is based on a Brookings defense analysis staff study on the role of the Sixth Fleet in the Mediterranean being made by Arnold M. Kuzmack and Leslie H. Gelb.

The U.S. Sixth Fleet, which has been stationed in the Mediterranean for twenty-five years, consists of about forty ships. Its striking power is provided by two carrier task groups, one of which has its home port in Greece. At a time of crisis these naval forces could be quickly strengthened by U.S. naval vessels from the Atlantic and by tactical air units drawn from Western Europe.

Continuous deployment of substantial Soviet naval forces in the Mediterranean began in 1965. These forces now consist of approximately fifty vessels, about half of which are warships; of the latter, submarines and cruise-missile-carrying surface ships predominate. In a war, providing reinforcements could be difficult for the USSR, since NATO would probably control both entrances to the Mediterranean. On the other hand, Soviet land-based aircraft could pose a considerable threat to NATO vessels in the eastern Mediterranean.

Apart from comparative size, there is an important structural difference between the opposing fleets in the Mediterranean. Sea-based aircraft and Marine detachments carried on naval vessels give U.S. naval forces a significant capability to project power ashore. Soviet naval forces, on the other hand, are designed to counter other warships. They might aim at deterring U.S. intervention in the Mediterranean region, but their own interventionary capabilities are very limited.

How will future developments affect this balance in the Middle East and its requirements for U.S. forces? Although American naval forces in the Mediterranean have been directed principally toward NATO contingencies, the necessity for keeping American ships there may not automatically diminish with a further easing of tension in Europe. Continuing instability in the Middle East and the associated danger of U.S.–Soviet confrontation will remain an important independent reason for keeping U.S. forces in the area, unless regional military disengagement agreements can be negotiated with the USSR or among the countries of the region.

Nevertheless, a continuing show of American arms in the Middle East does not necessarily pose an incremental requirement for total U.S. force levels. Under now foreseeable circumstances the naval forces maintained by the United States for the contingency of a war in Europe are more than enough to serve simultaneously as a peacetime naval presence in the Mediterranean.

The Military Balance in Asia*

The decision by the United States to go to war over the North Korean attack on South Korea inaugurated the Asian version of forward defense. As in Europe, the policy resulting from the Korean experience aimed at deterring war by (1) organizing treaty alliances committing the United States to military intervention in the event of aggression against allies, and (2) stationing substantial U.S. forces in the region to guarantee such commitments. However, U.S. political commitments in Asia were more ambiguous than arrangements in Europe, and peacetime U.S. forces in the region were not part of a closely integrated, multinational, and reasonably balanced military defense organization.

A U.S. containment policy in this form remained virtually undisturbed for twenty years, although striking changes occurred in the balance of forces on which it was based. Three developments were paramount: (1) the turnabout in the Sino-Soviet connection from an alliance to an adversary relationship; (2) the resurgence of Japan from economic dependency to world economic power and, potentially, to world military power; and (3) the growing economic and political strength of many of the smaller nations of East Asia, accompanied by a stronger sense of national identity and growing interest and progress in regional cooperation. Over and above these regional developments, the Vietnam war raised grave doubts in the United States about its ability to influence events in Asia by military means and about the wisdom of such involvement. These developments eventually led to a reassessment of the U.S. security relationship to the region. The outcome of this reassessment, as far as the administration is concerned, is expressed in the somewhat ambiguous terminology of the Nixon doctrine, which points to a cautious withdrawal of U.S. troops and increased future reliance on local forces in the area (at the least, on local ground combat forces). Alternatively, it can be argued that a more drastic reassessment is in order—specifically, that in defining U.S. security interests sharp distinctions should be drawn between the different parts of East Asia.

* The analysis of developments in East Asia in this section closely follows that appearing in Ralph N. Clough, "East Asia," in Henry Owen (ed.), *The Next Phase in Foreign Policy* (Brookings Institution, 1973). Material on the military balance in Korea is based on an assessment by William D. White of the Brookings defense analysis staff.

In Northeast Asia, U.S. security interests are closely linked to relations with Japan. If the relation prospers, it can be the basis of constructive U.S.-Japanese collaboration throughout the region, which could lead to reduced U.S. force levels and military expenditures. If the relationship goes badly astray, it could lead to an across-the-board buildup in Japanese military power that could once again make Japan a source of international instability in Asia and, in this sense at least, eventually increase U.S. force requirements.

Economic perhaps more than military considerations will affect the future course of U.S.-Japanese relations. Indeed, the manner in which the United States and Japan work out the economic issues that have recently plagued their relationship may be the most important determinant of whether relations between them proceed in an atmosphere of suspicion or of trust. So far as military factors are concerned, Japanese confidence in continuing to maintain a low military profile will depend not only on the U.S. nuclear guarantee, on the continuing U.S. conventional military presence in the area, and on the way U.S.-Japanese security relations are managed, but also on the maintenance of military equilibrium in Korea.

At present, the array of military forces in Korea points to continued stalemate. Without external help neither North Korea nor South Korea has the military resources or the productive capacity to be assured of a quick victory after launching an invasion, or to be able to fight a conventional war lasting more than a few months. During recent years, furthermore, neither the Soviet Union nor China has shown any inclination to encourage North Korean adventures; instead, both seem to have exerted a restraining influence. Similarly, U.S. military assistance to South Korea has concentrated on improving defensive rather than offensive capabilities.

A comparison of the military forces of North and South Korea is shown in Table 10-4. The main features of the present military balance are as follows:

• South Korean ground forces are probably superior to those of North Korea—at least numerically, and possibly in training as well. North Korean ground forces, however, may have greater firepower and, in the initial stages of a conflict, greater mobility.

• In the air, North Korea has a decided numerical advantage, but this may be misleading. Most of the aircraft on both sides are obsolescent. If only modern aircraft are counted, each side has about

Table 10-4. Comparison of the Current Military Forces of North and South Korea

Force	South Korea	North Korea
Divisions	21	23
Ground force manpower	590,000	360,000
Tanks	750	1,100
Trained military reserves	1,500,000	1,000,000
Fighter aircraft	220	510
(Modern aircraft only)[a]	(100)	(100)
Light bombers	...	70[b]
Other military aircraft	140	160

Sources: Dupuy and Blanchard, *Almanac of World Military Power*, and International Institute for Strategic Studies, *The Military Balance, 1972–1973*.
a. Over half the South Korean force and more than two-thirds of the North Korean force are composed of obsolescent aircraft of Korean war vintage.
b. Obsolete types with very limited offensive potential.

one hundred fighters, hardly enough to be decisive in offensive action.

• Naval forces on both sides are too small to play a significant role in conventional war.

In any new conflict, which now seems remote, the greatest danger probably would lie in a unilateral attack by North Korea aimed at the quick capture of Seoul and drawing in the USSR or China to provide support after the fact. The South Korean capital is only thirty miles from the border, and North Korean forces are probably trained to launch a surprise invasion. However, the approaches to Seoul have been heavily fortified and the opposing forces are such that any North Korean attack would have to be viewed as a desperate gamble.

What, then, is the role of the United States? It has been helping reequip South Korean forces through a five-year military assistance program costing about $1.5 billion and scheduled to be completed by 1975. Far more important, U.S. forces in Korea assure immediate U.S. involvement in the event of attack and thus have a deterrent value, not only against North Korean actions but against Soviet or Chinese supporting actions as well. They also give the South Koreans confidence in their security and thereby contribute to stabilizing the military situation by reducing the chances of South Korean preemptive action. To achieve these objectives the United States has approximately 43,000 men in Korea, including one infantry division and one tactical fighter wing. The disposition of U.S. ground forces—north of Seoul—almost guarantees American involvement in the event of an invasion. In addition, American airpower could be supplied relatively quickly from carriers of the Seventh Fleet and from squadrons based on Okinawa. Finally, the United States deploys tactical nuclear weapons in Korea for possible use should all else fail.

Taiwan also has a security treaty with the United States and, like Korea, poses issues affecting Japan, although on a lesser scale. Japan continues to have extensive links with Taiwan, but its concern about the future of Taiwan has recently diminished as a result of the renewal of its own and of U.S. relations with China. Nevertheless, a U.S. failure to respond to a Chinese attack on Taiwan would shock Japan and might erode Japan's confidence in its security arrangements with the United States. This contingency, however, appears remote. Apart from the protection afforded Taiwan by its insular position, China's present objective, stemming from its fears about the USSR, is to avoid a confrontation with the United States. China is likely, therefore, to continue to show restraint toward Taiwan and look toward a long-term resolution of the issue as an essential requirement for building new political and economic relations with the United States.

In Southeast Asia, a very different situation exists. The United States has no interests in the area comparable to its interests in Japan. Furthermore, unlike the situation in Korea and possibly in Taiwan, Japan's security relationship with the United States would not be seriously threatened by new conflicts in Southeast Asia, short of an attack by a nuclear power, since the Japanese do not believe they have vital interests in the region and do not regard U.S. action there as a touchstone of U.S. willingness to defend Japan.

Neither China nor the USSR is likely to launch an invasion against countries in Southeast Asia. The interest of both countries in broadening relations with the United States, as well as with Japan, constitutes a political constraint, and neither is in a favorable logistic position for such adventures. Moreover, the Soviet Union is a long distance away, and the Chinese do not appear to envisage direct military conquest as a main element of national policy. Both countries, as well as North Vietnam, could back internal rebellion in Southeast Asia, but the rivalry of the three for influence in the area would preclude a concert of their efforts and might diminish the effectiveness of each.

The greatest uncertainty surrounds the military and political outcome in Indochina in the aftermath of the U.S. withdrawal. Elsewhere, however, there is no local balance of opposing military forces that can appropriately be drawn. Threats to governments are most likely to arise from internal unrest and strife, and the outcome will depend principally on internal forces rather than on the extent or character of external military assistance.

Alternative General Purpose Forces

In light of the foregoing assessments it is evident that requirements for general purpose forces could vary widely to accord with differing views of U.S. interests abroad, differing assessments of the forces necessary to protect those interests, and even differences over whether a conventional, as opposed to a nuclear, defense is either militarily necessary or financially practical. To illustrate how widely force postures can vary, existing general purpose forces are compared with three alternative postures based on such differing assessments.

In considering the budgets corresponding to these alternative force postures, it is worth emphasizing that costs depend primarily on total force levels, not on the location of forces. Pay and allowances are much the same wherever troops are stationed, as are many other military operating expenses. Moving and housing men and their families overseas involve extra expenses, but these are at least partly offset by the fact that wages paid to foreign civilian employees at military bases abroad are lower than pay scales for civilian employees at military installations in the United States. Bringing troops home, therefore, saves a significant amount of money for the taxpayer only when the troops are deactivated or when their return makes a reduction in total forces possible in some other way.

The composition and projected cost of the alternative force postures discussed below are summarized in Table 10-5.

Alternative 1 is a projection of the administration's program. This posture defines the deterrence of war as requiring sufficient forces to conduct a forward defense of Western Europe with NATO allies or to be used in defense against a Chinese or Soviet attack in Asia; to assist Asian allies in conflicts not involving the USSR and China, principally by providing military equipment and naval and air support rather than by intervening with U.S. ground forces; and to maintain the confidence of allies in the determination of the United States to uphold its security commitments.

Under this strategy, most ground forces are oriented toward Euro-

Table 10-5. The Cost of Alternative General Purpose Forces, Fiscal Years 1974, 1977, and 1980

Total obligational authority in billions of 1974 dollars

Alternative	1974	1977	1980	Annual average, 1974–80
1. The present posture[a]	54.6	56.7	57.5	56.2
2. A lower profile in Asia[b]	53.1	52.0	53.0	52.0
3. A lower profile in Asia and a lower-cost force for Europe[c]	51.0	44.1	45.2	45.7
4. Minimum general purpose forces[d]	48.0	25.0	20.0	30.0

Source: Derived by authors using cost estimates in Chapter 9.

a. Projection of the cost of carrying out present ground combat, naval, and tactical air programs. See Chapter 9, pp. 314–28, for details.

b. Reduction in U.S. force levels of five Air Force tactical fighter wings, one Marine division/wing, one Army division, and six aircraft carriers with associated aircraft and escort ships. In addition, this program terminates the DD-963 and patrol frigate shipbuilding programs.

c. In addition to all the measures listed in note b, this alternative calls for the deactivation of the equivalent of three active Army divisions; cancellation of the F-14 and F-15 aircraft programs, but increased purchases of the A-10 close support aircraft; cancellation of the S-3A aircraft, the sea control ship, and a reduction in the nuclear attack submarine program; reductions in the Navy reserve of 70,000 men; reorganization of ground force reserves so as to maintain three Army reserve brigades (in hybrid divisions), three National Guard armored-mechanized divisions, plus 200,000 other National Guardsmen.

d. General purpose forces maintained under this program consist principally of six carrier task forces, the equivalent of six active divisions, twenty-five Air Force tactical squadrons, and about 200,000 National Guard reservists.

pean contingencies, but U.S. naval general purpose forces and tactical air forces are divided about equally between the two theaters. If enough time were available, however, forces oriented toward one theater could be moved to the other in the event of an emergency.

Present military planning calls for general purpose forces to be sufficient to deal principally with the initial phases of a protracted war; that is, to contain an attack until reserves can be mobilized and newly recruited forces can be trained and deployed. For example, the stockpile of ammunition and spare equipment that the United States maintains in Western Europe is sufficient for approximately ninety days of continuous fighting; stocks maintained by NATO countries would run out long before then. On the other hand, the size, mission orientation, and readiness of existing U.S. forces, as well as those to be mobilized, have been determined on the planning assumption that a conventional war in Europe would be relatively long. In general, present forces are probably adequate in size for a short war in Europe and in addition represent a large investment in capabilities for protracted conflict.

Under the administration's program, the annual cost of general purpose forces, as described in Chapter 9, is estimated to rise moderately, in real terms, over the balance of this decade, averaging $56.2 billion a year.

Alternative 2 would call for a lower military profile in Asia. This alternative rests on the assumption that the overriding U.S. security interest is to maintain a relationship of confidence with Japan and that the United States has no vital security interest elsewhere in Asia. This view, together with rising nationalist antagonism in the region, argues for maintenance of an effective military presence in Northeast Asia, disengagement from the defense of Southeast Asia, a general reduction in the U.S. military presence, and greater reliance on non-military options to exercise U.S. influence in the region. Specifically, this alternative calls for the following actions:

• Return and deactivation of U.S. forces in Thailand—about 50,000 men and four tactical fighter wings.

• Ceding of Clark Air Field and the Subic Bay naval base to the Philippine government within, say, three years, and the return and deactivation of U.S. forces now in the Philippines—17,000 men and one tactical fighter wing.

• Return and deactivation of the elements of the Marine division in Okinawa and Japan, thereby limiting the U.S. military presence in Okinawa to one air base and one tactical fighter wing as a backup for Korea.

• Return and deactivation of approximately 8,000 military personnel stationed in Taiwan to support the U.S. military effort in Indochina.

• Reduction of U.S. naval forces stationed in the Pacific from three to two carrier task groups, one of which would continue to make its home port in Japan. These naval forces would represent the principal evidence of the U.S. military commitment to the defense of Japan. All U.S. military facilities in Japan except the Yokosuka naval base would be turned over to the Japanese.

• Maintenance of one tactical fighter wing in Korea, for political reasons as well as deterrence. However, the U.S. Army division now deployed there would be returned to the United States and deactivated.

The effect of these actions on force levels and procurement programs might be summarized as follows:

• For ground forces, a reduction of two divisions, one in 1974 and one in 1975, and their supporting units. Savings are estimated to average $1.4 billion a year for the rest of the decade.

• For naval general purpose forces, a reduction in carrier force levels from fifteen to twelve in fiscal 1974 and to nine in fiscal 1975— the number consistent with reduced requirements in Asia under this alternative. Nine carriers would also be sufficient for NATO contingencies on the reasoning, outlined in Chapter 9, that greater reliance could be placed on land-based than on sea-based aircraft, both to protect shipping in the Atlantic and to provide air support in Central Europe. As a consequence, the CVN-70 would be the last nuclear carrier authorized in this decade. In addition, escort ship requirements would be lower, which would suggest termination of the Spruance class destroyer (DD-963) and patrol frigate (PF) programs. Estimated annual savings would average $1.7 billion.

• For tactical air forces, a reduction of eleven fighter wings (from thirty-eight to twenty-seven) by the end of fiscal 1975, leading to savings in operating and investment costs averaging $1.1 billion a year.

Under alternative 2, the annual cost of general purpose forces would average $52.0 billion for the rest of this decade, or $4.2 billion less than the present program. Savings would be relatively small in the first year. They would peak at $5.3 billion in fiscal 1976 and level off at $4.6 billion in subsequent years.

What risks might be involved? First, there might be concern in Japan about the adequacy of the U.S. security guarantee, although there would be some political advantage in the virtual removal of U.S. military bases in Japan, which have been a constant irritant in U.S.– Japanese relations. The Japanese probably would not be alarmed by the reduction in U.S. carrier strength in the Pacific, which they might see as a natural result of U.S. disengagement from Southeast Asia. Withdrawal of the U.S. division from Korea would pose a more serious problem since some Japanese view its presence as a symbol of the U.S. commitment to the defense of Northeast Asia. Second, worry might arise in South Korea that could be a source of instability. Third, heightened uncertainty in Southeast Asia would lead to a reappraisal by each country of its future orientation toward the major powers in the region.

Alternative 3 is a lower-cost general purpose force for conventional defense of Western Europe, together with a lower military profile in

Asia. This alternative retains strong U.S. participation in a NATO forward defense strategy but gears U.S. general purpose forces for a short, intense conflict in Europe rather than for a replay of World War II. That change in planning assumptions would call for three major modifications in general purpose forces: restructuring forces deployed in Western Europe so as to maximize the firepower they could bring to bear immediately; making sure that U.S.-based forces earmarked for Europe could be deployed to Europe quickly—within the first thirty days of mobilization; and reducing forces whose missions and capabilities are relevant principally to a protracted war.

The first requirement amounts to getting more quick combat power out of forces stationed in Europe and making sure they are located in the right places. One way of doing this would be to reorganize the four and one-third divisions now in Europe into six divisions, each of which would have two brigades in Europe and one brigade in the United States. Each of these six divisions would maintain in Europe the equipment needed for a full division; hence the brigade stationed in the United States could be flown to Europe and deployed there within seven days.[10] This reorganization would lend itself to rotating brigades in the United States with brigades of the parent division in Europe. Personnel in these brigades would have relatively short tours of duty in Europe, thereby making possible a reduction in the number of U.S. dependents living abroad.[11] This force posture could probably be sustained by approximately 250,000 U.S. troops in Europe—50,000 fewer than are currently stationed there. Reductions would be made possible by the diminished need for support troops and by the elimination of functions that are now marginal.

Additional though relatively modest investments might be required to carry out other measures aimed at increasing the combat effectiveness of U.S. forces in Europe. For example, some ground units should be relocated in areas that are both the most likely avenues of attack and opposite major concentrations of Soviet forces. Present lines of communication, which are too exposed, should be tied into a multinational logistic command, making it possible for U.S. forces to rely

10. All the necessary equipment is there now, for the United States has pre-positioned equipment for two and two-thirds divisions in depots in Western Europe. Under present arrangements, however, this equipment is excessively vulnerable and inadequately maintained.

11. Brigades in the United States would be attached to and supported by Army base commands. Literally, rotation would take place between battalions rather than brigades.

more heavily on the logistic systems of European NATO countries and encouraging greater use of joint basing arrangements. Eventually this would result in budgetary savings for the United States and greater efficiency for European NATO countries in their use of military resources.

Two Army divisions and one Marine division earmarked for Europe would continue to be located in the United States. To make sure they could be deployed to the Continent within the first thirty days of mobilization, equipment for one additional division would be pre-positioned in Western Europe. Under this plan, only the equipment for one Marine division would have to be transported by sea during the first thirty days of mobilization.

Planning for a short war in Europe points to other major changes in general purpose forces. For example, some of the active and reserve ground forces expected to reach Europe in the later phases of a conflict would become unnecessary and could therefore be deactivated. Tactical air forces, which are more easily redeployed, might be maintained at present levels, except for the reduction in Asian deployments specified in alternative 2. However, since the sole purpose of tactical air forces would be to support combat troops, procurement would shift from long-range multipurpose planes to low-cost planes designed for that purpose. In the case of naval general purpose forces, much less emphasis would be placed on forces whose primary mission is to keep Atlantic sea lanes open during a protracted war.

The effects of these changes on force levels and procurement programs, *over and above those noted for alternative 2*, would be as follows:

• For ground forces, a further reduction, from fourteen to twelve divisions, would be feasible (there are sixteen divisions in the present force). Nine divisions would be deployable in Europe within the first few weeks of a conflict and three would constitute a strategic reserve. Each of the latter three divisions could consist of two active brigades and one reserve brigade, which would save the equivalent of one additional division in active manpower. Ground combat reserve components would be substantially reduced in size and reorganized. They would consist of three armored or mechanized National Guard divisions, three reserve brigades integrated with active divisions, and about 200,000 other National Guardsmen (two battalions plus headquarters in each state for use in domestic emergencies and to provide a mobilization base). In all, savings in this decade, beyond those envisaged in alternative 2, would average $3.4 billion a year but would be about $5 billion a year from fiscal 1977 through fiscal 1980.

• For tactical air forces, the change in mission orientation would indicate termination of the F-14 and F-15 fighter programs, increased procurement of an all-weather version of the A-10, and a more serious effort to develop the lightweight fighter. Savings for the balance of the decade, beyond those envisaged in alternative 2, would average $1.5 billion a year, but would be larger in the 1980s, as aircraft that cost less to build and operate replaced present aircraft on an increasing scale.

• For naval general purpose forces, the diminished requirement for protection of shipping in the Atlantic would point to maintaining forces principally as a peacetime presence in Northeast Asia and the Middle East and as a moderate hedge against a longer war. This would suggest terminating the S-3A program to modernize carrier-based ASW aircraft and the sea control ship, and reducing construction of nuclear-powered attack submarines to perhaps two a year. Annual savings from these steps, beyond those projected for alternative 2, would average $1.4 billion, mostly from the reduced procurement program.

Implementation of these measures, together with those discussed under alternative 2, would lead to an average annual cost for general purpose forces, through the 1970s, of $45.7 billion. This amount would represent a saving of $10.5 billion a year, on average, as compared to our projection of the cost of the present general purpose force posture. Savings would be less than $4.0 billion in fiscal 1974 but would rise to a peak of $12.7 billion in fiscal 1978. They could be expected to remain near this level into the next decade.

Apart from any problems that might arise as a result of cutting forces for Asian contingencies, the main risk incurred under this alternative is that a war in Europe, contrary to expectations, could turn out to be protracted. In that event, U.S. forces would be poorly prepared, which is already the case with both America's allies and its potential adversaries on the Continent. Neither the ammunition stockpiles nor the tactical doctrine of European NATO countries permit or envisage a major conventional defense of much more than thirty days. And the severe logistical and organizational constraints plaguing Soviet and Eastern European forces compel a decisive resolution of hostilities long before substantial U.S. reinforcements are scheduled to arrive in Europe. Indeed, it appears that of all the various national military contingents deployed along both sides of the central front only the forces of the United States are deliberately geared for a prolonged conflict, and this at the expense of sufficient preparation for the more likely contingency of a short war.

Politically, U.S. efforts to reorient its forces to a short war in Europe and continued maintenance of large forces there would at least partly offset the concern European NATO countries might have about the reduction in total U.S. force levels. Political benefits could also occur since this reorganization would be interpreted in Europe as reducing the prospect of unilateral U.S. troop withdrawals from Europe and since it could help NATO to maintain its cohesion while negotiating about mutual force reductions with the USSR.

Alternative 4 places predominant reliance on nuclear deterrence and therefore maintains only minimum general purpose forces. A proponent of this alternative would draw a sharp nuclear line across Europe and argue that this alone would be sufficient to deter the full range of possible Soviet military pressures. It is commonly associated with, but not dependent on, a belief that a successful conventional defense of Europe is militarily impossible, financially impractical, or both.

Alternative 4 calls for sweeping reductions in U.S. general purpose forces and deployments. All forces in Europe would be withdrawn except for one division and enough tactical air squadrons to exercise a tactical nuclear capability and to serve as hostages guaranteeing the involvement of the United States (and implicitly, threatening the use of U.S. strategic nuclear weapons) should war break out.

Beyond that, perhaps six carriers might be maintained to demonstrate that the United States has continuing interests in Northeast Asia and the Middle East, and a small number of ground units and tactical air squadrons might be retained in the United States for coastal and air surveillance. Any attempt to add forces and a mobilization base as a hedge against a conventional war, it could be argued, would create doubts about the willingness of the United States to launch an immediate nuclear response to aggression and would thereby prejudice the strategy.

The estimated cost of general purpose forces under this alternative, once the forces had been phased down, might be roughly one-third their present cost, or perhaps $20 billion a year.

The military risks in this alternative are that the strategy would lack credibility to adversaries and allies alike and that even in the event of accidental war it would leave the United States with a nuclear option only. Politically it could lead to the disintegration of the NATO alliance and the emergence of a German nuclear force that would not only revive traditional antagonisms in Western Europe but also destroy the prospects for East-West détente.

Manpower Policies*

The discussion in Chapter 8 emphasized that the cost of defense manpower has been rising because of changes in its *use* (more manpower per force unit) as well as because of changes in its *price* (higher pay scales, pay grades, and benefits for retirees). This section examines five areas in which policy changes could result in reduced manpower costs. The first two suggest changes in support services and in the use of reserve components that could achieve savings fairly soon; the next two examine changes that could produce substantial savings over the longer term; and the fifth—a brief status report on the all-volunteer service—highlights the relationship between the number of active duty military personnel, their qualifications, and the cost of recruitment.

Can Support Expenditures Be Reduced?

Manpower has been used more intensively in recent years because support forces have risen in relation to combat forces. Analysis of what is a desirable support–combat ratio of forces is plagued by the problem of how to define each of these functions. For present purposes combat capability is assumed to be measured by an Army combat soldier, an Air Force flying hour, and a Navy ship steaming hour. Strictly speaking, these are not measures of military output, but they are the major elements of the demand for support. The cost of supporting combat capability has direct and indirect components.

Direct support consists of activities performed within a major combat command. Thus it includes support personnel in combat units (for example, clerks and drivers) and complete support units assigned

* Prepared with the assistance of Martin Binkin.

to a combat organization (for example, an engineering battalion in an Army division). *Indirect support* includes centralized or servicewide activities that are not identifiable with a single mission (for example, logistics, training, personnel, headquarters, communications, and intelligence).

Use of these definitions shows that support costs per unit of combat capability have increased since 1964 (see Table 10-6). Direct and indirect support costs, however, show strikingly different trends. In the

Table 10-6. Support Costs per Unit, Army Combat Soldier, Navy Steaming Hour, and Air Force Flying Hour, Fiscal Year 1974, and Change, Fiscal Years 1964–74

Unit	Support cost per unit, 1974 (thousands of dollars)	Percentage change (in constant dollars) 1964–74	1970–74
Army combat soldier			
Direct support	6.3	+4	−5
Indirect support			
Communications and intelligence	1.5	−3	−6
Central logistics	3.5	...	−20
Training and rotation	7.4	+47	−4
Medical services	2.2	+90	+76
Central headquarters	1.0	−2	+21
Total indirect	15.6	+28	−1
Navy ship steaming hour			
Direct support	1.3	+34	+16
Indirect support			
Communications and intelligence	0.4	+70	+11
Central logistics	1.4	+63	+3
Training and rotation	1.5	+60	+21
Medical services	0.4	+150	+67
Central headquarters	0.2	...	−5
Total indirect	3.9	+63	+14
Air Force flying hour			
Direct support	1.3	+11	+10
Indirect support			
Communications and intelligence	0.4	+58	+15
Central logistics	0.7	+50	+23
Training and rotation	0.7	+38	+48
Medical services	0.2	+163	+75
Central headquarters	0.1	+33	+33
Total indirect	2.1	+53	+33

Sources: Authors' estimates, based on *The Budget of the United States Government—Appendix*, various years; and for activity measures, *Department of Defense Appropriations*, Hearings before the Senate and House Committees on Appropriations, various years. Support costs include operations and maintenance costs and military personnel costs. Direct support costs are assumed to be in the same proportion to total direct operating costs as direct support military manpower is to total direct military manpower.

fiscal years 1964–74 direct support costs increased significantly for the Air Force and for the Navy; for the Army, however, they are now close to pre-Vietnam levels (after growing during the war). Indirect support costs for all three services, on the other hand, are much higher than they were in 1964, and for the Navy and Air Force higher than they were as recently as 1970.

This increase in support costs is attributed by the Defense Department to three improvements in military capabilities:[12]

• *Improved readiness.* Increased training and rotation of personnel is designed to ensure that the right people will be in the right place at the right time. Moreover, the trend toward more sophisticated weapons throughout the combat forces requires more elaborate maintenance.

• *Increased mobility.* New equipment for this purpose—for example, more helicopters and mechanized equipment for ground forces—requires a larger number of maintenance personnel and facilities.

• *Sustainability.* U.S. forces can stay in combat for a sustained period principally because substantial support forces are an integral part of combat organizations.

In addition, some growth in support spending can be related to making military life more attractive as a means of developing an all-volunteer service. This is one reason why housing and other facilities have been improved and why more attention is paid to career development and the diversification of assignments.

Notwithstanding these explanations for the increase in support costs, the fact remains that criteria for judging the most appropriate ratio of support to combat forces lack precision, more so than for other force planning issues. Moreover, variations imply substantial differences in costs. For example, the average length of specialized training courses is steadily increasing, but there are no clear answers to questions of how much training is in fact necessary and what form it should take. Specialized training courses now average twelve weeks; a one-week reduction would save $100 million a year. How long tours of duty should be is another issue. Although the average tour of duty has recently been getting longer, reassignment still occurs more frequently than it did in 1964. Increasing the average tour of duty by one month would save $200 million a year in administrative and

12. For example, see the discussion in U.S. Department of Defense, *Military Manpower Requirements Report for FY 1974*, Chap. 14.

transportation costs. Medical services are a third area where the relation between support costs and military preparedness can be somewhat obscure. The rise in the cost of these services has been very rapid in the past few years, with a sizable portion of the increase attributable to providing benefits to the growing number of retired personnel.[13] Finally, the influence on support costs of considerations other than military ones is evident from the political furor that arises whenever closings of excess military bases are announced.

All of this suggests that if the large bureaucratic and political obstacles could be overcome the trend toward increased support costs could be revised moderately without noticeable damage to U.S. military capabilities or foreign policy. Substantial savings could be achieved. For example, if present combat units were supported at their fiscal 1970 levels, support costs could be reduced by about $2 billion a year. The administration's decision to close military bases is a major step in this direction, and the estimate of savings offered here is in addition to an allowance of $700 million assumed to result from that decision. If all forces were supported at the 1964 level—a less realistic alternative—savings could easily double.

To illustrate what might be involved, outlined below is a list of measures that could eventually save $2 billion a year (other measures are of course possible, or the relative emphasis could be changed):[14]

Policy decision	Estimated savings (millions of FY 1974 dollars)
Close additional bases	300
Shorten specialized training courses by two weeks (average)	200
Increase reliance on on-the-job, rather than formal, training by 10 percent	100

13. Medical costs in fiscal 1974 will amount to $285 per capita (including active and retired military personnel and their dependents). This does not include the cost of medical units that are an integral part of combat organizations. Since fiscal 1970, the total cost of medical services (not including combat medical units) has grown from $2.0 billion to $2.4 billion in 1974 dollars, or by 20 percent. None of the increase can be attributed to Vietnam, since medical costs associated with the war declined after 1970. About two-thirds of this increase can be attributed to the growth in services provided to military personnel and their dependents in civilian facilities, which apparently occurred without offsetting reductions in the cost of military medical facilities.

14. The additional bases closed would be those necessary to bring the savings associated with base closings up to $1 billion—the amount former Deputy Secretary of Defense David Packard estimated could be saved in this area.

Increase average tour length by two months	400
Provide medical support at 1972 level	300
Overhaul and maintain weapon systems at 1970 standards	350
Provide headquarters and administrative support at 1970 level	150
Provide intelligence and communications support at 1970 level	200
Total	2,000

Most of the savings would be in manpower. It is estimated that a program on this scale would reduce Department of Defense personnel by 150,000, of whom one half would be civilians. Military reductions would be concentrated in the areas of training, communications and intelligence, medical services, and personnel administration. Reductions in employment of civilians by the Defense Department would be concentrated in the areas of logistics, headquarters, and base operations.

Economies in the Cost of Reserve Forces

The administration has steadily increased expenditures on reserve components as a way of building a supplementary source of military readiness at relatively low cost. In absolute terms, however, the cost of the program is sizable. For fiscal 1974, $4.4 billion is requested for reserve forces, 30 percent more, in constant dollars, than the 1968 level. Making a fairly modest allowance for the cost of equipment transferred to reserve forces and of support provided by active units could bring the total cost to more than $5 billion.

Critics argue that reserve forces are not worth this investment because (1) past experience indicates that political constraints would prevent their being mobilized in an emergency; and (2) even if they were mobilized, reserve forces would not be available in time to affect the outcome of a short war. For these reasons, in outlining general purpose force requirements under the strategy alternative predicated on a short European war, sharp reductions in reserve forces were assumed.

On the other hand, it can also be argued that improvements in reserve capabilities might make it possible to achieve economies by limited substitution of reserve for active forces. Examples include the formation of hybrid ground force divisions containing, for example, elements of two active brigades and one reserve brigade, the transfer of active air squadrons to reserve units, and the use of naval reserves to replace active forces in manning aircraft carriers and other naval vessels when they are being overhauled.

Apart from these major force planning issues, the size and cost of reserve forces can be questioned strictly on grounds of efficiency. Questions of this kind are discussed below.

MARGINAL FUNCTIONS. As a heritage of World War II, the United States continues to maintain reserve units organized to perform such functions as military censorship, postal service management, systems analysis, military government, and intelligence. The contribution of these operations to military preparedness is small.

Similarly, the merit of maintaining a large number of individual reservists is questionable. Some are kept in reserve status even though their skills would be readily available from the civilian manpower force after mobilization began. Others may no longer be needed because of organizational changes in the active forces. For example, the Navy has 100,000 individual reservists who would not be mobilized in reserve units. At one time, when naval vessels were not fully manned, these reservists were viewed as a quick source for meeting wartime requirements. Since 1970, however, most naval vessels are more fully manned, which makes the justification for individual naval reservists less clear. The other services also maintain individual reservists, but to a much smaller extent than the Navy.

Altogether, pay and allowances for these reserve force functions amount to $200 million a year, of which a large proportion appears to be devoted to activities that have now become marginal.

STREAMLINING MANAGEMENT. Proposals frequently have been made to merge the National Guard and the reserves, which, in the case of the Army and Air Force, are separately organized and administered (naval reserves are under one roof). Present duplication of command leads to wasteful management and excessive overhead, but proposals for merging invariably founder on political factors. State governments are opposed to relinquishing control over the National Guard, and the Army and Air Force are reluctant to give up control over the reserves.

Nevertheless, the obvious merits of action along these lines call for another try. One compromise would be to transfer Army reserves to the National Guard and transfer all National Guard air units to the

Air Force reserves. Even under this relatively modest proposal, the reduction of administrative duplication and the consolidation of training and recruitment facilities would save perhaps $100 million a year.

ARE ADDITIONAL RESERVE BONUSES NECESSARY? The end of the draft is causing a reduction in the rate of enlistment in the reserves. To maintain total strength and assure necessary skills, the administration is requesting $85 million in the 1974 budget to provide bonuses to attract and retain reservists. The cost of this program could soon reach $100 million a year.

Bonuses may eventually be necessary, but are they needed now? For example, a reduction in total reserve strength by eliminating marginal functions might make it possible to meet recruitment needs without additional pay incentives. Similarly, reducing the number of individual reservists would cut back formal requirements for some of the skills that under present concepts and listings are classified as scarce. More women might be used in the reserves, or qualification standards might be relaxed. Finally, greater reliance might be placed on noneconomic incentives such as more active participation in community programs and wider opportunities to use skills.

CHANGES IN RETIRED PAY FOR RESERVISTS. The burden of retired pay for reservists is now about $200 million a year, but it will reach $1 billion a year by 1990. Reservists receive a deferred annuity on retirement, to be paid when they reach the age of sixty. One of the most costly and most controversial features of the system is that benefits are computed on the basis of pay scales in effect at the time retired benefits begin to be paid, rather than at the time of retirement.[15] Computing annuities on pay scales in effect when the reservist retires would save an average of $100 million a year between now and the year 2000. Savings would be small in the beginning but reach $300 million a year by the end of the period.

In sum, these changes could greatly reduce the cost of reserve forces, even without altering the missions now assigned to them.

15. An interagency committee appointed by the President to study the Uniformed Services retirement system concluded: "A program providing more economic incentive than is necessary to meet its manpower requirements is not efficient. . . . The Committee believes that the present reserve retirement subsystem provides more economic incentive than necessary to meet its manpower requirements by permitting annuity computation to be based on future pay rates, unrelated to the pay level in effect while the member was participating in the reserve service." "Report to the President on the Study of Uniformed Services Retirement and Survivor Benefits by the Interagency Committee" (July 1, 1971; processed), Vol. 1, p. 3-2.

While data on costs are approximate, it is estimated that the policy changes described above could achieve savings of $500 million a year.

Computation of Military Pay Increases

A special formula incorporated in the military pay act of 1967 is resulting in higher pay increases for military personnel than are necessary to keep military pay competitive with the private sector. It also adds to the confusion surrounding the military pay system.

Calculations of comparability pay and of the incentives needed for an all-volunteer service are based on "regular military compensation," which includes the elements of pay that are viewed as equivalent to monetary income in the private sector.[16] Regular military compensation consists of basic pay (75 percent), quarters allowances (14 percent), subsistence allowances (6 percent), and a tax advantage (5 percent).[17] In 1967, Congress directed that (1) when federal civilian pay was increased the same percentage increase for military personnel was to apply to regular military compensation; and (2) the absolute increase was to be reflected in basic pay alone. Understandably, therefore, a given percentage increase in federal civilian pay is accompanied by a higher rate of increase in military basic pay.

A specific example may be helpful. In January 1973 the comparability pay index called for an increase of 5.14 percent in federal civilian pay. Increasing regular military compensation at that rate called for a total pay increase of $963 million, calculated as follows:

Component	Amount (millions of dollars)
Basic pay	14,390
Quarters and subsistence allowance (both cash and in-kind)	3,933
Tax advantage (imputed value)	869
Total regular military compensation	19,192
Comparability increase (5.14 percent of total, adjusted for tax advantage)	963

To increase total military pay by this amount, basic pay was increased by 6.69 percent.

16. Regular military compensation does not include special bonuses, fringe benefits (such as commissary and medical privileges), and a retirement fund to which the recipient makes no contribution.

17. The tax advantage derives from the fact that military quarters and subsistence allowances, whether in cash or in kind, are not subject to federal income tax. A specific monetary value, based on an assumed average military income, is attached to this element of pay.

This formula for calculating military pay increases has resulted in several anomalies, all of which have the effect of increasing military pay by more than the criteria of comparability with the private sector would require:

• Military personnel who receive quarters and subsistence in kind are being compensated through an extra increase in basic pay for the effects of increases in the cost of these services, even though it is the government that pays the higher prices for food, utilities, maintenance, and the other services it provides in kind.

• Under this formula, military personnel receiving cash allowances for food and quarters are understandably compensated for inflation by the extra increase in their basic pay. However, the cash allowances, which are left unchanged by this formula, then seem to be too low, resulting in pressures to increase them.[18] Because of this reasoning, allowances for quarters were increased substantially in fiscal 1972 as part of the volunteer incentive package, and allowances for subsistence were increased in fiscal 1973 to compensate for the rising cost of food. Those receiving cash allowances, therefore, are being compensated twice for the same purpose.

• Other elements of military compensation, such as reenlistment bonuses, separation pay, and the government contribution to social security benefits, are increased by more than is necessary because they are tied to basic pay.

• In addition, military retired pay costs are higher than they otherwise would be because they too are computed solely on the basis of basic pay.

Substantial savings would occur if this special formula was eliminated and each component of regular military compensation was increased by the same rate as the increase in federal civilian pay. An increase of 5.14 percent (see the data cited earlier) applied across the board would have reduced the first full-year cost of the most recent military pay increase by $200 million a year. This calculation is shown in Table 10-7.

Over a longer period the difference in costs between the two for-

18. For example, in 1971 the average allowance for Army enlisted men with dependents was $95 a month for quarters and $1.46 a day for subsistence. These amounts would obviously be inadequate if they were in fact the total allowances provided for these purposes. But they are not. Compensatory increases in basic pay have been paid since 1968; hence, there is no reason to increase the allowances themselves, small as they seem to be.

Table 10-7. **Estimated First Full-Year Savings in Military Pay and Allowances If Increases Are Held at the Same Level as Those in Federal Civilian Pay**
Millions of dollars

		Pay increase	
	Amount before pay	Current	Alternative
Category	increase	formula[a]	formula[b]
Regular military compensation			
Basic pay	14,390	963	740
Cash quarters allowance	1,848	...	95
Cash subsistence allowance			
Officers	191	...	10
Enlisted men	629	74	32
Other military compensation			
Other allowances	1,591	106	82
·Reserve forces	1,307	87	67
Total		1,230	1,025

Sources: Authors' estimates based on data from U.S. Department of Defense, Office of the Assistant Secretary of Defense (Comptroller), April 1973. Figures may not add to totals because of rounding.
  a. Increase of 6.69 percent in basic pay and "other allowances" tied to basic pay. Independently, cash subsistence allowances for enlisted men, which are pegged to food costs, were increased by about 12 percent.
  b. Across-the-board increase of 5.14 percent, equivalent to the increase in federal civilian pay.

mulas becomes strikingly large. If annual pay increases are assumed to be 5.5 percent a year, the present formula, by fiscal 1980, will require a total pay increase approximately $2 billion a year higher than the amount that would be paid under the alternative formula.

In his 1974 Budget Message the President indicated he would propose legislation to change the current formula so as to permit military pay raises to be applied separately to basic pay and to allowances. It is not clear how this is to be done. Present indications are that the administration will request broad authority to apportion the total military pay increase between basic pay and allowances as circumstances or management objectives might require. Savings then would depend on how the formula was applied.

This issue highlights the urgent need to reform the present system of military pay. There are now over 200 separate military pay accounts, including basic pay, numerous cash allowances, a wide range of services in kind, and fringe benefits. This complex system originally was geared to a small, relatively unskilled, peacetime force. Pay was low, especially monetary pay. Heavy emphasis was placed on services in kind, reenlistment bonuses, and liberal retirement benefits as means of encouraging a lengthy career service.

At present, the system is a patchwork. Legislators have difficulty determining how large an increase in military pay must be to be equitable, and military personnel now in the service or considering a military career have difficulty evaluating accurately the various elements—cash and in-kind—that go into military compensation. In 1967 a special Department of Defense study group (the Hubbell Committee) recommended an overhaul of the military pay system that would replace military basic pay and allowances with a salary system. This recommendation was subsequently endorsed by the Gates Commission. Making the method of military compensation more nearly comparable to practice in the civilian sector would avoid misunderstandings and, at the same time, improve the accuracy of comparisons between military and civilian pay. Monetizing all forms of military compensation would also enhance the possibilities of using differentials in pay as a management tool.

Reductions in Retired Pay Outlays

In Chapter 9 it was projected that the cost of retired pay, measured in 1974 dollars, would increase from $5.3 billion in 1974 to $7.0 billion in 1980. This trend is likely to continue thereafter. By 1980 the number of retirees will have grown to 1.3 million (from 1 million in 1974) and the newer entrants will have retired at higher salaries and will therefore receive higher benefits. If present force levels and the present retirement system are maintained, the retired pay obligation by the year 2000 will have increased to $12.8 billion a year (in 1974 dollars).

Partly because of this disturbing trend, the President established an interagency committee to study the military retirement system and prepare legislative proposals. The committee submitted its recommendations in 1971; it essentially proposed that military retirement should be aligned with the federal civilian retirement system. Altogether, its recommendations would have had the effect of moderately increasing costs throughout the 1970s and gradually achieving savings from 1980 to the end of that decade. Last year's budget contained funds to carry out some of the committee's recommendations, as amended by the administration, but for the most part the Congress deferred action. The 1974 budget contains $389 million for new measures affecting retired pay. Two distinct kinds of changes are involved: a proposal for recomputation and measures to reform the system.

Recomputation was the rule before 1958, and there is continuing pressure from military retirees to resume the practice. It concerns the thorny issue of whether military retired pay, which is now pegged to changes in the cost-of-living index, as is the case for federal civilian employees, should in addition be adjusted each time there is a real increase in active duty pay. The Court of Claims ruled in 1966 that the government is under no legal obligation to recompute retired pay.[19] Hence, the argument for recomputation comes down to a question of equity. Did the government, in changing the system in 1958, break faith with the retirees who entered military service before that time and presumably made their decision partly on the understanding that their retirement benefits would always be kept current with active duty pay scales? In terms of comparability with other systems, the argument for recomputation has no validity. Recomputation would be more generous than federal civilian retirement systems and virtually without precedent in private retirement systems.

In the 1974 budget the administration, as a compromise, has requested $360 million for a one-time recomputation, which in general would be made for older retirees only. This measure would increase retired pay by an average of $400 million a year for the rest of this century. The alternative would be to reject recomputation altogether, on the grounds that the equity argument is not sufficient to justify the cost and because passage of this legislation now could lead to pressures for similar "one-time recomputations" in the future.

Proposals to *reform* military retired pay generally are based on the principle that those already in the system must not be penalized. Hence, reforms undertaken on this premise would save little for the rest of the 1970s, but could substantially reduce costs in the longer term. In this area the administration proposes, with very small initial expenditures, to bring the military retirement system more closely in line with the federal civilian retirement system. The major features are:

• Military annuities would not be fully paid until retirees had had thirty years of service or, if they retired earlier, reached the age at which they would have had thirty years of service.

• Retirement pay would be based on the retiree's highest average pay for a full year rather than on his pay at the time of retirement.

19. See "Report by the Interagency Committee," p. 7-5.

• Social security benefits for military retirees would be reduced by one-half.

• Greater flexibility in manpower management would be gained by granting deferred annuities to those leaving the service before they were eligible for retirement.

In each case these proposals are significantly more liberal than the federal civilian retirement system and generally do not go as far as the recommendations of the Interagency Committee. Nevertheless, they would represent an initial step toward modernization of the military retirement system. Costs (−) or savings (+) in future years would be as follows (in millions of current dollars):

Year	Annual cost or saving
1974	29 (−)
1978	14 (+)
1980	55 (+)
1990	421 (+)
2000	1,571 (+)

If the major provisions of the military retirement system were aligned completely with the federal civilian retirement system, as recommended by the Interagency Committee, savings would be almost three times the amounts indicated above.[20] A far-reaching measure of this kind might be taken as part of a broader and much needed effort to recast the entire system of military compensation.

It is possible that no reforms will be initiated because of the complexity of the retirement system, the misunderstanding that surrounds proposals to change it, and the absence of large savings in the near future. If so, retired pay will continue to impose a growing burden on the defense budget—a burden that is independent of defense requirements.

The All-Volunteer Service: A Status Report*

The transition from conscription to an all-volunteer service has now been completed, at an annual cost of approximately $3 billion a

20. "Summary of the Report to the Secretary of Defense by the DOD Retirement Study Group" (Department of Defense, May 31, 1972; processed), p. S-6.

* This section is based on a Brookings defense analysis staff study by Martin Binkin and John D. Johnston, *All-Volunteer Armed Forces: Progress, Problems, and Prospects*, Report prepared for the Senate Committee on Armed Services, 93 Cong. 1 sess. (1973).

year.[21] These costs, though substantial, represent less than one-fifth of the increase in military manpower costs since 1968. The rate of enlistments is high enough to maintain present force levels. However, the Department of Defense, concerned about anticipated shortages in certain fields, has requested $225 million in the 1974 budget for special bonuses. Whether these bonuses are necessary is part of a larger issue—can the all-volunteer service be maintained over the long term without repeated increases in cost?

Long-term requirements may be stated as follows. At present force levels one out of six men would, at some point in their lives, have to volunteer for military service. Correcting for those not likely to volunteer—for example, students or veterans—and those not meeting present enlistment standards would reduce this proportion to one out of three.

Should enlistments eventually fall short of requirements, additional pay incentives might be offered. This is what the administration proposes to do now to attract more highly qualified volunteers, reservists, and doctors. There is a great deal of uncertainty about how enlistments will respond to future pay increases, but the possibility that such increases will spill over into all forms of military compensation could make this a costly method.

Alternatively, special bonuses could be avoided for the time being, if not indefinitely, by adopting measures to increase the pool of eligible manpower or to reduce the number of volunteers required each year. This might be done by relaxing enlistment standards, substituting civilian for military manpower, accepting more women in the armed services, and adjusting manpower policies to encourage longer periods of service. It is estimated that such measures, in combination, could easily reduce the magnitude of the enlistment problem by at least one-third and thus greatly improve the prospects of meeting present military manpower needs at present pay scales.

Finally, whether new monetary incentives are necessary, either now

21. This sum includes only the cost of incentive pay raises, bonus, and special recruiting programs. Not included are the cost of improvements in the military standard of living and in military personnel policies that have been justified in part as being necessary for the all-volunteer service. The General Accounting Office has estimated that these improvements may have increased military costs by $1 billion a year (Comptroller General of the United States, "Problems in Meeting Military Manpower Needs in the All-Volunteer Force," Report to the Congress [GAO, May 2, 1973; processed], p. 5). Such estimates, however, take no cognizance of whether the improvements were in fact tied to the all-volunteer service or whether they would have been made in any event.

Table 10-8. Summary of Cost Savings from Alternative Manpower Policies
Total obligational authority in billions of 1974 dollars

Policy change	1974	1977	1980	Average, 1974–80
Reduction in support costs[a]	0.8	2.0	2.0	1.8
Reduction in reserves[b]	0.2	0.4	0.4	0.4
Reform of military pay system[c]	0.1	0.8	1.6	0.7
Reform of retired pay system[d]	0.4	0.4	0.4	0.4
Deletion of volunteer service bonuses[e]	0.2	0.3	0.3	0.3
Total cost savings	1.7	3.9	4.7	3.6

Source: Authors' estimates using assumptions described in notes below.
a. Reduction of support services as follows: ground forces to 1964 level; Air Force and Navy to 1970 level; and medical costs for all services to 1970 level.
b. Reduction of 20 percent in reserve manpower, as described on pp. 377–80. Reduction in reserve manpower assumed to eliminate need for enlistment bonuses, with savings included in note e.
c. Alternative method of computing military pay increases, as described on pp. 380–83; savings estimate in current dollars is converted to 1974 dollars.
d. Assumes no recomputation of retired pay. Reform of retired pay system is not likely to produce significant savings until the 1980s.
e. Assumes that enlistment needs can be met through measures other than bonuses.

or in the future, will depend in large part on the total number of military personnel sought. For this reason the alternative force postures discussed earlier in this chapter have additional significance. Lower force levels would increase the probability that an all-volunteer service could be maintained without lowering enlistment standards and without increasing monetary incentives.

Summary of Manpower Alternatives

A summary of the budgetary savings that would result from the alternative manpower policies outlined here is shown in Table 10-8. Since the discussion has assumed the continuation of present military missions, these policies should be viewed as a means of carrying out such missions at lower cost. Also by assumption, manpower savings have been calculated on the basis of present force levels. Consequently, they cannot be added to savings shown for any of the strategic or general purpose force alternatives presented earlier in this chapter without adjustments for differences in force levels.[23]

23. These adjustments are made in the calculations underlying the alternative defense budgets shown in Chapter 11.

11. Major National Security Options

DEFENSE CONTINUES TO BE the largest single federal activity, absorbing 30 percent of the federal budget and 6 percent of the gross national product (GNP). Because of its size alone, the defense budget occupies a central position in the examination of national priorities. Furthermore, its justification is based on the concept of national security, which involves intricate judgments about relations between the United States and the rest of the world. Yet public discussion of the defense budget all too frequently fails to clarify the available choices. Often, the debate on military spending centers on peripheral issues, such as a particular weapon system. Or it is misleadingly incomplete, such as the controversy over keeping troops in Europe—a subject that yields no reasonable conclusions unless explicitly linked to positions on how large the total force structure should be and what foreign policy purposes military forces are to serve. At worst, the discussion can become sterile because extreme views are advanced, exemplified both by those who argue that the defense budget request cannot be cut in any way without catastrophic results, and by those who contend it can be massively reduced without significant consequence.

Defense expenditures, like those for other government programs, involve trade-offs between costs and benefits. In the case of the defense program, the calculation is analogous to deciding on the amount of insurance to carry. How much should the United States be willing to pay, as a society, to avert possible unfavorable political and military

388

developments and to be prepared for wars that seem unlikely to occur? This calculation, in turn, depends not only on assessments about the importance and probable course of political developments abroad, but also on judgments about whether given changes in the level of military expenditures can affect the direction of these developments. Since the cost of "deterrence and war insurance" is substantial, differences in judgments on these questions imply wide differences in military spending.

In this chapter, we seek to assess the defense budget in terms of such a calculation. After a brief discussion of factors that tend to constrain the area of choice, four alternative defense budgets are outlined. Each illustrates a general approach to determining the size of military forces and their cost. These budgets are based on the analysis of defense programs and issues in the preceding chapters; they are purposely designed to show that a few key issues have wide-ranging implitions for force levels and costs. In the final sections, the four illustrative defense budgets are examined in terms of their relation to arms control negotiations, their impact on the balance of payments, and their implications for congressional review of defense appropriations.

Constraints on the Area of Choice

Three factors that tend to narrow the range of choice among defense budgets deserve brief mention here: trends in Soviet military spending; changing relations between the United States, Western Europe, and Japan; and the sizable proportion of fixed costs in the defense budget.

Trends in Soviet Spending for Defense*

A large portion of the U.S. military force structure is justified as necessary to counter Soviet military capabilities. What, then, are the likely trends in Soviet military forces, and how might they shape the United States' view of its defense options?

At present, most Western observers estimate that the USSR spends about 10 percent of its GNP on defense and space, but estimates range as low as 6 percent and as high as 15 percent. There are disagreements as to whether this percentage has inched up or down during the

---

* The summary observations in this section are drawn in part from a background paper prepared by Herbert Block.

Brezhnev era, although there is a consensus that defense spending in absolute terms has been increasing moderately and steadily. Notwithstanding their differences, which are understandable in view of the absence of reliable data, most researchers tend to assume that the USSR produces a defense package roughly equal in value to that of the United States. In other words, if Soviet military manpower, equipment, and research and development were valued at U.S. prices, the two defense budgets would be nearly the same.

Although there may be equality in defense budgets, the distribution of expenditures among the major force components is likely to differ in the two countries. Both probably spend about the same proportion on strategic forces, but the USSR, having larger armies, presumably allocates a higher proportion to ground forces and the United States a higher proportion to naval and tactical air forces. In general, the USSR has sought quantitative superiority whereas the United States has sought superior military technology and other qualitative advantages.

A major shift in resources from the defense to the civilian economy is not to be expected, even though the present Soviet defense burden is heavy. The Soviet economy, to be sure, is in trouble not simply because of poor weather and a bad harvest, but because of the system's chronic inefficiencies. In these circumstances it is tempting to conclude that the debate over resources to be allocated to defense will take on more bite. However, it is more likely that neither military nor political leaders will be willing to risk the domestic uncertainties that would accompany a sharp change in the status quo.

The military in the USSR seem to be generally satisfied with their share of GNP, and might even be willing to moderate their claims to prevent consumer dissatisfaction from increasing and to help the economy return to more nearly normal growth. The political leaders, on the other hand, would be cautious not to go too far in pushing an austerity program on the military. Furthermore, in view of the rigidities in the Soviet economy, it is not easy to transfer resources from the efficient defense sector to the inefficient civilian sector without suffering disproportionately large losses in the process. And finally, with all its problems, the economy probably will grow at a rate of 4 to 5 percent a year, in which case the status quo in the defense share will still permit a continuing increase in per capita consumption.

A persistently unfavorable economic environment might well cause

Soviet leaders to be more responsive to proposals to limit arms programs or even to reduce forces. But no major policy shifts in this direction prompted by economic stringency are yet on the horizon. All elements of the leadership believe that negotiations with the United States must be undertaken from a position of strength. Although they would welcome military savings, they would be prepared to make concessions that promise economies only if they were convinced that the Soviet Union's presumed position as a military equal of the United States would not be jeopardized.

All this suggests very modest changes in Soviet defense budget trends, if any. Defense expenditures probably will continue to increase in absolute terms, although slowly and by less than the rate of increase in GNP. Expenditures might even remain fairly constant, but this is less likely. Defense as a share of GNP would then gradually decline, suggesting a modest shift in favor of the civilian sector. Where budget pressures required military choices, investments in future security (modernization of weapon systems) are likely to be favored over expenditures on measures to maintain or improve current military readiness.

Although this trend toward increased defense spending in the USSR warrants concern, it does not provide a basis for automatic responses on the part of the United States. Increased Soviet military spending in itself need not call for an increase in U.S. military spending or even forestall U.S. force reductions. The connection between the defense budgets of the two countries is more complicated than that, if only because each budget is partly based on factors independent of relations between them. In large measure, as noted above, the trend in Soviet military spending is structural in character, stemming from the highly conservative nature of the regime and its disinclination to change institutional patterns. Furthermore, part of the increase in Soviet military spending is for forces that would be directed against China and could not be readily deployed against the United States or its allies. Or Soviet military spending may reflect miscalculations about the importance of specific political objectives or the efficacy of achieving them through the buildup or deployment of military forces. Since specific Soviet defense measures could have adverse consequences for the U.S.–Soviet military balance and thus require U.S. countermeasures, Soviet military spending should be examined carefully. However, the U.S. response, if any, should depend on an analysis of the specific

military purposes and effectiveness of Soviet spending and their consequences for U.S. interests.

Total Soviet military spending, however, will set limits on the defense budget options open to the United States. In the short term,
these limits are likely to be broad. As long as the United States reduces
defense spending by efficiency measures or by eliminating forces that
would not in any event be particularly useful in a conflict with the
Soviet Union, the U.S. defense budget can be falling while the Soviet
defense budget is rising without appreciably affecting the U.S.–Soviet
military balance. Yet over the longer term this divergence in budgetary trends would not be sustainable. A steady increase in Soviet defense spending in the face of cuts in U.S. defense spending could be-
cloud the international atmosphere and raise suspicions about Soviet
intentions. Such a trend clearly could conflict with continued steps
toward economic and military cooperation between the superpowers
and could therefore threaten a reversal in the trend toward détente.
Eventually such divergencies could so significantly affect the U.S.–
Soviet military balance as to require offsetting increases in U.S. military capabilities.

Relations with Allies

The justification for U.S. forces is only partially based on an assessment of military threats from potential adversaries. It also has a
political dimension based on relations with allies. These political requirements revolve around the U.S. interest in sustaining the forces of
political moderation in Germany and Japan and in managing relations
with its allies so as to avoid further proliferation of nuclear weapons.

The present German and Japanese sense of security reflects in good
part those countries' confidence in U.S. military power—in its extent,
its deterrent capability, and its availability for their defense. This
sense of security makes it possible for them to follow policies aimed at
East-West détente, to maintain only nonnuclear and relatively modest
military forces, and to cooperate with the United States in economic
and political matters.

This relationship between the United States and its industrial allies
does not rule out reductions in U.S. forces and changes in their deployment. Indeed, long-term trends both in Northeast Asia and in
Western Europe could facilitate such changes. In Northeast Asia, the
movement toward détente with China and the opening of relations

with North Korea should make it easier for the Japanese to adjust to reductions of the U.S. military presence in the region. In Western Europe, progress toward closer cohesion and unity should permit a larger local military effort in the future—one in which Germany's national role is safely subsumed—and progress in East-West negotiations should allow mutual force reductions.

However, these trends will take time to work themselves out. In the meantime the United States faces a continuing need to act cautiously. Western Europe and Japan have the economic resources to underwrite their own security, but for the United States to press them too far and too fast in this direction might undermine the influence of moderate groups in both countries and risk a resurgence of German and Japanese nationalism, accompanied by rearmament on a scale that could threaten the international structure. Although these risks are now remote, the United States must take them into account in choosing among its defense options. They apply more strongly to decisions about U.S. forces deployed in and near Germany and Japan than to decisions about total U.S. force levels. Generally, however, the extent, character, and timing of changes in U.S. military forces should not get ahead of the political trends in Europe and Asia that make change feasible.

Fixed versus Variable Costs

An important factor influencing the consideration of alternative force levels is the sizable element of relatively fixed costs in the defense budget. Such cost categories include retired pay, research and development expenditures, and a portion of support costs. Each tends to be fixed for periods of different duration and for different reasons.

Retired pay, now approximately $5 billion a year, is of course the clearest example of fixed costs. Retired pay benefits are determined by the size of military forces in the past; reductions in force levels now will affect the retired pay appropriation only in the distant future.

Research and development expenditures, nearly $9 billion a year, largely represent an investment to hedge against future risks. At any given time, specific research and development programs may be questionable on the basis of cost-effectiveness considerations or other grounds. A reduction in force levels, however, probably would not result in proportionate reductions in the total appropriation for research and development since there would be continued, if not heightened, concern to keep up with military technology as a hedge against being wrong.

Support costs, which, broadly defined, constitute at least two-fifths of the defense budget, also contain elements of fixed costs. For example, a portion of support expenditures is for investment in global communications and intelligence systems, which for the most part would have to be maintained even when the size of forces was sharply reduced. In the case of training, supply and maintenance, and administrative services, costs do not go down proportionately with force levels, both because there are economies of scale and because a minimum overhead structure is required for almost any size force and for the maintenance of a base for mobilization in an emergency.

It is very roughly estimated that the elements of these three cost categories which would not vary in proportion to changes in force levels total perhaps $25 billion a year, or almost 30 percent of the defense budget. This amount would decline if the United States substantially reduced its forces and kept the level down for a considerable period of time, principally because much smaller forces might reflect a reassessment of the need for hedges such as a strong research and development program or the maintenance of a mobilization base. Over the short and medium term, however, these fixed costs represent a constraint on available choices in the sense that an attempt to reduce the defense budget by a given proportion will require a significantly larger proportionate reduction in variable costs and consequently in combat forces.

Defense Budget Options

In drawing up the following illustrative defense postures and budgets the above constraints were specifically taken into account. Furthermore, the alternatives presented rest on the assumption that there will be no sudden or drastic shift in the present pattern of international relations for the rest of this decade. Specifically, this means that there will be no reversion to cold war confrontation between the United States and the Soviet Union—for example, as a result of events in the Middle East, the succession problem in Yugoslavia, or developments elsewhere in Eastern Europe—and that there will be no reversal of the trend toward détente with China. Friction could grow in relations with Western Europe and Japan, but it is assumed that they would not be so serious as to break up the alliance of each with the United States. On the other hand, these assumed international conditions also mean that, though arms control and European security discussions will continue and modest agreements in both fields may be concluded, there will be no decisive breakthrough in relations with the USSR that would assure dramatic, large-scale, and early mutual reductions in strategic or general purpose forces. The assumption about Sino-Soviet relations is that neither war nor basic reconciliation lie in the near future.

The four defense postures outlined below consist of the defense program reflected in the 1974 budget and three lower-cost alternatives. They differ principally in their assessment of U.S. interests, the risks to those interests inherent in a continuation of present international trends, and the military forces that these interests and risks require.

Alternative 1, the administration's program, provides generally for maintenance of present force levels as described in Chapter 9. These force levels are not viewed as being fixed indefinitely; rather, the administration argues, they are necessary for the near term to encourage continuing improvement in East-West relations. Any reductions in military forces, therefore, should be made cautiously and gradually so as to avoid alarming allies or giving the wrong signals to potential adversaries. This reasoning implies that maintaining strong military forces now is the safest and surest route to having reduced military forces and smaller defense budgets in the future.

Under this alternative, strategic forces would make up a diversified deterrent, characterized by continuing modernization of its three offensive elements—sea-based missiles, land-based missiles, and bombers. The major components of general purpose forces consist of sixteen divisions, fifteen carrier task groups (eventually declining to twelve), and thirty-eight tactical air wings. Military manpower would stabilize at 2.2 million and defense civilian employment at 1 million. The cost in constant dollars of these forces is projected to rise steadily through the rest of the decade. In current dollars, the baseline defense budget would increase from $82 billion in fiscal 1974 to $104 billion in 1978.

Disadvantages in this program stem principally from its high cost. Defense would continue to absorb almost 6 percent of GNP, and there would be little room to shift budgetary resources from military to civilian activities. Moreover, as emphasized in Chapter 8, the combination of fiscal constraints and high manpower and weapon system costs probably will require reductions in forces eventually. Reductions made under these kinds of pressures, however, are likely to be haphazard and carried out in ways that would be inconsistent with the military and political purposes these forces are designed to serve.

Alternative 2 is a defense posture designed to serve present purposes at lower cost. It is based on the view that large economies can be made in defense costs without modifying the U.S. definition of its interests abroad or appreciably affecting present military capabilities to protect or advance those interests.

Major cost reductions would be concentrated in strategic forces and in manpower. In the case of strategic forces, the pace of modernization would be substantially moderated and the more marginal force elements, including the older model B-52 bombers and selected air defense units, would be eliminated.[1] Manpower savings would arise from moderate reductions in support services and reserve forces and from changes in military pay policies, including retired pay benefits.[2] The number of major force components—both strategic and general purpose—however, would remain virtually unchanged. But there would be reductions of over 100,000 in active military manpower and slightly less than 100,000 in defense civilian employment. In constant dollars, these economies would keep the defense budget at approximately the fiscal 1974 level for the rest of the decade. On the average, alternative 2 would cost about 8 percent less than the present program. In current dollars, the savings would be $3 billion in fiscal 1974, nearly $6 billion in 1975, and $10 billion in 1978.

Possible disadvantages in this course of action are political. It could be argued that U.S. unilateral reductions in strategic forces—even in the marginal elements of these forces—or a slowdown in strategic modernization programs may weaken the position of the United States in political negotiations with the USSR or cause anxiety in nations allied with the United States. Implementing economies in manpower costs also would require overcoming domestic political opposition such as that engendered when excess bases are closed or emanating from pressure groups protecting the interests of active and retired members of the armed forces and the reserve organizations.

1. See alternative 2, pp. 345–46.
2. See pp. 373–87, including the summary of cost savings from changes in manpower policies in Table 10-6.

Alternative 3 is based on a reassessment of U.S. interests in Asia and of U.S. force requirements for the defense of Western Europe. This course of action would substantially change both the political and military missions of U.S. forces. In Asia, the United States would limit its security interests to Japan and disengage from commitments to the defense of Southeast Asia. This would call for a reduction in the U.S. military presence and would limit forces in the Pacific to those necessary for the maintenance of a strong alliance with Japan based on mutual confidence and cooperation.[3] American forces earmarked for the defense of Europe would be oriented for the contingency of a short war instead of for protracted conflict, as they are now. Consequently, U.S. forces in both Europe and the United States would be reorganized so as to bring maximum defensive power to bear in the first thirty to sixty days following mobilization.[4] At the same time, those elements of U.S. forces geared to a long war in Europe would be substantially reduced. In the case of strategic forces, land-based missiles would gradually be phased out and reliance placed on a dyad composed of bombers and submarine-launched missiles, on the assumption that these two kinds of offensive forces would provide an invulnerable, flexible, and powerful strategic retaliatory capability indefinitely.[5]

Under this alternative, total conventional forces would be cut by roughly one-third. Army and Marine Corps divisions would be reduced from sixteen to the equivalent of eleven, carrier task forces from fifteen to nine. Air Force tactical fighter wings would decline from twenty-one to sixteen; procurement, moreover, would shift to lower-cost aircraft designed solely to support ground troops, and present programs for multipurpose, high-cost planes would be terminated. In general, military procurement in major weapon systems would be reduced by about $7 billion. Military manpower would drop to 1.7 million and civilian employment to 800,000.

For the period 1974–80, defense costs under alternative 3 would be reduced by an average of $12 billion a year below the spending levels implied by alternative 2. Of this amount, $2 billion is attributable to the additional reductions in strategic forces, $4 billion to the force reductions made possible by the adoption of a low military profile in

3. See alternative 2, pp. 367–68.
4. See alternative 3, pp. 368–72.
5. See alternative 3, p. 346.

Asia, and $6 billion to the reductions made possible by the reorganization of forces for Europe.

The combination of reductions based on the efficiency considerations outlined in alternative 2 and reductions based on a redefinition of the roles and missions of U.S. forces in Europe and Asia would make substantial cuts in the defense budget possible. In constant dollars, the defense budget would shrink steadily through the period, averaging about 20 percent less than the present program. In current dollars, savings would be $7 billion in fiscal 1974, $16 billion in 1975, and $26 billion in 1978. By the end of the decade, the defense budget as a share of GNP would decline from 6 percent to 4.5 percent.

A reduction of this magnitude, irrespective of its rationale, is likely to strongly influence the attitudes of adversaries and allies alike, although its specific effects are somewhat difficult to predict. A good deal would depend on U.S. actions in other fields and on the manner in which the defense cuts were managed, as well as on internal developments in the USSR and Western Europe, including rising military manpower costs and the intensity of pressures in those countries for reductions in defense costs.

In the case of the USSR, the basic issue is whether Soviet leaders would see these changes in the U.S. military posture as so altering the military balance in their favor that they would give up the advantages they now perceive in economic and political cooperation with the United States. On the one hand, so large a reduction in the U.S. defense budget might signal to the Soviet leadership a basic weakening of U.S. resolve; consequently, they might be tempted to explore the possibilities of pressing the United States in areas of potential conflict; for example, the Middle East. On the other hand, in the areas of major interest to the United States—Western Europe and Japan—the USSR would see little evidence of a change in the U.S. security commitment. In the strategic field, the USSR might be tempted to derive political gain from its numerical advantage in missiles by pursuing a more aggressive policy generally, but it would not wish to carry this policy to a point that would increase the risk of war since it would have no reason to question either the security or the flexibility of the U.S. retaliatory capability.

In the case of Western Europe and Japan, the large reduction in the defense budget might intensify doubts about the reliability of U.S. guarantees and lead to a weakening of military cooperation between them and the United States. These doubts would be tempered to the extent that the reduction and reorganization of U.S. military forces were seen as reflecting U.S. disengagement from peripheral commitments, which at the same time helped to place the U.S. contribution to the defense of the two main industrial areas on a fiscally manageable, and hence more enduring, basis.

Alternative 4 is a defense posture that places virtually exclusive reliance on nuclear forces to deter war. It is based on the view that the consequences of nuclear war are so catastrophic that the essential interests of the United States can be safeguarded at a far lower cost by relying more heavily on nuclear forces. While withdrawing most of its conventional forces from Western Europe and the Pacific, the United States would emphasize its intention to respond to any attack on its industrial allies with nuclear weapons. The reasoning is that no country, threatened with the possibility of U.S. nuclear retaliation, would risk initiating a chain of events that could lead to war. To make this strategy more credible, the United States would invest more heavily in its strategic forces—both offensive and defensive.

Under this alternative, the strategic force budget would be increased, principally because of investments in defensive systems, including the deployment of antiballistic missiles and air defenses designed to protect urban centers from nuclear attack. General purpose forces, on the other hand, would be drastically reduced. Indeed, it is difficult to construct firm guidelines for general purpose force levels under this strategy. These forces might consist, for example, of six divisions, six carrier task groups, and four Air Force tactical air wings; in this case, military manpower would decline to 1.3 million and civilian employment to 600,000. In constant dollars, the defense budget would go down sharply and steadily for the rest of the decade, averaging almost one-third less than the present program. In current dollars, savings would amount to $6 billion in fiscal 1974 and would rise to $38 billion by 1978.

Clearly, this change in strategy would generate profound foreign reaction, arising principally from questions about its credibility. The USSR would probably respond by initiating a strategic buildup of its own and might be tempted to test U.S. intentions by applying military pressures in small ways in Western Europe. Leaders in Western Europe and Japan would find it difficult to base the security of their countries on the willingness of the United States to accept millions of

Table 11-1. Projection of Costs of Alternative Defense Budgets, Fiscal Years 1974 and 1978, and Average for 1974–80[a]

Total obligational authority in billions of dollars

Type of force or cost factor	Alternative 1			Alternative 2			Alternative 3[b]			Alternative 4		
	1974	1978	1974–80 average	1974	1978	1974–80 average	1974	1978	1974–80 average	1974	1978	1974–80 average
Strategic forces	18	21	20	16	16	16	16	14	14	19	23	22
Baseline general purpose forces[c]	55	57	56	53	53	54	49	41	44	48	23	30
Other[d]	10	11	10	10	11	10	10	11	10	10	11	10
Allowance for real pay increases[e]	...	5	3	...	4	3	...	3	3	...	3	2
Total (constant FY 1974 dollars)	82	93	90	79	84	83	75	69	71	76	59	64
Pay and price increases[f]	...	11	8	...	10	8	...	8	6	...	7	5
Total (current dollars)	82	104	98	79	94	90	75	78	77	76	66	69
Outlays in current dollars corresponding to the above projections	75	102	95	72	92	87	69	78	76	70	66	68

Source: Authors' estimates based on the projections in Chapters 9 and 10. Figures may not add to totals because of rounding.

a. *Alternative 1* is the cost of the administration's program as reflected in the 1974 budget request and in congressional testimony. *Alternative 2* is designed to carry out present missions at lower cost. *Alternative 3* reduces missions in Asia, reorganizes forces for Europe, and maintains a strategic dyad. *Alternative 4* places almost exclusive reliance on nuclear deterrence.

b. Also includes the savings from the efficiency measures in alternative 2 adjusted for reductions in force levels.

c. Consists of the cost of ground combat forces, tactical air forces, and naval general purpose forces. Incremental Vietnam war costs for fiscal 1974 are excluded.

d. Consists of the cost of airlift, family housing, military assistance, and retired pay.

e. Assumes real pay increases of 3 percent a year corresponding to the average increase in productivity in the private sector.

f. Based on rates of increase in prices and in the cost of living shown in notes to Table 9-9.

casualties and the risk of total devastation in order to respond with nuclear weapons to attacks against their countries. It is possible that adverse consequences could be contained. The more likely outcome, however, would be the eventual dissolution of U.S. alliances with Western Europe and Japan, the proliferation of nuclear forces, and the reversal of the trend toward East-West détente.

The four illustrative defense budgets are summarized in Table 11-1 as they apply to strategic forces, general purpose forces, and other programs. The alternatives were designed for the specific purpose of showing that a wide range of national security options are at least conceivable. They are, of course, in no sense exhaustive, and each could be adopted in part or as a whole. Numerous other defense budgets, based on the efficiency criteria and foreign policy alternatives discussed in Chapter 10, could readily be developed.

Several observations emerging from a comparison of these four defense budgets deserve emphasis.

First, a significant part of the defense budget depends on decisions relating to cost and efficiency factors alone and does not involve considerations of foreign policy or national security.

Second, in today's international environment the purposes served by military forces are as much political as military. Carrying out these political purposes depends, perhaps more than do the military purposes, on the deployment of U.S. military forces in Western Europe and Asia. If these political interests were discounted or if the political environment was altered by such factors as a dramatic breakthrough in East-West negotiations or progress toward Western European unity, these overseas deployments could be substantially reduced. In this case it probably would make sense to reduce backup forces in the United States as well. Conversely, dismantling the U.S. military presence abroad without a change in the political rationale or environment would remove the justification for a sizable portion of the total U.S. force structure, because these forces, which would then be located entirely at home, could not effectively serve their intended purposes.

Third, insofar as considerations relating to the USSR are concerned, a sizable reduction in U.S. forces can be based on a realistic assessment of Soviet military capabilities rather than on a benign interpretation of Soviet intentions. Unilateral U.S. force reductions may in fact encourage the USSR to take similar action. While this would be desirable, decisions about reductions in U.S. forces need not be based on this expectation.

Table 11-2. Projected Cost of the Present Defense Program and Projected Yearly
Savings from Alternative Defense Postures, Fiscal Years 1974–78

	Outlays *(billions of dollars)*				
Program	1974	1975	1976	1977	1978
Cost of present program (alternative 1)	75	82	89	96	102
Savings from alternative programs					
Alternative 2	3	6	7	9	10
Alternative 3	6	12	18	23	25
Alternative 4	5	12	22	32	36

Source: Authors' estimates based on the projections in Chapters 9 and 10.

Fourth, the full budgetary effect of moving toward smaller military
forces is felt only after a few years. This is shown in Table 11-2, which
presents savings in terms of outlays rather than obligational authority.
Even the lowest-cost defense posture yields relatively modest savings
in the first year. This is due to a number of factors: (1) when programs
are reduced, outlays, which in part reflect past authorizations, decline
less rapidly than obligational authority; (2) the Congress usually does
not legislate appropriations until well into the fiscal year, which inevitably reduces the scope for savings in the first year; (3) cutbacks in
programs often involve one-time costs—for example, payment of
accrued leave and other termination expenses for manpower, cancellation penalties on procurement contracts, and resettlement expenses
in base closings; and (4) program reductions probably would be made
gradually, both for efficiency reasons and to minimize adverse political effects. In general, savings during the first year from the lower-cost
defense postures are about one-fourth those realized after five years.
For this reason alone an assessment of longer-term cost and policy
implications is essential to the consideration of alternative defense
budgets, as it is to the consideration of domestic programs.

Implications for Arms Control

Two arms control negotiations are currently under way: the second
round of the U.S.–Soviet strategic arms limitation talks (SALT) and
the discussions between NATO and Warsaw Pact countries about
mutual and balanced force reduction (MBFR) in Europe. The effect
of these two negotiations on U.S. defense spending has not been examined in detail in the preceding chapters. Both the SALT and the

MBFR negotiations are likely to be prolonged and thus have little effect on defense budgets in the next few years. In any case, these negotiations are not necessarily aimed at bringing about substantial immediate savings in military spending. Rather they should be viewed as means of avoiding an escalation in the arms race and, more important, of improving political relations by stabilizing the military balance. Creation of an improved political atmosphere, in turn, could enable both sides to reduce arms—unilaterally as well as by agreement—with greater confidence and as part of a continuing process.

How would the U.S. force postures described above differ in their effect on these negotiations?

Of the four alternatives, *alternative 1*, the administration's defense posture, at least nominally offers the best prospect for ultimately achieving agreements in arms control negotiations. Maintaining strong forces in general constitutes an inducement for the USSR to negotiate and specifically provides bargaining chips to trade off against equivalent reductions in Soviet forces. The development of new weapons, however, is usually accompanied by the growth of institutional pressures against abolishing them. The present defense posture, therefore, may lead the United States to be overcautious in the positions it takes in the SALT and MBFR negotiations and thus postpone or preclude arms reduction agreements that would otherwise be feasible on military or political grounds.

The extent to which *alternative 2*, the lower-cost version of the administration program, would differ from that program in its effects on arms control negotiations is subject to disagreement. The unilateral strategic force reductions outlined in this alternative might reduce pressure on the USSR to come to agreement in the SALT negotiations. In the last analysis, the United States brings two advantages to these negotiations: its technological leadership and its superior economic resources. From the Soviet Union's point of view, the danger arising from an impasse in the negotiations is that these advantages would allow the United States to step up its strategic programs, which would threaten to reopen the gap in U.S.–Soviet strategic capabilities. The reductions outlined in alternative 2 would not affect this basic source of U.S. bargaining leverage.

The sizable reduction in forces contemplated in *alternative 3* might reduce Soviet interest in arms control negotiations, since the Soviet Union could conclude that there was no need to accept reductions in its own forces to secure reductions in U.S. forces. To the extent the USSR wished to secure reductions in the U.S. strategic dyad, which would not be affected by alternative 3, it might still see strong reasons to negotiate on strategic arms control. In the case of MBFR, adoption of this alternative would provide greater leeway for NATO to reach an early first-round agreement with the USSR. A reorganization of its military forces that enabled the United States to deploy combat divisions to Europe more quickly would diminish the present negotiating complications caused by the proximity of the Soviet homeland to central Europe. And the possibilities for reducing U.S. support forces in Europe under this alternative would provide the basis for offering a sizable reduction in U.S. military manpower there without diminishing NATO defensive capabilities in a short war. A critical question is whether the USSR is more anxious to reduce its own military spending and pursue détente or to have the present apparent balance of East-West military power shift in its favor; in the first case, it might follow U.S. cuts with cuts of its own; in the second case, it would simply stand pat.

Alternative 4, moving toward heavy reliance on nuclear deterrence, would probably preclude reaching arms control agreements. Investments in strategic defensive forces envisaged in this posture could be undertaken only by abrogating the SALT agreement. Furthermore, a policy that relied heavily on nuclear forces to deter war would make the issue of the conventional military balance in Europe—and therefore the MBFR negotiations—of little significance.

The impact on arms control negotiations is, of course, only one of a number of factors that need to be taken into account in choosing among alternative defense postures. Mutual arms reductions are obviously desirable, but there should be a presumption in favor of not deferring unilateral reductions where they make sense and where U.S. ability to secure agreement with the USSR on mutual reductions is uncertain.

Implications for the Balance of Payments

Balance-of-payments consequences of stationing forces abroad have preoccupied the U.S. government for more than a decade. However, the issues involved are for the most part related to the functioning of the international monetary system rather than to the operation of military alliances. For this reason the fundamental changes now taking place in the international monetary system will inevitably transform the military balance-of-payments questions into financial questions and, in the process, largely solve them.

But the subject continues to be prominent in discussions of military dispositions abroad, so it is useful to review the numbers. American military activities abroad in 1972 involved gross foreign exchange expenditures of $4.7 billion a year. Net foreign exchange outlays were less because (1) part of these foreign exchange expenditures were for products purchased for U.S. forces abroad, such as petroleum, which would have had to be imported in increased quantity if these forces were stationed in the United States; and (2) collective defense arrangements increased U.S. sales of military equipment to allies in Western Europe and Japan, and this increase in military sales can be viewed as a partial offset to U.S. foreign expenditures on military account. If adjustments for these two factors are made, it is estimated that the net military foreign exchange deficit was about $3 billion a year. How would the alternative defense postures outlined above affect this portion of U.S. international financial accounts?

Gross military foreign exchange expenditures in 1972 were distributed, geographically, as follows: $2.2 billion in Europe, principally for U.S. activities in support of NATO; perhaps $1 billion for forces and installations in Japan and Korea; $1 billion for Vietnam-related activities and for U.S. military dispositions elsewhere in Southeast Asia; and $500 million for U.S. military facilities in other parts of the world. The withdrawal of U.S. troops from Vietnam will reduce foreign exchange costs there; on the other hand, the February 1973 devaluation of the dollar will increase the foreign exchange cost of U.S. military forces in Western Europe and Japan. As a result of these two changes, it is estimated that the net military foreign exchange deficit in fiscal 1974 will decline to approximately $2.5 billion. This amount can be taken to be the foreign exchange cost of alternative 1 (the present defense posture) and of alternative 2 (its lower-cost version).

Alternative 3 would probably reduce the net foreign exchange deficit by at least $1.5 billion. Of this amount, perhaps $1 billion would come from the removal of U.S. military forces in Southeast Asia, the reduction of military forces in Japan and Korea, and the closing of most military bases throughout East Asia. In addition, at least $500 million in foreign exchange would be saved as a result of the reduction in the number of American troops and dependents in Western Europe and from greater reliance on joint military basing arrangements in Western Europe and on the logistical systems of allied countries. Sales of military equipment to Western Europe might be reduced, though only by relatively small amounts.

Alternative 4, which envisages the almost total withdrawal of U.S. military forces overseas, probably would eliminate the net foreign exchange deficit on military account. There would be a drastic reduction in gross military expenditures abroad and an equally drastic reduction in sales of military equipment to Western Europe and Japan, the effects of the former outweighing the latter.

These direct effects, however, are probably the least significant aspect of the relationship between defense postures and the U.S. balance of payments. How rapidly the United States regains equilibrium in its balance of payments and whether it does so in circumstances that maintain economic gains or produce economic losses will depend in large measure on cooperation between the United States, Western Europe, and Japan in current efforts to reform the international financial system and to improve prospects for increased international trade and investment. None of the first three alternatives would diminish the possibilities for such cooperation. Alternative 4, however, which could disrupt political and security relations between the United States and its industrial allies, would also reverse the steady trend toward economic collaboration. Paradoxically, therefore, this alternative, which would eliminate the U.S. foreign exchange deficit on military account, would have a seriously adverse impact on the international economic position of the United States.

Congressional Review of the Defense Budget

By fiscal 1978 the three lower-cost options outlined in this chapter would achieve reductions ranging from 10 to 35 percent from the projected cost of the present defense posture. Based on post–World War II experience, changes of this magnitude in peacetime defense budgets would be unusual. Military spending declined drastically, of course, following World War II and rose sharply during the Korean and Vietnam wars. From 1955 to 1964, however, the defense budget in constant dollars was remarkably stable, and for the post–Vietnam war period the prospect is for maintenance of present spending levels on a moderately rising trend. This record raises questions as to whether the process of formulating and reviewing defense budgets within the government is suitable for assessing the desirability of large changes in peacetime military forces in light of changing international conditions and U.S. interests.

Procedures for such an examination are well established within the executive branch. The President's foreign policy report, the report submitted by the secretary of defense, the five-year defense program, and the underlying studies carried out under the direction of the National Security Council provide a logical framework in which the executive branch can examine relationships between foreign policy objectives, military forces, and other determinants of defense spending. However, interservice log rolling within the Department of Defense and bureaucratic inertia in other relevant parts of the executive branch constrain the effectiveness of these procedures—perhaps to an overriding extent.

In the Congress, on the other hand, the review process tends to be limited. For fiscal years 1960–69 Congress changed the administration's defense budget request by an average of little more than 1 percent. For the fiscal years 1970 to 1973, when dissatisfaction with Vietnam became more pronounced and concern about budget priorities became more serious, the Congress reduced the administration's defense budget request by an average of 4 percent.

Congressional review has usually focused on specific weapon system issues, which at best represent only a partial view of the defense budget and its central questions. Sometimes congressional support for or opposition to specific weapon systems has had, or could have had, a substantial impact on the defense posture.[6] For example, Congress authorized increased spending on the B-70 strategic bomber against the administration's wishes because it had no confidence in the missile programs then under way; on the other hand, it refused to fund the fast deployment logistic ships requested by the administration in the 1960s because of its concern about increasing U.S. capabilities to intervene abroad. The fact remains, however, that major weapon systems account for only about 15 percent of the defense budget. In contrast, the Congress has usually left manpower programs and poli-

6. See Arnold Kanter, "Congress and the Defense Budget, 1960–70," *American Political Science Review*, Vol. 66 (March 1972).

cies unchanged, even though they account for over half the defense budget and also involve issues that shape the defense posture. It was not until fiscal 1972 that the Congress authorized specific military manpower ceilings, and only now is it requesting the data necessary for systematic review of manpower needs. And most significantly, Congress rarely if ever addresses the question of force levels.

Consideration of defense budget options along the lines outlined in this chapter, therefore, would require changes in congressional procedures for reviewing the defense budget.

First, Congress would have to base its review on a longer perspective. As pointed out earlier, the first year's savings from even sizable reductions in military forces and programs are relatively modest. More congressional attention would have to center on the longer-term implications of current decisions. Multiyear authorizations would help to bring this about.

Second, the Congress would have to develop more effective procedures for examining the relation between defense budgets, on the one hand, and alternative foreign and defense policies, on the other. Efficiency changes of the type included in alternative 2 could readily be considered in the current congressional review process. The sizable force reductions suggested in alternative 3, however, would require means of (1) reassessing U.S. foreign policy interests (for instance, in East Asia) and relating that reassessment to military force requirements; and (2) examining alternative military strategies (for example, short versus long war in Europe) and relating that examination to U.S. military force requirements. Similar reassessments would be required for options that moved in the direction of alternative 4.

Both changes suggest the need for an integrated review procedure that would permit congressional consideration of orderly changes in the defense program in light of alternative definitions of U.S. foreign and defense policy. Indeed, this need is part of the larger problem of devising procedures that could improve congressional review of the budget as a whole.

12. Alternative Budgets for the Future

PRESIDENT NIXON'S 1974 BUDGET is quite unlike most of its predecessors. Few budgets envisage major changes in the scope and role of the federal government in society. Important changes, often unperceived while they are happening, usually occur over many years as the cumulative result of many individual decisions, each relatively modest in itself. But the 1974 budget explicitly aims at a major redirection of government.

In part the "radical" nature of the 1974 budget proposals stems from the magnitude of the problem the budget framers faced. As pointed out in Chapter 1, a budget that simply continued existing federal expenditure programs and tax policies and reintroduced earlier presidential initiatives was out of the question. Such a course would have led to full employment budget deficits on the order of $15 billion to $20 billion over the next four years. In an economy already recovering rapidly from recession, and projected to continue on that path, full employment deficits of this magnitude would have entailed unacceptable inflationary pressures.

There were three ways to reduce the projected deficits: to cut domestic spending, to cut defense spending, or to increase revenues through tax reform or tax rate increases. The administration rejected defense cutbacks and revenue increases, choosing to avoid projected deficits by cutting domestic spending from the levels it would otherwise have reached.

409

But the President's budget reflects more than simply a low priority for domestic spending. It indicates a strong view about the appropriate role of the federal government in the domestic area. The President proposes to reduce the degree of federal control over the use of grant funds provided to state and local governments and to rely more heavily on state and local decision making. The budget eliminates many narrow-purpose categorical grants, consolidates others into block grants for more general purposes, and emphasizes the new general revenue sharing program. This view of the federal role was clearly spelled out in the President's 1974 budget message:

> The 1974 budget proposes a leaner federal bureaucracy, increased reliance on State and local governments to carry out what are primarily State and local responsibilities, and greater freedom for the American people to make for themselves fundamental choices about what is best for them. . . . Two years ago, I spoke of the need for a new American Revolution to return power to people and put the individual *self* back in the idea of *self*-government. The 1974 budget moves us firmly toward that goal.

If the philosophy reflected in the 1974 budget proposals were consistently applied over a period of several years, the budget would be profoundly altered: domestic spending would increase only as needed to accommodate rising workloads, wages, and prices under existing programs; categorical grants would shrink in favor of revenue sharing; and incremental budgetary resources would be devoted principally to additional revenue sharing or to reducing federal tax rates. Compared with previously projected budget trends, the 1974 budget philosophy implies a smaller domestic budget and less federal intervention.

However one views their specific content, these moves by the President clearly open up the possibility of a major debate about alternative paths down which the federal government should travel in the next few years. Indeed, such a debate is inevitable, since return to the status quo is impossible. Simply restoring the budget programs cut by the President is not a feasible choice because of the large full employment budget deficits that such a course would entail. Given the necessity for major changes in direction, however, there is no reason to limit consideration to the magnitude or the direction of the changes proposed by the President. Each of the major decisions reflected in the 1974 budget can and should be questioned and debated.

The decision not to seek more revenue through tax reform or tax rate increases was by no means inevitable. As discussed in Chapter 3, substantial reform of the federal tax structure can be advocated as a means both of raising more revenue and of making the tax system fairer.

Similarly, the decision not to cut defense spending was far from inevitable. As discussed in Chapters 10 and 11, substantial savings in defense spending might be accomplished by pursuing current national security objectives more efficiently without modifying the objectives themselves. Even more substantial cuts would be possible if some basic assumptions about the role of the United States in Asia and the missions of its armed forces in Europe were reexamined and altered.

If both tax reform and defense cuts were carried out, substantial resources would be available for other uses. But then the fundamental questions about what role the federal government should be playing would be even more open to debate. How should the additional resources be used? What basic strategies should be followed and what specific programs undertaken?

Rejection of the administration's decisions about tax reform or defense spending would not necessarily imply rejection of the administration's view of the appropriate role of the federal government in domestic affairs. One could argue that the additional resources derived from tax reform or defense cuts should be devoted to additional revenue sharing, to tax rate reduction, or to both. There is nothing inconsistent in favoring cuts in *both* domestic and defense spending or in making the tax system more progressive through tax reform and simultaneously lowering tax rates. Nor is it inconsistent to argue both for more federal support for state and local governments and for less federal intervention in state and local decisions.

If more resources were made available, however, other strategies for using them would deserve consideration. As demonstrated in Chapter 3, a strong case can be made for giving priority to the redistribution of cash income and devoting additional resources to increasing cash transfers designed to reduce or eliminate poverty. Alternatively, as discussed in Chapter 4, an argument could be made for giving priority to helping people buy essential goods and services by channeling incremental resources into health insurance, housing allowances, and similar programs. Still another set of arguments could be marshaled in defense of categorical aids to state and local governments, especially the grants for social programs discussed in Chapter 5 and physical investments discussed in Chapter 6. These various strategies, translated into budget decisions over several years, would result in profound differences in the nature of the budget and the role of the federal government in national life in the last half of this decade.

The President in his 1974 budget has opened the way for serious discussion of the proper size and role of the federal government. The major objective of this book is to advance that discussion by laying out some feasible alternative budget options for the next five years—to illustrate the possibilities so that they can be examined and debated. Earlier chapters described alternative domestic strategies and the programs they imply, and suggested two major ways of increasing the resources available for carrying out those strategies. This chapter will put these building blocks together and show in broad outline several illustrative budgets for the years 1974–78. In developing these illustrative budgets we have made three alternative assumptions about the future availability of resources: (1) continuation of the "current posture" of no tax reform and no defense cuts; (2) a moderate increase in resources, attributable to moderate defense reductions and tax reform; and (3) a large increase in resources, attributable to major tax reform and defense cuts. For levels of resources corresponding to these assumptions we have developed budgets that reflect both the administration's view of the appropriate role of the federal government in domestic policy and alternatives to that view.

Several points should be kept in mind about these budget options. First, they are illustrations of the range of possibilities, not projections of what the authors believe is likely to happen. The alternatives were deliberately chosen to illustrate widely divergent outcomes in both the size and the role of the federal government. Compromise positions—a little of this and a little of that—are doubtless more likely to occur, but less helpful in clarifying the issues to be decided.

Second, out of the huge array of conceivable alternative resource levels and budget strategies, we have chosen a small number for display and discussion. We chose options that were in our judgment interesting, distinct, and capable of commanding substantial political support. Other people will no doubt make different judgments. We did not, for example, show any budget option that involved a general increase in tax rates because in our judgment such an increase is unlikely to command political support and because substantial revenues can be raised through tax reform. Similarly, we do not show budget options that involve cuts in broad categories of domestic spending beyond those already made in the President's 1974 budget proposals. Further cuts in major categories, such as cash transfers and grants for social programs, seem to us unlikely to have enough support to be worth discussing. Hence, the illustrative budgets shown for future years take projections of the President's 1974 domestic budget as a base and show alternative allocations of additions to that base. Within the broad categories, there is plenty of room for cutting or redirecting specific programs.

Finally, there are some parts of the federal budget we have not examined at all: civilian research and development, federal energy programs (both current and potential), space, law enforcement, and the general housekeeping functions of the government. A comprehensive review of the budget would require attention to these areas. In all the alternatives presented below, however, we have provided an "allowance for contingencies" that could accommodate program initiatives in these areas, should that be found desirable. Cuts in some of the programs we have not covered are also conceivable. For example, some would urge sharp reductions in funds for manned space flights or further cuts in agricultural price supports. Even drastic cuts in the areas we have not covered, however, would not produce budgetary savings large enough to change the basic shape of any of the alternatives.

Three Resource Levels

Two projections of the full employment budget through fiscal year 1978 are shown in Table 12-1. Federal revenues are the same in both projections—current tax laws are presumed to remain unchanged. Expenditures in the first projection assume the continuation of federal programs and policies as they existed before the administration's 1974 budget proposals, and they include the cost of the new programs, such as welfare reform and health insurance, that the President proposed last year. The second set of estimates (which are lower) project expenditures to 1978 under the programs and policies in the 1974 budget. They reflect the President's cuts in existing programs and his withdrawal of last year's new initiatives. The projected rise in expenditures over the next five years allows for no new programs and for no expan-

Table 12-1. Full Employment Revenues and Expenditures, before and after Budget Reductions Proposed by the Administration, Fiscal Years 1974–78

Billions of dollars

Budget items	1974	1975	1976	1977	1978
1. Before budget reductions					
Revenues	268	290	315	342	370
Expenditures	284	311	334	357	378
Existing programs	(280)	(303)	(325)	(347)	(368)
Proposed new programs	(4)	(8)	(9)	(10)	(10)
Surplus (+) or deficit (−)	−16	−21	−19	−15	−8
2. After budget reductions					
Revenues	268	290	315	342	370
Expenditures	267	288	308	329	348
Surplus (+) or deficit (−)	+1	+2	+7	+13	+22
Major expenditure categories[a]					
Defense, space, foreign affairs	89	91	99	107	113
Cash income maintenance[b]	79	90	96	103	111
Helping people buy essentials	27	30	33	35	37
Grants for social programs	14	15	15	15	16
Investment in physical environment	15	16	17	19	20
General revenue sharing	7	7	7	7	7
Subsidies to producer groups	6	6	6	6	6
Net interest	19	20	21	22	22
All other	21	17	18	20	21
Financial adjustments	−10	−4	−4	−4	−4

Source: Authors' estimates.
a. May not add to total expenditures because of rounding.
b. Adjusted to full employment level.

sion in existing programs beyond that necessary (1) to carry out the defense policies currently in force; (2) to meet the expansion in numbers of beneficiaries and workloads under existing domestic programs; and (3) to pay for projected moderate increases in wages and prices. This set of lower projections forms the base on which the budget alternatives shown in this chapter are built.[1]

Although economic growth can be expected to generate slightly more than $100 billion in additional revenues over the next four years, rising expenditures under current programs and policies would absorb four-fifths of this increment. Of the $80 billion rise in expenditures, more than $60 billion would come in three areas: defense, cash transfers, and programs to help people buy essentials.

1. Recent larger-than-anticipated price increases would raise both the revenues and the expenditures projected in Table 12-1 but would not change the basic budgetary situation depicted in the table. See Chapter 1, note 5, pp. 19–20.

We have chosen three different levels of resources to illustrate budget options.[2] The first of these is the projection of the 1974 budget outlined above. It implies continued adherence to two critical and controversial judgments that underlie the President's budget: (1) that the currently projected increase in defense spending is essential for national security; (2) that major revenue-yielding tax reforms would penalize economic growth too severely to warrant adoption. As the projections show, when changes in tax or defense policy are ruled out there is no room for the expansion of domestic programs, for the introduction of new programs, or for tax cuts in 1974 or 1975. Even by 1976, the growth of revenues relative to expenditures will yield only a modest fiscal dividend available for other uses. Only by 1977 and 1978 will significant leeway appear—$13 billion and $22 billion respectively. For purposes of convenient reference in later discussion, we have labeled this alternative the "current posture."

The second and third alternatives draw upon the analysis of tax reform in Chapter 3 and of defense budgets in Chapter 11 to suggest means of making additional budget resources available for discretionary use. The second alternative is based on the adoption of defense budget reductions and tax reforms sufficient to yield, in combination, $17 billion in additional resources by 1976 and $22 billion by 1978. More specifically, this alternative assumes that one-half of the revenue increase implied by the smaller tax reform package outlined in Chapter 3 is realized and that steps are taken along the lines presented in Chapter 11 to increase the efficiency of defense programs without fundamentally altering the roles and missions of the armed forces. This alternative we have called "moderate additional resources."

As a third possibility we have examined a very large reallocation of resources that might be achieved by greater reductions in defense than under alternative 2 and a major restructuring of the tax system. This alternative assumes realization of at least two-thirds of the revenue increase implied by the more ambitious tax reform package outlined in Chapter 3 and adoption of the larger defense budget reduction spelled

---

2. In all cases we have assumed a balanced full employment budget—expenditures are limited by the revenues obtained from a full employment economy. This does not imply that a balanced full employment budget is desirable under all economic conditions. In any particular year either a surplus or a deficit may be warranted as a means of restraining or stimulating the economy. But the kind of changes in revenues or expenditures needed to stabilize the economy in a particular future year should be made at that time. They cannot be built into long-run plans looking five years ahead.

Table 12-2. Excess of Receipts over Expenditures Available for Discretionary Use, Fiscal Years 1974–78

Billions of dollars

Option	1974	1975	1976	1977	1978
1. Current posture	1	2	7	13	22
2. Moderate additional resources	5	13	24	33	44
Current posture	1	2	7	13	22
Defense budget reductions	3	6	7	9	10
Tax reform	1	5	10	11	12
3. Large additional resources	9	21	40	60	77
Current posture	1	2	7	13	22
Defense budget reductions	6	12	18	23	25
Tax reform	2	7	15	24	30

Sources: Authors' estimates based on tables in Chapters 3 and 11.

out in Chapter 11, which includes not only efficiency measures but also changes in the roles and missions of U.S. forces in Asia and Europe. This alternative we have called "large additional resources."

Table 12-2 summarizes the budget resources that would be available under each of the three alternatives for discretionary use in domestic programs or for tax cuts. In all cases the data include projected price changes between now and the year in question. Moreover, the time lags that normally occur in translating legislative or executive decisions into actual changes in expenditures have been taken into account. Similarly, the tax reforms have been phased in over the next few years; the reforms in the smaller package become fully effective by January 1, 1975, and in the larger package by January 1, 1977.[3] As a result of these time lags, even the third alternative, which contemplates major changes in the tax structure and the defense budget, provides only a modest leeway in fiscal 1974.

In some of the specific examples given below, part of the additional funds is used to reduce tax rates. Rather than show this as an offset to the tax reforms, we have kept the gross revenue yield from reforms as a *source* of additional resources and listed general tax cuts as a *use* of those resources.

For each of the three levels of resource availability there is a host of potential ways in which the discretionary funds might be used— reducing taxes, restoring funds to programs cut by the President in the 1974 budget, expanding existing programs, or initiating new ones.

3. In both packages constructive realization of capital gains at death does not become fully effective until January 1, 1977.

Within each of these categories the possibilities are numerous. The alternatives outlined below, though limited in number, illustrate major potential differences both in the overall size of the federal sector and in the various strategies or roles the government might pursue.

Options under the Current Posture

For the next two budget years, there are for all practical purposes no discretionary funds available under this alternative. Reasonable planning must also assume that a projection based on no expansion in existing programs and no initiation of new ones is too austere to be adhered to with complete fidelity. Some unforeseen contingencies requiring federal funds are bound to arise and some modest increases in existing programs will surely occur even in a budget dedicated to holding the line. As a consequence, in determining what funds are available for major new purposes, an allowance for contingencies must first be set aside. Although under the current posture some free resources ($7 billion) do begin to appear by 1976, a reasonable allowance for contingencies would absorb at least half of this, leaving only a very small amount available for other purposes. Thus not until 1977 would any truly interesting possibilities open up. Looking ahead to that period, we have examined two variants of the current posture.

VARIANT 1: A SMALLER ROLE FOR THE FEDERAL GOVERNMENT. This approach reflects the view that the federal government is already doing enough and the fiscal dividend ultimately yielded by economic growth ought to be used principally for tax reductions. Priority in the use of available resources would be given to tax cuts and remaining resources would be used to expand general revenue sharing, giving state and local governments the major voice in determining how the funds are to be used (see Table 12-3).

Table 12-3. Use of Available Resources under Current Posture Option, Variant 1, Fiscal Years 1974–78

Billions of dollars

Item	1974	1975	1976	1977	1978
Available resources	1	2	7	13	22
Used for:					
Personal and corporation tax cut	0	0	4	5	12
Allowance for contingencies	1	2	3	3	4
Expanded general revenue sharing	0	0	0	5	6

Source: Authors' estimates.

With this approach, personal income taxes could be reduced by about 3 percent in 1976 and by another 4 percent in 1978. An expansion of general revenue sharing could begin in 1977, almost doubling the current program. The addition to general revenue sharing could be made simply by increasing the funds available under the current programs or by using a different distribution formula to emphasize one or the other of the various objectives discussed in Chapter 7.

Although the contingency allowance would permit some small new initiatives on the part of the federal government (an increase in research and development for energy resources, for example), this alternative basically foresees nothing significant in the way of domestic program expansion over the next four years.

VARIANT 2: INCREASE IN DOMESTIC PROGRAMS. This alternative, like the one above, reflects the judgment that other priorities do not warrant changes in current defense programs or in the tax structure. But it would give the expansion of domestic programs priority over tax cuts in the use of the fiscal dividend. The problem is that significant new resources would not become available for this purpose until fiscal 1977.

Clearly, given the current tax structure and defense policies, it would not be possible to restore even a small part of the President's proposed budget cuts in existing programs in the next two years (see Table 12-4). Only by 1978 would there be leeway for full restoration, and even this assumes no requirements in the interim for additional federal spending for any other purpose. If the cuts were not restored, some new program initiatives could be undertaken by 1977. But even then the amounts available would not be very large. By 1977, for example, it would be possible to launch a new health insurance program costing $11 billion along the lines discussed in Chapter 4. And by 1978 a program of federal aid to equalize educational expenditures among

Table 12-4. Impact on Available Resources of Restoring Funds Cut by the 1974 Budget, Fiscal Years 1974–78
Billions of dollars

Item	1974	1975	1976	1977	1978
Available resources	1	2	7	13	22
Restoration of funds	12	15	17	18	20
Resulting deficit (−) or surplus (+)	−11	−13	−10	−5	+2

Source: Authors' estimates.

and within states, as outlined in Chapter 5, could also be undertaken. But these two initiatives alone, together with a small contingency allowance, would entirely absorb the resources available. Nothing else would be possible.

While a number of other combinations of federal programs might be undertaken, the chief lesson to be drawn from this variant is that realistically, without changes in tax structure or defense spending, there is little room for initiative in the domestic budget before 1977, and even then the leeway is modest.

Moderate Additional Resources

To provide any budgetary resources for significant discretionary use before 1977, and to have the kinds of sums necessary to adopt more than one or two major program initiatives at any time in the next five years, the current posture on the tax structure and the defense budget would have to be abandoned. One moderate alternative would be the adoption of tax reforms yielding one-half of the revenue gained in the smaller tax reform package outlined in Chapter 3 and making the efficiency-oriented defense cuts discussed in Chapter 11. Together, these two policy changes would add only a small amount of resources in 1974 but would increase the total discretionary funds by $22 billion a year in 1978. Combining these sums with those available under the current posture would provide a total of $44 billion. We have developed four different variants of how these funds might be used. Each emphasizes, though not exclusively, one major strategy.

VARIANT 1: ADMINISTRATION APPROACH PLUS MORE MONEY. This variant carries out the basic philosophy of (1) reducing the size of the federal government and (2) favoring approaches that minimize federal control over how funds are spent. The newly available budgetary resources could be used as follows:

1. Cut personal and corporation income taxes by an amount equal in 1975 to the yield from the tax reform, and go beyond this to provide some net tax relief after 1976. When fully in effect, this would mean a 9 percent cut in personal and corporation taxes. It would mean higher effective rates for those who now take advantage of the tax preferences removed by the reform but lower rates for most people.

2. Provide a credit on the federal income tax to offset property taxes for low-income elderly people (see pages 63–68, above).

3. Raise the minimum Aid to Families with Dependent Children

Table 12-5. Use of Moderate Additional Resources, Variant 1, Fiscal Years 1974–78
Billions of dollars

Item	1974	1975	1976	1977	1978
Available resources	5	13	24	33	44
Used for:					
Personal and corporation tax cut	0	5	15	21	22
Property tax relief for the elderly	1	1	1	1.5	1.5
Raise minimum AFDC benefit	0	0	1	1.5	2
Expanded general revenue sharing	2	4	4	5	7.5
Educational equalization grant	0	0	0	0	6
Allowance for contingencies	2	3	3	4	5

Source: Authors' estimates.

(AFDC) benefit to $2,600 (for a family of four) in 1976 and to $2,800 in 1978, paying for this completely with federal money. Food stamps would be maintained, with a value of about $900 to a family of four.[4] The combination of welfare and food stamps would guarantee a minimum of $3,500 for AFDC recipients in 1976, but no new benefits would be available for the working poor. States would be required to supplement the federal program to prevent a reduction in benefits where, in combination with food stamps, they exceeded $3,500, and the federal government would share 30 percent of the supplementation cost (pages 89–90).

4. Gradually expand general revenue sharing from the current $6 billion to $7 billion to more than $14 billion in 1978.

5. Undertake a program of educational equalization grants to states to go into effect in 1978, but without a maintenance-of-effort provision (pages 201–06). The federal government would pay 10 percent of educational outlays in the average state. This program is likely to induce some reduction in local property taxes.

These proposals are shown in Table 12-5. In general their basic thrust is consistent with the administration's philosophy of holding down the size of the federal government and providing cash to persons and to state and local governments with relatively few federal strings attached.

VARIANT 2: CONCENTRATE ON REDISTRIBUTING INCOME THROUGH CASH TRANSFERS, TAX CUTS AND PAYROLL TAX REFORMS FOR LOW-WAGE EARNERS, AND SOCIAL SECURITY BENEFIT

4. Throughout this chapter it is assumed that benefits under all the various cash and in-kind transfers are periodically raised to keep pace with price increases.

INCREASES. This approach might be described as emphasizing income redistribution while minimizing the degree of federal intervention. Three-fifths of the available resources (after allowance for contingencies) would be used for cash income redistribution. Other programs would be expanded principally as they were necessary to fit into a cash transfer approach (day care so mothers could work, manpower training vouchers, and so forth) or as a minimal substitute for certain kinds of programs left out of this approach (restore Medicare and Medicaid funds and continue financing certain public health services because no health insurance program is made available). More specifically, under this variant the following measures would be instituted:

1. A universal negative income tax with a minimum guarantee of $4,000 and a marginal tax rate of 50 percent would be adopted, beginning on January 1, 1975; food stamps would be abolished at that time. State supplementation for current AFDC beneficiaries, with 30 percent federal matching, would be required (pages 80–85).

2. A personal exemption of $750 and a $1,300 standard deduction would be allowed on both employer and employee payroll taxes, phasing out as income rose (pages 57–63). This would raise the take-home pay of the low-wage earner. The cost would be financed by a transfer of general revenues to the social security trust fund rather than by increases in payroll tax rates or increases in the wage ceiling.

3. Starting in 1977, taxes on low incomes would be reduced by increasing the minimum standard deduction from its present $1,300 to $2,300. This would raise the level below which a family of four pays no income taxes from $4,300 to $5,300, and would reduce taxes principally for families earning incomes of less than $20,000.

4. Social security benefits would be raised by 5 percent in 1976 and another 5 percent in 1978. Since the current program already provides for automatic adjustments to meet increases in the cost of living, the increases proposed under this variant would be on top of such adjustments. The larger benefits would be financed by increases in payroll taxes. Table 12-6 shows the availability and distribution of resources after including these payroll tax increases.

5. A "structured" public service employment program—one designed to provide career public service jobs for disadvantaged workers —would be introduced in 1975 and expanded in 1978 (pages 90–94).

6. In the absence of a health insurance program with comprehen-

Table 12-6. Use of Moderate Additional Resources, Variant 2, Fiscal Years 1974–78
Billions of dollars

Item	1974	1975	1976	1977	1978
Available resources	**5**	**13**	**24**	**33**	**44**
(Including payroll tax increase)	(5)	(13)	(27)	(36.5)	(51)
Used for:					
Income redistribution (from general revenues)	**0**	**6**	**15**	**21**	**24**
Universal negative income tax	0	5	9	9	9.5
Payroll tax reform	0	0	5	5	5
Tax cut for low-income families	0	0	0	6	7
Structured public employment	0	1	1	1	2
(Increase in social security benefits)	(0)	(0)	(3)	(3.5)	(7)
(Total, including social security)	(0)	(6)	(18)	(24.5)	(31)
Helping people buy essentials	**1.5**	**2**	**4**	**5**	**7.5**
Restore Medicare and Medicaid funds	1.5	1.5	1.5	2	2
Child care vouchers	0	0.5	1.5	2	4
Manpower training vouchers	0	0	1	1	1.5
Grants for social programs	**0.5**	**1.5**	**1.5**	**2**	**5.5**
Health services and development	0.5	0.5	0.5	1	1.5
Compensatory education	0	1	1	1	4
Investment in physical environment	**0.5**	**0.5**	**0.5**	**1**	**1.5**
Urban mass transit	0.5	0.5	0.5	1	1.5
Allowance for contingencies	**2**	**3**	**3**	**4**	**5**

Source: Authors' estimates. Figures may not add to totals because of rounding.

sive benefits for the poor, the proposed increase in deductibles and coinsurance under Medicare and Medicaid would *not* be enacted. Funds for health service delivery programs which were reduced in the 1974 budget would be restored.

7. A day care voucher program would be introduced in 1975, at first just for children under six in single-parent families; eligibility would be gradually expanded until, in 1978, it covered such children in all families with working mothers. The amount of the subsidy would correspond to the "low-cost" plan outlined in Chapter 4 (pages 166–68). Manpower training vouchers would be introduced in 1976 and gradually expanded also (pages 227–32).

8. The compensatory education component of the education special revenue sharing program would be enlarged, beginning in 1975, and expanded further in 1978 to provide an effective grant of about $400 per disadvantaged child. The urban mass transit program would be redesigned along the lines described in Chapter 6 and moderately expanded (pages 248–52).

Except for the urban mass transit program, virtually all of the available resources in this variant are used for redistribution, and as pointed out earlier, most of the redistribution would take place through taxes and cash transfers. Low-income and lower-middle-income working people in particular would benefit under this variant (compared with other variants). The universal negative income tax with its 50 percent marginal tax rate would provide benefits to working families that had incomes up to the $8,000 level; the payroll tax reform and the reduction of taxes on low incomes would also help this group.

VARIANT 3: EMPHASIS ON HELPING PEOPLE BUY ESSENTIALS. Like the preceding variant, this one stresses redistribution, but cash transfers are not the principal means. Instead, it concentrates most of the available resources on helping people buy essential goods and services produced in the private market. AFDC would be reformed, but the aid would be at a much lower level than in the previous alternative. In the case of services such as day care, manpower training, higher education, housing, and health care, people would receive vouchers or insurance so that they could choose where to buy the services they needed. The alternative strategy of providing these services through federal support of public institutions would not be followed.

More specifically, as shown in Table 12-7, this variant would use the available resources as follows:

1. Minimum AFDC benefits would be raised to $2,600 in 1976 and to $2,800 in 1978. State supplementation would be required. Food stamps would be continued and appropriations increased, so that a larger proportion of the eligible population could take advantage of them. A structured public employment program would be initiated and gradually expanded.

2. A national health insurance system would be initiated in mid-1975 with income-related deductibles and coinsurance, along the lines of the illustrative plan described in Chapter 4 ("plan 1," discussed on pages 124–26). In the period before the introduction of the insurance system, the cuts in Medicare and Medicaid proposed by the administration would *not* be made.[5]

5. Once health insurance was introduced, the current income tax deductions for medical expenses would be eliminated, and federal revenue would increase. The costs shown in Table 12-7 are net of this revenue gain. The increase in federal expenditures, therefore, would be larger than the amount shown in the table, but revenues would also be larger.

Table 12-7. Use of Moderate Additional Resources, Variant 3, Fiscal Years 1974–78
Billions of dollars

Item	1974	1975	1976	1977	1978
Available resources	**5**	**13**	**24**	**33**	**44**
Used for:					
Income redistribution	**0**	**1**	**2**	**3**	**4**
Raise minimum AFDC benefit	0	0	1	1.5	2
Structured public employment	0	1	1	1.5	2
Helping people buy essentials	**1.5**	**7**	**17**	**23.5**	**30**
Health insurance	1.5	1.5	9.5	10	11
Food stamps	0	1	1	1.5	2
Housing allowance[a]	0	1.5	1.5	4.5	5
Child care vouchers	0	1.5	3.5	5.5	7.5
Manpower training vouchers	0	0.5	0.5	1	1.5
Basic opportunity grants	0	1	1	1	3
Grants for social programs	**1.5**	**2**	**1.5**	**2**	**4**
Health development	0.5	0.5	0.5	0.5	0.5
Urban community development	0.5	1.0	0.5	0	0
Community action programs	0.5	0.5	0.5	0.5	0.5
Compensatory education	0	0	0	1	3
Investment in physical environment	**0**	**0.5**	**0.5**	**0.5**	**1**
Urban mass transit	0	0.5	0.5	0.5	1
Allowance for contingencies	**2**	**3**	**3**	**4**	**5**

Source: Authors' estimates. Figures may not add to totals because of rounding.
a. The elderly would receive a larger housing allowance.

3. A small housing allowance would be introduced in 1975 and expanded in 1977 to a medium-sized allowance (pages 138–44).

4. The Basic Opportunity Grant program for higher education would be enlarged starting in 1975 (pages 155–59). Manpower training vouchers would be initiated in the same year. Vouchers for child care would be introduced in 1975 and thereafter expanded fairly rapidly, so that by 1978 eligibility would be extended to all working mothers.

5. The community action program would be restored, grants for health development and for the training of minority health personnel would be undertaken, and additional funds made available during the transition to the new urban community revenue sharing program. Grants for urban mass transit would be redesigned and later expanded. The compensatory education component of education special revenue sharing would be expanded starting in 1977.

Under this approach, by 1978 an AFDC family of four with no other income would receive cash, housing allowance, and food stamps worth about $4,400—slightly higher than the $4,000 guaranteed under the negative income tax in variant 2. The value of health insurance would add a substantial amount to this minimum income. The working poor and lower-middle-income groups would receive no additional cash transfers under this approach, but would benefit from the expansion of the food stamp program, the housing allowance, day care, health insurance, and related voucher programs.

The approach in variant 3 does involve more federal intervention than variant 2—instead of simply providing cash to people, the federal government would earmark its assistance for particular goods and services. Adoption of this alternative would move the country toward a society in which the distribution of goods and services was split into two parts. For one set of goods and services—principally housing, health care, food, child care, and access to education and training—everybody would be assured of at least a reasonable minimum. To some extent, therefore, the distribution of these goods would be divorced from the distribution of income. The distribution of all other goods and services among the population would continue to be governed by the distribution of income. At the same time, this approach would allow people maximum freedom to secure the subsidized goods and services wherever they chose. In that sense, it would be an interventionist approach on the demand side of the market but not on the supply side.

VARIANT 4: CONCENTRATE ON FEDERAL GRANTS FOR SOCIAL PROGRAMS. This variant differs from its predecessors in two ways: it emphasizes the provision of public services by the government, and it emphasizes delivery through public or nonprofit institutions rather than the private market. Thus many of the essential services that the federal government would support through voucher schemes under variant 3 would be supported through grants to public or nonprofit institutions in variant 4—child care, manpower training, and student aid for higher education are the chief examples. Some provision is made for improving the current welfare system through a family assistance plan. Generally, however, the scope of federal assistance given directly to people, either in cash or in kind, is much less under this variant than under either variant 2 or variant 3 (see Table 12-8).

1. A family assistance plan, for which all families with children would be eligible, would start January 1, 1975. The plan would incorporate a minimum guarantee of $3,000 and a marginal tax rate of

Table 12-8. Use of Moderate Additional Resources, Variant 4, Fiscal Years 1974–78
Billions of dollars

Item	1974	1975	1976	1977	1978
Available resources	5	13	24	33	44
Used for:					
Income redistribution	0	2.5	4	4.5	6
Family assistance plan at $3,000	0	2	3.5	3.5	4
Structured public employment	0	0.5	0.5	1	2
Helping people buy essentials	1.5	1.5	3	3.5	4
Restore Medicare and Medicaid funds	1.5	1.5	1.5	2	2
Small housing allowance	0	0	1.5	1.5	2
Grants for social programs	1.5	5.5	12.5	18.5	25.5
Compensatory education	0	1	3	3.5	4
Health services and development	0.5	0.5	1.5	2	3
Targeted urban development	0.5	1	1.5	2.5	4
Manpower training grants	0	0.5	1	1	1.5
Social service	0	0.5	1.5	2	3
Child care institutional grants	0	1.5	2.5	5	6
Community action programs	0.5	0.5	0.5	0.5	0.5
Aid to institutions of higher education	0	0	1	2	3.5
Investment in physical environment	0	0.5	2	2.5	3
Urban mass transit	0	0.5	1	1	1
Waste treatment	0	0	1	1.5	2
Allowance for contingencies	2	3	3	4	5

Source: Authors' estimates. Figures may not add to totals because of rounding.

50 percent; state supplementation, with federal assistance, would be required. Food stamps would be abolished for all of those eligible for the family assistance plan. A small housing allowance would be introduced and integrated into the family assistance plan. In total, for a family of four with no other income, the two schemes would provide a minimum income of about $3,300 by 1977. A structured public employment program would be initiated in 1975 and gradually expanded.

2. Since no national health insurance is foreseen under this variant, the funds for Medicare and Medicaid that the administration has proposed to reduce would be restored, and federal support for neighborhood health centers, hospital-based ambulatory facilities, and other health services would be sharply expanded.

3. Support for manpower training, child care, and higher education would be enlarged but, as outlined above, through federal grants to state and local governments and nonprofit institutions rather than through vouchers.

4. The revenue sharing grants for urban community development would be redesigned along the lines suggested in Chapter 5—federal requirements for targeting some of the grants to low-income neighborhoods would be introduced and the principle of maximum cash flow would be applied (pages 215-17). The program would be expanded over the period. The day care component of social service grants to states would be transferred to the expanded child care program, and grants for other services would be increased. The compensatory component of education special revenue sharing would be steadily enlarged, until in 1978 it provided effective grants of about $400 per disadvantaged child. The support grants for community action agencies, terminated in the 1974 budget, would be restored (pages 252-57).

5. Urban mass transit grants would be redesigned along the lines discussed in Chapter 6 and increased in size. Grants for municipal waste treatment plants would be enlarged to a point about halfway between the program now contemplated by the administration and the level authorized last year by the Congress.

All four variants foresee a modest reduction in the share of federal expenditures devoted to defense. All imply some redistribution of income through tax reform. In addition, the expenditure increases in variants 2, 3, and 4 are all heavily redistributive in nature. These three variants differ much more in method than in objective. Variant 2 relies on a redistribution of cash income. Decisions about how to spend the money are left to the individual and few additional resources are devoted to grants that change the ways in which private or public institutions deliver goods and services. Variant 3 also redistributes income, but the federal government decides what goods and services it is important to provide for the poor and near-poor. The techniques using insurance, vouchers, and housing allowances, however, imply a willingness to rely principally on existing institutions to deliver those goods and services. The final variant goes one step further by allowing for substantial federal intervention not only in determining what goods and services it is important to redistribute, but also in specifying, through its grants, what institutions are to deliver them and how. Moreover, compared with other variants, this one emphasizes the improvement of opportunities for the disadvantaged through public services—education, urban development, and social services.

The variants lie along a spectrum. Variant 1 reflects a preference for private over public consumption and for local over federal decision making. Variant 2 maintains government spending but minimizes the inefficiencies and difficulties that accompany detailed federal involvement in the demand for and supply of goods and services; it does little to improve the current institutions by which goods and services are now delivered. Variant 3 implies a judgment that the benefits of federal intervention are worth the costs on the demand side but not on the supply side—in other words, the federal government should have a voice in determining what is bought but not how it is supplied. Variant 4, at the other end of the spectrum, is based on a judgment that changes in the institutions supplying goods and services are critical, that redistribution in cash or in kind is not enough, and that the potential benefits of intervention on the supply side, through the grant system, outweigh the possible costs in red tape and complexity. While several of the chapters on domestic programs have discussed how federal intervention could be undertaken more efficiently, the basic choices posed here still have to be made, after the benefits of intervention have been weighed against its costs.

Large Additional Resources

Another set of illustrative alternatives has been developed to show the implications of a much more ambitious change in priorities than that contemplated in the options discussed above. Chapter 11 outlined several alternative defense budgets. One of those was based on a redefinition of American national security interests in Asia, a change in defense planning for Europe, the phasing out of land-based strategic missiles, and the achievement of a number of economies in the defense structure, particularly in the use of manpower. The adoption of these changes in military planning would lead to substantial reductions in defense spending, bringing it by 1978 some $25 billion below the levels implied in current policies and programs.

Chapter 3 identifies a comprehensive series of tax reforms, the largest of which would result in major additions to federal receipts from taxes on personal income and corporation profits. Fuller taxation of capital gains (including constructive realization at death), elimination of deductions for mortgage interest and property taxes, and substantially increased taxation of preference income are the largest items on the list in terms of revenues yielded. If all the reforms were undertaken, the revenue gain would indeed be sizable, amounting to approximately $27 billion in 1974 and rising to about $45 billion in 1978. For purposes of illustrating a major change in national priorities, we have assumed that a combination of reforms yielding approximately two-thirds of this large "package" is adopted. Together with the savings in defense spending identified above, these actions would add $55 billion to the amount of discretionary resources available by 1978 over and above the $22 billion built into the baseline projections.

As explained in Chapter 11, changes in defense policies affect the level of spending only after a time lag, which in the case of many components of the defense budget is quite long. And even if the full roster of tax reforms were enacted in this session of Congress, which is highly improbable, they would produce little revenue in fiscal 1974. We have assumed that the reforms are introduced gradually over four years, making their first full impact in fiscal 1977. For these reasons, even though the added resources made available by the assumed changes in defense policies and tax structure are ultimately quite large, they provide only modest amounts for discretionary use in 1974 and 1975.

As in the "moderate resources" case, we have constructed four widely different patterns of how the discretionary resources might be used. Again, the variants outlined below differ partly in the objectives they imply for the federal government and partly in the degree of federal intervention. The first variant would use the bulk of the added resources for a major tax cut and for a large expansion in general revenue sharing. The remaining three variants would stress redistribution, but would differ in the degree to which the federal government became involved in specific decisions about the demand and supply of particular goods and services. Since more funds are available than in the "moderate resources" case, each variant envisages programs dealing with both public and private goods and services. Variant 2 stresses the redistribution of income and the adoption of programs to equalize the distribution of public services in ways that minimize federal control over how the funds are used. Variant 3 emphasizes helping people buy essentials through insurance, vouchers, and other similar techniques, and also provides grants to equalize the distribution of public services, with somewhat greater federal control over the uses of grant funds. Variant 4—the most interventionist—makes essential services available principally through grants to selected institutions and similarly stresses the provision of public services through specific grant programs. In all the variants, however, the availability of relatively large additional resources makes it possible to emphasize a particular strategy while providing funds for other areas. Thus variant 2, which emphasizes cash transfers, incorporates a health insurance plan. The variants are therefore not as conceptually distinct as those in the "moderate resources" case, but they still differ substantially among themselves and represent quite divergent strategic choices.

VARIANT 1 : LARGE TAX CUT AND A LARGE EXPANSION IN REVE- NUE SHARING. This is the "big brother" of the first variant outlined in the previous section. Personal and corporation tax rates would be cut sufficiently to offset the yield of the tax reforms. A large expansion in general revenue sharing and educational equalization grants would absorb another sizable fraction of the added resources; the remainder would be used for a small health insurance system and a family assistance plan (see Table 12-9).

1. Tax cuts would keep pace with the increasing yield from tax re- form. Ultimately a 12 percent reduction in individual income and corporation profits taxes would be possible. The corporation tax rates could be cut from 48 to 42.5 percent. Top bracket rates in the individ- ual income tax could be reduced to 50 percent and then other rates cut, by 3 percentage points in the lower brackets and 2 percentage points in the remaining ones. The new bracket rates would range from 11 to 50 percent (the present range is 14 to 70 percent).

2. A family assistance plan with a minimum guarantee of $3,000 and a 50 percent marginal tax rate would be introduced on January 1, 1975.

Table 12-9. Use of Large Additional Resources, Variant 1, Fiscal Years 1974–78
Billions of dollars

Item	1974	1975	1976	1977	1978
Available resources	**9**	**21**	**40**	**60**	**77**
Used for:					
Personal and corporation tax cut	2	7	15	24	30
Family assistance plan	0	2	6	6	6
Health insurance	1.5	2	4	4	5
Educational equalization	3	3	6	12	17
General revenue sharing	0	4	6	10	14
Allowance for contingencies	2	3	3	4	5

Source: Authors' estimates. Figures may not add to totals because of rounding.

3. A small health insurance program emphasizing protection against catastrophic illness would be inaugurated on January 1, 1976. The proposed increases in Medicare and Medicaid deductibles and coinsurance would be rescinded.

4. An educational equalization program would be introduced in 1974, and gradually expanded to the point at which in 1978 the federal government was matching 35 percent of state and local education tax efforts. No maintenance of-effort provision would be included; as a consequence, part of the federal grants would undoubtedly be used for property tax relief.

5. General revenue sharing would be sharply enlarged, so that by 1978 the federal government would be contributing $20 billion to state and local government revenues. The expanded program would use the same distribution formula as that applied in the current program.

Under this variant the total yield of the tax system would remain unchanged, but it would become significantly more progressive. Both the educational equalization and the general revenue sharing program, through the current distribution formula, would result in a modest redistribution of resources favoring poorer state and local governments, and in combination the two measures would undoubtedly lead to a substantial reduction of property taxes. Middle-income groups would receive protection against catastrophic illness, would experience some reduction in state and local taxes, and would gain from the tax reduction. Poor persons in families with children would receive (by 1976) a minimum income guarantee of $3,900, with a combination of food stamps and the family assistance plan, and the low-income worker would benefit from the 50 percent marginal tax rate provisions in the plan.

Quite different approaches to budgetary futures are presented in the remaining three variants. In all of them, substantial sums would be raised through tax reform, affecting principally upper-income taxpayers and corporations, and none would be returned in tax cuts for those taxpayers. Some reduction in business investment might be anticipated in response to these changes, but we do not have any reliable means of forecasting the magnitude of the reaction. A moderate reduction that lowered the ratio of net business investment to national income by, say, one percentage point would have only a small impact on the rate of economic growth[6] and no serious repercussions. A large reduction in investment outlays would have more serious consequences for future living standards. It would be possible to lower the probability of this by the choice of tax reforms adopted. The "large additional resources" alternative assumes that not all of the reforms outlined in Chapter 3 would be adopted. Enough would be enacted to produce revenues equal to two-thirds of the total. Within that framework, it would be possible to leave the investment credit intact and to include in the tax reform legislation a provision setting a 50 percent ceiling on the highest individual income tax bracket (lower than the 70 percent maximum now applicable to other than earned income). These adjustments, combined with the gradual phase-in of the tax reforms, should substantially soften or, in the view of many, eliminate the impact of the program on investment and growth.

Those who wish to see the kinds of resource shifts outlined below but are still fearful of the effect of a large tax reform package on investment, even in the version outlined above, would have to propose other means of raising the resources, which presumably would be through a general tax increase. One way of generating the budgetary funds included in the "large additional resources" alternative, for example, would be to cut the tax reforms in this alternative by half—to yield $15 billion by 1978 ($9 billion at 1974 income levels) —and substitute a 9 percent increase in individual income taxes, under which all groups with taxable income paid some part of the added tax bill.

VARIANT 2: EMPHASIS ON INCOME REDISTRIBUTION AND EQUAL- IZATION OF STATE AND LOCAL PUBLIC SERVICES. Table 12-10 summarizes the elements of this approach, which are outlined below.

1. A universal negative income tax program would be introduced, along the lines discussed in Chapter 3. The minimum guarantee for a family of four would be set at $3,600 in 1975 and raised to $4,400 in 1977; a marginal tax of 50 percent would be applied against earnings. Personal exemptions and deductions would be applied to both the employer and employee portions of the payroll tax and the cost financed from general revenues. Individual income taxes for people

6. Edward F. Denison, in a study of long-term U.S. growth, has estimated that a 1 percent reduction in the ratio of investment to national income would slow the rate of growth by one-tenth of one percent a year. Edward F. Denison, *The Sources of Economic Growth in the United States and the Alternatives Before Us*, Supplementary Paper 13 (Committee for Economic Development, 1962), p. 277.

with low and moderate incomes would be reduced by raising the minimum standard deduction to $2,000 in 1975 and to $2,500 by 1977 (which would make incomes below $5,500 tax free for a family of four). Social security benefits, in real terms, would be raised by 10 percent in 1975 and another 5 percent in 1977, the increase to be financed by added payroll taxes. Manpower training vouchers would be introduced and the basic opportunity grants for higher education enlarged. A structured public service employment program would be initiated in 1975 and, if successful, expanded gradually throughout the period.

2. A small health insurance program, designed principally to give protection against catastrophic medical expenses, would be initiated in 1976, and in 1978 expanded into a more generous system with low or zero deductibles for the poor. Until that latter stage was reached, the funds for Medicare and Medicaid cut in the 1974 budget would be restored.

3. An educational equalization program, with strong redistributive

Table 12-10. Use of Large Additional Resources, Variant 2, Fiscal Years 1974–78
Billions of dollars

Item	1974	1975	1976	1977	1978
Available resources	**9**	**21**	**40**	**60**	**77**
(Including payroll tax increase)	(9)	(26)	(46)	(70)	(88)
Used for:					
Income redistribution (from general revenues)	**0**	**8**	**14.5**	**31**	**32**
Universal negative income tax	0	5	5.5	15	15
Payroll tax reform	0	0	5	5	5
Tax cut for low-income families	0	2.5	3	9.5	10
Structured public employment	0	0.5	1	1.5	2
(Increase in social security benefits)	(0)	(5)	(6)	(10)	(11)
(Total, including social security)	(0)	(13)	(20.5)	(41)	(43)
Helping people buy essentials	**1.5**	**3**	**6.5**	**7.5**	**15**
Health insurance	1.5	1.5	4.5	5	11
Manpower training vouchers	0	0.5	0.5	1	1.5
Basic opportunity grants	0	1	1.5	1.5	2.5
Grants for social programs	**6**	**7**	**12**	**14**	**19**
Health services and development	0.5	0.5	0.5	0.5	0.5
Community action programs	0.5	0.5	0.5	0.5	0.5
Educational equalization	5	6	11	13	18
General revenue sharing (compensatory distribution formula)	**0**	**0**	**4**	**4**	**6**
Allowance for contingencies	**2**	**3**	**3**	**4**	**5**

Source: Authors' estimates. Figures may not add to totals because of rounding.

features and maintenance-of-effort provisions, would be introduced in 1974 and expanded to the point where, by 1978, the federal government matched 35 percent of the state and local tax effort devoted to elementary and secondary education. A new component, along the lines described at the end of Chapter 7, would be added to general revenue sharing—the funds would be distributed according to the number of poor persons residing in a jurisdiction, weighted by the per capita public expenditures of that jurisdiction.

In this variant the major stress is placed on redistributing income through cash transfers and the tax system and on the equalization of public services provided by different political jurisdictions. Of the $88 billion in additional resources (counting the social security tax increase), $66 billion would be used for these purposes. Strong maintenance-of-effort provisions in the educational equalization program would prevent the federal grants from being used to any great extent for state or local tax relief. Low-income families would receive a substantial minimum income guarantee but one that would still fall short of the poverty line by about 10 percent. The value of health insurance, however, would make up for this gap. Wage earners in the lower-middle-income range would receive substantial benefits as well, through the operation of the low marginal tax rates in the negative income tax plan, the payroll tax reform, the income tax cut, the health insurance system, and the voucher plan for manpower training and higher education. The substantial redistribution of public and private goods and services contemplated in this variant would be accompanied by little federal intervention in how the funds were used or how the goods and services were supplied. Redistribution with a minimum of federal intervention is the theme of this variant.

VARIANT 3: PRIMARY EMPHASIS ON HELPING PEOPLE BUY ESSENTIALS WITH SOME ADDED RESOURCES FOR TARGETED GRANT PROGRAMS. This variant proposes very limited welfare reform and concentrates redistributive efforts on helping people buy essentials. It would also put resources into grant programs explicitly aimed at providing specific public services for the disadvantaged. A modest amount of the added funds would be devoted to transportation and the environment (modest in terms of the total resources available, but fairly substantial in terms of the funds now budgeted for those programs). Table 12-11 summarizes the elements of this variant.

1. A family assistance plan, with a $2,800 minimum and a 50 per-

Table 12-11. Use of Large Additional Resources, Variant 3, Fiscal Years 1974–78
Billions of dollars

Item	1974	1975	1976	1977	1978
Available resources	**9**	**21**	**40**	**60**	**77**
Used for:					
Income redistribution	**0**	**0.5**	**3.5**	**6**	**7.5**
Family assistance plan	0	0	2.5	4.5	5
Structured public employment	0	0.5	1.0	1.5	2.5
Helping people buy essentials	**3.5**	**13**	**25**	**37**	**47**
Large health insurance plan	1.5	5	10.5	19.5	21
Medium housing allowance[a]	0	2	4.5	4.5	5
Food stamps	1	1	1.5	2	2
Manpower vouchers	0.5	1	1.5	2	3
Basic opportunity grants	0.5	1	2	3	5
Child care vouchers	0	3	5	6	11
Grants for social programs	**3**	**3.5**	**7**	**9.5**	**14**
Compensatory education	1.5	1.5	2.5	3.5	6
Targeted urban development	0.5	1	3.5	5	6
Community action programs	0.5	0.5	0.5	0.5	1
Health services and development	0.5	0.5	0.5	0.5	1
Investment in physical environment	**0**	**1**	**1.5**	**3**	**4**
Urban mass transit	0	0.5	0.5	1	1.5
Waste treatment	0	0.5	1	2	2.5
Allowance for contingencies	**2**	**3**	**3**	**4**	**5**

Source: Authors' estimates. Figures may not add to totals because of rounding.
a. The elderly would receive a larger housing allowance.

cent tax rate, would be adopted. Food stamps would be continued and expanded to reach a larger proportion of poor families. A medium-sized housing allowance would be introduced on January 1, 1975. For the elderly, who would not benefit from the family assistance plan, a larger housing allowance would be provided.

2. On January 1, 1975, the smaller of the two major health insurance plans outlined in Chapter 4 would be initiated. In 1977 a much more generous plan with even lower deductibles and coinsurance would go into effect. The Medicare and Medicaid cuts proposed in the budget would not be made until the insurance program was operative, and the health services and development grants would be initiated in 1974.

3. A voucher plan for child care would be adopted in 1975; standards of eligibility would be made more liberal and the value of the vouchers increased steadily over the period. Manpower training and higher education vouchers would also be introduced and expanded.

4. Two major targeted social grant programs would be emphasized, both aimed at helping the disadvantaged—compensatory education and urban community development.

5. The redesigned urban mass transit grant would be undertaken and waste treatment grants expanded.

Programs to help people buy essential goods and services supplied by the private market and to support public services for the disadvantaged would absorb $59 billion of the $77 billion in additional resources. Although the family assistance plan contemplated under this variant would have a relatively low minimum guarantee, in combination with food stamps and the housing allowance, it would provide a quite substantial minimum income of about $4,400; the value of health insurance would raise this to about $5,000. Although the working poor and those in the lower-middle-income range would benefit, somewhat more of the aid in this variant would be concentrated on the lowest-income groups than would be the case under variant 2. The cumulative marginal tax rates implied by the "in-kind" transfers envisaged under this variant might pose significant incentive problems.

In general, this variant implies substantial redistribution of public and private goods and services and a significant voice for the federal government, on the demand side, in deciding what goods and services should be purchased. But it does not envisage large federal intervention on the supply side through grants that influence the way in which goods and services are provided.

VARIANT 4: EMPHASIS ON GRANTS FOR SOCIAL PROGRAMS. This variant pursues roughly the same objectives as the previous one—redistribution of specified goods and services. But wherever feasible, it does so through a grant strategy under which the federal government provides assistance to the supplier, rather than the purchaser, and exercises some degree of control over the way in which goods and services are delivered (see Table 12-12).

1. A family assistance plan, with a minimum guarantee of $2,800 and à 50 percent marginal tax rate, would be initiated on January 1, 1975. Food stamps would be continued and expanded.

2. A health plan offering insurance against catastrophic expenses would begin in 1975 and in 1977 be converted into a more comprehensive plan, with deductibles and coinsurance at very low levels for the poor but rising along with income.

Table 12-12. Use of Large Additional Resources, Variant 4, Fiscal Years 1974–78
Billions of dollars

Item	1974	1975	1976	1977	1978
Available resources	9	21	40	60	77
Used for:					
Income redistribution	0	3	6	6.5	7.5
Family assistance plan	0	2.5	4.5	4.5	5
Structured public employment	0	0.5	1.5	2	2.5
Helping people buy essentials	2	4.5	6	11.5	13
Health insurance	1.5	4	5	10	11
Food stamps	0.5	0.5	1	1.5	2
Grants for social programs	5	9.5	22	33.5	46
Child care institutional grants	0.5	3	6	8	11
Manpower training	0.5	1	2	2	3
Aid to institutions of higher education	0.5	1	3	4	5
Compensatory education	1.5	1.5	3	4	5
Educational equalization	0	0	2	8	12
Targeted urban development	0.5	1.5	2	3	4
Community action programs	0.5	0.5	1	1	1
Health services and development	0.5	0.5	1	1	2
Social service	0.5	0.5	2	2.5	3
Investment in physical environment	0	1.5	3	4	5.5
Urban mass transit	0	0.5	1	1	1.5
Waste treatment	0	1	2	3	4
Allowance for contingencies	2	3	3	4	5

Source: Authors' estimates. Figures may not add to totals because of rounding.

3. Child care, manpower training, and aid to students would be furnished, on a gradually expanding scale, through grants to institutions. Social service grants to states would also be increased throughout the period.

4. Urban community development grants would be revised to target part of the funds on low-income neighborhoods and expanded considerably. Community action programs would be restored and enlarged.

5. The compensatory education program would be substantially enlarged during the period to provide effective grants of $500 per child by 1978. An educational equalization program with strong maintenance-of-effort provisions would be introduced; under this program the federal government would match 20 percent of the state and local educational tax effort in a state with average fiscal capacity.

6. A revised urban mass transit grant would be adopted and grants

Table 12-13. Federal Expenditures on Defense and Domestic Programs under Alternative Budget Options, Fiscal Years 1974 and 1978

		1978							
		Current posture		Moderate additional resources			Large additional resources		
Expenditures	1974	Variant 1	Variant 2	Variant 1	Variant 2	Variants 3 and 4	Variant 1	Variant 2	Variants 3 and 4
				Billions of dollars					
Total expenditures	267	358	370	359	377	382	370	396	400
Defense[a]	89	113	113	103	103	103	88	88	88
Domestic	178	245	257	256	274	279	282	308	312
				Percentage of GNP					
Total expenditures	20.0	20.4	21.1	20.5	21.5	21.8	21.1	22.6	22.8
Defense[a]	6.6	6.5	6.5	5.9	5.9	5.9	5.0	5.0	5.0
Domestic	13.4	14.0	14.7	14.6	15.6	15.9	16.1	17.6	17.8

Source: Authors' estimates. Figures may not add to totals because of rounding.
a. Defense, space, and foreign affairs.

for waste treatment plants expanded to the levels authorized by the Congress last year.

By 1978 two-thirds of the total discretionary resources available would be devoted to expanding federal grants-in-aid for both social programs and preserving the environment. Except for the educational equalization program, the federal government would retain significant control over either the targeting or the specific services involved. Provision of public services would be emphasized; only a modest fraction of the additional resources would go directly to people.

The Federal Budget in the National Economy

Table 12-13 summarizes the effect of the various alternatives discussed in this chapter on defense and domestic spending and on the overall size of the federal budget.

Even with no changes in current tax laws, the progressivity of the federal tax system would slightly raise the proportion of gross national product (GNP) flowing to the federal sector between 1974 and 1978. With no policy changes, defense spending would retain its present share of GNP. The tax cut assumed in variant 1 of the current posture would keep the federal share of GNP from rising significantly; under variant 2 the federal share would be increased.

Under the "moderate additional resources" alternative, the normal growth in the federal revenue share, the yield from tax reform, and the cut in defense spending would make available about 2.5 percent of GNP for discretionary use. Under variant 1, about 1.3 percentage points would be returned through tax cuts and the other 1.2 points would be added to domestic spending. The remaining three variants would use most or all of the 2.5 percentage points for additional domestic expenditures.

In the "large resources" alternative, the combination of economic growth, tax reform, and defense cuts would make 4.4 percent of GNP available for discretionary use. Variant 1 would return 1.7 percentage points through tax cuts, and devote the remainder to additional federal expenditures. The other three variants would use the full 4.4 percent of GNP for domestic expenditures (variant 2 would return a small amount via tax cuts).

Other Alternatives

One possibility that some observers might find attractive has not been considered here—namely, adopting either of the two alternative defense postures without undertaking any of the tax reforms.

The smaller, efficiency-oriented defense cut would provide budgetary savings amounting to $6 billion in 1975, rising to $10 billion in 1978. If these savings are combined with the fiscal dividend and an allowance for contingencies is set aside, the following implications emerge: by 1975 a small ($5 billion) leeway has appeared for new initiatives, and by 1978 this has grown substantially, providing an amount equal to about two-thirds of the discretionary funds available under the "moderate resources" alternative. From the tables and discussion in this chapter, the reader can examine the implications of pruning the various different strategies shown in the "moderate resources" alternative to fit the smaller sum. After 1976 in the projection, however, one important fact emerges: the resources available without tax reform in any year are almost the same as those available in the prior year with tax reform.[7] Hence a possible way of dealing with this situation would be simply to delay for a year each of the program initiatives or expansions contemplated earlier in the "moderate resources" variants.

Adoption of the larger of the two defense-cut alternatives, unaccompanied by any tax reform, would make roughly the same discretionary resources available as are contemplated in the "moderate resources" alternative. In other words, the large defense cut is roughly the same in magnitude each year as the combination of the small defense cut and the small tax reform package.

Conclusions

The budget options illustrated in this chapter represent a few of the divergent views about what the federal government ought to do. A large number of other alternatives could be conceived to represent different judgments about priorities and about the appropriate role of the federal government. The discussion, however, has brought out four central points.

7. In other words, the tax reforms contemplated in the "moderate resources" alternative are equal to about one year's growth in the fiscal dividend.

First, barring major changes in current tax policies and expenditure programs, there will be little room for maneuver in the federal budget during the next three years. Despite the large rise in revenues to be expected from economic growth and the cuts in domestic programs proposed in the 1974 budget, there are no significant discretionary resources available until fiscal 1977.

Second, a series of modifications in defense policies and the tax structure can be identified that, if adopted, would greatly change this outlook and provide a large and growing volume of resources for discretionary use. These changes in defense policies and tax structure are of such a nature that they can be pursued at various levels—they do not require an all-or-nothing choice. Even if adopted only in part, they can still significantly alter the budgetary outlook.

Third, even with additional resources available, there are difficult choices to be made among competing strategies in the use of these funds.

Fourth, many of these important and difficult choices have to do not with the ultimate objectives the federal government should seek but with the role it should play in pursuing them. The chief distinctions we have drawn in this book, stated in perhaps oversimplified form, hinge on the extent to which the federal government goes beyond providing funds to persons or governments and intervenes in decisions about the demand or supply of particular goods and services.

Looking at the federal budget year by year, one is impressed with its inertia and the difficulty of changing anything important. But if one looks five years ahead, the budget is not uncontrollable. Over that period the size and scope of the budget, the objectives the federal government pursues, and the strategies it follows can be altered—and significantly. The projections that show little room for new initiatives in the foreseeable future are only extrapolations of current priorities. They do not set limits on what can be done by deliberate actions to provide additional budgetary resources or to change priorities.

What Happened to the 1973 Budget

THE BUDGET submitted in January 1972 for fiscal 1973 forecast federal expenditures of $246.3 billion. It included a large volume of transactions that counted as negative expenditures, mainly receipts from the leasing of rights to offshore oil deposits, the sale of financial assets, and sales from the stockpile of strategic materials. Expenditures net of these transactions would have been $256.3 billion according to the original forecast.

During the year, congressional action and other developments added $12.3 billion to fiscal 1973 outlays. This was partially offset by a $3.8 billion reduction in other expenditures, as can be seen in Table A-1. Congress reduced the defense request for new obligational authority by $5.2 billion, but the impact on expenditures is expected to be only $1.9 billion in fiscal 1973. Several programs proposed by the administration were not enacted—among them, welfare reform and special revenue sharing—and coverage of the disabled under Medicare was delayed until fiscal 1974.

The largest increase in fiscal year 1973 stemmed from an increase in social security benefits that was greater than requested (20 percent rather than 5 percent). There were also sizable increases in other beneficiary programs, such as those for veterans, railroad retirees, disabled coal miners, and welfare recipients. Enactment of general revenue sharing was delayed until October 1972 but made retroactive to the first of the calendar year. Consequently, some of the money expected to be spent in fiscal 1972 fell into fiscal 1973. Net interest payments were larger than originally anticipated. Disaster relief resulted in another $1 billion of increased expenditures.

The net effect of these changes was to raise the preliminary estimates of total 1973 expenditures (net of financial transactions) from $256.3 billion to $264.8 billion. To reach the announced goal of expenditures no higher than $250 billion, the administration last January submitted a revised 1973 budget incorporating a $3.6 billion reduction of funds for domestic programs and increasing the volume of financial transactions, which count as negative expenditures, to $11.4 billion.

Table A-1. Major Changes in Federal Budget Expenditures from Original Estimates, Fiscal Year 1973

Billions of dollars

Description		1973
1973 outlays (original estimate, January 1972 budget)		246.3
Receipts from financial transactions		10.0
Adjusted total, original estimate		256.3
Decreases		−3.8
Defense	−1.9	
Programs not enacted or delayed	−1.4	
Other	−0.5	
Increases		12.3
Social security benefits	3.9	
Veterans' and other retirement programs[a]	1.2	
Black lung disease benefits	0.9	
Welfare and social services[b]	1.6	
General revenue sharing	1.8	
Net interest	1.9	
Disaster relief	1.0	
Revised 1973 outlays (before January 1973 budget)		264.8
Actions taken to reduce expenditures		−15.0
Executive program reductions	−3.6	
Financial transactions	−11.4	
1973 outlays shown in January 1973 budget		249.8

Sources: *The Budget of the United States Government* and accompanying *Appendix* and *Special Analyses* for fiscal years 1973 and 1974, and authors' estimates.

a. Includes veterans' compensation and pensions, military, civilian, and railroad retirement.

b. Includes cash assistance, grants for social services, and the Work Incentive Program.

How Large Are the Administration's Proposed Expenditure Reductions?

THE ESTIMATES in Table 1-7 of expenditure reductions undertaken by the administration are lower than those shown in the 1974 budget document. The estimated savings from expenditure reductions published there are $6.5 billion for fiscal 1973, $16.9 billion for 1974, and $21.7 billion for 1975. Examination of the 108 proposed reductions indicates that some of the proposals do not truly represent reductions in the level of federal programs: some hinge on apparent overestimates of the original level of a program; some arise from financial transactions counted as negative expenditures; and some are reductions that would have occurred anyway.

Of the total reductions estimated for each of the fiscal years 1973, 1974, and 1975, $2.3 billion, $2.7 billion, and $4.7 billion are the respective amounts claimed as a reduction in the program of grants to the states for social services. These grants had increased from less than $400 million in 1969 to $1.9 billion in 1972 and were expected to reach almost $5 billion in 1973. Last year, as part of the general revenue sharing bill, the Congress, with administration support, put a ceiling of $2.5 billion a year on this program. Savings of the magnitude listed in the budget document assume that these grants would have continued to grow at a rapid pace between 1972 and 1975, even though a congressional ceiling had already been enacted. A more realistic estimate of the cut in these programs would be the amount by which expenditures were held below the $2.5 billion ceiling.

An estimated $2.7 billion is listed by the administration as having been cut from military expenditures. Part of this reduction is a result of the volunteer army being less expensive than originally anticipated and part is the result of stretching out procurement and research and development.

444

How much the original estimates of defense expenditures overshot the mark is, of course, a matter of judgment. However, if the $2.7 billion reduction claimed all resulted from cuts in programs, then the increase initially planned for defense was quite large. Defense expenditures are estimated at $79.0 billion for fiscal 1974, an increase of $4.2 billion over 1973. Thus the increase planned before the cutback would have been $6.9 billion, which appears to be more than necessary to fund the proposed program.

Included in the proposed reductions are further sales of leases on offshore oil deposits. Receipts from these transactions are counted as negative expenditures and do not represent reduction in ongoing programs. Also of an accounting nature is the proposal to allocate retirement costs to the postal service. The postal service was made independent in 1971, but employees still are covered by civil service retirement. If the post office were a completely self-financed government-sponsored operation, this proposal could save money. However, the postal service will receive a subsidy of nearly $1.4 billion in fiscal 1974. The increased retirement costs could be paid from these funds.

In 1958, the United States contributed to a European Fund run by the Organisation for Economic Co-operation and Development (OECD). The fund granted credits to countries having temporary balance-of-payments problems. It has been terminated, and OECD is returning the contribution. This is a financial transaction that probably would have occurred anyway.

Savings of $1.2 billion in agricultural subsidies are estimated for both fiscal 1974 and 1975. With the worldwide shortage of farm products, the amount of subsidy paid to farmers in fiscal 1974 would in any event have been less than in previous years. In part, therefore, the savings listed in the budget stem not from positive actions but from the force of outside events. How large these "automatic" reductions in agricultural subsidies would have been is a matter of judgment. Our estimates disallow half of the amount shown in the budget document as savings for fiscal 1974 and one-third of the amount estimated for fiscal 1975.

Two other proposed reductions probably would also have happened without a special effort to reduce expenditures. One is the saving in highway expenditures attributable to delay in enacting the enabling legislation. The other is the saving to be realized by requiring that federal agencies offset the 1973 pay increase by seeking additional economies in fiscal 1973. The requirement that federal agencies absorb pay increases in the year they become effective is not new and is very often a part of normal budgeting procedures.

Finally, whereas the termination of the model cities, urban renewal, and other urban development programs is listed as a reduction in expenditures, the budget in fact proposes to replace these programs with special revenue sharing for urban community development, with no net change in expenditures.

Even after adjustments have been made to produce a more realistic picture of savings (Table B-1), the reductions proposed by the President are nonetheless quite large, amounting to $3.6 billion, $12.2 billion, and $15.2 billion in fiscal years 1973, 1974, and 1975, respectively.

Table B-1. Adjustments of Official Estimates of Expenditure Reductions in the Federal Budget, Fiscal Years 1973–75

Millions of dollars

Official estimate and adjustment	1973	1974	1975
Total reductions estimated in 1974 budget document	6,515	16,893	21,739
Adjustments	−2,965	−4,714	−6,494
Social service grants	−2,343	−2,100	−4,100
Defense expenditures	...	−700	−700
Sale of off-shore oil leases	...	−1,010	−510
Post office retirement adjustment	...	−285	−105
Repayment of advances to Agency for International Development	−242	...	...
Reduction in agricultural subsidies	...	−619	−334
Delay in highway expenditures	−100	...	...
Absorption of 1973 federal pay increases	−280	...	...
Termination of expenditures for urban programs replaced by urban special revenue sharing	...	...	−745
Adjusted reductions used in this book	3,550	12,179	15,245

Sources: *The Budget of the United States Government, Fiscal Year 1974*, pp. 50–57, and authors' estimates.

TYPESETTING *Monotype Composition Company, Inc., Baltimore*

PRINTING & BINDING *R. R. Donnelley & Sons Company, Chicago*